BRYAN WYNTER

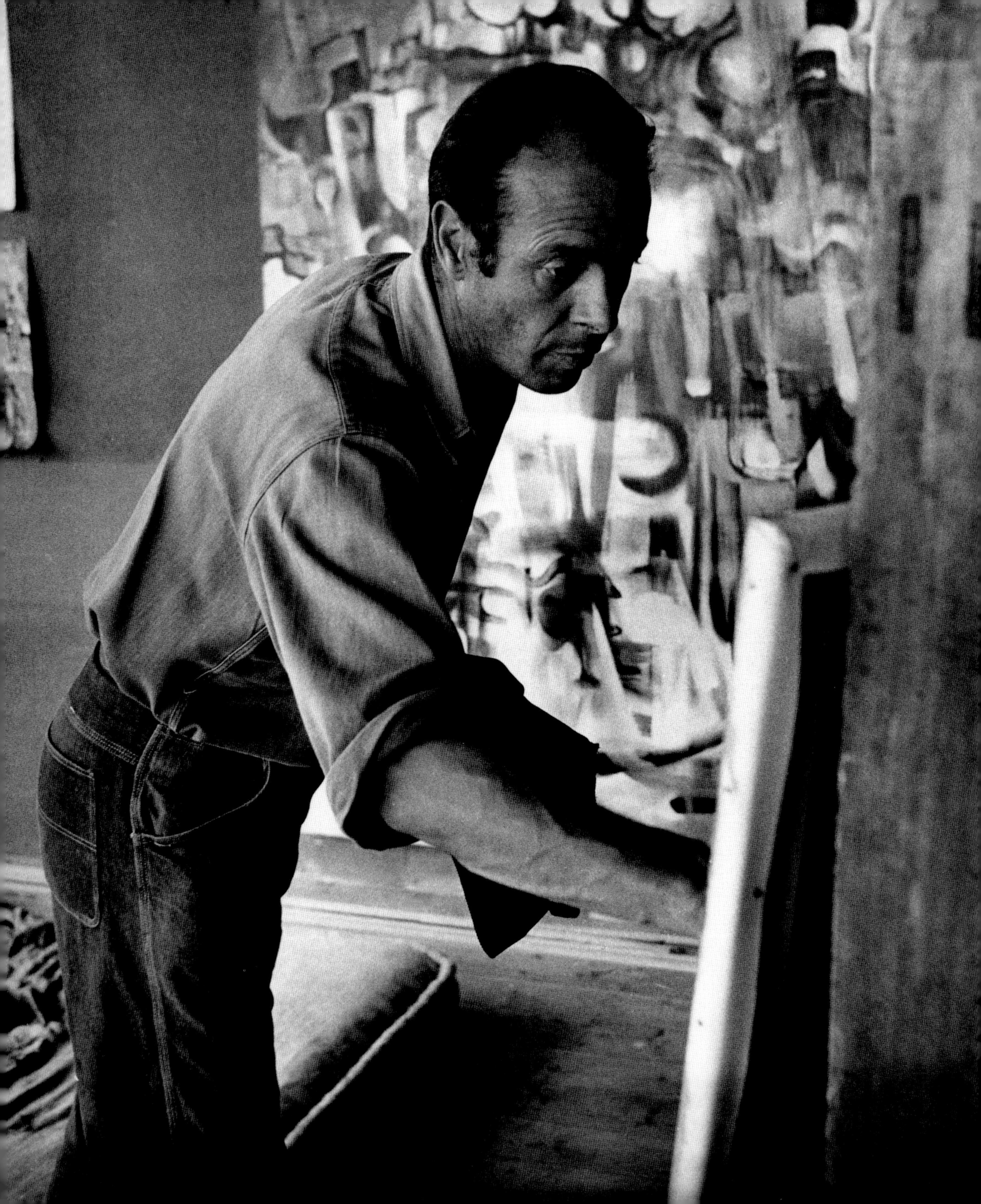

BRYAN WYNTER

Michael Bird

LUND HUMPHRIES

For Monica

First published in 2010 by Lund Humphries

Lund Humphries
Wey Court East
Union Road
Farnham
Surrey
GU9 7PT
UK

and

Suite 420
101 Cherry Street
Burlington
VT 05401-4405
USA

www.lundhumphries.com

Lund Humphries is part of Ashgate Publishing

British Library Cataloguing-in-Publication Data:

Bird, Michael.
Bryan Wynter.
1. Wynter, Bryan, 1915-1975—Criticism and interpretation.
I. Title II. Wynter, Bryan, 1915-1975.
759.2-dc22

ISBN 978-1-84822-009-6

Library of Congress Control Number: 2009930083

Edited by Matthew Taylor
Designed by Nigel Soper
Set in FF-DIN
Printed in China

Frontispiece:
Bryan Wynter in his studio, 1959
Photograph by Roger Mayne

Jacket captions:
Front: *Kayak*, 1961
Back: Bryan Wynter with *IMOOS*, 1971
Front flap: *Confluence VIII*, 1967

Contents

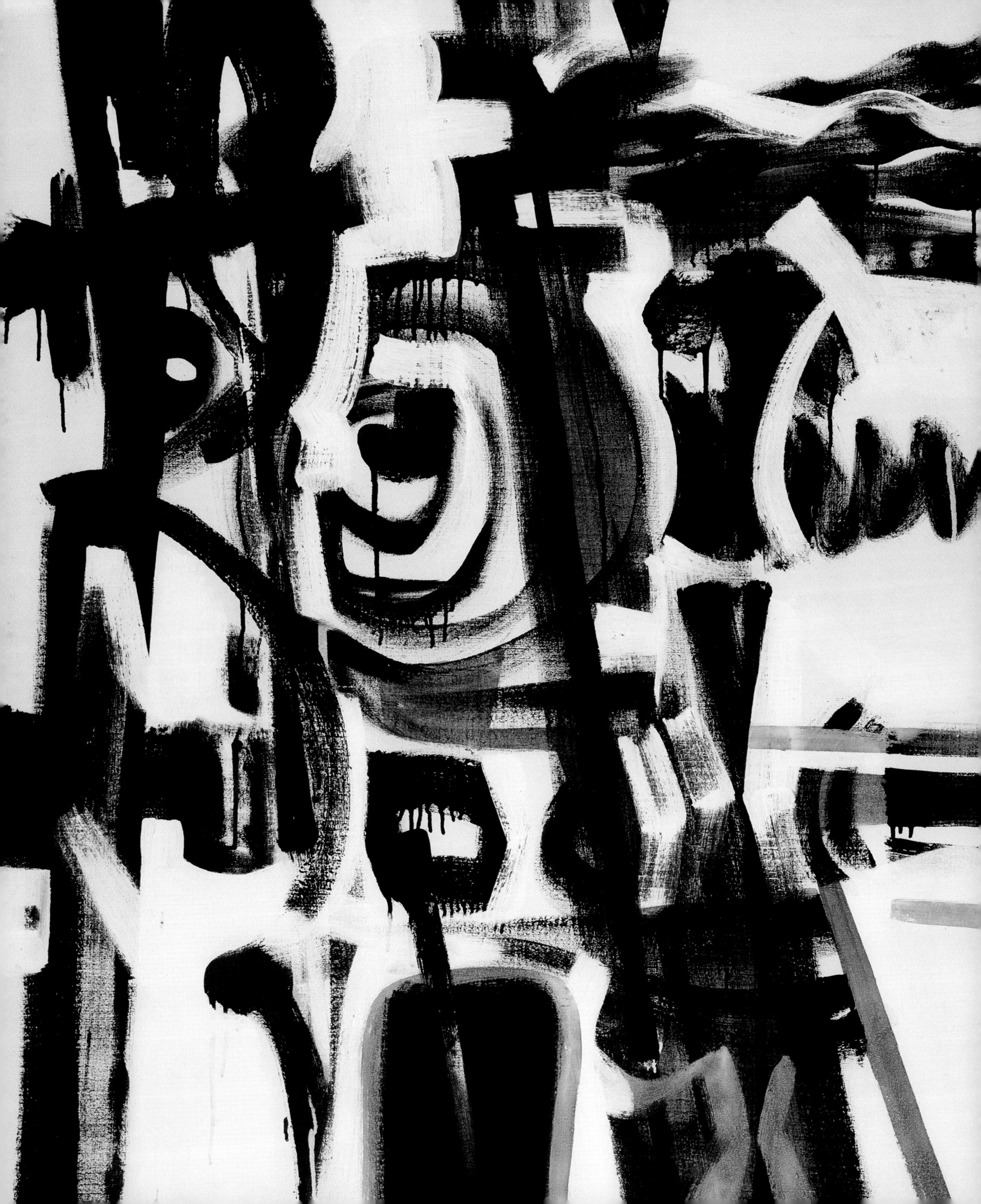

Acknowledgements

I have been struck by how vividly, despite the passage of more than thirty years since his death, Bryan Wynter remains present in the recollections of those who knew him. In this connection I especially wish to thank Tom and Billy Wynter, Sue Murray, Sir Alan Bowness, Graham Coles, Milein Cosman, Paul Feiler, Rose Hilton and Sheila Wynter. Most of all, I thank Monica Wynter, for her wise and (it has seemed to me) remarkably impartial consideration of things past.

As the first full-length survey of Wynter's career, this book builds on foundations expertly laid by Chris Stephens in his 1999 monograph and by Elizabeth Knowles in her catalogue of the artist's estate and archive. At Jonathan Clark Fine Art, the gallery that represents the Wynter Estate, Simon Hucker's enthusiasm for and practical assistance with this project have been invaluable, while Galina Valavani made deceptively light work of permissions enquiries and picture credits. I am also grateful to David King, who kindly provided copies of more than 200 pages of Wynter's letters to Hedy Hoffmann; to Michael and Margaret Snow for permission to quote from W. S. Graham, *New Collected Poems* (2004) and *The Nightfisherman: Selected Letters of W.S. Graham* (1999); and to Adrian Gibbs at the Bridgeman Art Library, Susanna Heron, Gillian Jason, Sheila Lanyon, Roger Mayne, Gordon Samuel, Robert Travers and James Wynter for providing particular images. Once again, I owe much to the Lund Humphries team – Lucy Myers, Miranda Harrison, Alex Hitchins, Matthew Taylor and Nigel Soper – for their flair and attention to detail. And to Felicity, as always my most perceptive critic and necessary encourager.

I gratefully acknowledge the support of a grant from The Authors' Foundation, which helped with the research costs for this book.

detail of **137**, *Black White*, 1964

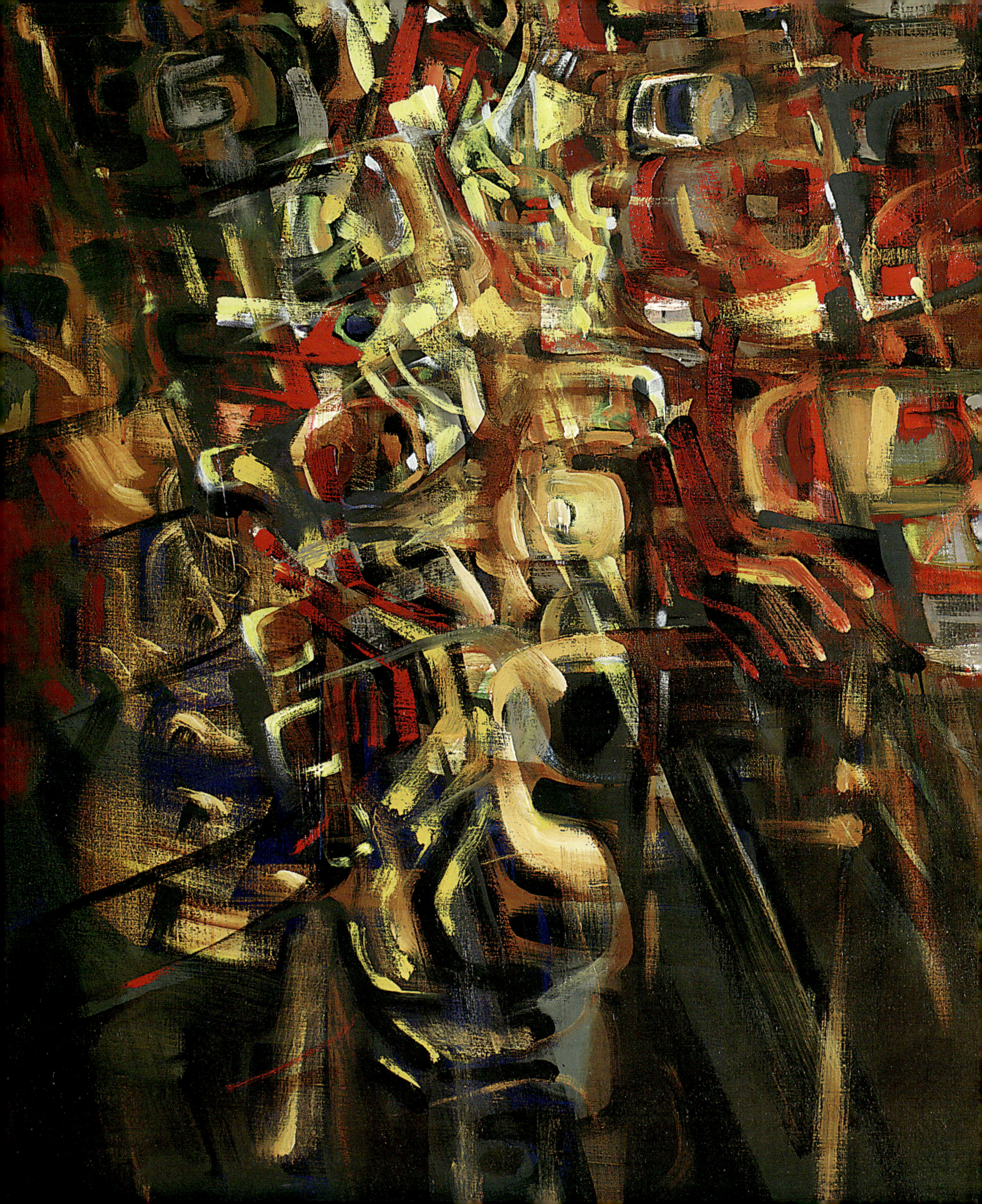

Introduction: Doors of Perception

Twice, maybe three times, a year during the latter half of the 1950s Bryan Wynter set a day aside for psychedelic self-experimentation. There was nothing casual or impulsive about these sessions; rather, they were planned with Wynter's characteristically practical approach to liberating the unconscious. After making sure that he had twelve hours or so clear of any other arrangements, he took a mescalin dose in the form of white powder carefully measured by a pharmacist, and waited to observe its effects. From his wartime laboratory work in Oxford he was familiar with standard procedures for drug trials. He was, in general, a dedicated observer of natural phenomena and, more sporadically, a meticulous record-keeper, filling page after page of notebooks with detailed observations in his distinctive lanky script on subjects as diverse as dreams, itineraries for river kayaking and recipes for rice wine. The results of Wynter's mescalin sessions, however, remained undocumented. Instead, we have anecdotes told by people who happened to be around at the time – visiting friends, other artists – whom he enthusiastically invited to participate in the experience.[1] These stories developed a crazy posterity of their own, eventually merging with a wider stream of post-war artistic folklore. Here is Terry Frost, groggily coming round on the moors outside Wynter's cottage in Cornwall. Perched on a tumbledown field wall, a large black bird – a raven – mischievously eyes Frost up before speaking. 'Come on! Come on!' it admonishes him, in a spookily accurate imitation of Wynter's voice. Or here is Roger Hilton, wandering through the bracken, exclaiming that he is an orange and that people are trying to peel him. And it is still only 1957 or 1958, some years before the countercultural revolution of the 1960s made such sorts of 'experiments' commonplace.

Yet Wynter's hallucinogenic forays merit the term 'experimental' in a stricter, more scientific sense than is usual in the context either of modern art or of post-war counterculture. Like the other extra-artistic projects in which he was, at various times, passionately absorbed (including three-dimensional photographic projection, amateur aqualung construction, pyrotechnics and raven-training), they combined methodical, dispassionate enquiry with a risky spirit of subversion. The mescalin episodes make good stories; in a more serious sense they stand for much else in Wynter's life and work. 'By temperament', his friend and sometime art-world advocate Alan Bowness believed, 'he was an explorer, with a curiosity about natural things, and this was to become exactly the base for his own painting.'[2] 'Natural things', in any discussion of Wynter, is a very wide category; it embraces animals, landscapes and hydrology, as well as the nature of his own existence, in particular the elusive psychic borderlands between seeing and recognition. 'I find it helpful', he once wrote of his working practice, 'to think of the moment at which the eye looks out at the world it has not yet recognised, in which true seeing has not yet been translated into the useful concepts with which the mind immediately swamps it.'[3]

Wynter had a voracious, unconventional intelligence. As will become clear, he was an artist for whom the life of the mind was at once a continual, self-renewing source for his art and a side of his personality that he was forever trying to outwit in the quest for 'true seeing'. In this game of psychological hide-and-seek, art abetted the unconscious in its attempts to avoid being swamped by the rational mind. Few British artists of Wynter's generation were as well read, yet when it came to art he had little patience for intellectualisation. 'We talk far too much', Aldous Huxley had approvingly quoted Goethe in the *The Doors of Perception* (1954), a book that Wynter knew well: 'We should talk less and draw more. I personally should like to renounce speech altogether and, like organic Nature, communicate everything I have to say in sketches.'[4] For those who are not artists and, Wynter might have added, for any artist intent on 'true seeing', mescalin – according to Aldous Huxley's account of his own first trip in *The Doors of Perception* – sets our minds

detail of **101**, *Tumult*, 1958

free to behave in the way the human mind naturally would, if it hadn't been conditioned over millennia to serve the more prosaic requirements of day-to-day living. 'We must preserve and, if necessary, intensify our ability to look at the world directly and not through that half-opaque medium of concepts, which distorts every given fact into the all too familiar likeness of some generic label or explanatory abstraction', wrote Huxley.[5] This was the sort of idea that appealed intensely to Wynter, the sort of idea he felt compelled to put to the test, to see whether it could work as well in practice as it sounded in print.

And the mescalin did work, at least for a few years. As with Wynter's many other experiments, the results found their way into his art. In addition to the trail of gossip and anecdote, and a few drawings he made on the spot (possibly not his best), there exists weightier testimony in the form of the transformation in style and scale that took place in his painting during 1956, initiating the most intense and productive phase of his career. It was not the only time that Wynter completely changed the way he did things – and not just the type of work he made but his whole working method. This particular development, however, was definitive. It marked a point at which Wynter's irrepressible compulsion to experiment seemed at last to bring together his experience and his art within a single frame. This is too neat a way of putting it; but it is still true that Wynter had for some time been deliberately attempting a fusion, a confluence of this kind. 'Experience' and 'experiment' have the same root meaning: to discover by trying things out. It may occasionally seem as though Wynter was trying too hard 'to fox the intention, the conscious ordering',[6] as if thoughtful ingenuity could release the *daimon* on its own. Mescalin, by contrast, opened the door to visual sensations of extraordinary beauty and immediacy while bypassing the conscious process. Although there would be other explorations and further transformations, the great series of canvases Wynter produced in the four or five years after 1956 has the unmistakable aura of an artist who has hit his stride. Works such as *Impenetrable Country* and *Gust*, from 1957 and 1959 respectively (figs 91 and 6), blazed in the brief high noon of gestural abstract painting in Britain. But half a century later it is also clear that they are in many ways so different from what other British abstract painters were doing at the time that it is only with some difficulty that Wynter's work can be aligned with theirs.

Throughout his career Wynter repeatedly surprised and slightly unnerved his supporters by absconding, apparently without warning, from the categories to which they had assigned his work. Around 1950, for example, people who wanted to buy 'a Wynter' (and there seemed to be plenty of them) would have visualised a smallish painting with a title like *Cornish Harbour* (fig. 3), *Still Life with Cow's Skull* (fig. 1) or *Foreshore with Gull* (fig. 2). Describing Wynter's gouaches in an essay published in 1955, Patrick Heron was of the opinion that 'No English artist living excels him in this medium'.[7] These paintings were marked by a 'haunting accuracy of mood' in their evocation of 'the bleak, bony, stony mysteriousness of the Celtic moors'. Another Wynteresque trait was their ability to be at once sombre and strangely lurid: 'The squat, tipping church tower catches, suddenly, a lemon shaft of mad light from a hidden sun or moon far out to sea somewhere.'[8] Nevertheless, however insistently the varied paint textures and restless contours threatened to become ends in themselves, you could still reliably make out the forms of buildings, windows, birds, bones, field walls. Within a year of Heron's essay, which, under the title 'Modern English Romantics', had placed Wynter alongside Graham Sutherland and Keith Vaughan, Wynter was associated with a kind of painting that, on the face of it, seemed completely alien to the work on which his earlier reputation had been based. His new large, non-representational oil paintings were constructed from intricate networks of thousands of paintmarks. Brush-signs,[9] *taches*, paint gestures, calligraphic marks – whatever you called them, Wynter's new approach evidently belonged heart-and-soul to what the American

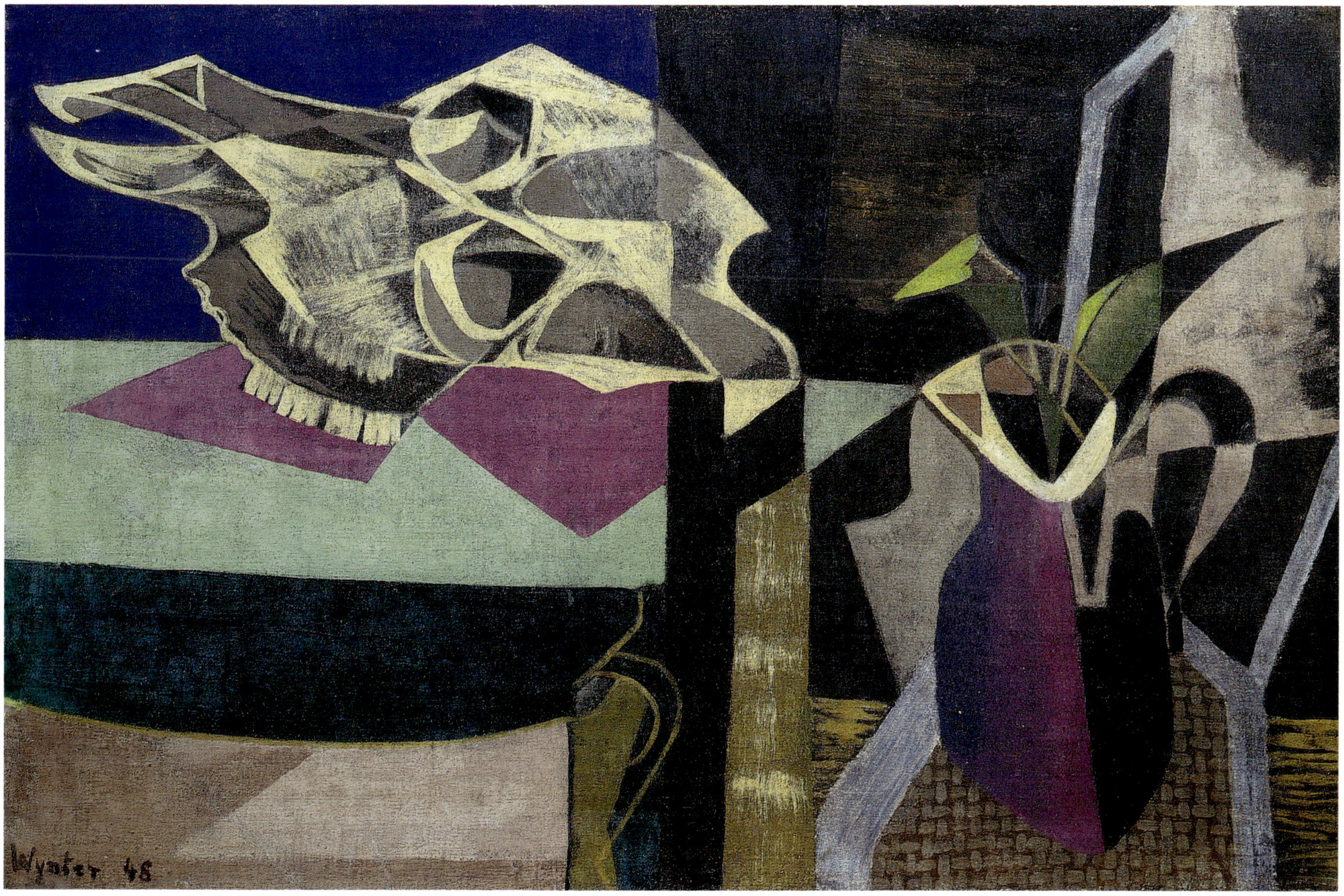

1
Still Life with Cow's Skull
oil on canvas
51 x 75.5 cm (20¾ x 29¾ in)
1948
Artist's estate

critic Harold Rosenberg described as 'a new painting consciousness'. From now on, pronounced Rosenberg in 1952, putting his own highly quotable interpretation on the artistic movement known as Abstract Expressionism, 'What was to go on the canvas was not a picture but an event.'[10]

As events on canvas, Wynter's abstract-calligraphic paintings of the later 1950s could be, and often have been, readily interpreted as mescalin trips to hang on the wall. There it all is: the dancing, stereoscopically layered surfaces, the slow, arterial visual pulse, the jewel-like colours of drug-induced hallucination. Seen in such a light, these canvases have an ancestry that stretches back to early twentieth-century Cubism, whose development by Braque, Picasso and others is thought to owe something – possibly a lot – to mescalin use. Closer to Wynter's own era, the Belgian-born poet and painter Henri Michaux, who experimented with the drug over several years, recorded its effects on his mind and art in three books published between 1956 and 1959. The inkstorm calligraphic images for which Michaux is best known, and which find an echo in some of Wynter's contemporaneous works (figs 5, 8) without there being much question of influence either way, are usually termed 'abstract'. Francis Bacon, who owned one, flatly disagreed: Michaux, he said, was 'a very, very intelligent man', whose '*tachiste* or free marks' were not abstract at all but rather 'about delayed ways of remaking the human image, through a mark which is totally outside an illustrational mark but yet always conveys you back to the human image'.[11]

Wynter gave the first of his 'new consciousness' paintings, on which he was working in January 1956, the title *The Interior* (fig. 4). It's just over 4 feet high and 3 feet wide (127 x 101.6 cm): not enormous but the size at which a painting begins to feel large to the viewer. 'Abstract', you have to admit after a few minutes' looking, is not a particularly useful term to describe what's going on here. The narrow braids, ladders and little trellises of 'free marks' are full of activity, cascading, overlapping,

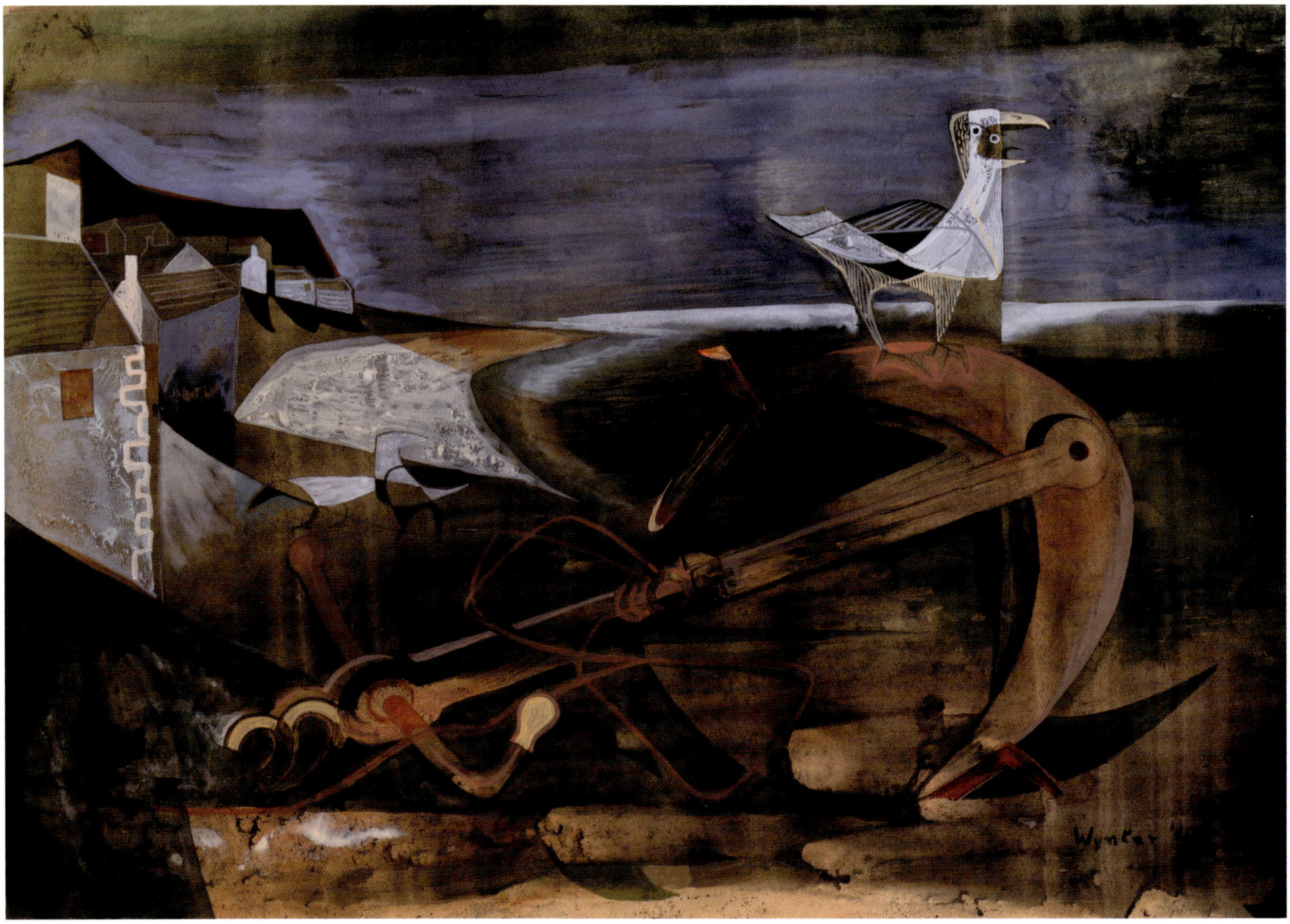

intermingling. Yet all this seems to be happening within an atmosphere of enthralled contemplative stillness. There is something, too, that 'conveys you back to the human image'. Maybe this feeling comes from the patchy foregrounding of flesh and earth tones, imparting a gentleness to the trails of cusped, scything paint marks, or from a steady verticality that, somewhere in the background, echoes the poise of a standing figure – perhaps the artist's or the viewer's own. Heron, always Wynter's most observant critic in terms of exactly how he was using paint and forming images, saw 'the glimmer of a window near the top edge of the canvas, and the broken silhouette of a table near the right centre'.[12] If not an image of the human body, then, this is a painting deeply suggestive of human habitation, with its touches of ember red, its play of white, blue and creamy highlights as though picking out the textures of a lived-in space.

The Interior was an apt title; but the interior of what, or where? A room, a cave, a burnt-down fire, the artist's own mind – or all of these? In its mesmerising, holographic completeness, which appears more like the summation of a long series of experiments than a first attempt in a new manner, *The Interior* bears out Frank Auerbach's observation that 'all good painting looks as though the painting has escaped from the thicket of prepared positions and has entered some sort of freedom where it exists on its own, and by its own laws, and inexplicably has got free of all possible explanations'.[13] Freedom, whether personal, creative or physical, was a concept that preoccupied Wynter from his student years

2
Foreshore with Gull
monotype and gouache on paper
29.2 x 45 cm (11½ x 17¾ in)
1949
British Council Collection

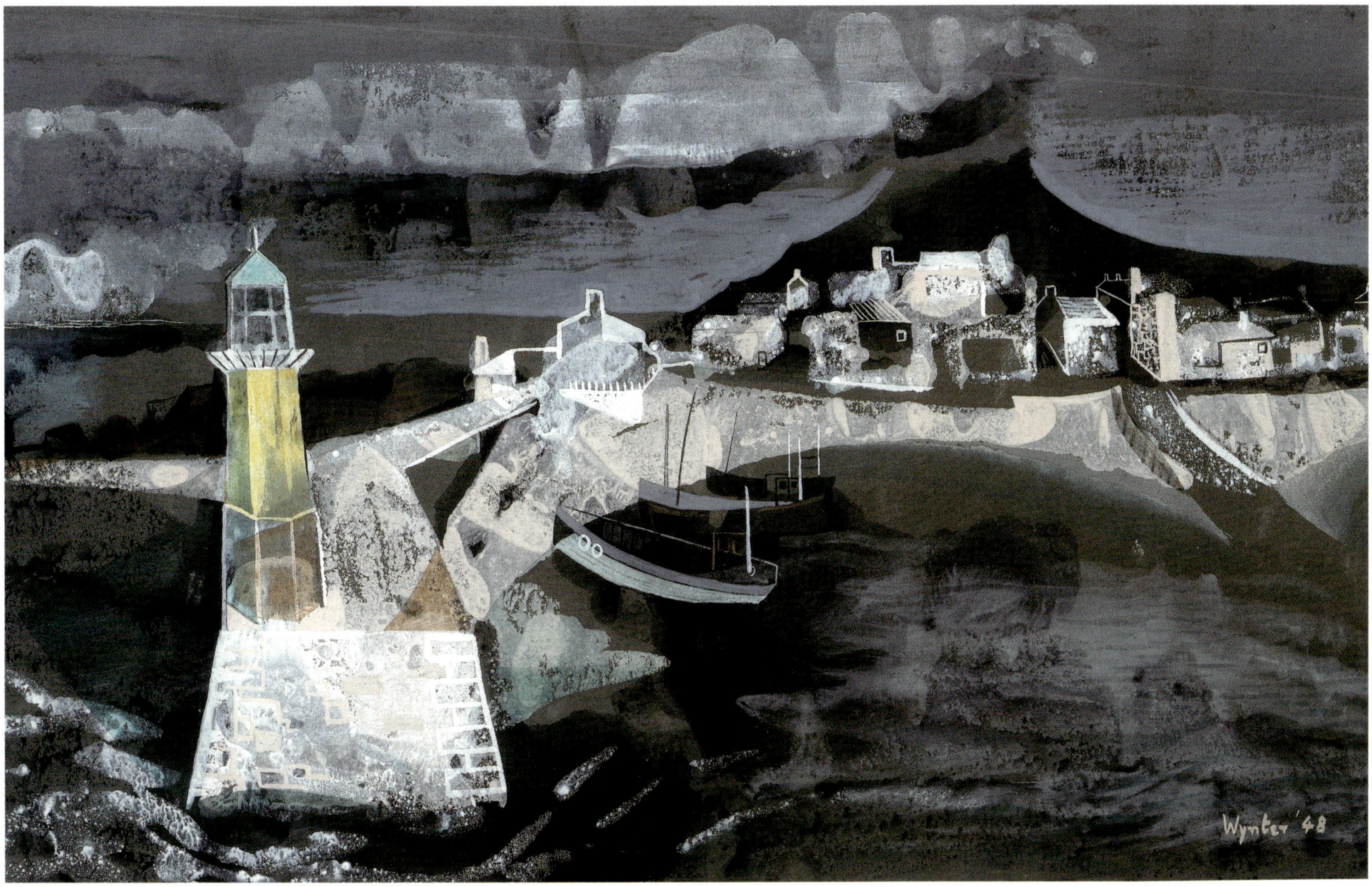

3
Cornish Harbour
gouache on paper
35.6 x 55.9 cm (14 x 22 in)
1948
Private collection

onwards. Much later, for those who lived through the 1960s but who were old enough to have experienced the preceding post-war era as adults, Wynter's whole attitude to life seemed in retrospect always to have been ahead of its time. It was an attitude, wrote Alan Bowness in 1976, shortly after Wynter's death, 'more common among young people today than it was among Wynter's generation'.[14] Psychedelic experimentation – one of the main countercultural activities that, in popular perception, made the 1960s seem so mind-blowingly different from the previous decade – was just one of the ways in which Wynter had been in on the action early. If he had also – like Peter Blake, say, or Richard Hamilton – met Paul McCartney, designed an album cover,[15] guested in a film or appeared on television, his posthumous reputation might have shaped up very differently. 'I can't help feeling', Bowness mused, 'that he might now become, in some strange way, a hero-figure.'

Wynter certainly inspired respect and loyalty – Heron's heartfelt obituary mourned the loss of 'a prince of friends'[16] – but a 'hero-figure' he never became. Which British artist of his generation ever did, or could? Until at least the 1990s, and probably later, the audience for contemporary art remained simply too limited; art occasionally made the headlines, but, with rare exceptions such as Hockney, artists remained personally almost invisible to the general public. Moreover, Wynter lived much of the time far from cities. Apart from a spell between 1951 and 1955, and again briefly in the early 1970s, he seldom taught and therefore left few student

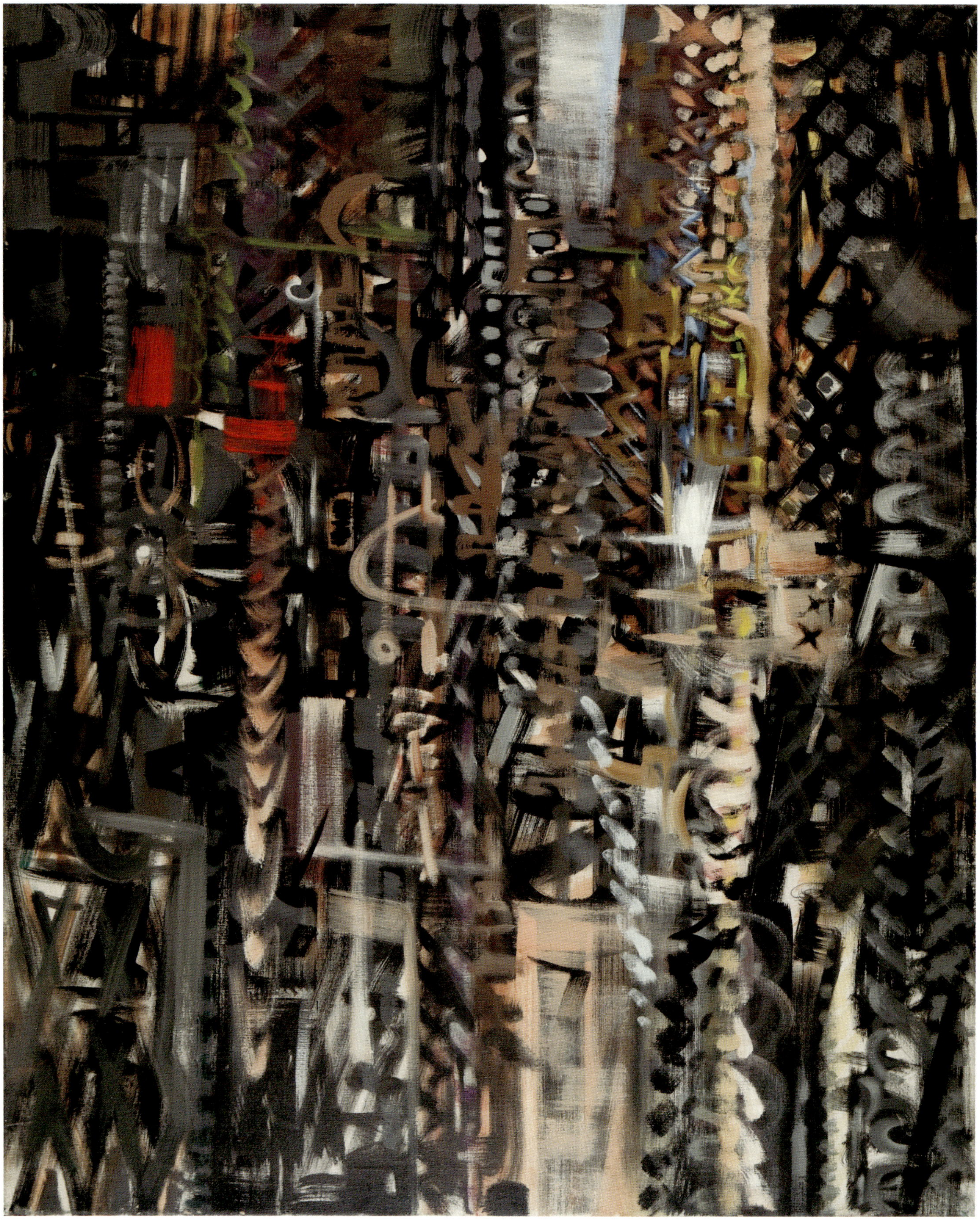

4
The Interior
oil on canvas
127 x 101.6 cm (50 x 40 in)
1956
Private collection

5
The Watchers
gouache on paper
77.8 x 56.5 cm (30½ x 22¼ in)
1959
Whitworth Art Gallery,
University of Manchester

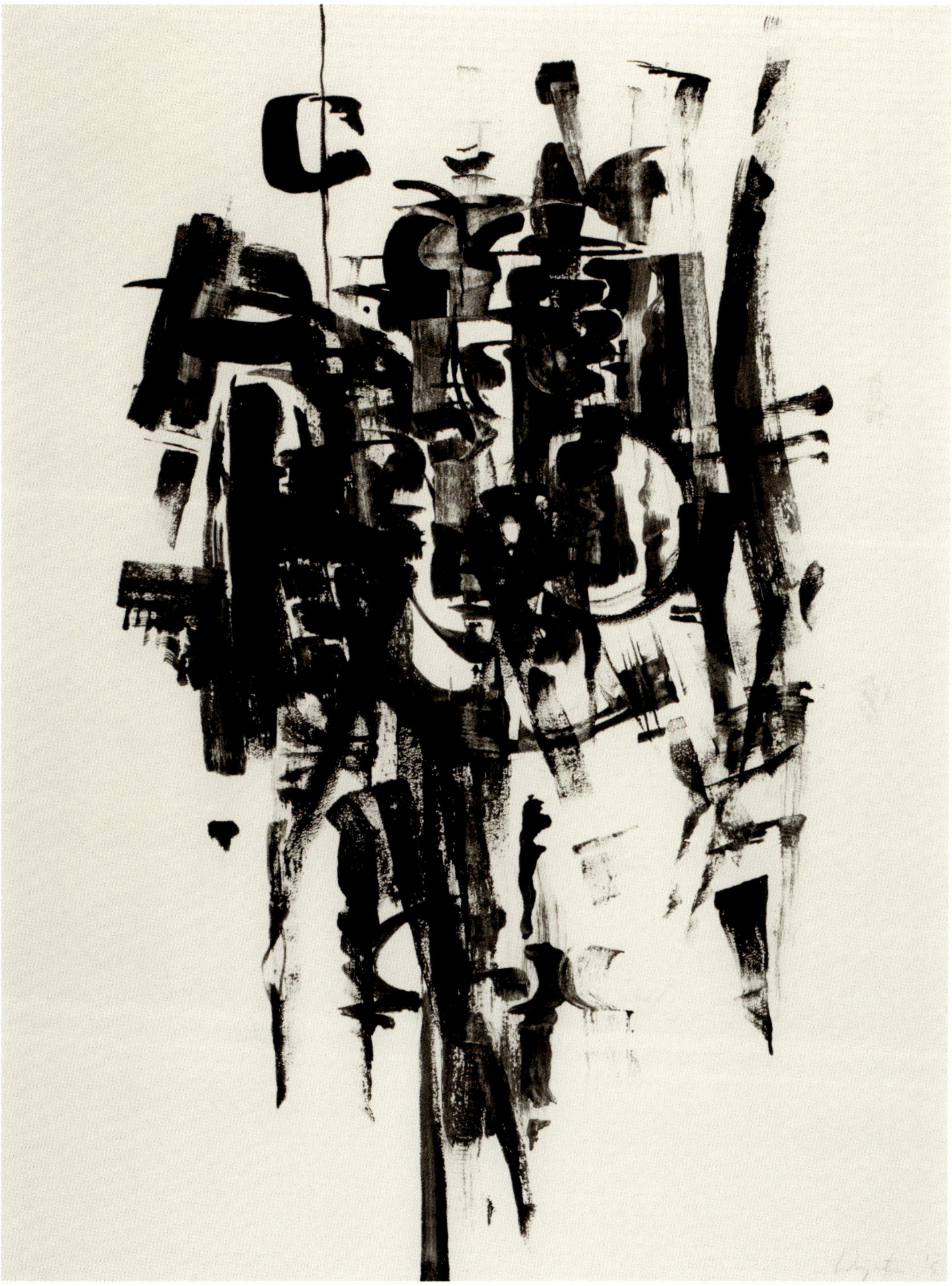

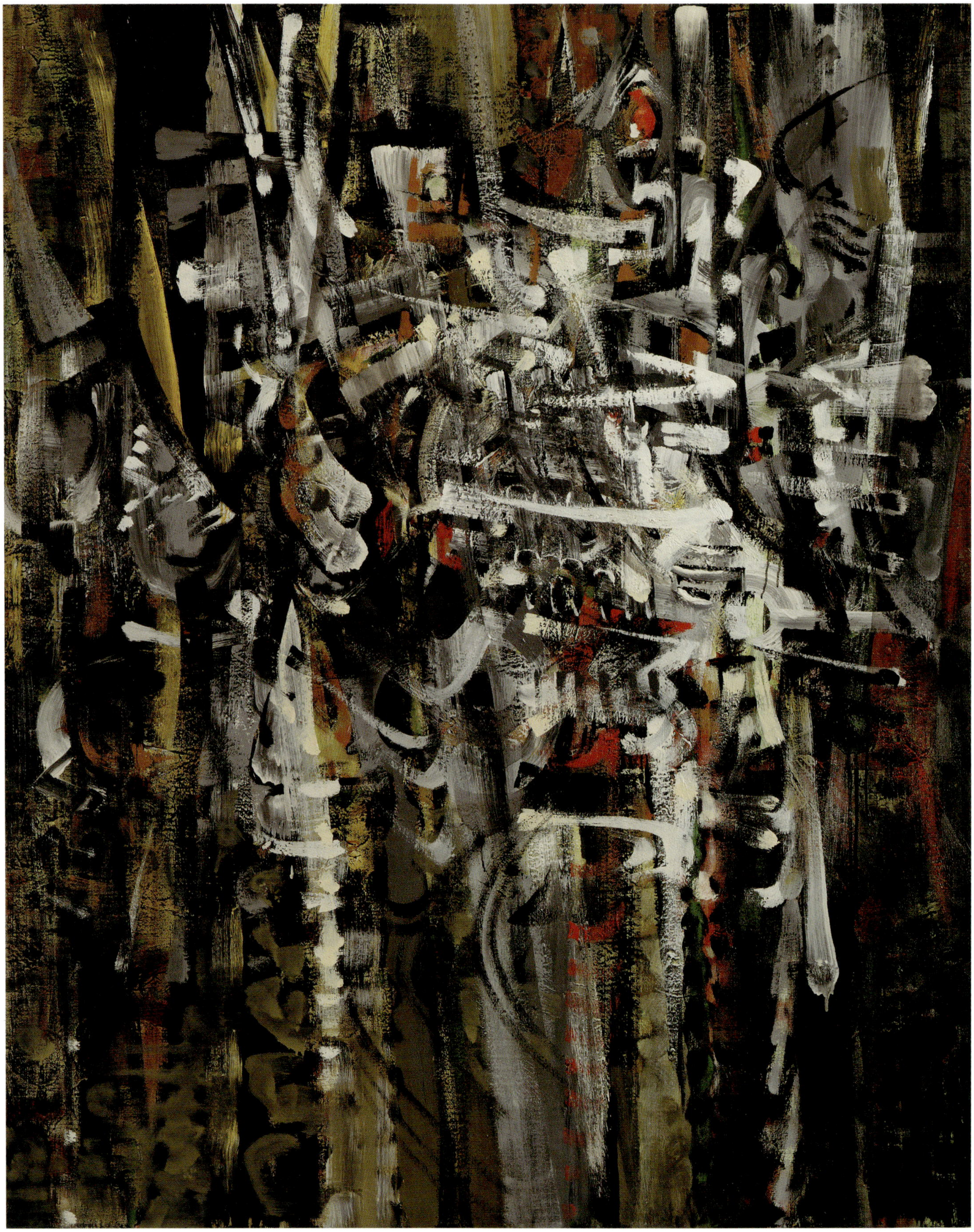

6
Gust
oil on canvas
142.5 x 112 cm (56 x 45 in)
1959
Jonathan Clark Fine Art

disciples; and, though socially adept, he lacked (again in common with many artists of his generation) much interest in self-promotion. 'Seldom has there been an artist of such great inventive intelligence', wrote Heron, 'whose professional stance was so lacking in that egocentricity of which many a great painter had been personally guilty.'[17] This picture is confirmed in other recollections of Wynter, in which he appears singularly unconcerned with *being an artist* or with any idea of art as a special, elevated sphere of action. Nor can he have been over-excited about the ascendancy of liberal social attitudes during the 1960s and 1970s. His own pursuit of the over-arching permissive theme – the quest to become a free individual – had begun so much earlier, with his reading of Huxley in the 1930s. When people began talking about 'the new permissive society', Wynter's friend, neighbour and indomitable drinking companion the poet Sydney Graham observed that they and their circle in Cornwall 'were permissive years ago'.[18] Wynter's personal philosophy was based, in any case, on a perception that the sought-for freedoms had more to do with his own state of mind and way of life than with a desire for political or cultural change.

This attitude – both ahead of its time and, in other ways, very much of its time – informed Wynter's longest-lasting experiment, which took place between September 1945 and May 1964. For most of these nineteen years he lived in a primitive granite cottage on the exposed, bare outcrop of Zennor Carn, high above the small coastal village of Zennor in west Cornwall (fig. 7). In full widescreen view to the north lay the Atlantic; on the other three sides stretched the Penwith downs, or moors. There were still a few functioning farms in the district – a jigsaw of any-shaped stone-walled fields where livestock grazed but where the soil was too thin for cultivation – and the remains of buildings that had once served the area's tin- and copper-mining industry, long roofless and gutted of their machinery. For the most part, though, this ancient agricultural and industrial landscape had returned to the wild. Surrounding Wynter's eyrie at Carn Cottage, or the Carn, a carpet of almost impenetrable gorse and bracken scrub bristled against enormous granite slabs and boulders. A dirt track led down to the switchback coast road several hundred yards below; there was no running water or electricity.

In practice, Wynter came and went fairly regularly. For some years he worked in a former cowshed beside the cottage, but he also occasionally rented studios in London, where he might stay for weeks at a time. Like the mescalin tales, however, people came to see the Carn as an essential aspect of Wynter's identity, an experiment in living that was integral to his wider creative endeavour. Although he made the place quite habitable by fixing up a system of tanks for gathering rainwater, which fed the house through his own ingenious plumbing arrangements, and installing a wind generator for electricity, conditions remained very basic, as Wynter intended they should. When in 1945, after years in wartime lodgings, the Carn became his first place of his own, it seemed vital that his way of life there should be as antithetical as he could make it to his bourgeois upbringing. Later, perhaps, as he reached mid-career and middle age around 1960, it represented a bastion of personal freedom and integrity, at a remove from the consumerist forces that were reshaping British urban life. Down in the nearby seaside town of St Ives, meanwhile, the counter-attack on materialism was gathering. Like other such small resorts, St Ives was a magnet for beatnik drifters, who could be seen any day strumming guitars and rolling spliffs along the harbour front. Wynter, as so often in his determination to put his ideas and ideals into action, had got there first.

By choosing to live on Zennor Carn, Wynter may further have enhanced his countercultural credentials through local association. According to the pub gossip that regaled him when he first moved in, his cottage was haunted. It was, moreover, rumoured to have hosted a fatal act of black magic performed in 1938 by the egoma-

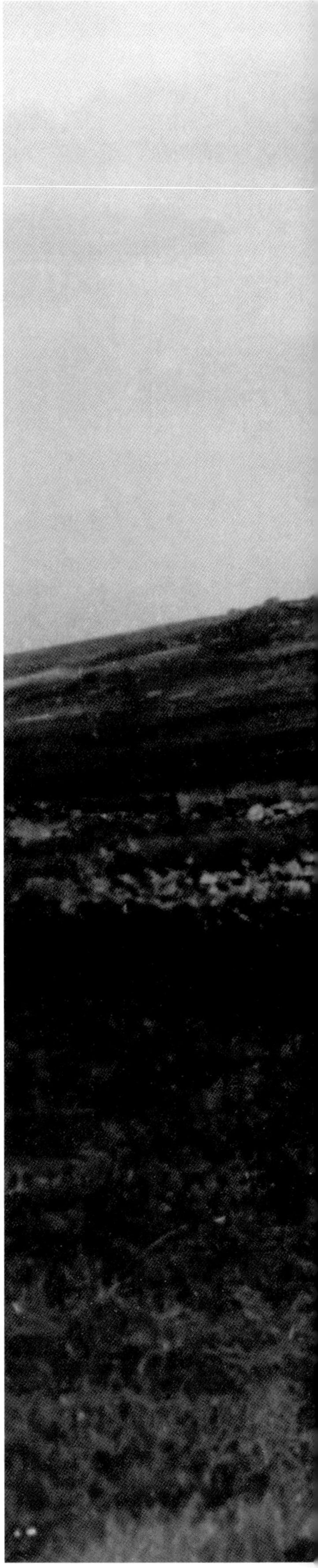

7
The Carn, Zennor, 1940s

niacal occultist, mountaineer and author Aleister Crowley, whose lurid sobriquets included 'the Picasso of the occult' and 'the Wickedest Man in the World'. Part of Crowley's satanic fame rested on the greedy depravity of his drug abuse – the author of the novel *Diary of a Drug Fiend* (1922), he was reputed to have introduced Huxley to the peyote cactus (the natural source of mescalin) when the two men met in Berlin in 1930. Almost equally notorious, at least in the environs of Zennor and St Ives, was a row of cottages half a mile down the slope, on the other side of the coast road, known as Higher Tregerthen. During the First World War these had been the temporarily home to D. H. Lawrence (the dedicatee of one of Crowley's books), his wife, Frieda, and – rather more briefly – Katherine Mansfield and John Middleton Murry. Lawrence's attempt to establish his fantasy colony of kindred spirits, Rananim, right there in Zennor, had fizzled out when Mansfield and Murry fled the equally unbearable intensity of his friendship and his rages. While Wynter didn't exactly identify with either of these antecedents, he enjoyed the sense that the place he had chosen had a potent *genius loci* – an amalgam of the supernatural, the idealistic and the plain bizarre.

Somehow, too, this rough corner of the Penwith moors, with its farmsteads crouching out of the wind and its scattered, barely habitable hovels, never lost its improbable links to the wider world. In 1961, towards the end of Wynter's time there, Lawrence's star was high in the national consciousness. The *Lady Chatterley* obscenity trial was under way in London, and the long-reviled author of 'dirty' books was about to be reborn as a guiding spirit of the permissive society. Wynter, meanwhile, was occupied by yet another experiment, involving the manipulation of colour, light and shape by the use of distorting mirrors. He called the box-like contraptions that eventually resulted Images Moving Out Onto Space, or IMOOS, 'in default of any other more ordinary satisfactory names' (fig. 172).[19] These home-made generators of visual sensation are among the most effective and beautiful products of 1960s' kinetic art, precursors of much that, as technology advanced, was later to be developed in the form of holograms and computer visuals. By the early 1970s, however, when kinetic art had become fashionable, Wynter had tired of the IMOOS and moved on to other investigations. Always intrigued by new products that could be co-opted as artists' materials, he was experimenting with Pentel fibre-tip pens, using a light-box to create multiple series of superimposed designs. Captivated by the science of water flow, he wanted to find out whether its dynamic patterning and rhythms could be emulated through a mechanical-intuitive process. The drawings piled up, yet the eureka moment remained elusive. At the same time, the works Wynter based on the twists and turns of a watery 'meander' motif (fig. 9) took him back for the first time in almost twenty years to a painterly idiom involving strong, flat colour that was both extrovert and subtle. Where he would have gone from here is an open question.

Wynter remains one of the most difficult modern British artists to categorise. There are themes that connect *Still Life with Cow's Skull* and the 'Meander' series, the 1950s' calligraphic abstract paintings and the IMOOS, across thirty years, but you have to follow Wynter through his life as well as his art for these to become clear. The world of the Carn, the mescalin, the kayaking, photography and fireworks – all these found their way into his art, but they would have engaged him just as intensely if they hadn't. One student contemporary at the Slade remembered Wynter as a 'Renaissance man', a 'polymath'[20] whose breadth of interests – more common, perhaps, in the fifteenth century than the twentieth – singled him out from the other artists she knew. What Heron called his 'extraordinary originality of mind' informed the whole gamut of Wynter's pursuits; but, while he delighted in dissolving disciplinary boundaries and turning an abstract idea into a construction on a workbench, art was always, finally, the synthesis he sought.

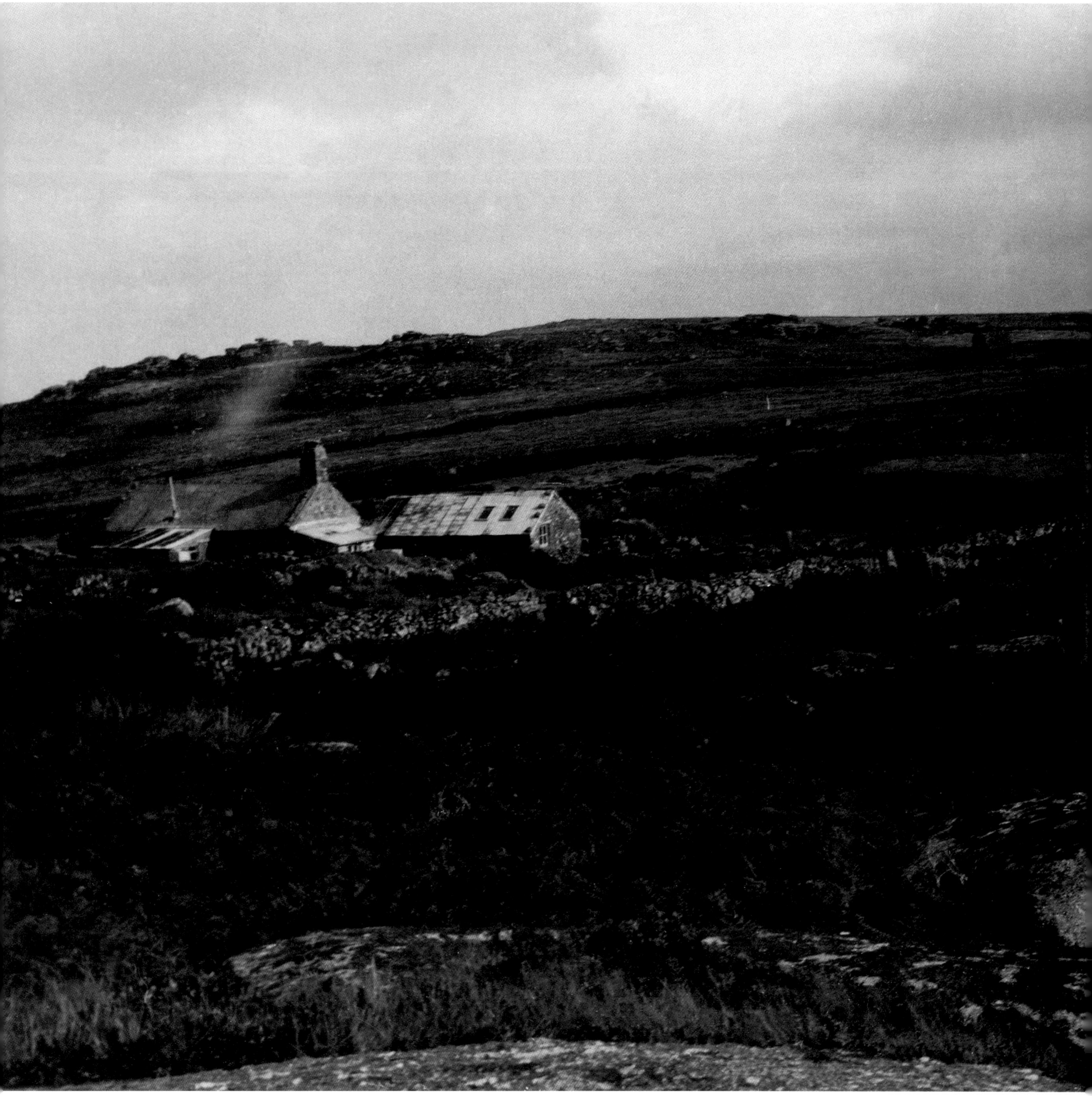

8
Black Coast
lithograph
58.5 x 38 cm (23 x 15 in)
1958
Artist's estate

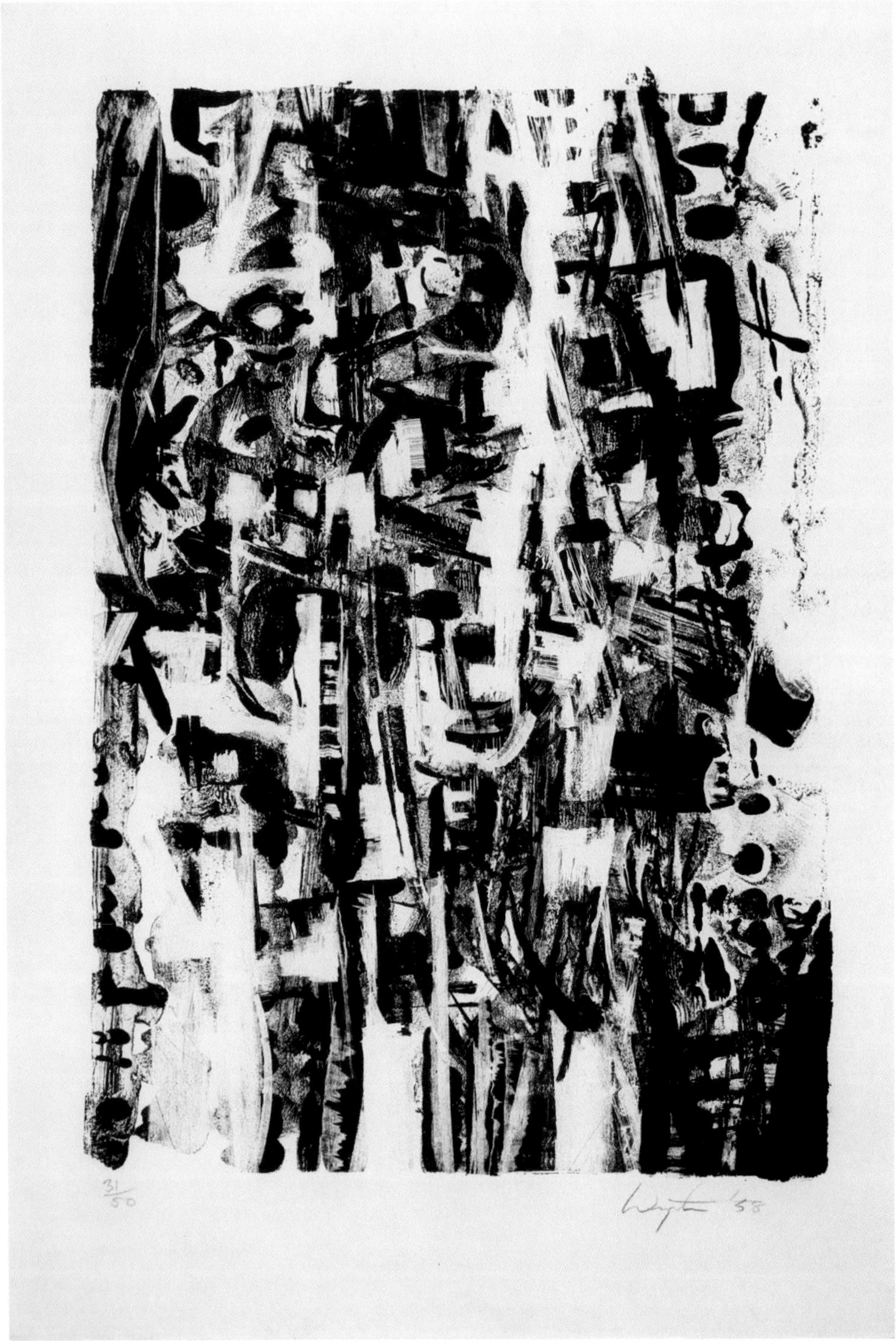

9
Confluence V
oil on canvas
132 x 122 cm (72 x 48 in)
1966
Private collection

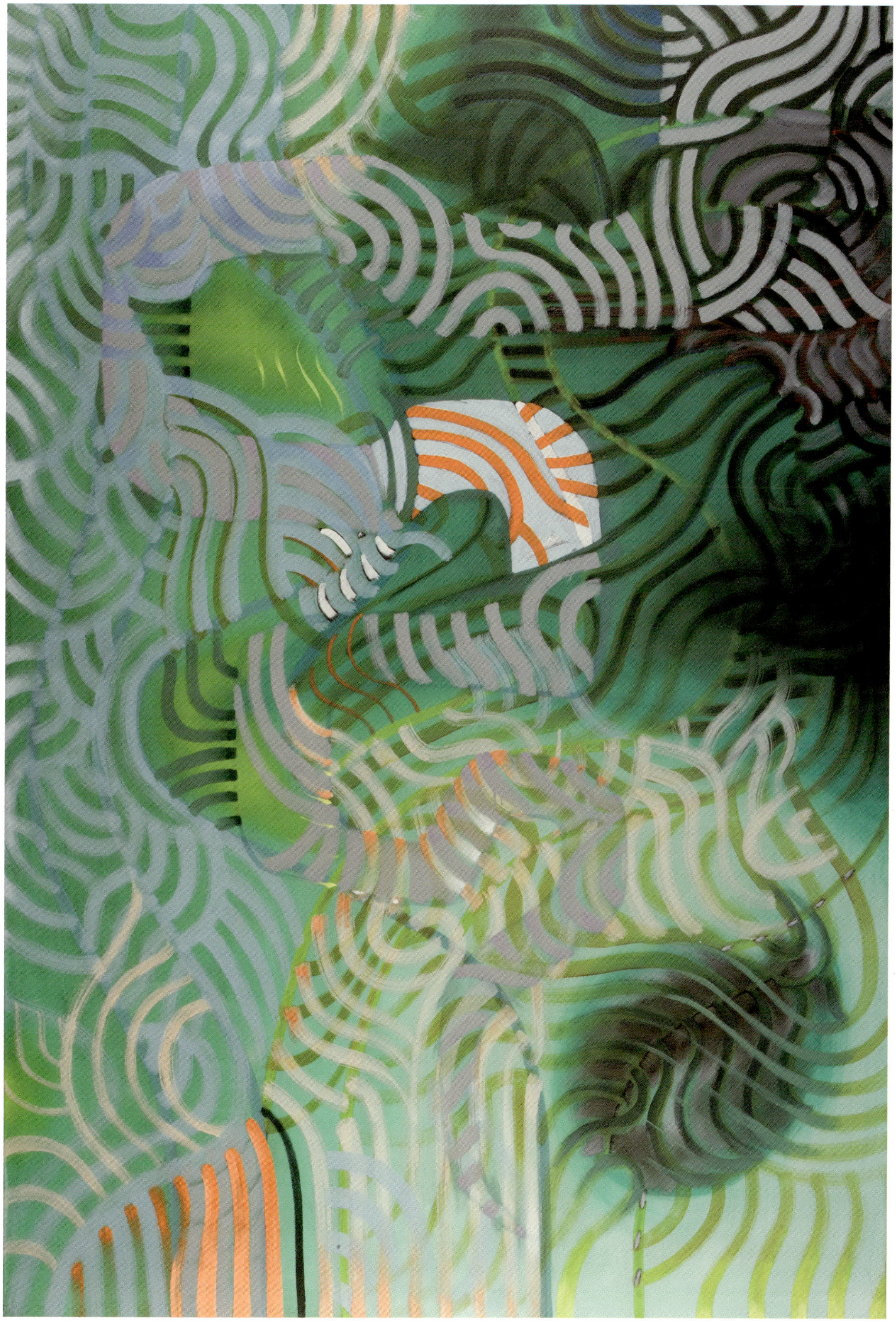

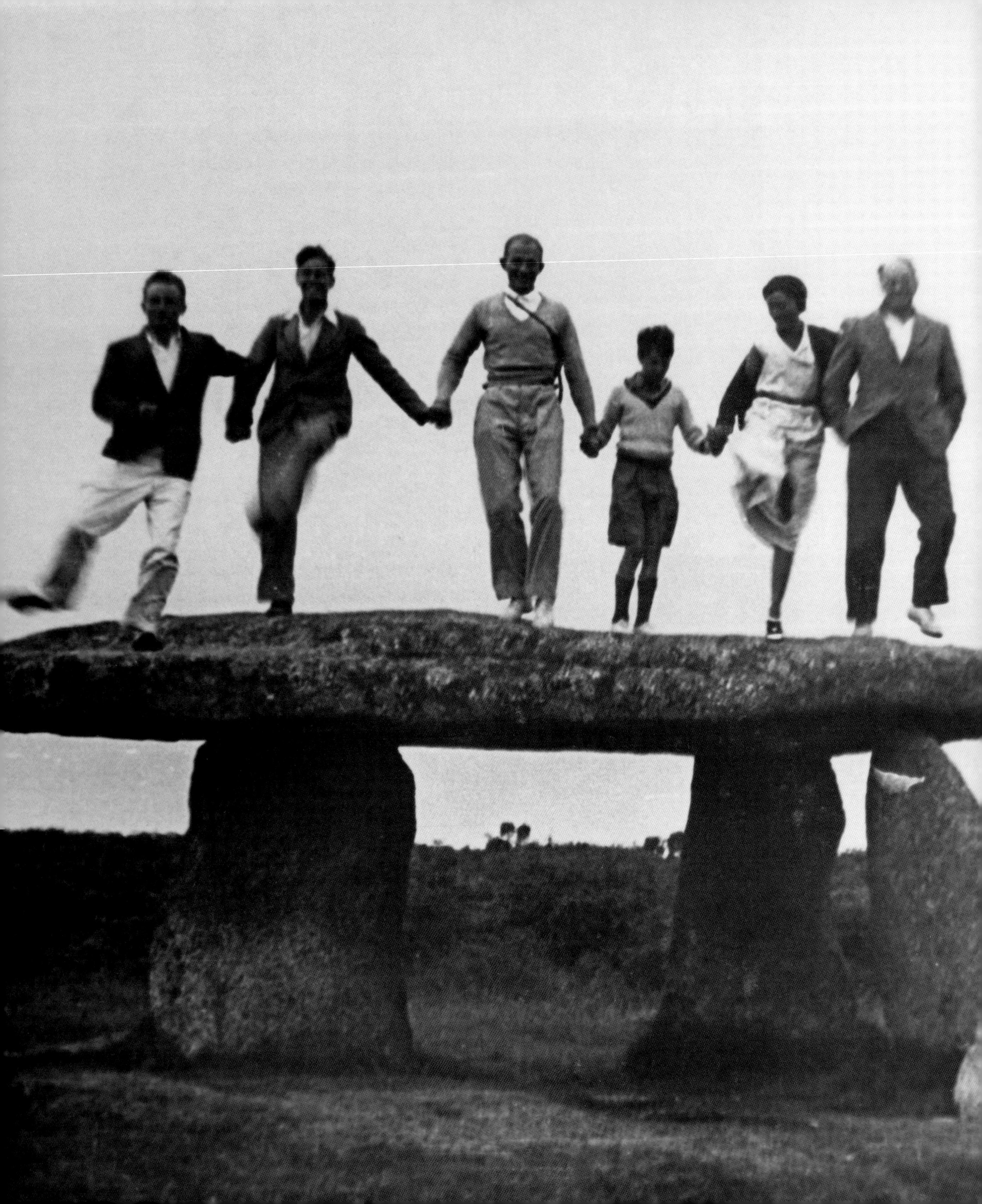

1 Swedenborg and Steam Laundry: Family Values, 1915–38

It was not until Wynter was well into his twenties that it began to seem likely that he would become an artist at all. If his father, James (Jim), could have had his way, his elder son would have succeeded him as head of the family business. This was the path he had himself felt bound to follow, and his determination to secure the Wynter succession by seeing Bryan duly installed at the Times Laundry Co. Ltd was flushed with a certain simmering resentment on his own account. That his twenty-two-year-old son insisted, with equally intractable determination, on quitting the firm in order to go to art school in 1938 can hardly have come as a surprise, but it touched a raw nerve all the same. Temperamentally, Wynter senior had never been suited to office existence. With a passion for hearty, outdoorsy activities, he hankered – so other family members were convinced – after life on the land, rather than as head of the laundry business that had been founded by his own father, David, in the 1890s. With its industrial-scale depots and smart fleet of horse-drawn vans, the Times Laundry had expanded to become a household name in early twentieth-century London. It was an inheritance whose demands and rewards were not lightly to be set aside.

David Winterbotham (fig. 10) was born in Oldham, Lancashire, in 1855. He worked as a schoolmaster before moving in 1893 to London, where he had previously spent two years as a trainee teacher. Changing his unmistakably northern surname to the more socially and professionally versatile Wynter, he proved a gifted entrepreneur. His machine-powered steam laundries performed for a small cost one of the most unrelenting and physically demanding of household chores, at a time when women were increasingly seeking work outside the traditional confines of family home and domestic service. The business grew rapidly; by 1909 Wynter was rich enough to move into Bishopswood, a mansion on the fashionable upper slopes of Highgate Hill, on the northern fringes of London.

In the extensive grounds of his new domain the following summer David Wynter hosted a garden party for almost a thousand guests. This was the kind of epic hospitality for which he became known – in his own circle, at least, which centred on his lifelong affiliation with the New Church and the Swedenborg Society. The teachings of the Swedish eighteenth-century scientist, philosopher and mystic Emanuel Swedenborg had inspired a Christian religious movement that took root early in the growing industrial centres of the north-west. With its dual emphasis on the scientific investigation of nature and revelatory journeying into supernatural realms, the New Church constituted one of the more intellectually complex trends of nineteenth-century nonconformism. More broadly, Swedenborgianism had a strong appeal for many thinkers and writers, including Blake, Baudelaire, Coleridge and Emerson. The 1910 Highgate garden party was, in fact, part of that summer's celebrations of the centenary of the Swedenborg Society, whose main event was an international conference in London under the patronage of the King of Sweden. One of the conference's vice-presidents, who was therefore likely to have been among the crowds circulating on Wynter's lawns to the accompaniment of the Grenadier Guards' regimental band, was the novelist Henry James.

During the later 1920s David Wynter effectively bankrolled Swedenborgianism in London. In 1926 he funded the Swedenborg Society's acquisition and fitting out of large new premises in Bloomsbury, while Bishopswood served as a venue for New Church council meetings and as an open house for Swedenborgians passing through the city. In the midst of all this, Wynter's three children, his unmarried sister and sister-in-law somehow made their home. His grandson Bryan was to recall early impressions of resonant Lancashire accents amid the *haut bourgeois* luxury of Bishopswood as well as his grandfather's anxious concern that this small boy should have been permitted to run around on the grass in bare feet. It was from his grandfather, if anyone, that Bryan was to inherit his intellectual eclecticism.

detail of **13** The Wynter and Bosshardt families on holiday

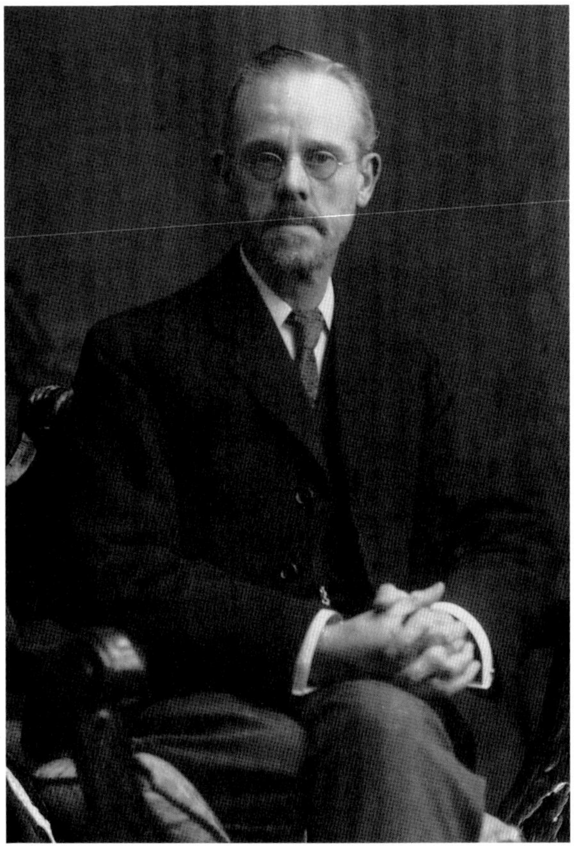

10
David Wynter (formerly Winterbotham), c.1906

While a young teacher, David Wynter had introduced extra subjects, such as physiology, chemistry and astronomy, into the curriculum. As a businessman, he kept up a serious amateur interest in science and in later life travelled widely (for those times), becoming a Fellow of the Royal Geographical Society. He visited Europe, the USA, Egypt and finally Palestine, where he was struck down by an unspecified but ultimately fatal illness.[1]

Some years before his father's death in 1931, Jim Wynter commissioned Windyridge, his own family seat in Hertfordshire. The house was designed in a plus-sized version of inter-war suburban Tudor, with a timber-frame façade and diamond-paned windows. Bryan Wynter was ten or eleven when his family moved here in 1926 (fig. 11); although its social atmosphere came to epitomise for him the worst excesses (or lack of excess) of middle-class boringness and repression, Windyridge was also a place of much-relished – if irredeemably privileged – freedoms. There were always ponies to ride (a particular enthusiasm of Bryan's), a river for swimming and boating, wide gardens set in farmland and a shifting menagerie of dogs, cats and sundry exotic pets. Photographs from the 1920s and early 1930s show Bryan and his younger brother, Eric, splashing around in a canoe, constructing a kind of penitential horse-drawn pallet on which their mother poses, smiling gamely, or attempting to mollify a glaring baby owl. In other snapshots a badger mucks in with the family's dogs, and a strange beast identifiable as a kinkajou scuttles and scrambles unhindered around the house. A vein of gamesy anarchy rises amid the stockbroker-belt stolidity, the kind of gentle madness in Metroland that so fascinated the poet John Betjeman. Though art and culture are utterly absent from the scene, these Wynters are all – you get the impression – individually strong-willed people who know their own tastes.

Bryan Wynter's childhood background has similarities to that of Patrick Heron, later his contemporary at the Slade School of Art and, later still, his neighbour on the west Cornwall moors. Heron was the doted-on eldest son of a successful entrepreneur from a northern nonconformist background, the Yorkshire garment-manufacturer Tom Heron, who, after a spell running the Cryséde silk-printing works in St Ives, pioneered 1930s' high-street fashion through his chain of Cresta Silks shops. The big difference was that Heron's parents jointly and assiduously nurtured their son's precocious artistic talent. Through his membership of the Leeds Art Club and visits to the Café Royal on London business trips, Tom Heron knew personally many leading artists and writers, including Jacob Epstein, Henri Gaudier-Brzeska and Herbert Read.[2] No one in the family doubted, let alone opposed, the idea that Patrick would become an artist, and that art was a noble occupation, necessary to building the fairer, more enlightened society dreamed of by Fabian socialists such as Tom Heron: 'Finding freedom in creative work,' he wrote to his fourteen-year-old son, 'this idea of freedom is what we have to carry into our social organisation.'[3]

The prevailing ethos at Windyridge, by contrast, was one of unselfconscious philistinism. After following the conventional educational route – prep school at Seafield Park, near Fareham, from the age of eight, then, from

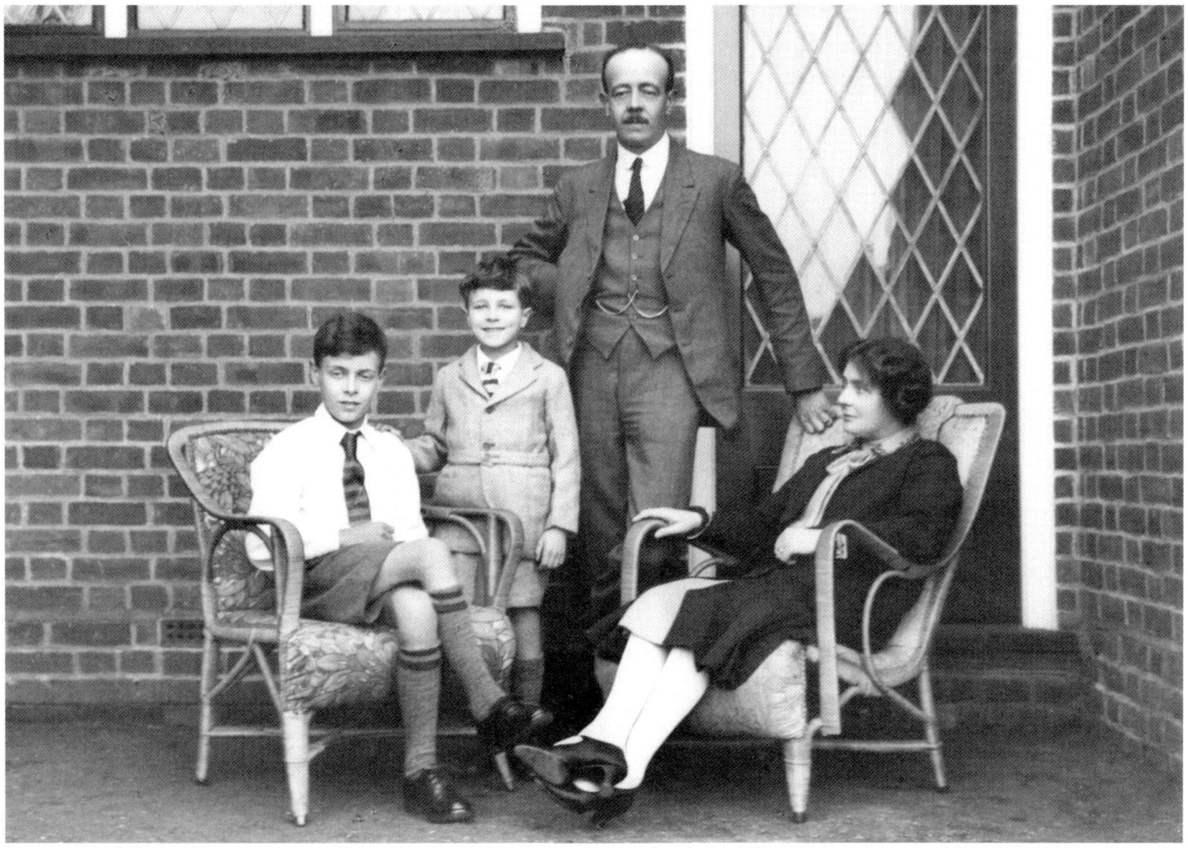

11
Bryan Wynter (seated left) with his parents and brother, Eric, Windyridge, Hertford, *c.*1927

thirteen to seventeen, public school at Haileybury in Hertfordshire – Bryan was expected to assume his place in the laundry business, along with the complaisant acceptance of material prosperity and social status that would come with it. The one adult in the family who saw things differently was his father's twin sister, Jessie, who, in a Swedenborgian spirit of rapt creativity, enjoyed art, wrote poetry and put a spanner in the works by encouraging the aptitude for these improvident pursuits that she detected in her nephew. Bryan's school career was marked more by his success as a gymnast (he was never a willing team player) than by his academic work, where his progress was thought slow, although his housemaster pronounced him 'a very sound boy';[4] at the age of sixteen he passed his school certificate in English and French. His art master at Haileybury was the charismatic Wilfrid Jasper Blunt, a former student at the Royal College of Art whose art historian brother Anthony later achieved notoriety as a Cold War spy. Howard Hodgkin, a pupil of Wilfrid Blunt's at Eton in the 1940s, remembered him as 'a great enthusiast, an eclectic collector, a brilliant talker about art'.[5] He was also responsible for promoting a change in the handwriting taught in English schools to a script based on Renaissance humanist models. That Wynter's handling of a drawn line so often has the feel of a calligraphic statement may owe something to Blunt's orthographic interests. Although a few of Wynter's early drawings and a prize-winning poem survive, there is nothing resembling Heron's adolescent output of unnervingly precocious oil paintings in styles adroitly assimilated from Cézanne and Braque. Yet Wynter's conviction that there were alternatives to the future that was being mapped out for him must already have been stirring. He was later to interpret much in his life as a reaction both to his parents' bourgeois habits and to certain unexpressed, and therefore all the more stifling, tensions in their relationship.

The small farm attached to Windyridge allowed Jim Wynter belated satisfaction of his agricultural leanings, but in other areas of his life he felt less fulfilled. His wife, Dora, came from a large family in Newbury, where her father was a 'factor', or dealer in farm produce. The couple met while she was working as David Wynter's secretary; after a five-year courtship Jim finally persuaded her to marry him. It was only once the knot had been tied – irrevocably, at a time when divorce was still a subject of profound shame and scandal – that he discovered his wife's unshakeable aversion to sex. She evidently submitted to what she privately called the 'sacrifice' on at least two occasions, probably connected with the departure and return of her husband in the First World War, since their first son, Bryan, was born in September 1915, and a second, Eric, followed in 1919. For the first three years of Bryan's life his father was almost entirely absent, serving as a private in the army in North Africa (he refused to accept a commission, suggesting a certain principled resistance to the offer of unearned privilege). During this time Dora transferred the full beam of her affection and needs on to her first-born (fig. 12). Even at a time when the English middle classes possessed only the most primitive terminology for discussing such things, it was noticed that, after Jim Wynter's return from the war, relations with his small son, who until then had been oblivious of his father's existence, were abysmal and apparently irreparable. When, as a young adult, Bryan encountered Freud's interpretation of the Oedipus myth, he must almost have felt its weight in his palm, like a long-sought key.

For the time being, Wynter's late teens went according to plan. He was initiated into every aspect of the laundry trade, from the shop floor up. After the tightly guarded social horizons towards which his education had been directed, he relished the chance to mix with people from other backgrounds. His apprenticeship also entailed being dispatched for several months to Switzerland, to see how things were done at Waschanstalt Zürich, where the modernist factory buildings and streamlined machinery were the last word in laundry technology. The firm's owners, the Bosshardts, were family friends; in summer 1933, after Bryan left school, they and the Wynters had shared a touring holiday in west Cornwall. Photographs show various members of the party climbing cliffs at Land's End and Gurnard's Head, sunbathing, horsing around on Bronze Age megaliths (fig. 13) and stopping off for tea and snapshots at scenic locations along the way, including St Ives, Zennor, Porthcurno and Cadgwith. Long days of sporty sociability – this time on the ski slopes – were similarly a feature of Bryan's stay with the Bosshardts in Switzerland. Though he came to loathe the slightest hint of any such connection, he evidently threw himself into these activities with a jokey, companionable gusto not unlike his father's. At the same time, the technical, scientific side of the Bosshardts' business genuinely engaged his interest. It was not until after his return to England, when he started work for the Times Laundry Co. in London, that art seriously entered the equation.

In 1936 Wynter enrolled in evening classes at Westminster School of Art, in Dean's Yard, beside

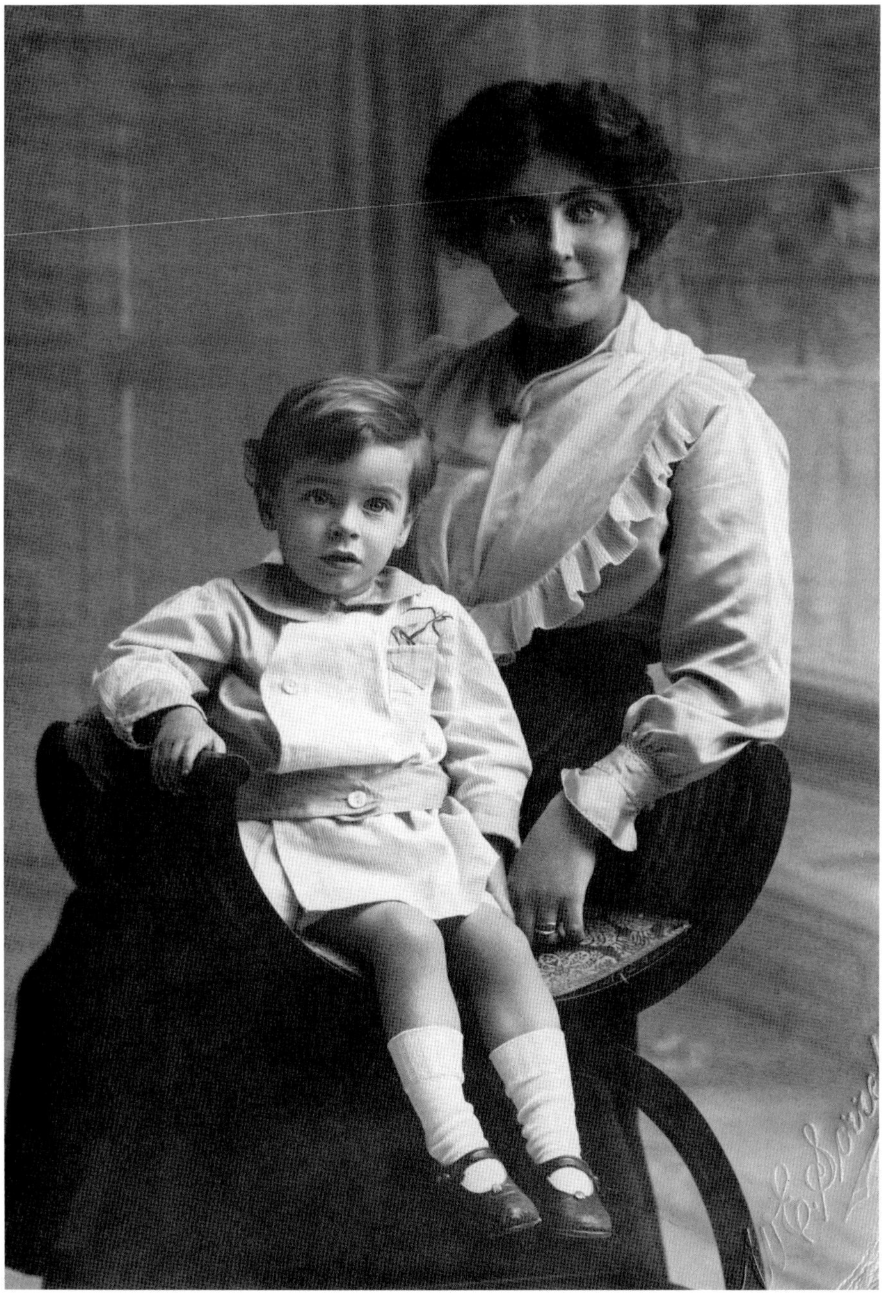

12
Bryan Wynter, aged three, with his mother, 1918

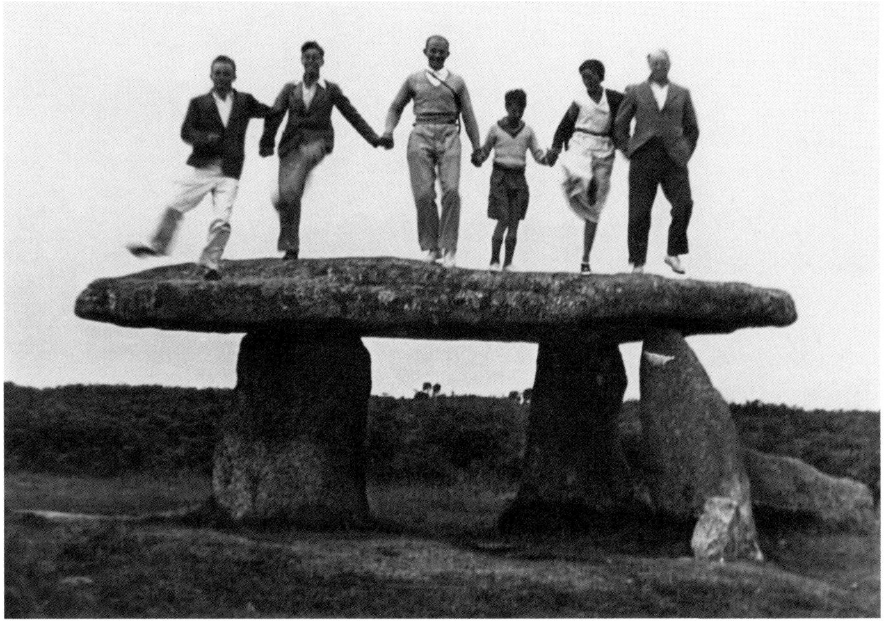

13
The Wynter and Bosshardt families on holiday, Lanyon Quoit, Cornwall, summer 1933

Westminster Abbey. The classes were held in rooms that led off from galleries still cluttered with exhibits from the architectural museum that had formerly occupied the building. Wynter may have attended the life classes taken here by Mervyn Peake and seen the idiosyncratic costume designs Peake produced that year for the Capek brothers' *The Insect Play*. These struck a cartoonishly surrealistic note, which was very much in the London air in the summer of 1936. In June the first International Surrealist Exhibition opened at the New Burlington Galleries. Surrealist art had been seen in London before, but on nothing like this scale. In the twelve years since André Breton had produced his *Surrealist Manifesto* the movement had been firmly based in Paris. Breton defined Surrealism as 'psychic automatism in its pure state, by which it is intended to express ... the true functioning of thought. Thought expressed in the absence of any control exerted by reason, and outside all moral and aesthetic considerations.'[6] The practice of 'automatism' (a term adopted from psychiatry) involved artistic techniques in which chance rather than intention governed the outcome. Deeply influenced by Freud's psychoanalytic theories, in which the conscious mind is seen as socially programmed to suppress or distort the deeper (unconscious or subconscious) workings of the psyche, Surrealism emphasised the creative importance of dreams, hallucinations and, more generally, an intuitive, impulsive, subversive approach to life and art.

Alongside European Surrealist heavyweights including Max Ernst and Salvador Dalí, both of whom made a profound impression on Wynter, the show featured a large British contingent, including Henry Moore, Paul Nash and Graham Sutherland. Whereas Breton had striven to maintain a certain ideological unity (as suggested by his sobriquet 'the Pope of Surrealism'), British Surrealism had far less discipline in its ranks. When the critic Herbert Read declared in his opening address that 'Surrealism in general is the Romantic principle in art',[7] gathering Blake, Coleridge, Shelley and pastoral visionaries such Samuel Palmer into the fold as honoured proto-Surrealists, the drift away from Breton's hardline leftist-Freudian stance must have been embarrassingly evident. Any such suggestion of internal fracture lines was lost on the British public, however; unusually for a modern art exhibition in London, the show was popular as well as controversial, attracting about a thousand visitors a day. A series of talks by leading Surrealists included a notorious event when Dalí, accompanied by two borzoi hounds, nearly perished from suffocation inside the deep-sea diver's helmet in which he was delivering his lecture and from which he had to be hastily unscrewed. For Wynter, who was intrigued by the whole Surrealist phenomenon, the exhibition coincided with, and was probably the catalyst for, his first serious move towards a career in art.

Surrealism's attraction for Wynter had much to do with its debt to Freudian psychoanalysis and its left-wing, assertively anti-bourgeois stance. Both became crucial to his youthful intellectual life, his attempts to secure 'the essential I ... this centre of myself'[8] from the claims

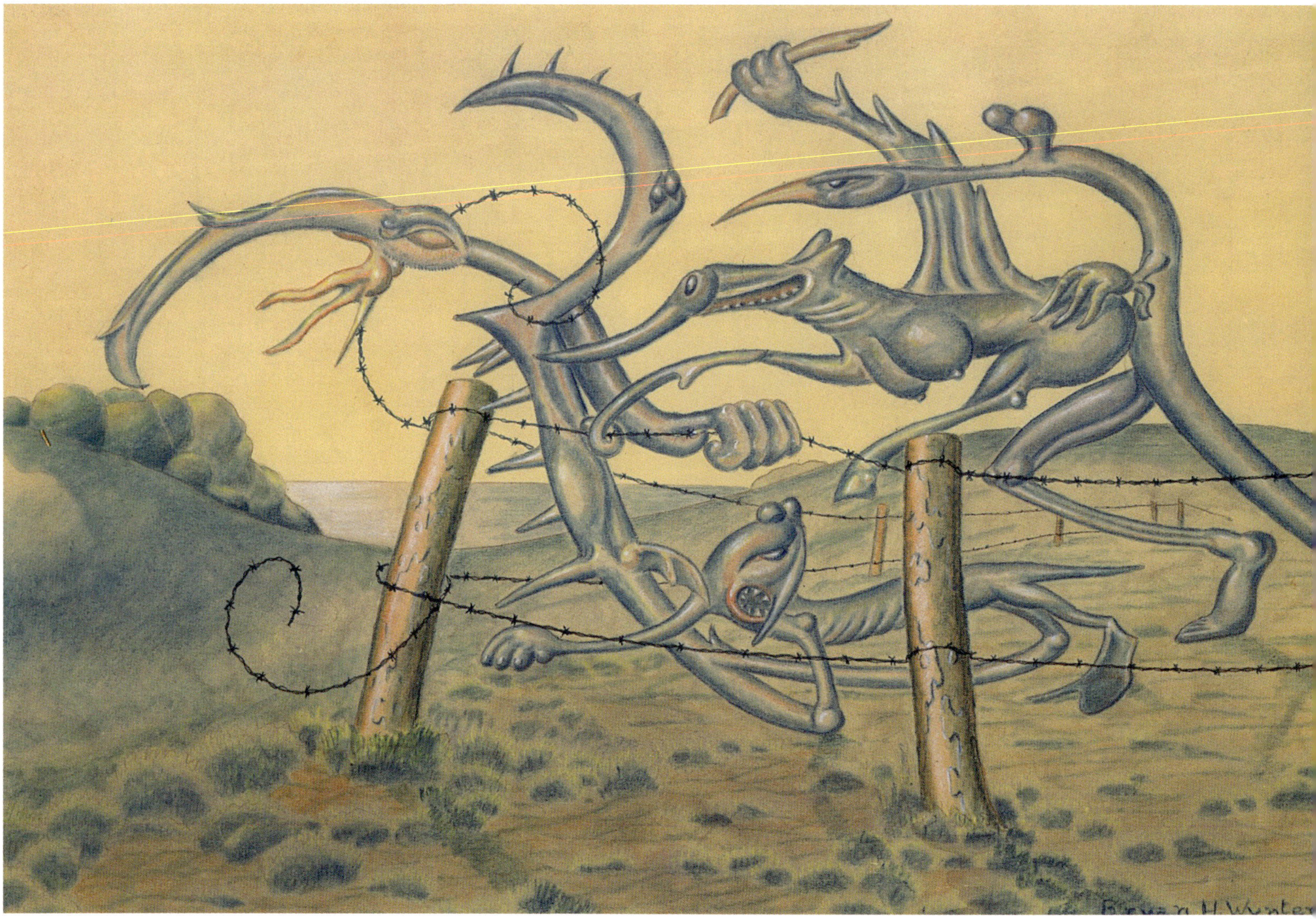

of upbringing and convention. In a crayon and pastel drawing he made in 1937, titled *Fantastic Figures Imprisoned by Barbed Wire* (fig. 14), he put his own interpretation on a familiar Surrealist trope, involving the dreamworld's ambiguous symbolic population of anthropomorphic animals and theriomorphic humans. On a tussocky hillside, behind a barbed-wire fence that could equally suggest a battlefield or a Windyridge paddock, caricatured, etiolated monsters, bearing more than a passing resemblance to Peake's costume design for Capek's Ichneumon Fly, strain forwards, frozen in tangled movement like a rubbery ideograph. Their erectile postures and gland-like breasts are a reminder of Surrealism's manic embrace of sexuality, another aspect of the movement that offered a compelling contrast to life in the Wynter family home.

Around the time he painted *Fantastic Figures*, Wynter made it clear to his father that he intended to quit the laundry and go to art school. On this issue years of mutual distrust came spectacularly to a head; yet more bitterness accumulated on both sides before Eric's intercession induced a furious Jim Wynter to accept defeat. Although Bryan finally took up a place at the Slade School of Art in 1938, this wasn't the end of the story. For years to come, after he had 'used money to try to keep Bryan out of the art world',[9] his father continued to provide financial support, while making his contempt for the whole enterprise clear. This was a fairly common state of affairs: a similar kind of curdled privilege underwrote Roger Hilton's art school career and those of several other mid-century British artists. The Slade, meanwhile, was hardly a springboard for progressive art. The teaching programme was, as in French academies, based on the life class rather than, as at the Royal Academy

14
Fantastic Figures Imprisoned by Barbed Wire
coloured crayon and pastel
37.5 x 55.2 cm (14¾ x 21¾ in)
1937
Victoria and Albert Museum, London

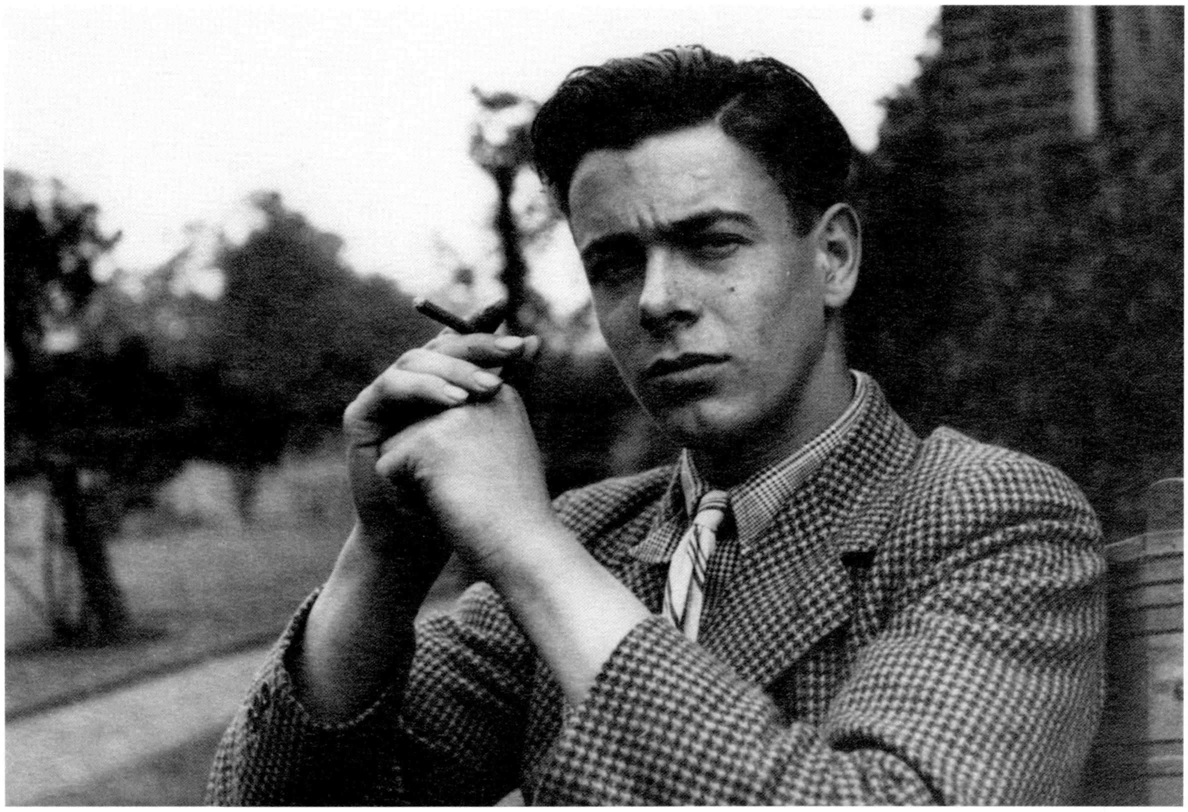

15
Bryan Wynter, *c.*1935

Schools, on drawing grime-caked casts of Classical statuary. Staff in both institutions, however, had a passionate loathing of modern European art.

In 1934, for example, the formidable Henry Tonks, whose regime as Slade Professor of Fine Art continued to set the tone under his milder-mannered successor, Randolph Schwabe, had welcomed news of the death of the avant-garde champion Roger Fry, remarking that it was 'as though Hitler and Mussolini had passed away'.[10] Fry's unforgiven atrocities included the introduction into England of Post-Impressionist painting a quarter of a century earlier. Modern European art had outraged audiences and, in Tonks's view, corrupted young British artists ever since. Students of Wynter's generation adapted to the situation, becoming skilled in academic drawing and in painting nudes while making their own extra-curricular discoveries in contemporary art, which they shared among themselves. Wynter's contemporaries at the Slade included Paul Feiler, who had arrived in Britain from Germany a few years earlier, and Patrick Heron, both of whom were later, like Wynter, to base their working lives in Cornwall. Heron attended only a couple of days each week, commuting from the family home in Welwyn Garden City; at the age of eighteen he had already absorbed Post-Impressionist and later French art so thoroughly that he found the Slade training worse than futile and soon dropped out. For his part, Wynter seems to have enjoyed student life. He was, recalled Feiler, 'not exactly a playboy', but he dressed well (fig. 15) drove a smart open-top car and had a flat in Gower Street, close to the Slade.[11]

Starting art school at the age of twenty-three (there would have been students of sixteen or younger in the classes), Wynter had a lot of time to make up. His art education was soon to be cut short, however. If his father had thrown at him the usual expostulations – What on earth could art school lead to? How would he ever earn his living? – by summer 1939 the idea of an assured future of any kind, for anyone, was rapidly dissolving. On 3 September, after several years of nervous prevarication over the Nazi threat, the German invasion of Poland finally triggered Britain's declaration of war. Air raids on London were expected to begin at any time, and by the end of the year the Slade had been evacuated from its city-centre premises to safer quarters at the Ashmolean Museum in Oxford, where the Ruskin School of Art occupied two studios. Unlike younger students, Wynter was already eligible for military service when the move took place; he did not have long in Oxford before his time as an art student came to an end.

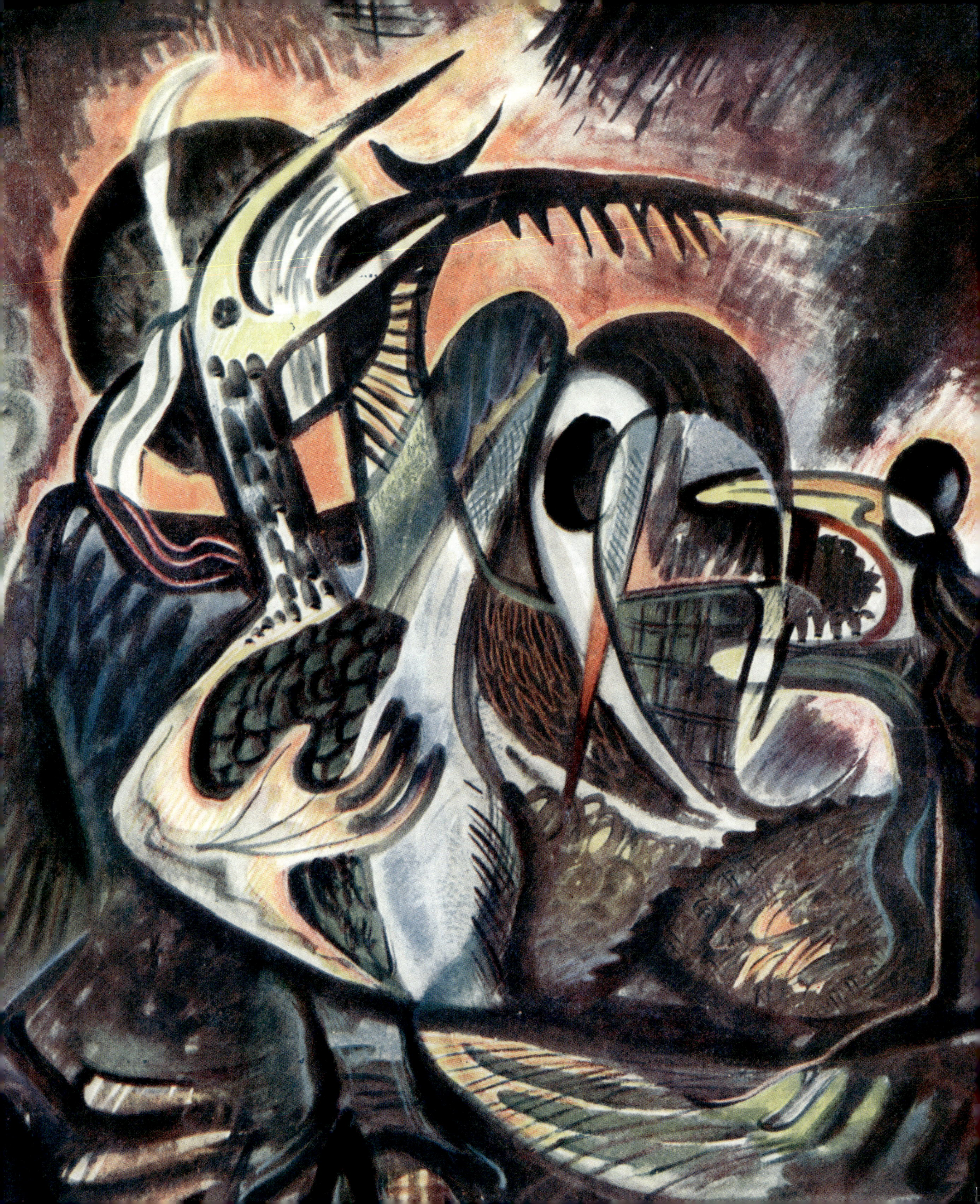

2

'The Tendency to Look Deeper': Wartime and Oxford, 1938–45

When his call-up papers came, Wynter decided to refuse military service and to register as a Conscientious Objector (CO). The motives for his decision were complex but were clearly informed, once again, by convictions to do with individual freedom and integrity. Moreover, Wynter belonged to a generation that, during the later 1930s, had come to accept as a given the association between progressive art, whether Surrealist or Constructivist, and anti-fascist politics. Art during these years was part of the ideological battleground. How could anyone doubt this, on seeing Picasso's monumental protest painting *Guernica* (shown in London at the New Burlington Galleries, then the Whitechapel Gallery, in the winter of 1938–9) or on hearing news of the 1937 Nazi blockbuster show 'Degenerate Art', in which works by modern artists were sneeringly juxtaposed with the productions of mental patients and 'primitive' peoples? However improbable it now seems that, by opposing state propaganda and militarisation, free intellectuals and artists could stall the momentum of war, this hope was earnestly shared by many of Wynter's contemporaries.

Like other young idealists, too, Wynter was fired by his reading of Aldous Huxley, whose *Ends and Means* (1937) set out the case for non-violence as a moral and courageous means of opposing war – in fact, the *only* effective way to achieve a peaceful future. Eric Wynter recalled how his discussions of the book with Bryan helped to form their joint determination to register as COs. In other ways, too, Bryan's thinking was influenced by Huxley, especially his reframing of the Buddhist concept of non-attachment for an educated Western readership. In Huxley's view, non-attachment specifically entailed the rejection of state authority and its manipulation of 'the sub-human world of crowd emotion'. 'The most nearly free men', he declared, 'have always been those who combined virtue with insight ... The ideal man is the non-attached man.'[1] By contrast, those who embraced 'military slavery, or conscription' allowed themselves to become pawns in the sinister machinery of the modern planned state. Such a course was little better, he implied, than becoming a fascist yourself, since 'All Fascist planning has one ultimate aim: to make the national society more efficient as a war machine'.[2] In this context, said Huxley, Conscientious Objectors were 'men of exceptional moral force'.[3]

Huxley was not, to be sure, solely responsible for such beliefs. The Romantic tradition identified by Herbert Read (himself a hardy anarchist) as a core element in Surrealism – or, at any rate, British Surrealism – had its own tough political credentials. Wynter's extensive reading of poetry may have included Wordsworth's exhortation in *The Prelude* to 'Build social freedom on its only basis,/ The freedom of the individual mind', a freedom whose authoritative self-sufficiency he evoked a few pages later, reflecting that 'the mind is to herself/ Witness and judge'.[4] Many men and women of Wynter's age who opted to become COs were also, of course, influenced by their experience of the First World War – not at first hand but through those fathers and uncles who, twenty years earlier, had returned alive but whose enforced participation in the world's first great experiments in mechanised mass slaughter had in so many cases left them physically and mentally broken.

The government's attitude to COs in the Second World War was more humane than it had been during the previous conflict, when they were routinely humiliated and their objections cavalierly overruled. In any case, the armed forces were not keen to enlist too many articulate young people who had tanked up on Huxley or Marx. Those who did not want to register for military service had to put their case in person to a tribunal, but this time the assessments were made by civilian boards not military personnel. After attending a tribunal in Reading – a rowdy affair in which members of the Oxford Playhouse company vociferously declared their pacifism – Wynter was assigned to work on the land, one of the Ministry of Labour's standard occupations for COs. He dug and cleared ditches along the Thames Valley and,

detail of **27**
Birds, 1944

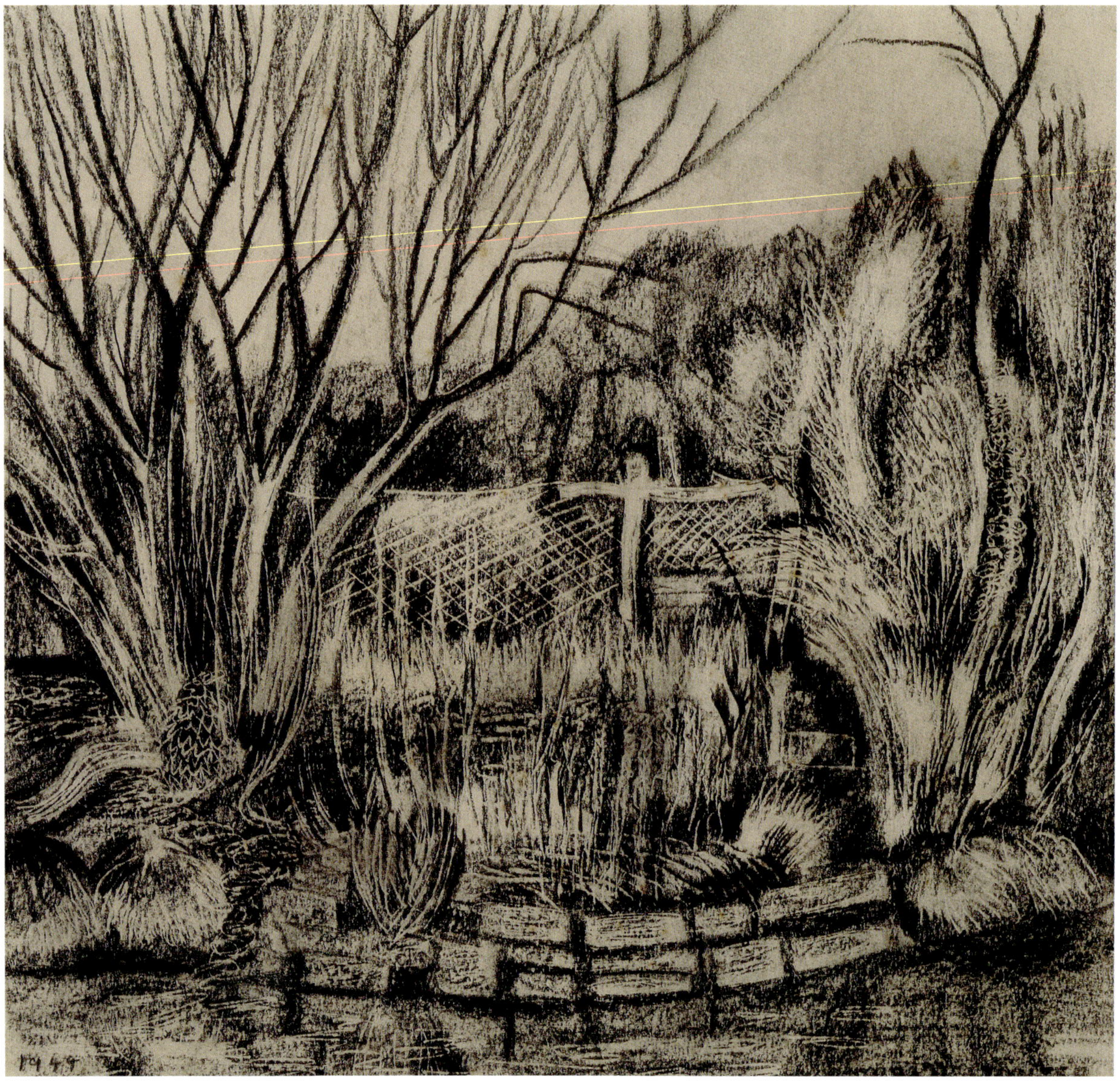

16
Riverbank near Oxford
pencil on paper
22.9 x 23.5 cm (9 x 9¼ in)
1944
Artist's estate

more congenially, worked as a labourer on a smallholding at Noke, north of Oxford, run by Edward and Rachel Walton, a young couple who shared many of his views. When he had the chance, Wynter went out drawing in Oxford and in the surrounding countryside (figs 16, 20). Noticeable in some sketches is the restless variety of his line – not as violent or frenetic as Ernst (fig. 34) or André Masson but comparably energetic, quite unlike the smooth draughtsmanship expected in the Slade life room.

From around 1943 Wynter and a Slade friend, Hugh Mellor, worked as keepers in the laboratories of Oxford University's Department of Human Anatomy, tending the animals housed there for vivisection. Under the direction of a senior government scientist, the endocrinologist Solly Zuckerman, rhesus monkeys were used for experiments into synthetic hormones. Zuckerman's researches also focused on air-raid casualties, and animals were required for testing the effects of explosives (one of the first such trials had involved pinioning primates to the ground on Salisbury Plain at varying distances from a bomb blast). In the monkey house Wynter and Mellor struck up an alliance with their charges, taking the animals' part against the scientific staff and encouraging rebellion (one old rhesus monkey, nicknamed Tchaikovsky, discovered how to unlock the cages, triggering a general jailbreak). Wynter noted the monkeys' increased reproductive rate under his care, which he took as a sign of their greater contentment. The cruelty and craziness of monkey house life are captured in Wynter's cartoons (figs 17, 18, 19) and in the surrealistic collaborative drawings he

This page:
(clockwise from top left)

17
Monkey House cartoon
pencil on paper
25.4 x 20.3 cm (10 x 8 in)
*c.*1944
Private collection

18
Monkey House cartoon
pencil on paper
25.4 x 20.3 cm (10 x 8 in)
1943–4
Private collection

19
Monkey House cartoon
pencil on paper
25.4 x 20.3 cm (10 x 8 in)
*c.*1944
Private collection

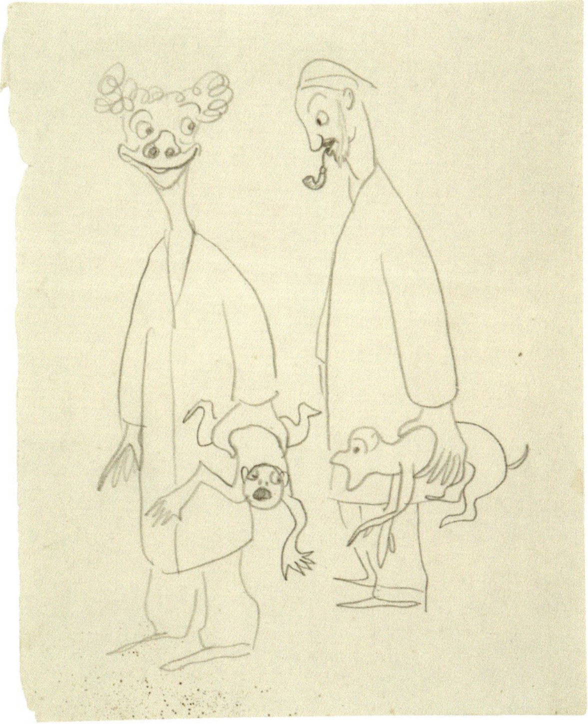

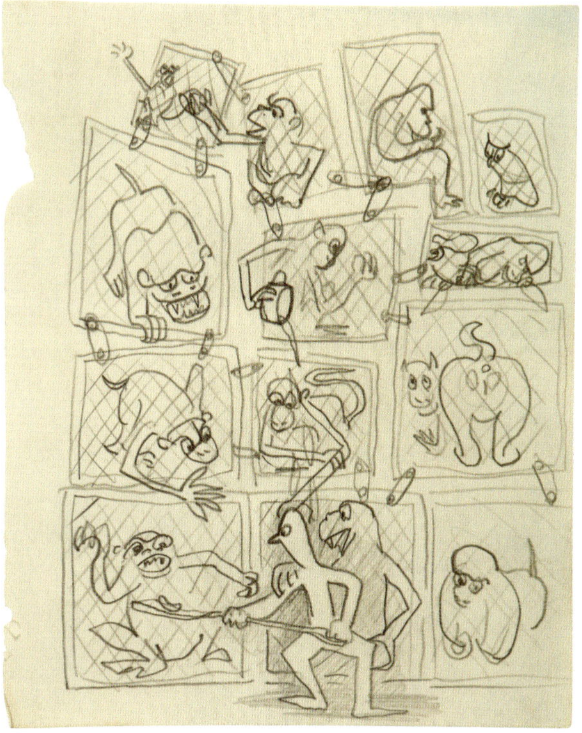

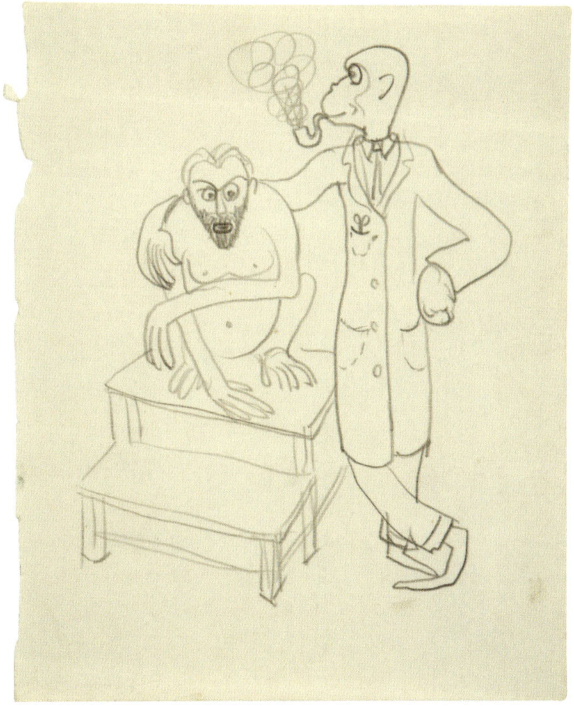

produced with Mellor and other Slade friends. Monkeys and scientists swap roles; naked victims are pinned down and probed with syringes – a crude graphic version of a motif later adopted by Francis Bacon. Recalling the time served by Wynter in the monkey house, his brother observed (as others were to observe of Wynter in different contexts):

> There was a good deal of savagery in his elaborate and bizarre practical jokes which curiously endeared him to the people he worked with. They respected his integrity, perhaps envied it and they loved his humour. But the 'short-haired mad executives' disliked him, for his satire put their fortresses at risk.[5]

When he wasn't slaving on the land or in the lab, Wynter's social life revolved around his Slade contemporaries and the actors and staff at the Oxford Playhouse, which stood just across the road from the Ashmolean's august classical portico. Among this group were several young refugee students from Nazi Germany, including Milein Cosman, Vera Leslie and Hedwig Hoffmann (known as Hedy or, to her English friends, Heidi). Cosman's sketchbooks, full of drawings rapidly executed in studios, concert halls, streets and tearooms, include portraits of Wynter and other members of Oxford's wartime intelligentsia, including Iris Murdoch, Lord David Cecil, the monk-turned-art-historian Bernard Denvir and the young poets Sidney Keyes and John Heath-Stubbs. Leslie, meanwhile, shared with Wynter her enthusiasm for Franz Kafka, whose stories she translated and illustrated, and Carl Gustav Jung ('To Bryan's subconscious with love from mine', runs her dedication in a Christmas gift of *The Psychology of C. G. Jung*). She and Wynter were evidently close, but it was with Hedy Hoffmann that he fell in love. He must have had earlier girlfriends – women tended to find him both physically attractive and easy to talk to – but it is his relationship with Hoffmann that leaves the first paper trail. They probably became lovers in 1941 or early 1942; after the affair ended some three years later, they continued to correspond until about 1950. Apart from Wynter's drawings and watercolours, of which few survive from before 1944, it is his letters to Hedy that provide the most consistent and revealing source for his development as an artist during the war.[6]

Their correspondence testifies to a passionate and intellectually intimate relationship. Emotions, sex, dreams, art – they seemed able to discuss most things in a straightforward, uninhibited way quite alien to the conversational register Wynter had grown up with. Several years older than Hedy, he found himself adopting a paternal, protective role. A drawing he gave her, which she kept all her life, illustrates her pet name, Mouse, but also shows Wynter on best behaviour as a Slade-trained draughtsman (fig. 21). There were clearly tensions; 'I must seem to you a hopelessly confused person', he wrote after an early contretemps. 'I want to be alone sometimes to work & collect myself, but when I am alone I miss you so much. I want us to be together & yet to remain separate individuals.' To qualify this plea for what we'd now call personal space, he acknowledged 'I know ... that you need a great deal of affection ... but I must express it in my own way & I know you find this a little bit distant.'[7] Still, if Wynter wanted to remind himself of the alternative to such emotional pressures, he had only to visit his parents. During a stay at Windyridge in early 1945 he described a typical scene on the Wynter home front. After quoting his mother's sunset paean of praise to 'those dear boys' of Bomber Command flying east above the garden, perhaps on their way in mid-February to incinerate Hedy's home town of Dresden (the rebuke to

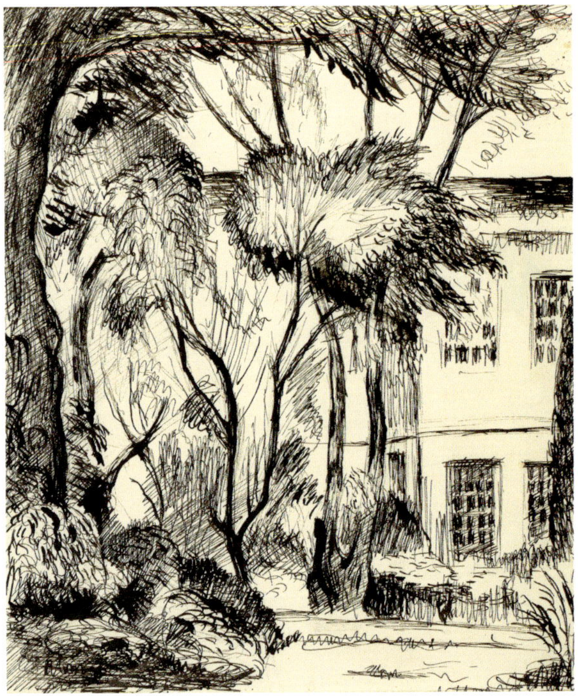

20
Botanic Gardens, Oxford
ink on paper
20.2 x 24.6 cm (8 x 9¾ in)
c.1944
Fitzwilliam Museum, Cambridge

Wynter's pacifism was sorely felt even if unintended), he reflected, 'to live trivially is bad enough but to do it on such a vast and expensive scale is utterly dismal. Materially they have gained all they ever wanted & all it has brought them is disappointment & a constant round of fatuous occupations.' He ruefully concluded, that 'cynicism is the necessary complement of idealism ... You must recognise that people *are* bloody but redeemable. If you expect them to be perfect then you yourself become embittered.'[8]

From Hedy he learned about a very different kind of life. Her father, the sculptor Eugen Hoffmann, had taught at the Hochschule für Bildende Künste in Dresden. An active Communist, he was imprisoned immediately after Hitler's accession as German chancellor in January 1933. On his release in 1936 he was forbidden to teach or exhibit, although three of his works were included the following year in 'Degenerate Art', which opened in Munich in the summer and then toured throughout the Reich. In the catalogue for the show, his sculpture *Girl with Blue Hair* was instructively twinned with a goggle-eyed fetish shaped from masticated bread by an asylum inmate. After war was declared, Hoffmann and his wife

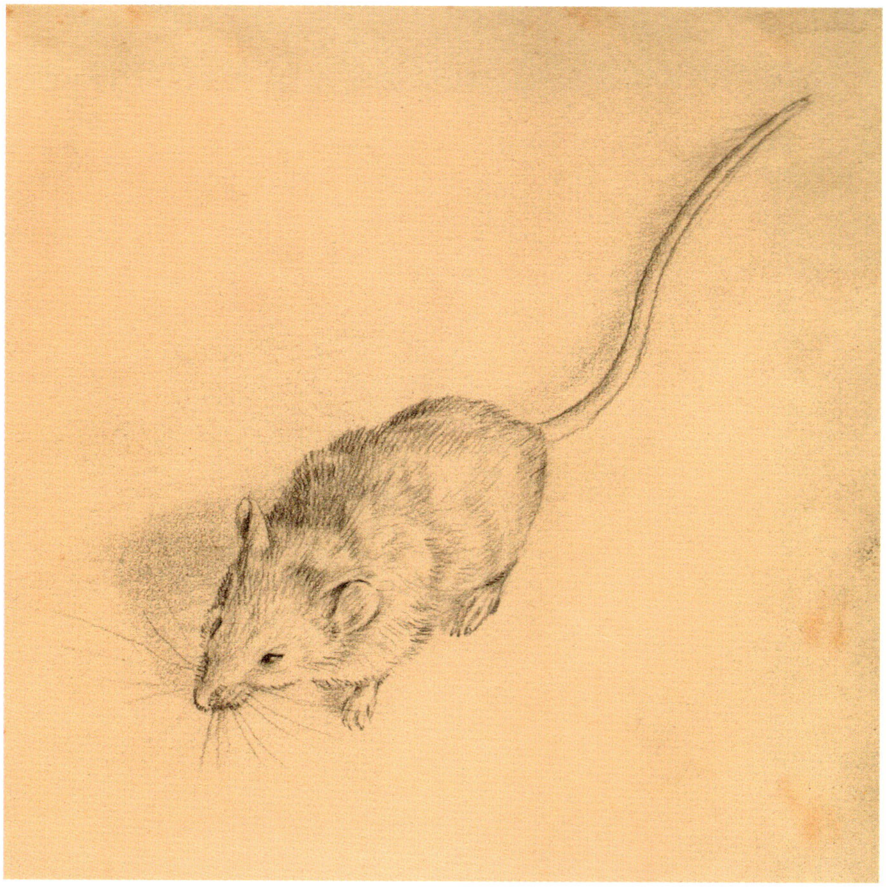

21
Mouse
pencil on paper
12.3 x 12 cm (4¾ x 4¾ in)
*c.*1940
Hedy Hoffmann Estate

narrowly escaped into exile, with the help of the Communist Party underground network. Some time before this, Hedy had been given temporary safe haven as an assistant in a Quaker home for children near Prague. When it became too dangerous to remain in Czechoslovakia, Oskar Kokoschka, a Dresden colleague of her father's and a family friend, arranged her escape on a *Kindertransport*, one of the last such trains to leave Prague before the borders closed. Once in Britain, she must have spent anxious weeks awaiting news of her parents.

Hedy had grown up amid a European artistic intelligentsia whose political engagement and (by English standards) classlessness were sharply distinguished from the sottish, dandified bohemianism Wynter associated with the 'cardboard Baudelaires' of London's Soho and Fitzrovia.[9] From Hedy, and no doubt from other refugee students, Wynter would have heard first-hand accounts of German Expressionist art, for which Dresden had been an important centre earlier in the century. Expressionism had put the sort of emphasis on emotional directness that Surrealism later placed on automatism; in contrast to Paris-based Surrealism, which drew heavily on Freudian theory, Expressionism had its roots in a more mystical approach to the psyche. Such an approach could be found in Jung's theories (another European thinker, incidentally, who acknowledged his debt to Swedenborg), which combined scientific observation with mythological symbolism. 'What to the casual view is *fact* to the final view is *symbol*, and vice versa', declared Jung. 'Certainly it is necessary for science to know how things are "in themselves", but even science cannot escape the psychological conditions of knowledge.'[10]

Jung became as influential on Wynter's circle in Oxford during the war as Huxley had been for him personally around 1940. Wynter owned and annotated numerous volumes of Jung's works, including *Psychology of the Unconscious*, *The Integration of the Personality* and *Modern Man in Search of a Soul*. A feature of such texts was their reference to illustrations, notably the concentric diagrams termed mandalas, with which Jung represented the unconscious self and which conveyed a persuasive conviction that psychological processes had visual equivalents. Wynter's access to actual examples of Expressionist art, meanwhile, was limited. For him, the artist who probably came closest to the Expressionist spirit, at least in the intensity of his colour and in his works' potent yet veiled intuitions of meaning, was Paul Klee. Like Hoffmann and many other progressive artists in Germany, Klee had been expelled from his job and publicly ridiculed in 'Degenerate Art'. Wynter may have seen the Klee exhibition at the Leicester Galleries in London in February 1941, the year after the artist's death in exile in Switzerland. He was certainly attracted by Klee's combination of lucid graphic definition and rich, luminous tones. Some of Klee's paintings of the later 1930s, such as *Oriental Sweet* (1938), contain configurations of what seem like hieroglyphs, which give the strong impression of signifying, without being actually readable.

Despite lack of time, materials, privacy and

opportunities to study or exhibit, Wynter continued to draw in the landscape; he also created non-naturalistic images using Surrealist techniques, such as frottage (creating patterns by rubbing a sheet of paper laid on a textured surface, such as floor planks, with a pencil or crayon; fig. 23), as well as narrative or theatrical scenes that seem illustrative without being clearly identifiable (fig. 22). It was partly in anticipation of finding terrain more stimulating than the Thames Valley that he and Eric arranged a holiday in St Ives in July 1942. In Cornwall, Wynter found his enjoyment of the countryside's more athletic pleasures undimmed since his teenage holiday there: he swam, cycled and scrambled over the cliffs as well as sunbathing and loafing around in cafes. Writing to Hedy after his first few days in a guest house, he confessed that he'd been unable to buy paper for drawing or painting (not quite such a poor excuse as it sounds, given wartime scarcities). In reply she gently nagged him, 'Have you managed to get some paper and do some work? I do wish you would do something otherwise it would somehow seem such a waste of time'.[11] (She herself had no means of support other than the succession of menial jobs she was able to find as a refugee, and had little time or energy to pursue her own art; fig. 24.) The two of them often dreamed about their post-war future, living and working together. Wynter noted that St Ives was 'full of potential "studios" – some of them in use as such & others just empty shacks formerly used as dumps for fishing tackle'. On the whole, though, the tone of this long-established art colony struck him as conservative and pretentious: 'There are the usual summer exhibitions (Dod Procter R.A. etc. etc.). Altogether rather an "arty" town still with its "Bo'emian rendey-vous".'[12] A few miles to the west, where high granite moorland drops to the coast, it was a different story. In Wynter's report of exploring the verdant stream valley that runs seaward from Zennor village to spill precipitously into a small, steep cove, he sounds more excited by the imagination of a Robinson Crusoe-ish existence that could be lived there than by anything to do with the art of St Ives:

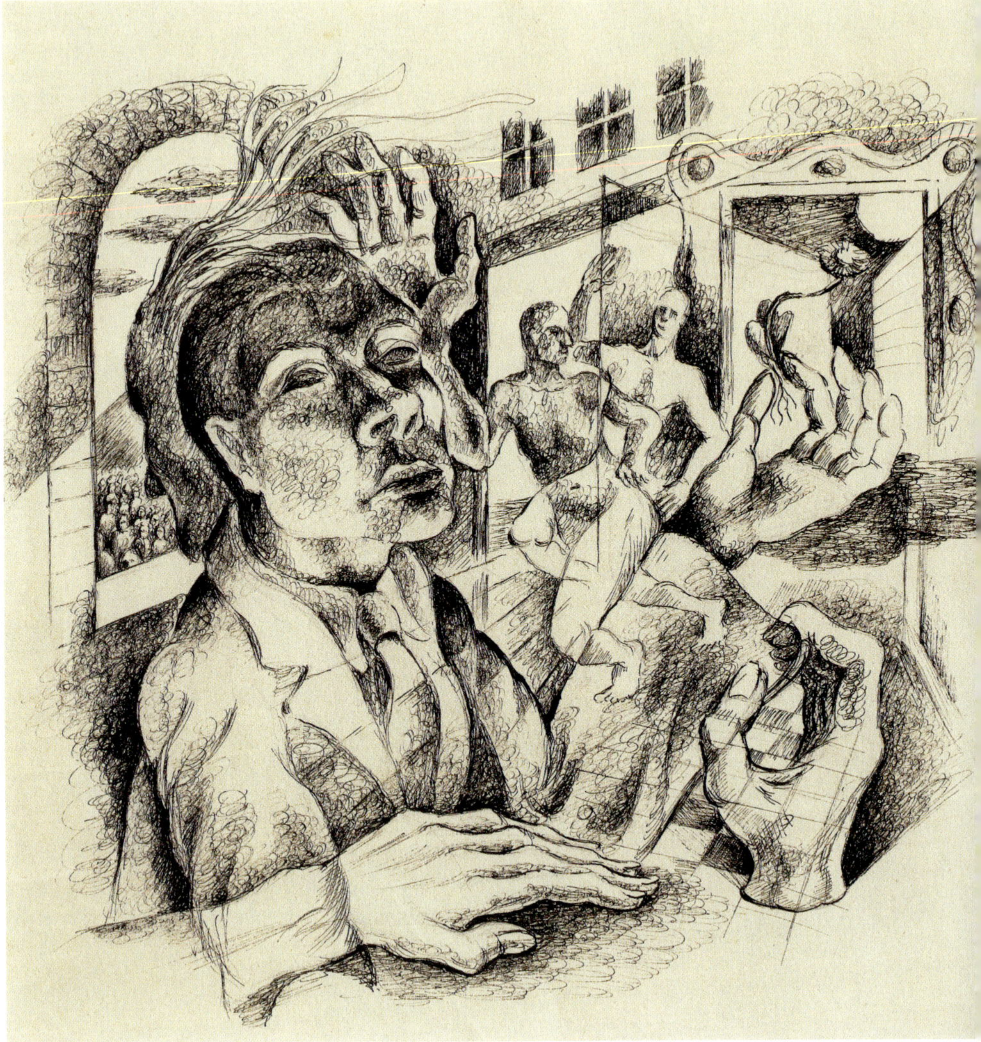

22
Illustration for 'Houses'
21.6 x 21 cm (8½ x 8¼ in)
1944
Artist's estate

> One could build here & live an almost self supporting life, terracing the flanks of the ravine for vegetables irrigating them & deriving power from the stream for electricity and other uses. One would have drift-wood for firing & the sea would provide fish, crabs & other food. I had a feast of raw mussels there, which eaten like this are rather like oysters. [13]

With its image of all-providing nature, this passage shows Wynter fantasising about a life free from wartime restrictions. But the daydream also contains practical calculations about what it would take to realise this fantasy.

Wynter's vision of a 'self supporting life', with water, fire, food and bucolic luxuries such as mussels to be

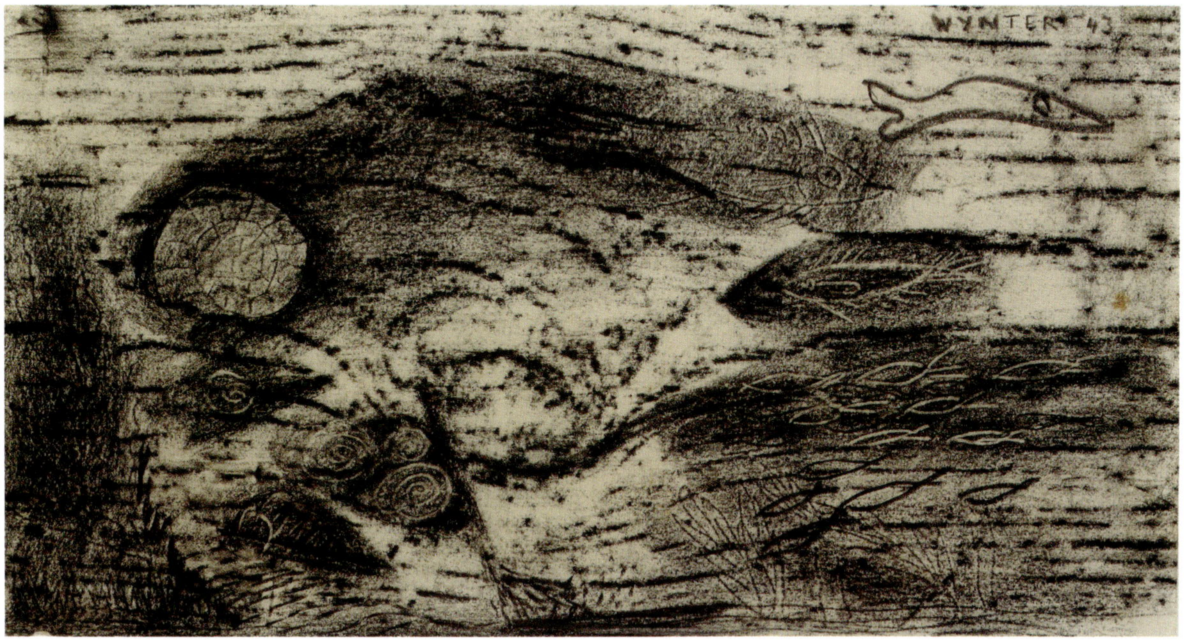

23
Fish Swimming
monotype, frottage and pencil on paper
12.7 x 22.8 cm (5 x 9 in)
1943
Artist's estate

taken straight from nature's hand, could hardly have been more different from his daily routine in Oxford. Here his sporadic early work, together with his developing idea of himself as an artist, was fuelled as much by discussions, books and art seen in reproduction as by contact either with wild nature or with professional artists. The Ashmolean, however, continued to stage exhibitions of contemporary British art throughout the war, including work by the Slade and Ruskin students. Between 1939 and 1944 Wynter was regularly able to see examples of work by Moore, Sutherland, Paul Nash, Ben Nicholson and other leading British artists. In 1942 a selection of masterworks from the Tate collection was shown (unmistakable Van Gogh-isms duly crept into Cosman's drawings and are detectable in Wynter's too). Nash had a solo exhibition in April 1943, and Sutherland lectured at least once. In the mid-1930s their names had been associated with the emerging British Surrealist faction; now, with European contact more or less severed and a mood of defiant yet vulnerable patriotism affecting all the arts, such Surrealist tendencies as they had earlier shown had reverted to their Romantic roots. 'Neo-Romanticism' was the term applied to the increasing number of artists whose work seemed doubly imbued with quasi-surrealistic anxiety and a pastoral yearning remote from everything that avant-garde art seemed to stand for.

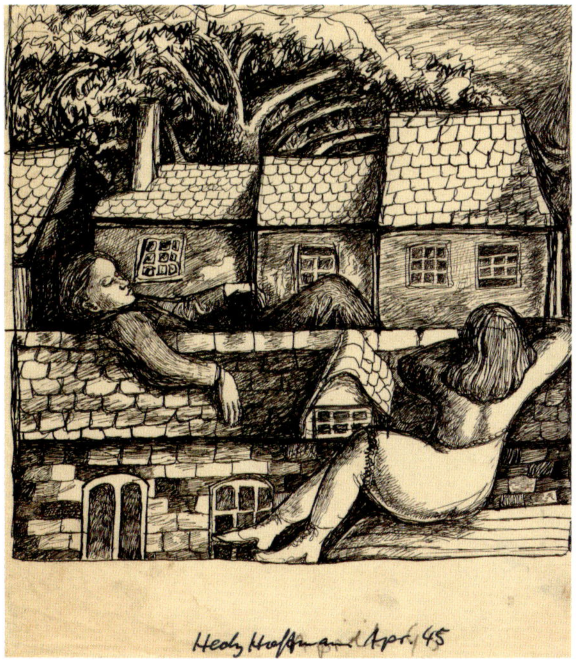

24
Hedy Hoffmann, drawing
ink and pencil on paper
25.3 x 22.3 cm (10 x 8¾ in)
1945
Private collection

In general, though, for all its distinguished cultural history, Oxford had never been much of a centre for visual art. In wartime it was a city in limbo, populated by students in their late teens awaiting call-up, a thinned-out cohort of dons who were either too elderly or deemed otherwise unfit to fight, and the motley assortment of *émigré* academics who featured in Milein Cosman's drawings. Almost untouched by air raids (it was said that Hitler had decided to spare its ancient colleges for future inhabitation by his generals), Oxford was an island of unreal normality between savagely blitzed cities – London to the south and, to the north, the industrial Midlands. In this atmosphere, 'stifling as a cocoon, and noisy with trivialities',[14] interesting ideas were nevertheless circulating among one smallish group of art students and undergraduate poets. Cosman recalled her feeling of being 'plunged into an astonishing web of intelligence ... the brimming buzz of allusions to saints, kings, martyrs, myths, miracles, bishops, ghosts and quotations, Yeats and Clare, Eliot, Blake ...'. Much of this buzz seemed to emanate from her studio in St John Street, behind the Ashmolean, which became

> a meeting point for tea after our divergent work; or later, after lectures or concerts, until the College gates shut. It was a rickety place with gas light – no electricity, so we preferred candlelight for our gatherings – where the newly- or half-baked poems were read in the meagre light. John Heath-Stubbs, Drummond Alison, and Sidney [Keyes], most memorably reading 'The Wilderness'. Once or twice we played Consequences, where you have to find a rhyming line to the end bit of the previous line – folded over – and it was handed around between seven or eight of us sitting on the floor. No need to see the handwriting: every single line would evoke its author.[15]

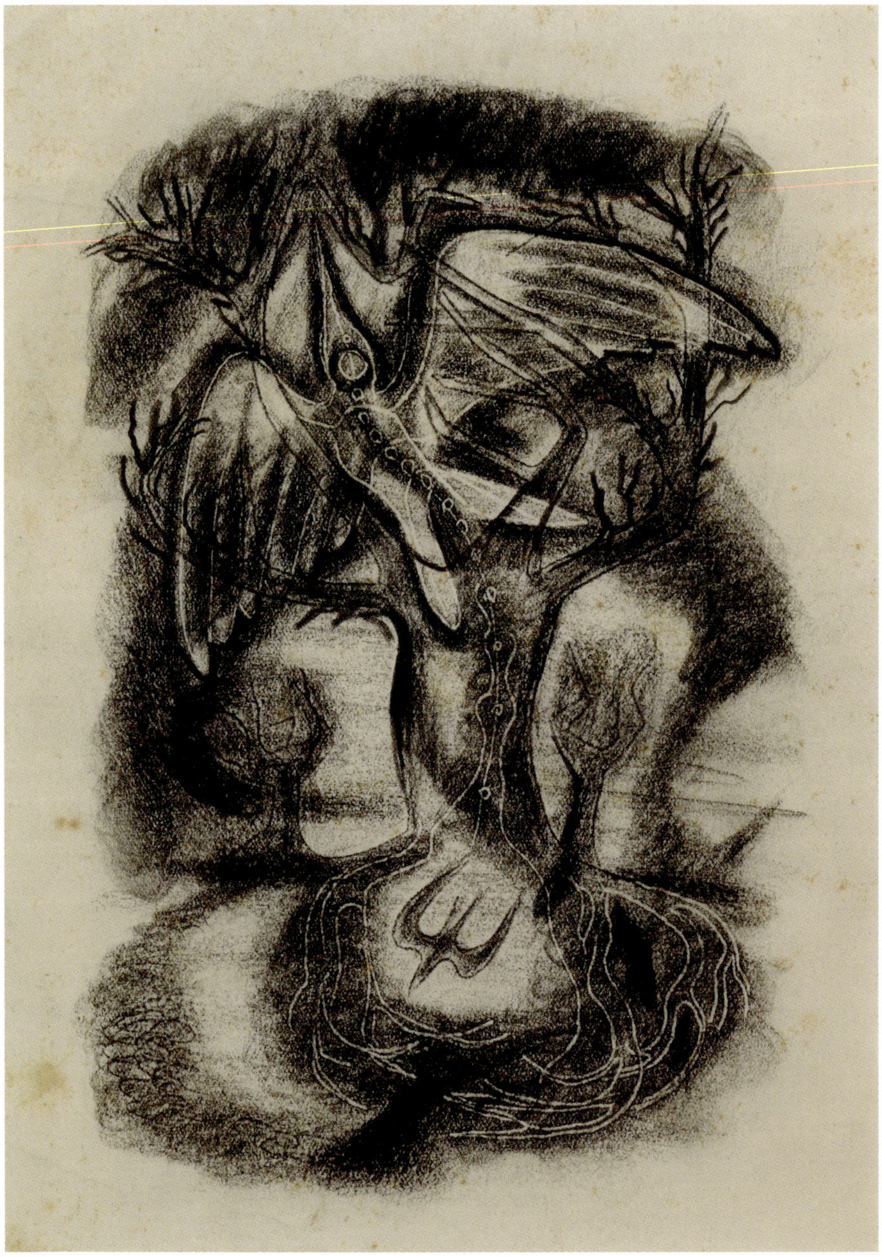

25
Bird Tree
charcoal on paper
22.9 x 15.2 cm (9 x 6 in)
1944–5
Artist's estate

Among Wynter's papers are dozens of such collaborative texts, either composed in Oxford with Mellor, Leslie and other friends or written at different times with Sven Berlin, David Wright or Sydney Graham when he was later living in Cornwall. It's not certain whether Wynter attended any of the St John Street sessions (his lodgings in Walton Crescent were near by), but his enjoyment of these word games, to which the Surrealists gave the name 'The Exquisite Corpse', began in Oxford, where a fascination with tapping the unconscious combined with the *longueurs* of nights during the black-out, when Wynter was regularly posted on firewatching duty at the Ashmolean. Hedy was a close friend of Cosman, to whom an infatuated Sidney Keyes addressed numerous poems. Keyes, in his turn, was the Keatsian shooting star of his poetic generation; they greeted his Romantic, death-fixated poems, composed during exams, at parties, anywhere and everywhere, with spellbound admiration. Talk among this group was indeed laced with references to 'saints, kings, martyrs, myths, miracles', reflecting their shared poetic manner – a lyrical compound of history, symbolism and jagged emotional gestures. Keyes, who declared Jung to be his 'only non-poetic influence', felt that life was not merely interpretable through symbols but was essentially symbolic: 'All I know is that everything in a vague sort of way means something else, and I want desperately to find out *what*!'[16]

In conscious opposition to W. H. Auden's urbane

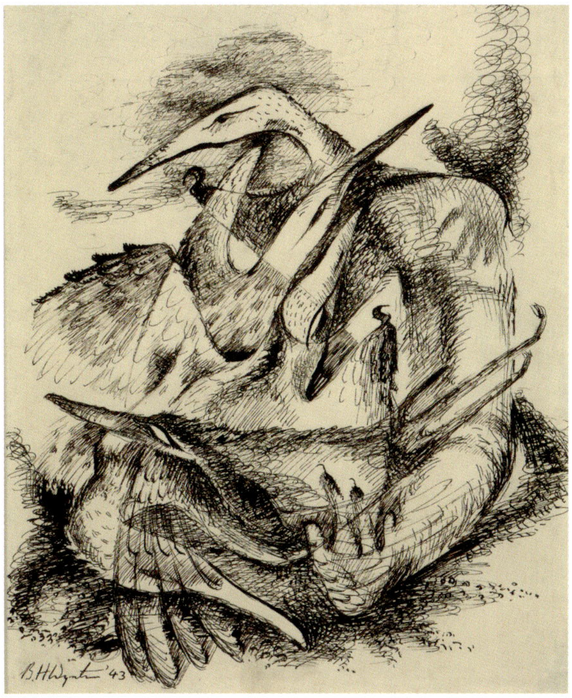

26
Birds
ink on paper
24.8 x 19.7 cm (9¾ x 7¾ in)
1943
Artist's estate

contemporaneity, these young poets wielded a language of heightened Romantic expressiveness. Keyes's *Collected Poems*, published after his death at the age of twenty while on active service in North Africa in April 1943, includes images that evoke the whole symbol-laden, spikily crepuscular imaginative atmosphere breathed by Wynter's Oxford circle. Birds fly and shriek portentously above sombre landscapes; there is an agony-in-the-garden stridency articulated against earthy, inhospitable backgrounds:

> The gulls
> Come inland from the marshes, scream and drift
> Over my landlocked city ...

Or again, Keyes's long poem 'The Wilderness', which he'd recited to the group in the St John Street studio, speaks of 'that last great meeting among mountains/ Where the metal bird sings madly from the fire', of 'sunlight shattered under the dark bridge/ And many tongues of rivers in the past'.[17] Wynter, who considered becoming a writer rather than an artist in the early 1940s, was himself writing poetry not so unlike Keyes's. One untitled draft runs:

> The blackbird rattles in the oaks of death
> And lifts her wings to meet the morning sun.
> Can I avert the tide or halt the wind?
> Delay the rivers feverish farewell?[18]

Of the few of Wynter's works on paper that survive from the last years of the war, apart from his landscape sketches, several are populated by strange imaginary birds (fig. 25). Despite their debt to Ernst's avian Surrealism (for example, in *Attirement of the Bride*, 1940), these creatures had been so thoroughly assimilated by Wynter that contemporaries thought of them as his personal *leitmotiv*. Wynter himself apparently viewed the recurrence of birds – whether imaginary, dead or alive – throughout his early work in Jungian terms, as symbols of the psyche.[19] (Feiler thought them 'a kind of conscience'.[20]) It was with reproductions of such images (figs 26, 27), published in early 1945 in the short-lived Oxford journal *Counterpoint*, that Wynter first came to public attention as an artist – and not just any emerging artist but the chosen representative of a generation for whom a post-war dawn of hope and changed perspectives was imminent. In this world, announced the Foreword to *Counterpoint*'s inaugural issue, 'there is of course, and will continue to be, a war', namely 'That bigger struggle against social orders negligent of individual freedom'.[21] The idealistic new journal weighed straight in by eschewing 1930s'-style factionalism. 'We take no sides politically', it announced – an unthinkable statement five years earlier.[22]

In May the previous year *Counterpoint*'s editor, Conrad Senat, had written to Paul Nash, explaining that he was interested in Wynter and would like 'to contrast his attitude, his problems, with those of an artist of your generation'.[23] He suggested that, since Nash was also in Oxford, the three should meet for a conversation from which Conrad might then print 'choice remarks ... together with reproductions of his works, and a few of yours'. 'So many of your ideas are shared by your contemporaries,' he explained, 'so many of his by his, that I think a discussion would be of great value.' He conceded, however, that Nash might be 'horrified at the

27
Birds
gouache on paper
*c.*76 x 50 cm (30 x 19¾ in)
1944
Untraced

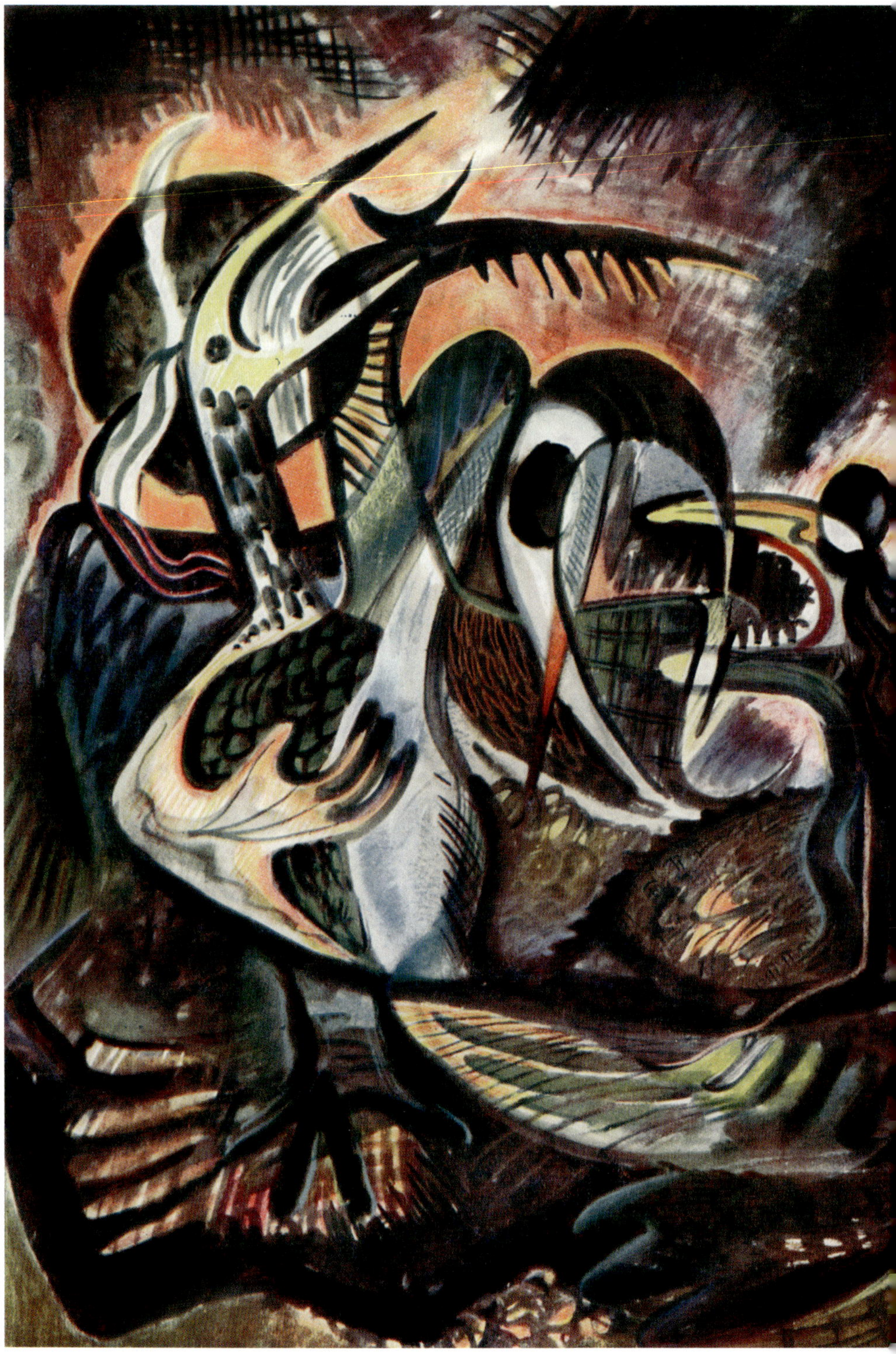

idea'. For whatever reason, the proposed conversation seems not to have taken place, and when 'Young English Painters, No.1: Some Paintings by Bryan Wynter' finally appeared, it was in the form of an article authored by Senat. Nash was featured separately, with works from his late 'Aerial Forms' series. Elsewhere he described these images of enormous airborne blooms, such as *Flight of the Magnolia* and *Cumulus Head* (1944), as 'a direct result of my imagining in my subconscious search for flight expression'.[24] Like Nash, the other senior artists in *Counterpoint* – Cecil Collins and Eileen Agar – had both been represented in the 1936 Surrealist exhibition in London. In this company, Senat singled out Wynter for his 'restatement of vital collective symbolism'. His bird series ('typical of Wynter's work') was marked by 'the tendency to look deeper than say the bird forms of Max Ernst' and to transcend the familiar language of Surrealism, which Senat dismissed as 'rooted in the bric a brac [*sic*] of infantile traumata'.[25]

In his early career Wynter put a high value on observational drawing. Yet his *Counterpoint* birds are in no sense naturalistic. One cries out or sings with a wide-stretched beak, its humanoid right hand gesturing with operatic pathos. Another gazes in cat-like vigilance while embracing a smaller bird with strangely predatory protectiveness. There is drama within the summary, fantastic landscapes these birds inhabit. Like the unicorn in a poem by John Heath-Stubbs – 'savage,/ And solitary in his solitary forest' – a Wynter bird is a 'bright, impossible beast of the mind'.[26] Wynter's imaginary birds and landscapes may owe something to John Craxton, who had also studied in the late 1930s at Westminster School of Art and whose work he admired. Craxton's drawing *Dreamer in a Landscape*, reproduced in *Horizon* in March 1942, is a Neo-Romantic classic (fig. 28).[27] The foreground figure of the dreamer sits within a kind of uterine pastoral envelope; its enmeshed roots, leaves and branches combine echoes of Samuel Palmer with a surreal aura of menacing distortion. The tusk-like appearance of some of Craxton's plant forms, sprouting with animalistic energy, can be found in Wynter's bird series in the pointed curves of beak and wing, and in more abstract angled shapes. This 'tusk' shape, at once dangerous and protective, also appears in the work of other British artists throughout the post-war decade. As time passed, the lingering Neo-Romanticism of the war

28
John Craxton, *Dreamer in a Landscape*
ink with pen and brush and chalk on paper
54.8 x 76.2 cm (21½ x 30 in)
1942
Tate

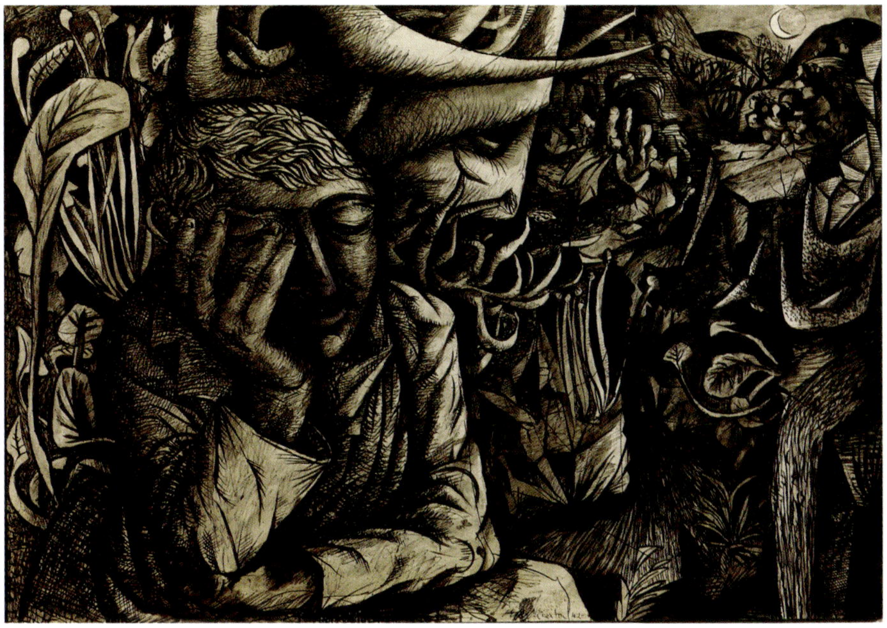

years lent its darker, Gothic, skeletal qualities to the more technological, science-fiction idiom to which Herbert Read gave the phrase 'geometry of fear'.[28]

Senat's confident advocacy of an artist unknown outside a small group in Oxford was in one sense no more than the callow overkill typical of student journalism; it can, in the end, have been based on only a few optimistic conversations over Wynter's portfolio of drawings and gouaches. In other ways, its characterisation of Wynter as an artist seeking 'to build up a classical art in keeping with the technical explorations of contemporary painting'[29] caught the mood of the moment as the war in Europe entered its final phase – the dual desire for tradition's safe refuge and modernity's hope and aspiration. In any event, it led to an invitation to exhibit at the Redfern Gallery in London. It was some seven years since Wynter had won the battle with his father and started at the Slade. Now, at the age of twenty-nine, he was finally getting his first professional break.

The early months of 1945 were a troubled time for him. His notebook speaks of a 'Hedy crisis' as their relationship foundered. The emerging news of Nazi atrocities, meanwhile, made him re-examine his decision to follow the path of non-attachment and non-violence. The stories were, he knew, exploited by the British press at a time when huge military and civilian casualties were being inflicted on Germany as British and American forces converged with the Red Army's advance from the east. Even so, photoreportage from the newly liberated concentration camps, such as Lee Miller's graphic reports from Dachau and Buchenwald for *Vogue*, soon made it impossible to doubt the scale of the atrocities that had taken place. As this realisation took hold, it definitively recast the story of the war; it had not been, after all, as Huxley had persuaded his readers in the late 1930s, a combat between equally amoral militaristic industrial powers, but a struggle of good against evil.

These doubts and difficulties, combined with Wynter's existing interest in psychoanalytic literature, led him to undertake several months of regular Jungian analysis in late 1944 and early 1945. During this time he diligently kept a dream diary, recording his dreams immediately on waking and occasionally adding an interpretation, either his own or his analyst's, on the facing page, left blank for this purpose. Some dreams still seem eloquent long after the event, as when Wynter dreamt vividly that he was stuffing his mother and aunts into a sack destined to be sent to a crematorium. His interpretations often focus on what he took to be sexual symbolism, arising, for example, from anxiety that he and Hedy had been overheard making love in the bathroom by lodging-house neighbours, or that his attempts to conceal the signs of their cohabitation from his visiting parents had been unsuccessful. He was intrigued by the settings of his dreams; many, he observed, took place in the London Underground, and some in Zurich and St Ives, which he described as 'symbols of war free towns'. For Wynter these towns were also symbols of a war-free future, now tantalisingly close at hand.

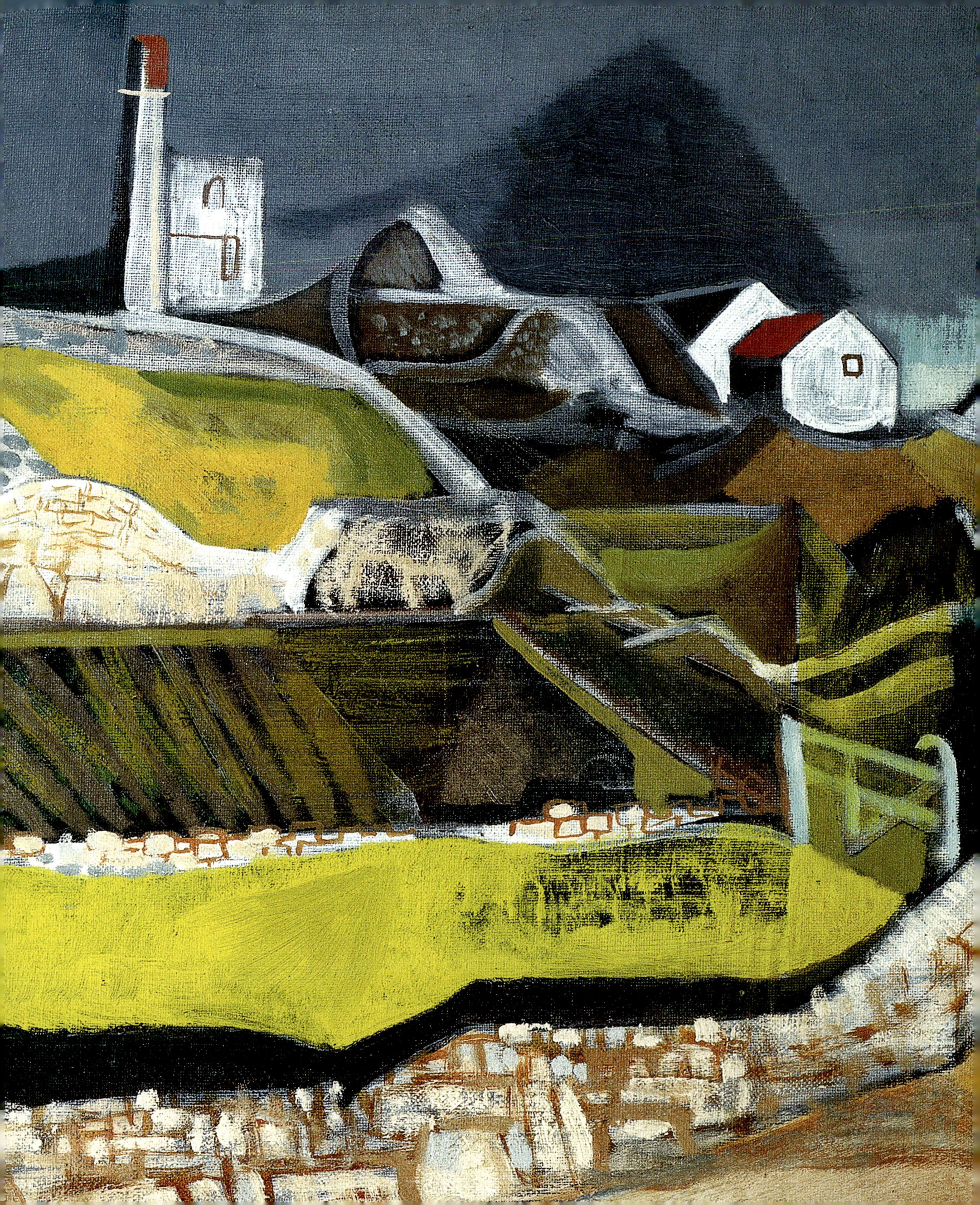

3

'Here, in this Landscape': Early Years in Zennor, 1945–9

With the fall of Berlin and the surrender of the German high command in early May 1945, the war in Europe was over. In Oxford town centre Hitler was burnt in effigy atop a huge bonfire while a blazing wagon was hauled through the streets. The jubilation verged on mayhem. It was, wrote Wynter, 'exhilarating to see those grey dreary crowds of people really wildly happy for once'.[1] By the second night of celebrations the city's pubs had run dry. After breaking into a house with Hugh Mellor and looting a cider barrel, Wynter awoke next morning to survey his party-trashed lodgings and the prospect of freedom. By the spring of 1945 his love affair with Hedy was over too. Though the tone of his letters to her remained affectionate, the break had been painful. 'All the hostility we have felt for one another these last months', he reflected, 'is largely due to our attempt to get disentangled emotionally, like a charge of gunpowder to blow us apart.'[2] Hedy was now in London, looking for work as an illustrator; for himself, Wynter planned that, after a detour via Windyridge to 'borrow' petrol (which remained rationed until 1950) from his father, he would escape Oxford for Cornwall. 'It is all rather adventurous as I haven't the least idea where I shall stay ... if I have to spend a night or two in a cave, a cave it will have to be.'[3]

Officially he needed permission to quit his war work – to go unauthorised was to risk arrest – but he took a chance that, in the bureaucratic overload that would accompany full-scale demobilisation, he was unlikely to be hunted down like a deserter. Even so, heading off 300 miles south-west may have been a sensible precaution. Thinking of his Cornish summer holiday three years earlier, he mused optimistically, 'I like to visualise myself arriving in brilliant sunshine through the whitewashed streets of St Ives & crawling straight off my motor bike into the sea ... I can almost smell the crushed lobsters & tar of the harbour & hear the gulls screaming.' The trip would be a breathing space: 'I shall probably stay in Cornwall through July and August', he informed Hedy, 'afterwards returning to London & perhaps the Slade.'[4]

This seemed reasonable enough. Wynter was pushing thirty; he had had to wait for the chance to go to art school, then been unable to complete the course before war broke out. Nevertheless, he was starting to build a reputation: there was the *Counterpoint* feature, a portfolio of work being considered by the publishers Nicholson and Watson, and the offer of a London exhibition at the Redfern. Pointless to think of living anywhere other than in the capital. It was this kind of future he had in mind when he arrived in St Ives around the end of June 1945. Pitching camp in a field on the western slopes above the town, he found it 'rather strange after all the chatter & clutter of intellectual Oxford to be living in a tent on a hill with no other company but the bluebottles buzzing & banging against the canvas'.[5] On the other side of the field stood a ramshackle huddle of workshops and kilns that turned out to be Bernard Leach's pottery. The nearby stream-bed was tiled with the shards of countless misfired pots chucked in over the past twenty-five years.

In the event, Wynter was to settle in Cornwall for even longer than this, spending most of the next thirty years – the rest of his life, in fact – within a few miles of St Ives, the town he had mocked for its arty pretensions and 'Bo'emian rendey-vous'. Had he foreseen that, by mid-career, he would be labelled a 'St Ives artist',[6] that his posthumous reputation would become inextricably entangled with his putative membership of a St Ives School of modern painters, he might have struck camp and left without delay. The motivation for his impulsive change of plan in July 1945 was complex, but one strand undoubtedly involved the ideas he had been developing in Oxford about personal development or 'growth'. By the 1960s this concept would become commonplace, but in the 1940s it marked its proponents out as minority aficionados of psychoanalytic thought. For Wynter the cultured urbanity that he seemed, by all accounts, to wear so easily meant nothing without a desire for more extended self-realisation, allied to what Huxley had called 'that non-attachment in the midst of activity, which

detail of **46**
Cornish Landscape, 1947

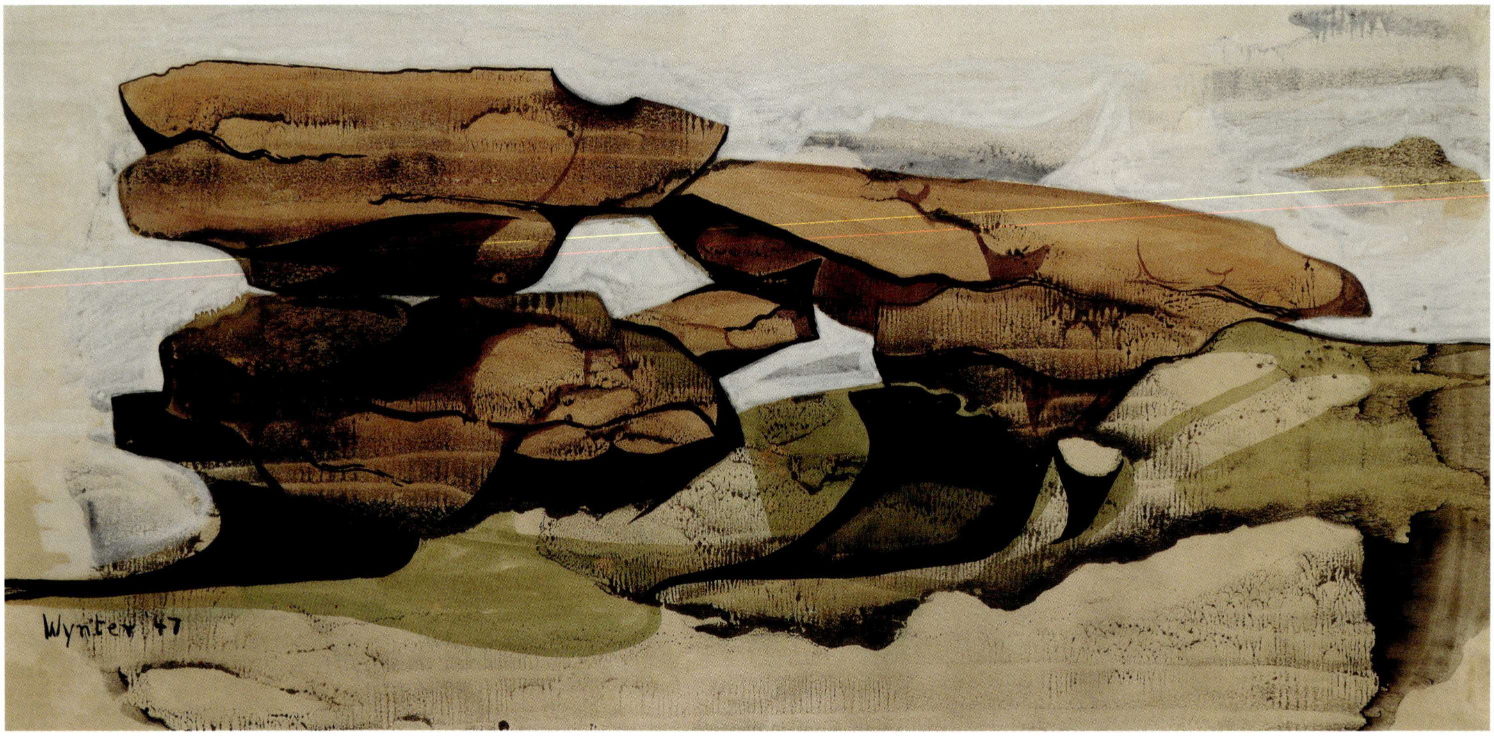

is the distinguishing mark of the ideally excellent human being'.[7] Where the pursuit of such aims was involved, Wynter viewed London – especially the bohemian enclaves of Soho and Fitzrovia in which Hedy was now ensconced – as a generally toxic environment. Beware, he told her, of the posturing 'urban gypsies' who would try to inveigle her. Instead, the important thing was always to 'Guard your intrinsic personality. Let it dictate quietly its own patterns. Let it grow and become strong.'[8]

This advice to his ex-girlfriend sums up a guiding principle of Wynter's life: the imperative to allow the 'intrinsic personality' to 'dictate its own patterns', in other words to create outward forms that mirror an inner reality. Here was the root of his affinity with Surrealism (although, as Conrad Senat pointed out, Wynter's instinct was to impart a warmer, more humane colouring to the expression of psychological 'traumata'). All this was a long way from the prevailing spirit in St Ives – characterised by Heron as 'pseudo-Impressionist'[9] – where the paintings you were most likely to encounter were concerned with replicating the effects of sunlight on sea, with the picturesque clustering of masts and sails, rather than with raiding the psychic hinterland. Nevertheless, a week into his visit, he'd decided to stay on for much longer than originally envisaged. 'Every day', he told Hedy, 'I set off in search of cottages exploring the coast & moors. There is just a chance I may get hold of a cottage in Zennor.'[10] This

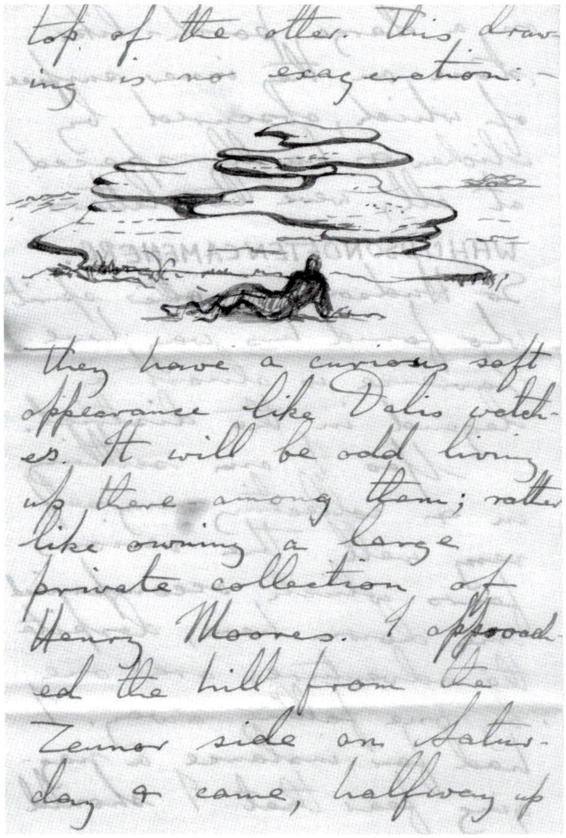
top of the other. This draw-
ing is no exageration:-

they have a curious soft
appearance like Dalis watch-
es. It will be odd living
up there among them; rather
like owning a large
private collection of
Henry Moores. I approach-
ed the hill from the
Zennor side on Satur-
day & came, halfway up

29
Rock Piles
monotype and gouache on paper
24.1 x 48.3 cm (9½ x 19 in)
1947
Private collection

30
Page from a letter to Hedy Hoffmann
ink on paper
22.9 x 14 cm (9 x 5½ in)
1945
Private collection

landscape (fig. 31) had exerted a pull on him since the family holiday there in 1933. Beyond Zennor, he'd walked to Gurnard's Head, where his Oxford friends the Denvirs had booked a holiday cottage and were soon due to arrive. His mood of adventure seemed wholly in tune with the times: on every level people felt a desire for change. Even in the 'old liberal constituency' of St Ives, Wynter reported of the general election in July, 'there seems to be a fair chance of Labour getting in'.[11]

In this context, Wynter's nearest artistic company, the team of disciple-assistants at the Leach Pottery (among whom Heron had served some of his time as a Conscientious Objector), seemed to be living on another planet:

> The 'art world' which surrounds the Leach Pottery is a very young & naïve one, serious without being intense & more enthusiastic than critical. Its idealism has not yet thrown its shadow of cynicism & perhaps it never will ... It may go on through life saying 'how beautiful' to the end without conflict or growth or decline.[12]

31
Landscape, Zennor
gouache on canvas
48.3 x 73.7 cm (19 x 29 in)
1948
Arts Council Collection

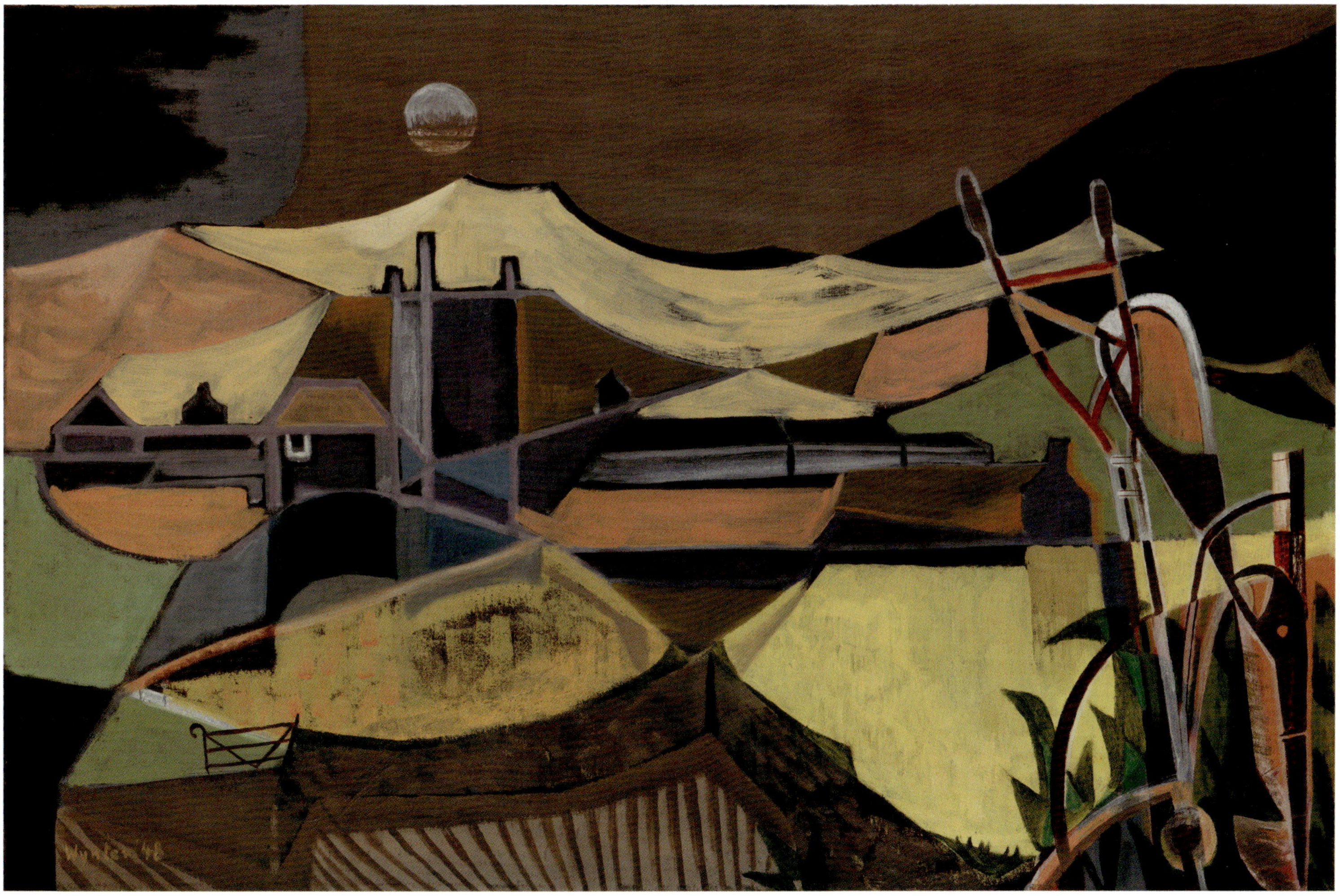

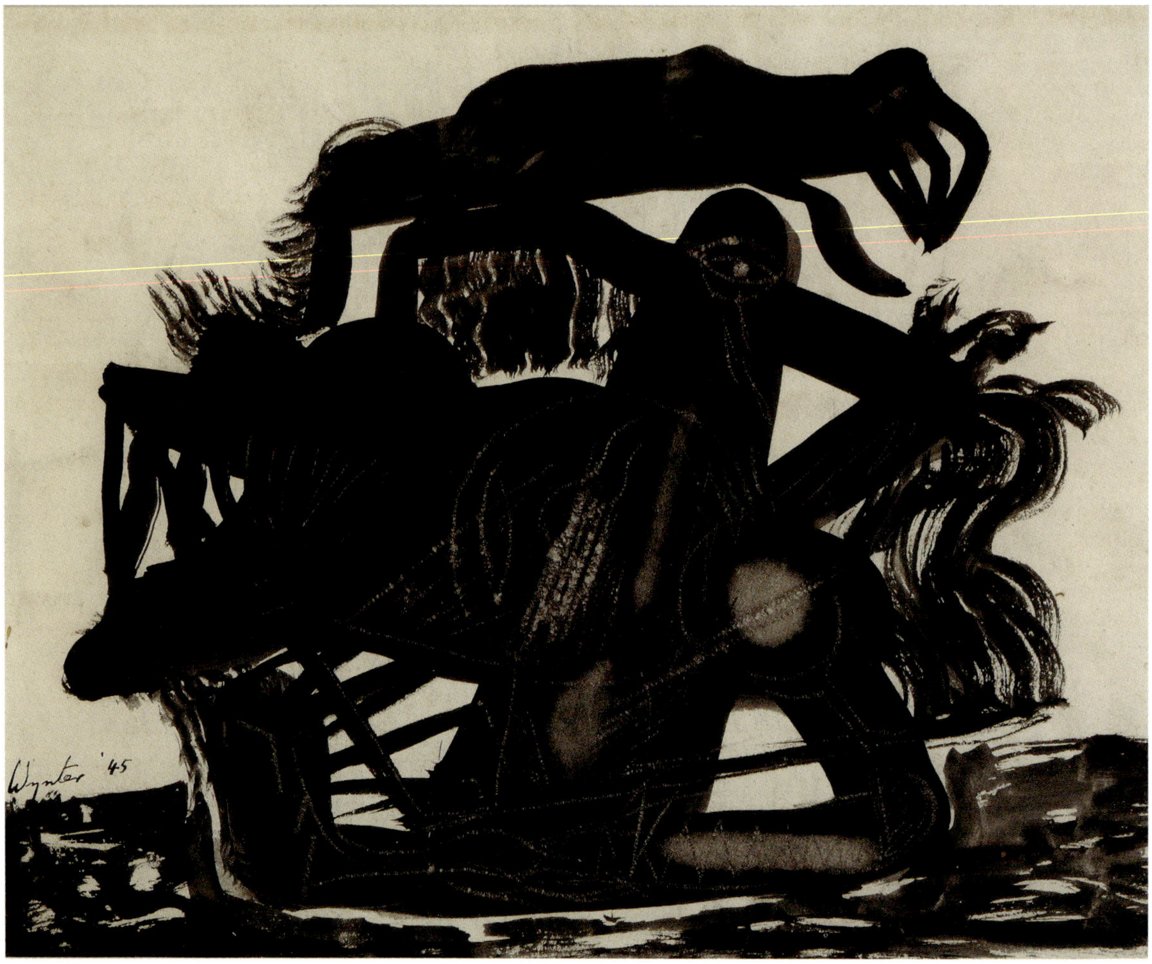

32
Threatening Figure
ink and scratched line on paper
24.1 x 29.8 cm (9½ x 11¾ in)
1945
Artist's estate

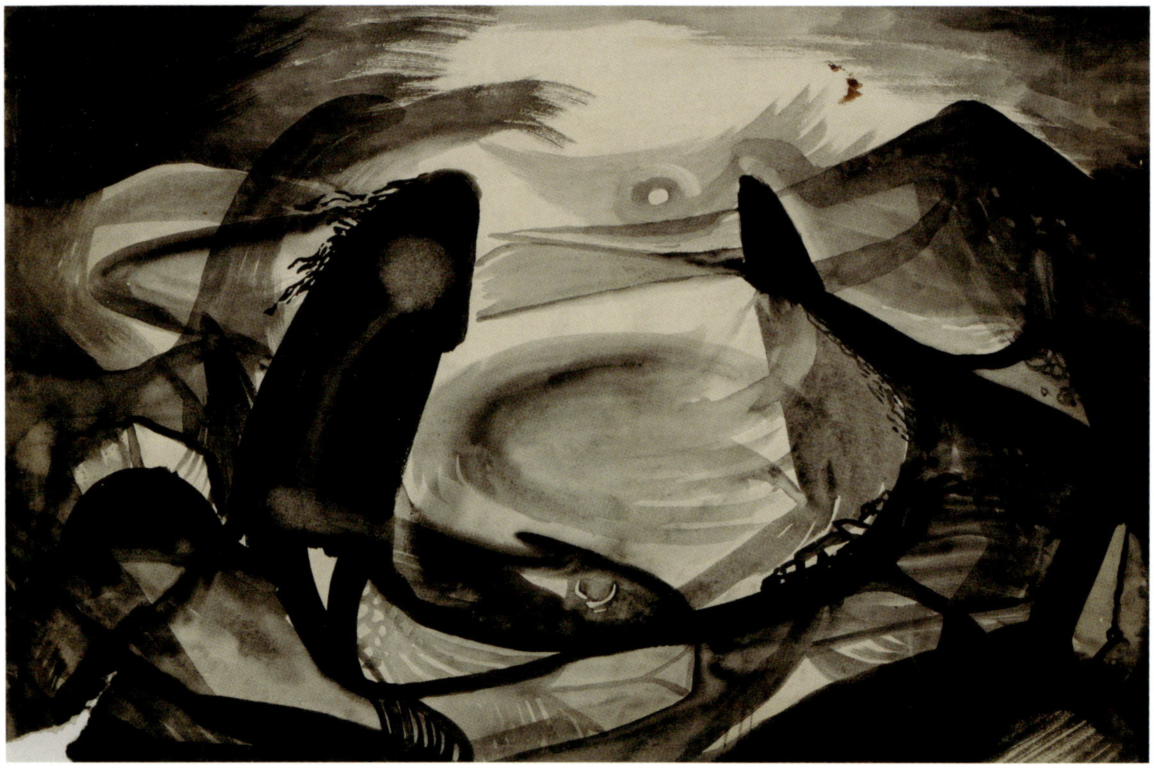

33
Landscape with Watery Moon
ink and wash on paper
38.1 x 56.2 cm (15 x 22¼ in)
*c.*1945
Artist's estate

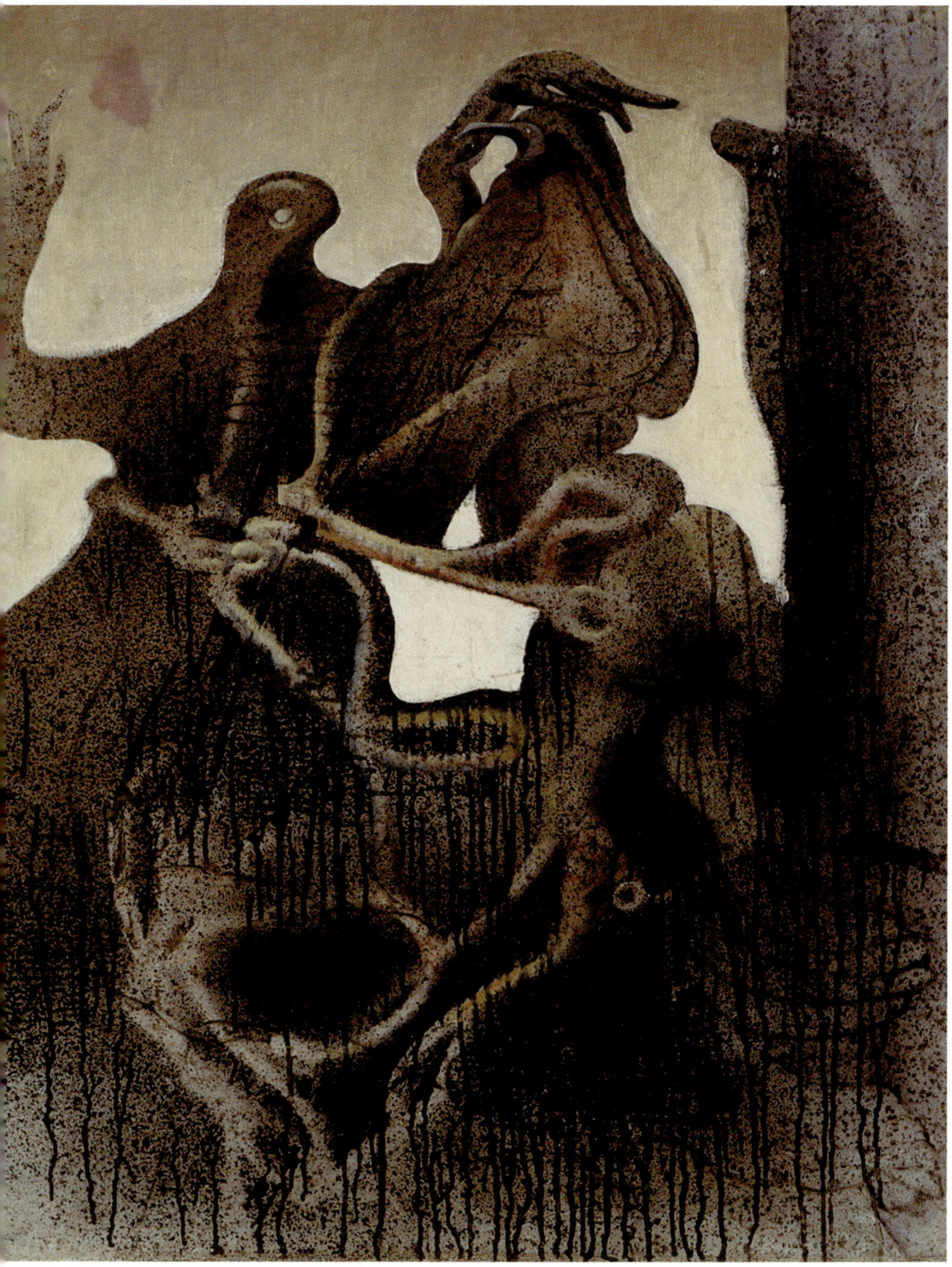

34
Max Ernst, *Zoomorphic Couple*
oil on canvas
91.9 x 73.3 cm (36¼ x 28¾ in)
1933
Peggy Guggenheim Collection, Venice/Solomon R. Guggenheim Foundation, New York

This quest for beauty struck him as anodyne – 'rather a weak cup of tea & not mine'. Instead he was finding stronger creative nourishment in the wild unsociable moorland stretching west from St Ives towards Land's End, a place of 'queer rocks, broken ruins, cromlechs & burial grounds' (fig. 29). With their brutal, glittering granite bedrock, their roughshod slippage through gorse and bracken down to the Atlantic cliffs, the Penwith moors opened out for Wynter like a compendium of all the things he'd lacked in Oxford. They were even a kind of savage art gallery; he was intrigued by the way the eroded rock piles resembled Henry Moore sculptures, as though shaped by the same spirit that animated Moore's fusion of monolithic abstraction and surrealistic dream-distortion. These protean rock formations at other times assumed the guise of Dalí watches (fig. 30), weirdly brittle yet sinuously organic. 'If Dali had been a Celt,' he enthused, 'this is the kind of landscape he would have painted. As for me, I am wagging my tail ... my persistence has been rewarded.'[13]

The landscape is like the art that Wynter admires. Yet it is not arty or artificial. Its strangeness keeps him at arm's length while at the same time he's immersed in its sensations – its rains, heat and gales. It felt as though Wynter had been preparing for such experiences throughout his wartime years in Oxford: the Surrealist games, the yearning for anti-suburbia, the mystique of the Jungian idea that human experience is founded on universal, symbolic psychic entities or archetypes. He confessed to having had 'a nagging fear that I should find I was no longer able to work; that the excuse "Of course I don't do anything now because of the war" would, when it no longer obtained, find me still unable to do anything'.[14] Instead, he was working 'with a good appetite' and producing work 'which goes a long way towards satisfying me'. The satisfaction may have come from the bold, semi-automatistic ink drawings that succeeded the *Counterpoint* birds (figs 32 and 33), or perhaps more conventionally from the prolific series of observational still-life and landscape drawings dating from Wynter's early years in Cornwall.

He had been anxious that the enjoyment of the Cornish landscape, remembered from holidays, might pall with longer familiarity. Not so, for 'although the novelty has worn off, behind the novelty is a much stronger enthusiasm. My solo expeditions onto the moors or to the coast are almost feverishly exciting ... It is like an enthralling book which I cannot lay down.'[15] The simile reminds us how deeply Wynter's reading impregnated both his art and his thinking about art. Trying to explain to Hedy what it was that appealed to him so strongly about the landscape, he revisited what was evidently an earlier

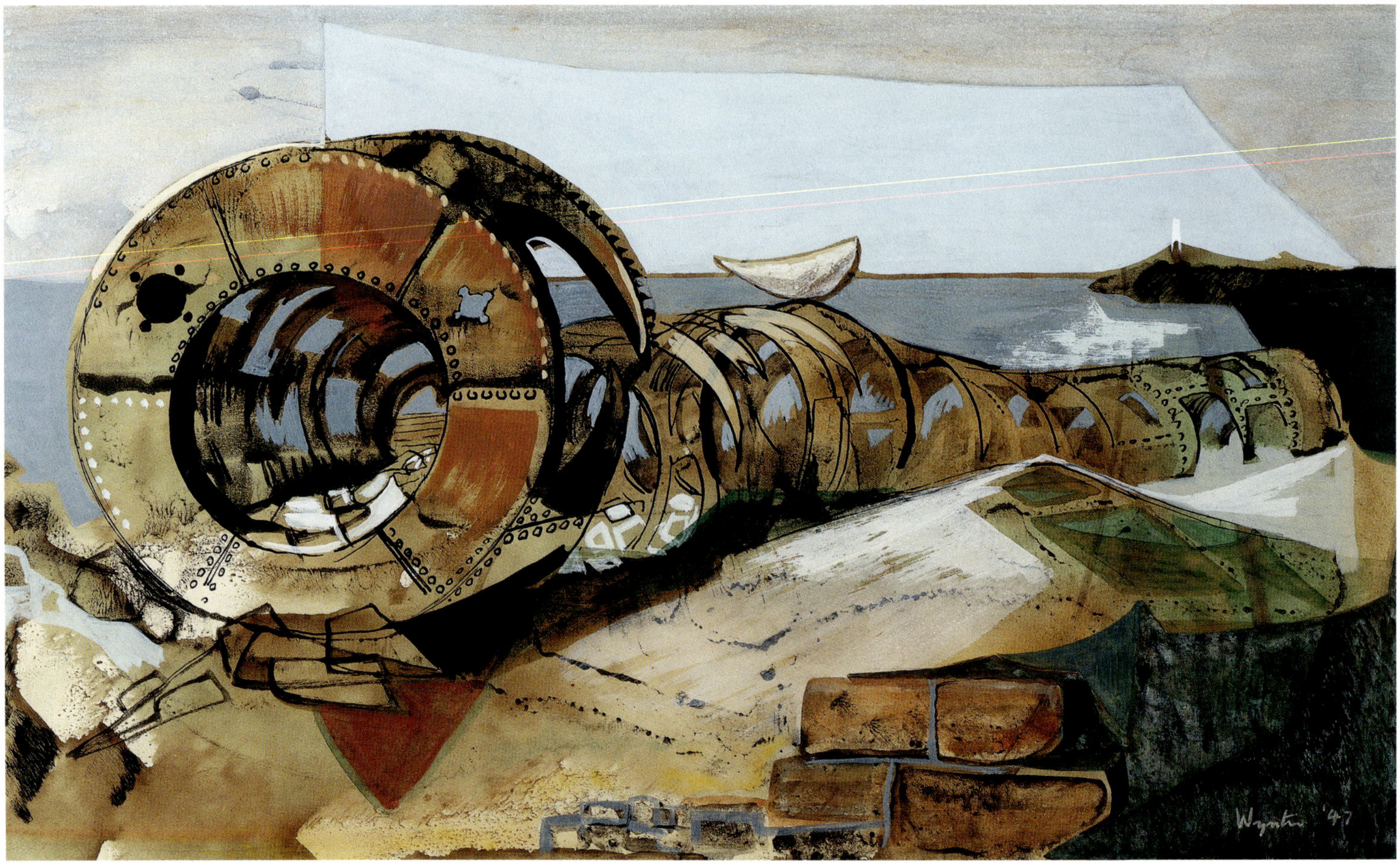

discussion of theirs, a theoretical figment from the 'intellectual chatter & clutter of Oxford' now powerfully embodied by the landscape in which he found himself:

> I mentioned as a theory of art the linking of the inner and outer worlds, as though it were a question of breaking down an artificial barrier & experiencing the two on the same plane at once, seeing it not in terms of inner & outer, of observer and the thing observed, but as one thing – the 'experience', probably the only humanly possible approach to reality. Well here, in this landscape, even when you are not drawing or painting, it happens, quite of its own accord. The real landscape overflows into the unconscious & the unconscious wells up peopling the real landscape with its own images. This is particularly so at dusk when the rocks and gorse shapes seem to come alive ... Then history & prehistory irrupts everywhere so that the present appears as a recent growth upon the past whose bones project wherever you go.[16]

Behind this letter can be felt the intensity of Wynter's awareness that he is drawn to this landscape in more than a temporary, recreational sense. Hadn't the idealistic young assistants at the Leach Pottery felt the same thing? Apparently not, since his letter to Hedy is motivated, too, by the need to communicate to another person what had evidently struck him as a revelation. If art unites the inner and outer 'on the same plane', as in Surrealism or Expressionism, the post-industrial moorland landscape acts in a very similar way. It 'overflows', while the unconscious 'wells up', an image of confluence that recalls Wordsworth's definition of 'good poetry' in his preface to *Lyrical Ballads* as 'the spontaneous overflow of powerful feelings'.[17] Dusk is the hour of transformations, such as those Wynter had recorded in his dream diary and images of fantastical birds. Here in Cornwall, he seemed to be saying, such transformations happen without volition and in the waking consciousness. In the image of a past 'whose bones project wherever you go', there's a hint, too, of the taste for Gothic sensationalism that had been current among the young poets he'd known in Oxford (Keyes had

35
Derelict Boiler
gouache on paper
30.5 x 52.1 cm (12 x 20½ in)
1947
City of Bristol Museum
and Art Gallery

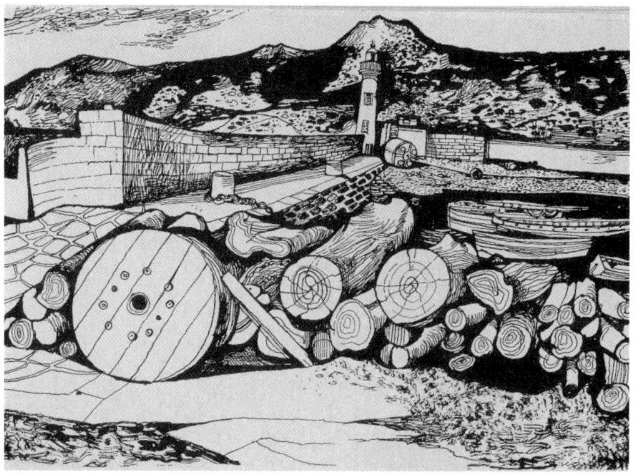

36
John Minton, *Propriano: Timber and Lighthouse* (1948)
book illustration

37
Bryan Wynter at the Carn, *c.*1950

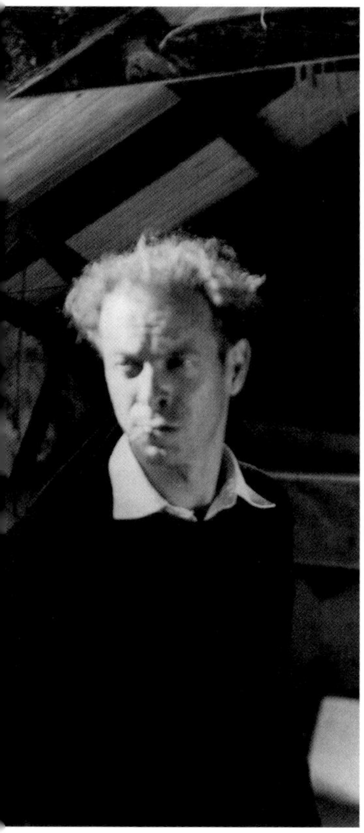

written of a 'hard garden where earth's ribs/ Lie bare'[18]), mixed with an echo of the phantasmagoric wasteland, 'This broken jaw of our lost kingdoms', in T. S. Eliot's poem 'The Hollow Men'.[19]

Even before she received this letter, Hedy must have been aware that Wynter was unlikely to return to life in London any time soon. He was already talking of moving into an isolated cottage he'd found on Zennor Carn in September. During the late summer his isolation had been pleasantly interrupted by visits from Oxford friends Edward Walton and Vera Leslie, and the Denvirs: 'It was odd to see them down here divorced from the Playhouse, Ashmolean & all the other well known focal points ... It was also odd to hear Bernard's voice raised above the wind, the cry of gulls & the rumble of sea saying "Of course, towards the middle of the nineteenth century, Russian society etc etc".'[20] Once the summer visitors had left, and he had moved into the cottage on the hill, Wynter's social rhythm changed. Days of solitude, which he relished, alternated with visits to St Ives for provisions and pubs. If he was aware that a trio of senior modernists – Ben Nicholson, Barbara Hepworth and Naum Gabo – had spent the war just along the road in Carbis Bay, Wynter made no mention of it. He had not been drawn to their kind of Constructivist abstract art (Surrealism's rival movement in 1930s' London); even later, after meeting Hepworth and Nicholson personally and becoming familiar with their work in St Ives, he never really engaged with the tradition of geometric abstraction. He did, however, get to know some of the younger progressive artists who, from the end of the war onwards, were regularly turning up in town.

One of the first to welcome him was Sven Berlin, on whose studio floor Wynter soon found himself sleeping when the five-mile hike back to Zennor after a night's drinking seemed a step too far. Berlin had had pre-war careers as a music-hall dancer, heating engineer and gardener, among other jobs; when war broke out, he was pursuing a new vocation as a self-taught sculptor. Like Wynter, he registered as a Conscientious Objector but ended up enlisting, after witnessing the sinking of a ship off the Cornish coast by German planes. In his 1994 'autosvenography', *The Coat of Many Colours*, Berlin recalled, with a raconteurish smoothing of hindsight, 'It was at the pottery I first met Bryan. He was simply there one day in a huge mackintosh with a haversack':

> he was very tall with dark wiry hair – 'mossy' as he put it – and a rather loose skin to his face and large eyes which lit up every now and then with an illuminating smile. There was a kind of Rex Harrison charm about this unusual person dressed in low tones of brown, umber, sullen green and ochre. He sat in a chair in the middle of the room talking with great vitality and humour, every now and then flicking his cigarette ash into the turn-up of his cord trouser leg. He gave one the feeling of belonging nowhere, a classless traveller who spoke in a low cultured voice almost as though he were making it up as a satirical means of dealing with life's fantasy.[21]

Wynter passed muster as a fellow bohemian (fig. 37), though he devoted nothing like Berlin's energy to acting the part. He seems not to have been put off by Berlin's

38
Zennor Coast from the Sea
monotype and gouache on paper
33 x 73.5 cm (13 x 29 in)
1949
Private collection

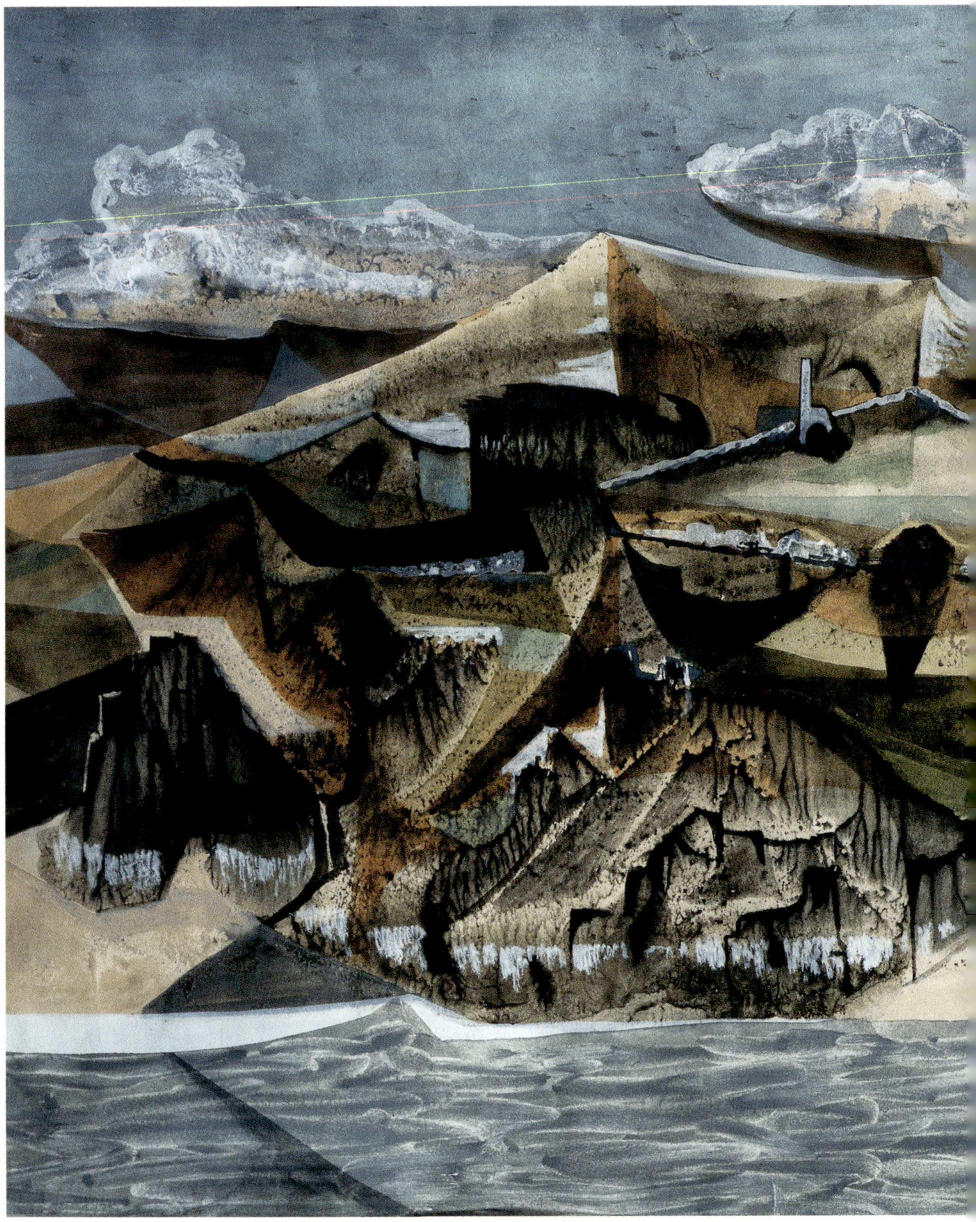

corny rhapsodies about the creative 'Spirit of the Moors' or the clunky, rather inept earnestness of his stone carvings, which fortunately could be readily interpreted as the outcome of a passionate primitivism.

Around this time Wynter met the Scottish poet Sydney Graham and his partner, Nessie Dunsmuir, also a poet. They were living in two caravans, dubbed 'the Wheelhouse' by Graham, near the village of Germoe on the opposite coast of the Penwith Peninsula from St Ives, about eight miles distant. Graham had published two volumes of verse and had a fairly wide acquaintance among artists and writers in Glasgow and London, most of whom at some point found themselves obliged to lend him money. Growing up in working-class Greenock, he had left school at fourteen and, by the time Wynter met him, had dedicated his life to poetry with a single-mindedness that usually excluded the possibility of earning a living by other means. On one occasion, marooned in the Wheelhouse during stormy weather (life at the Carn involved a lot of long-distance walking and hitch-hiking), Wynter stayed several days with Graham and Dunsmuir, many hours of which were spent by the three of them reading poetry aloud. It was here on another visit, in August 1945, that he was introduced to the artist John Minton, a friend and loyal benefactor of Graham's. Minton was two years younger than Wynter but already a well-established Neo-Romantic artist in London, where he taught at the Central School and was a stalwart of Soho bohemia. His work of the 1940s has strong affinities with Wynter's own; it isn't always possible to detect which way the influence was flowing. Wynter's 1947 gouache *Derelict Boiler* (fig. 35), for example, is remarkably similar in composition to an illustration titled *Propriano: Timber and Lighthouse* (fig. 36), which Minton published the following year in Alan Ross's Corsican travelogue *Time Was Away* (which could, of course, have been based on an earlier sketch).

In their shared social contacts, their cultural background and professional interests these poets and painters were deeply, essentially urban. Yet here they were, camping out in musty abandoned hovels, wind-rocked caravans and fish cellars in Cornwall as though the place were destined to become the epicentre of Britain's reborn post-war artistic life. Class-consciousness played a part in this Celtic epiphany: Graham remained pugnaciously sensitive all his life to the slightest hint of middle-class condescension; Wynter, for his part, was intent on leading a life that was the opposite in every way of 'the constant round of fatuous occupations' he associated with the privileged ambience of his upbringing.

By September, in return for a rent of £25 per year, Wynter was installed in his 'mountain retreat'. Here, as his brother Eric later recalled,

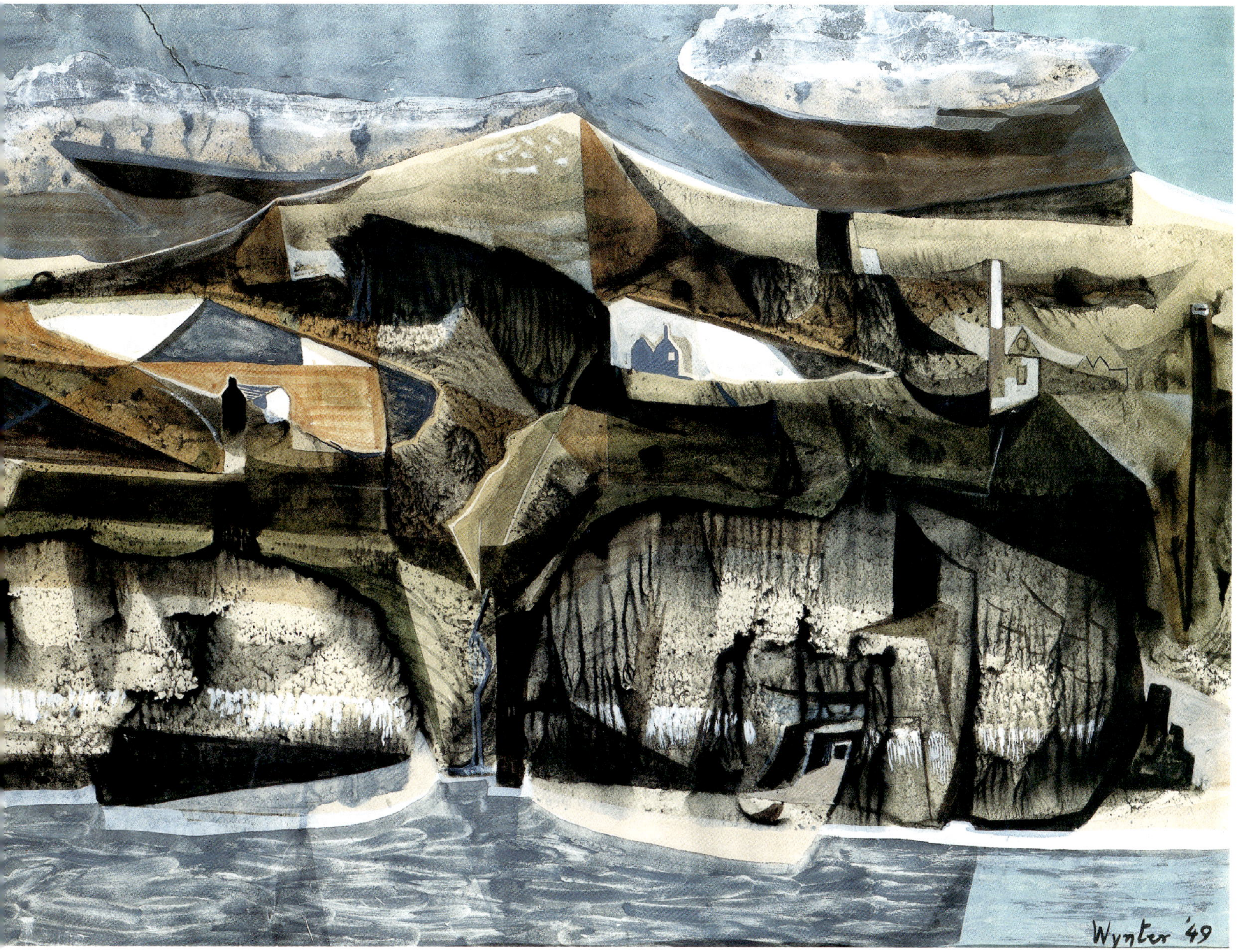

> in his thirtieth year he found release to work as he wanted ... He also befriended the wild animals, climbed the great Cornish cliffs, skin-dived, drank in the St Ives pubs and mooched around on the moors, coming to know their communities of wildlife as an appreciative observer without wishing to take a scientific interest in them. He teased the animals and ate the plants.[22]

On several fronts the move to the Carn marked a point of final transition from wartime Oxford. In his relationship with Hedy, Wynter had been harbouring an almost latent hope that they would eventually get back together; in August her announcement that she was pregnant by her new lover put paid to that. As far as his own family was concerned, he felt as though he had made a decisive break. In answer to his mother's concerns about how he was going to manage without running water, electricity and other domestic comforts that, while standard in the Home Counties by 1945, were still rare in Penwith upland cottages, he confidently assured her that

> What for you would be 'amenities' are just a nuisance to me. The Carn provides me with my own particular brand of amenities, an enormous access to & experience of this wild corner of England which still holds out against the slow insidious invasion of garden suburbs and slum.[23]

The mock-Tudor mod-cons of Windyridge had been replaced by life on a bare, rocky ridge where the winter gales, he had been told, 'drove over the hill like tornados'.[24] In contrast to Wynter's rosy holiday fantasy of living on the slopes of Zennor cove, where food and fuel would be delivered by nature, free of charge, the Carn entailed an exhausting routine of hauling coal for the fire, oil for the stove and provisions from the shops in St Ives up a steep dirt track from the coast road with, initially at least, a bicycle as the only mechanical aid. Plans to domesticate the wild goats he claimed to have found up on the moors came to nothing, and twenty years later Wynter was still to start work on the vegetable patch he had enthusiastically described to Hedy.

The effects of his move to Cornwall became almost immediately apparent in Wynter's prolific production of Cornish landscapes. As before, however, it was still primarily through drawing that he explored his motifs. It was as though landscape were now guiding his hand, as he had encouraged the unconscious to do in his Surrealist-inspired work in Oxford. And there remained, as in the dream diary he'd kept during his final months there, a pervasive sexual undercurrent. In an ink-and-wash drawing probably datable to 1945, *Landscape with Watery Moon* (fig. 33), the tumescent forms surrounding a sunken tarn or valley compose an erotic *mise-en-scène* in which landscape references are almost incidental. In a pencil drawing of a ruined engine house (an emblematic Cornish subject) (fig. 39) the gaping mineshaft in the foreground, surrounded by unkempt Neo-Romantic vegetation, has a frankly vaginal appearance – the 'deep, romantic chasm' at the heart of the paradisiacal wilderness in Coleridge's 'Kubla Khan'. Wynter's exposition to Hedy of the way the Penwith landscape revealed itself to him as a meeting-place of inner and outer sounds very like early nineteenth-century Romantic visions of art as the point of convergence between imagination and reality: 'The Imagination', Keats reflected in a letter to a friend, 'may be compared

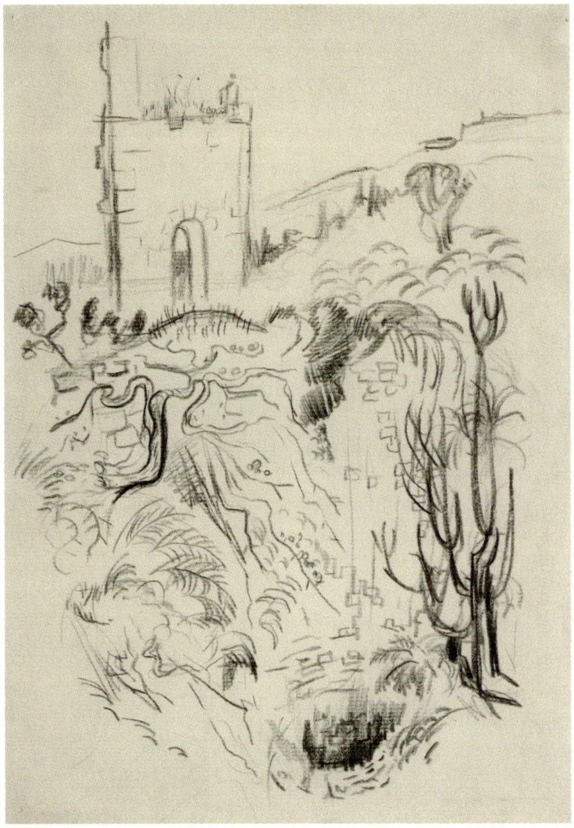

39
Engine House and Mineshaft
pencil on paper
39.4 x 26.7 cm (15½ x 10½ in)
c.1945–6
Artist's estate

to Adam's dream – he awoke and found it truth.'[25] There was also a practical motive for Wynter's change of subject. With the offer of a London exhibition, which eventually took place in April 1947, he had the chance to sell, and the British taste for landscape paintings could always be relied on. His father still gave him a weekly allowance of £4; although this was a living wage – factory workers and farm labourers in 1945 took home something similar for a full week's work – Wynter was determined not to depend on parental hand-outs, gift-wrapped as they were in a disapproval that was no less humiliating for being tacit.

In Oxford, Wynter had produced numerous frottages. This was one of Max Ernst's favoured automatistic methods, allowing suggestive forms to emerge involuntarily. Ernst also made extensive use of decalcomania, a technique for transferring images from one surface to another by pressing a sheet of paper face-to-face with another sheet or a glass slab that had been inked or painted. The effects created when the top sheet was peeled away could be incorporated into a painting, or even suggest its entire content. Following Ernst's lead, Wynter often began a work using this form of monotyping process, then developed it in a conventional painterly manner. He discovered how to produce a ground for a landscape painting that, before he had superimposed any deliberate marks, already seemed imbued with the forms, colours and tactile qualities of stone or water, earth, lichen, bracken. This technique perfectly embodied the 'theory' he had sketched to Hedy, and he brought it to a high pitch in works such as *Zennor Coast from the sea* (fig. 38). 'He knows how to pull paper off a glass slab, upon which paint or ink are spilt or drawn', observed Patrick Heron, 'in such a way that the veins of a pressed blob of colour can be instantly read as the veins, or strata, in rock – the rocky cliff in the picture.'[26] Wynter installed a small lithography press at the Carn, on which he pulled a few prints, although ultimately he preferred the less mechanical, more unpredictable, monotype process (fig. 51). He also made photomontages (another favourite Surrealist medium, which he had first explored in the late 1930s), often from topical photos he'd found in the illustrated magazine *Picture Post*. In these beautifully crafted one-off images, a sense of menacing incongruity is relished for its own sake, rather than in the service of, say, political or social satire (figs 40, 41, 42).

It's easy to imagine Wynter pursuing his work at the Carn without giving much thought to what was going on down in St Ives. Inevitably, though, he became involved with several of the younger artists who were collectively stepping up the tempo of the old art colony, initiating a new phase in its history that Sven Berlin liked to refer to as 'Disturbance in the West'. Some of the recent arrivals had served in the armed forces; others, like Wynter, had been COs. They all shared a slightly desperate awareness of six lost years, and their heady sense of release at being able to work again at last was tinged with a more than usually pressing determination to get their art shown and their careers taken seriously. In September 1946 Wynter took part in the first exhibition of the Crypt Group, which had been formed for the occasion and was so called because these five young artists had been permitted by the traditionalist St Ives Society of Artists to show their more progressive or unconventional work in the crypt beneath the deconsecrated Mariners' Church that served as the Society's gallery.

The group's other founder members were Sven Berlin, Peter Lanyon, John Wells and Guido Morris. Lanyon had grown up St Ives, where he had been befriended by the refugee artists from wartime London, Nicholson, Hepworth and Gabo, shortly before, aged twenty-one, he joined the RAF and served for the duration as an aircraft engineer. His contributions to the Crypt Group show included abstract sculpture, landscape painting, a box construction and a photomontage. Berlin showed primitivistic animal carvings, while Wells, who had spent the war as a doctor on the Scilly Isles, had been producing his own spare, tasteful interpretations of abstract Constructivist themes and painting intense little landscapes in which, as in Wynter's work, could be seen the influence of both Paul Klee and Graham Sutherland. Guido Morris was a craftsman-typographer, making a precarious living in St Ives by printing exhibition catalogues, posters and other jobbing commissions in the style of Renaissance treatises.

Dramatically lit by specially installed fluorescent lamps, a novelty in 1946 (fig. 43), the show was as notable for its uneven, quirky eclecticism as for its modernity. But it made its point. No one, at this early stage, was sure how or where modern art would revive in post-war Britain. To most observers Nicholson and Hepworth were, along with Henry Moore, the obvious names to watch. Though their marriage was all but over, both Nicholson and Hepworth had decided to remain in St Ives, where they contrived to transmute the story of their wartime exile from London, and the almost accidental circumstances of their arrival in Cornwall, into a narrative of providential self-realisation rather than haphazard flight. Hepworth, especially, began to describe the relationship between her art and the Penwith landscape in quasi-mystical terms uncannily similar to Berlin's effusions about the 'Spirit of the

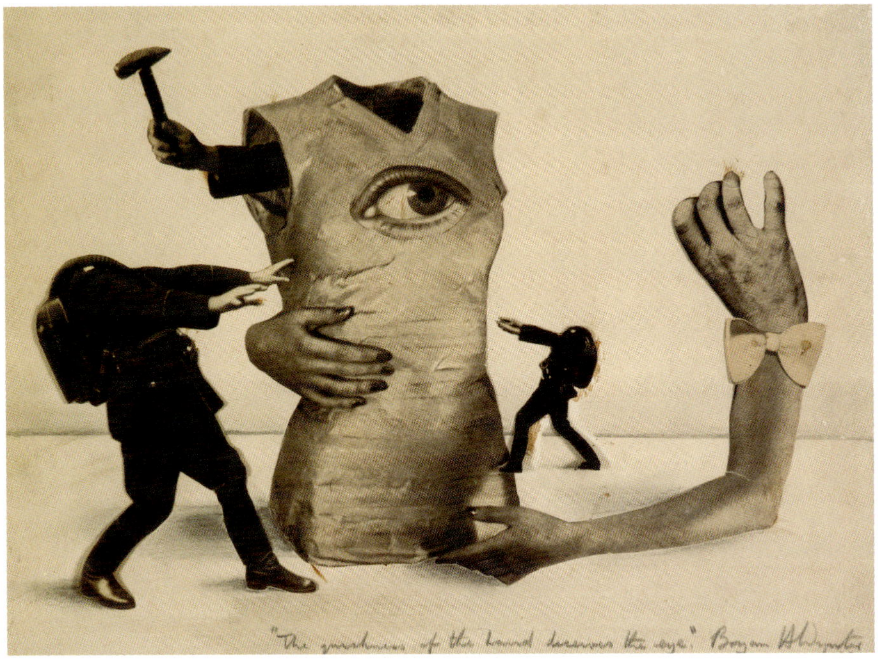

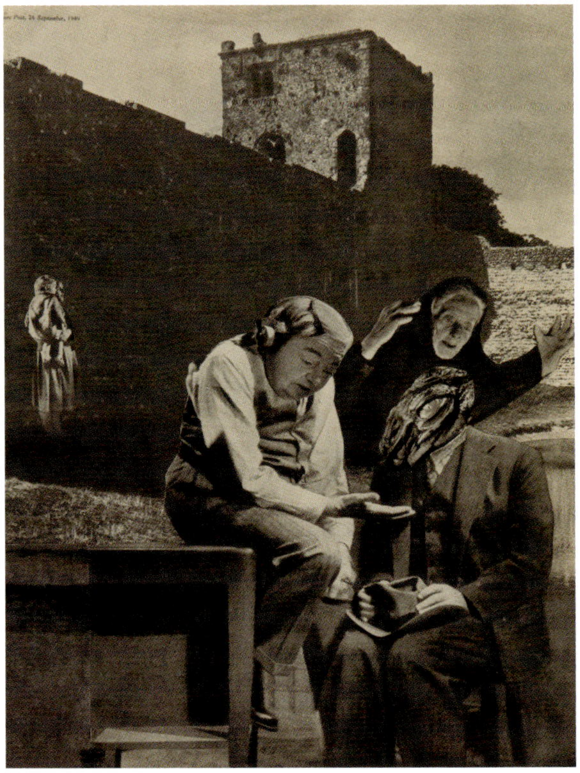

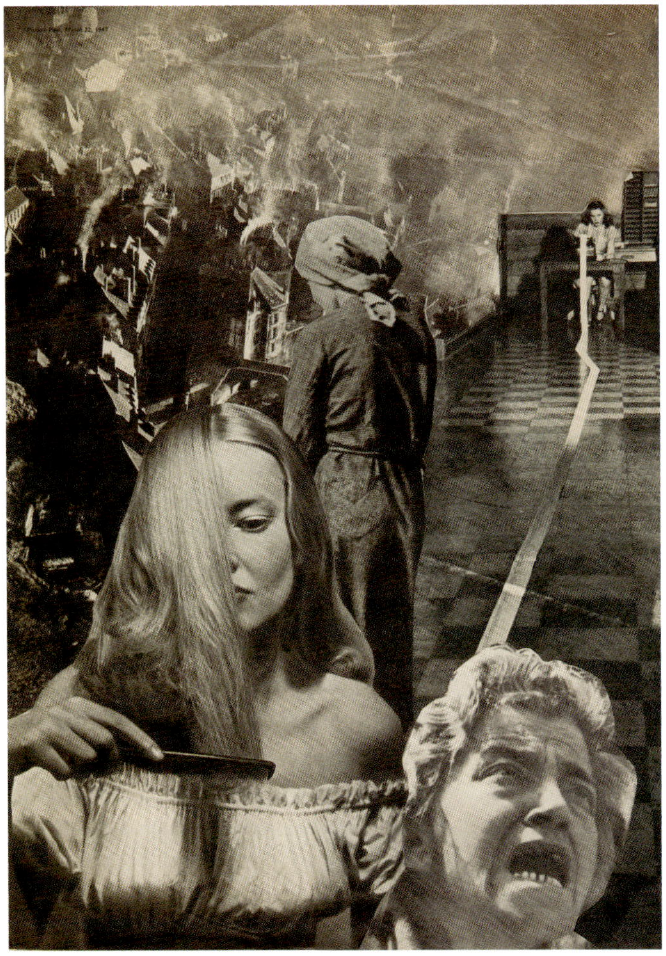

40
The Quickness of the Hand Deceives the Eye
photomontage on paper
29.5 x 38.8 cm
(11½ x 15¼ in)
1939
Private collection

41
Photomontage on *Picture Post* page (24 Sept 1949)
photomontage on paper
31.2 x 25.3 cm
(12¼ x 10 in)
1949
Private collection

42
Photomontage on *Picture Post* page (22 March 1947)
photomontage on paper
36 x 25 cm
(14¼ x 9¾ in)
1947
Private collection

Moors' and Wynter's excited outpourings in his first letters from St Ives to Hedy. She spoke feelingly of the landscape's miraculous 'withinness of form', of the way the tides 'made strange and wonderful calligraphy on the pale granite sand' and of how this environment 'induced a thousand fantasies of form and purpose, structure and life which had gone into the making of what I saw and what I was'.[27] In other words, there could be no better place than Cornwall in which to realise her life's work.

It seemed to Hepworth and Nicholson's influential supporters, including critics such as Herbert Read and the various officers of the British Council and recently formed Arts Council who regularly appeared in St Ives, quite natural that the presence of two of Britain's greatest modern artists should encourage the formation of a nucleus of younger followers in the area. It hardly mattered that the Crypt Group had no common plan of campaign or that, with the exception of Wells, none of its members saw themselves as allied to Hepworth or Nicholson. For Wynter, as for his new-found colleagues, the rather surprising reinvention of St Ives's gentlemanly art colony as a seed-bed of advanced contemporary practice was professionally useful, even if it had as yet very limited impact on the way he thought or painted. By temperament, however, he was not a natural group member; nor did his anarchic sense of humour (fig. 48) sit easily with the lofty theoretics with which veteran 1930s' modernists tended to infuse the discussion of art.

Taking his turn invigilating the Crypt Group show, Wynter passed the time reading the Spanish poet Lorca and eavesdropping on visitors' comments. 'We get one or two groups every day who go round growling "degenerate" "disgusting" etc.', he told Hedy. Of his own contribution, which included the *Counterpoint* drawings (competitively priced at 2 to 3 shillings, or 10 to 15 pence, each), 'One man said he thought the paintings were "austere & Nordic". I said the usual accusation was that they were Jewish. "Yes," he said "They are! They're Jewish as well."'[28] The pairing of terms 'degenerate' and 'Jewish' at a local art exhibition, so soon after the supposed defeat of all that Nazism stood for, had a significance of which both Wynter and Hedy were well aware. As the 'usual accusation' aimed at Wynter's painting, the word 'Jewish' may have meant simply too emotive, too expressionistic or even too Germanic for British tastes. If so, it suggests that at this date people more readily associated Wynter's work with modern European art than with British Neo-Romanticism, whose illustrative, nostalgic response to landscape made it easily palatable to a conservative public hungry for both hope and reassurance.

43
Hanging the First Crypt Group Show, September 1946 (L to R: Sven Berlin, John Wells, Peter Lanyon)

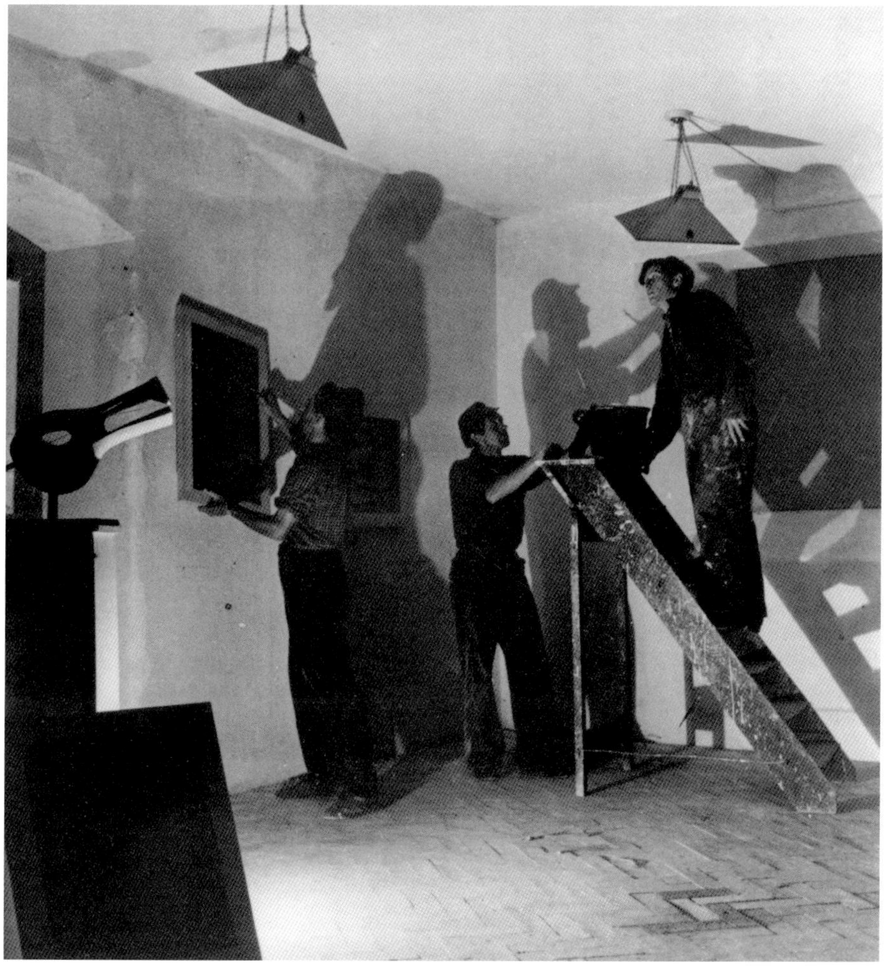

While his fellow Crypt Group members Lanyon and Wells were engaged in two quite different dialogues with the legacy of Constructivist abstraction, as personified by Hepworth and Nicholson (of whose influence in St Ives Lanyon became increasingly resentful), and Berlin carved away at his stone toads and fish as the spirit moved him, Wynter's 'Jewish' Eurocentrism made itself felt in his growing admiration for Braque, especially the French master's most recent 'Atelier' paintings (fig. 44). The wartime absence of contemporary French art from London had ended with an exhibition of work by Matisse and Picasso at the Victoria and Albert Museum in December 1945, quickly followed in April by the Tate Gallery's combined showing of Cézanne watercolours with a joint exhibition by Braque and Rouault. Wynter almost certainly saw these shows (he suggested to Hedy that they might visit together while they were in London in early July), and he probably also read a review of Braque's work in the *New English Weekly* in July by his Slade contemporary Patrick Heron, who wrote with spellbound eloquence of Braque's 'immensely powerful art'.[29] By autumn 1946 Wynter had acquired an expensive book of Braque reproductions.

Heron's descriptions of Braque's handling of form and colour incidentally illuminate Wynter's debt to the 'Atelier' paintings in the Cornish landscapes he painted around 1946–51. Braque's vision, wrote Heron, was 'essentially involved with *flat* areas of *even* tone colour'. He praised its qualities of 'matt stain' and 'stony opacity', observing that 'Dividing and bounding these carefully plotted areas run channels and low walls of paint, dragged on by a hand miraculously sensitive and expressive in its touch.'[30] This could equally serve to describe a landscape Wynter painted in 1947 (fig. 46). The drawing on which it is closely based (fig. 45) shows a Braquean 'surface consciousness' in its relish of the interplay between mass and pattern. The snaking rubble bastions that form the field walls, for example, are summarily rendered in glyph-like reticulations (of drawing walls in general, Wynter's dictum was 'You have to do it so it stands up'[31]). The scene resembles the plan of an archaeological excavation; within its table-top flatness, you sense the past's projecting bones, and a strange instability ('the real landscape overflows'), as though the fieldscape were about to slide forwards. In the painting, which would have been completed in the studio rather than out of doors, Wynter heightened certain elements to impart a surreal intensity ('the unconscious wells up') to this familiar Cornish scene. Deep, scything shadows stretch in different directions across the fields' variegated heraldry, as though cast by theatrical lighting rather than by natural, low-angled storm light.

Painted a year or so later, Lanyon's *Headland* has a similar S-shaped rhythm, but in place of Wynter's 'surface consciousness' there's a sinewy, tactile restlessness; in this case the painter seems to be physically trying to grapple the landscape rather than contemplate it. Lanyon described his practice in terms of quasi-erotic intimacy with his chosen terrain: its shapes, its touch, its history of human association. Where Wynter found archetypal symbols, Lanyon found sex: 'Having experienced this long line say from the armpit down over the ribcage down to the pelvis', he once confessed, 'that line might take me out in the car into the landscape and I might experience this again.'[32] Wynter and Lanyon were both known for their athletic approach to landscape, which involved much exploratory rambling and climbing around the cliffs and moors. Both liked to drive along the twisting coast road at racetrack speeds. But the theories and metaphors to which such experiences gave rise were in each case quite different.

In April 1947 Wynter had the first of a long series of shows that the Redfern was to give him over the next ten years. As was customary before London galleries adopted the fashion for solo exhibitions in the later 1950s, he shared the space with other artists and on this occasion showed only smallish drawings and watercolours.[33] The atmosphere in commercial art galleries just after the war was (as it often still is) as understated and exclusive as a Savile Row tailor, and critics tended to appraise the work in a suitably plush connoisseurial spirit. Wynter, wrote one, was

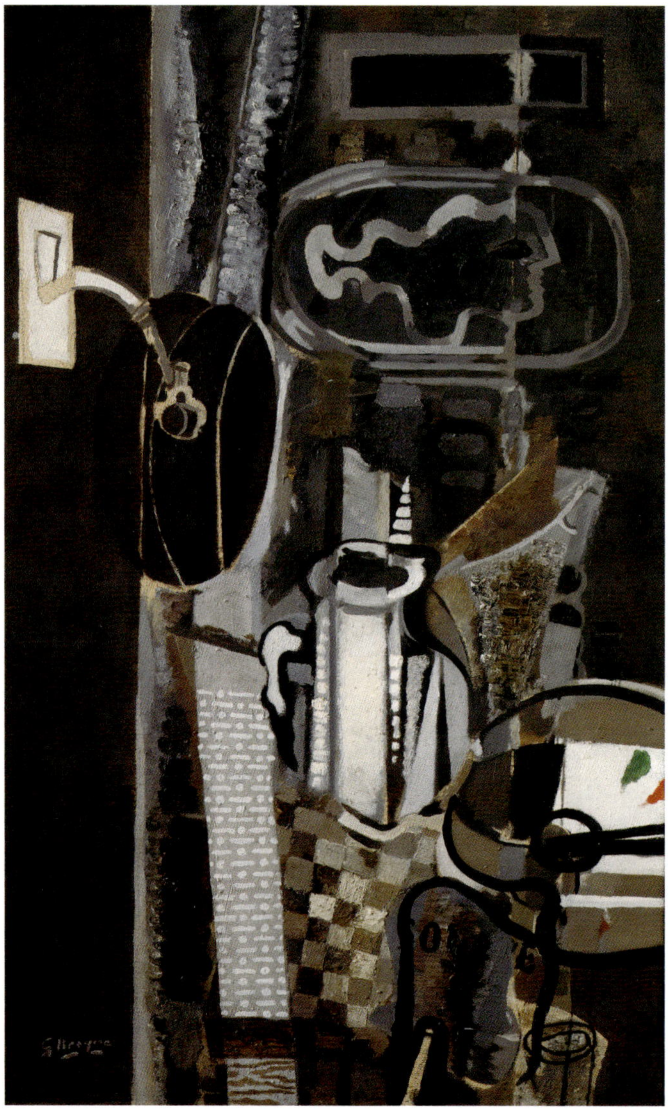

44
Georges Braque,
L'Atelier
oil on canvas
1949
The Metropolitan Museum of Art, bequest of Florene M. Schoenborn, 1995

45
Cornish Landscape
pencil on paper
24.1 x 42 cm (9 ½ x 16 ½ in)
1947
Artist's estate

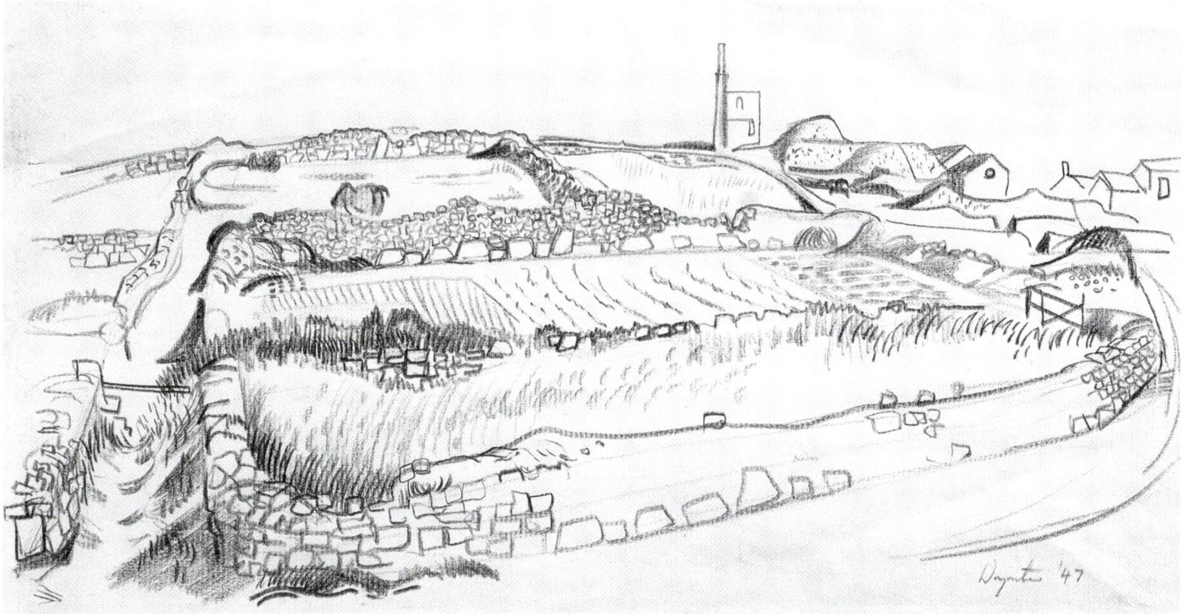

46
Cornish Landscape
oil on canvas
49.5 x 75 cm (19 ½ x 29 ½ in)
1947
Private collection

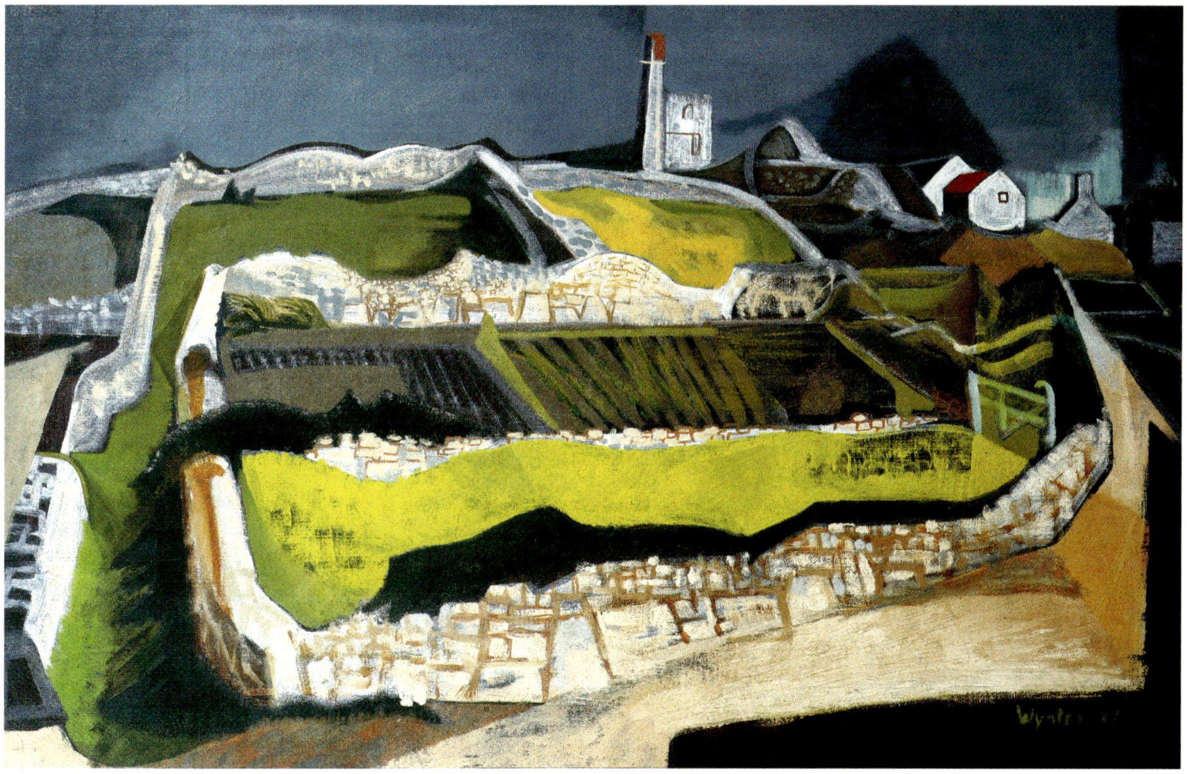

'impressive' for his 'quiet assurance';[34] another found him 'more remarkable for his technical resources than for his spontaneity' but approved of the way he had 'digested' Klee and Sutherland, and his professional mastery of 'certain receipts for texture, arrangement, and stylization'.[35] A fairly low-key debut, then – yet almost everything sold, grossing 293 guineas (£307.65), considerably more than Wynter's annual allowance.

A second show followed, in June 1948, this time reviewed by Heron, with whom Wynter had renewed his acquaintance either in London or St Ives, where Heron was to be found every summer between 1947 and 1955, staying with his young family in a rented harbourside cottage. He had had his own first show at the Redfern the previous October and, as art critic for the *New English Weekly* (1945–7) and then the *New Statesman and Nation*

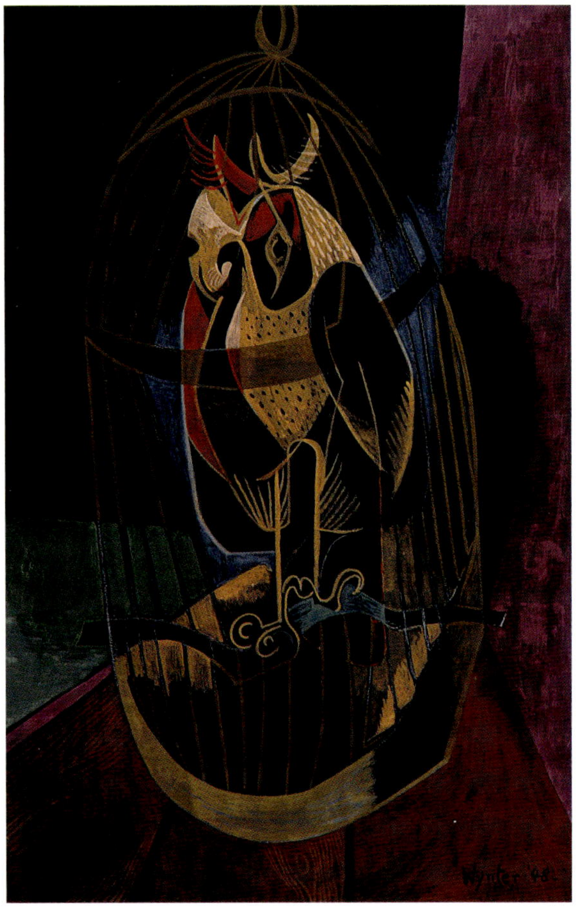

47
Bird in a Cage
00 x 00 cm (00 x 00 in)
c 1948
Private collection

(1947–50), was developing a distinct critical agenda. Heron loathed Surrealism, and he drew the co-ordinates carefully when positioning Wynter, placing him between the kind of French painting he admired and native Neo-Romanticism: 'His painting combines the formal ingenuity of cubism with the mood of a romantic; the discipline in abstract form of a still-life artist with the subjects of a landscapist.' This is spot-on as far as appearances go; but in his avoidance of any analysis of content (which might have revealed a Surrealist subtext in Wynter's images), Heron ran on blithely into bathos: 'Dead birds and the properties of the Cornish moors and beaches inhabit the dramatic twilight of his accomplished gouaches.'[36]

Heron wrote as though a painting need have no other justification, required no more probing analysis, than that afforded by a description of the artist's handling of colour and form to create spatial illusion. It was as if contemplating the effect of placing violet next to yellow had an ethical import equivalent to casting a vote. The *New Statesman*'s earnest left-wing readers might reasonably have asked how, in Heron's view, an artist of the 'impressive talent' he claimed for Wynter could content himself with painting 'Dead birds and the properties of the Cornish moors and beaches'. Such motifs recur in Wynter's work of the late 1940s, such as *Foreshore with Gull*, with an emphasis verging on caricature. Sometimes, as in his monkey-house cartoons or in *Bird in a Cage* (fig. 47), Wynter's animals have an autobiographical gleam in their eye. At others he explored Braquean themes, as in the coffee pot and cup in *Still Life with Kipper*; but even here the title adds a backhandedness to the tribute. More often, on table-tops where Braque, or indeed Heron, would have placed a bowl of fruit, coffee pot or wineglass, Wynter dumped a sheep or cow's skull – a Cornish spectre at the middle-class feast of Continental culture (see fig. 1). Some of the still-lifes he painted in the late 1940s have a lurid vitality and variation of colour that are absent from his earlier work in Cornwall or his contemporary landscapes, such as *Breaking Wave* (fig. 49). Their artistic avatar is not Braque, Sutherland or Klee but Picasso, oscillating in a mood of virtuoso jokery between classical good taste and Surrealist mischief.

Even in the form of bones, Wynter's animals are born subversives; a skull on a kitchen table remains as undomesticated as the screaming flock in *Birds Disturbing the Sleep of a Town* (fig. 50). In this 1948 gouache a small harbour town lies blanched in moonlight, like an illustration in a children's book, against a sombre, earthy monotype ground – more cave than sky. The posse of sharp-beaked, spectral birds disturbs the town, perhaps, not so much through its cries (the beaks are shut) as by breaking and entering the dreams of the human population asleep below. If this were an image from Wynter's dream diaries, how would he have interpreted those birds? As messengers from the unconscious, as symbols of anxiety or despair? Wynter reportedly told Sven Berlin that the painting arose from a mood of 'suicidal' depression one evening, which was suddenly alleviated by the cry of a curlew

48
Bryan Wynter with mask, *c.*1950

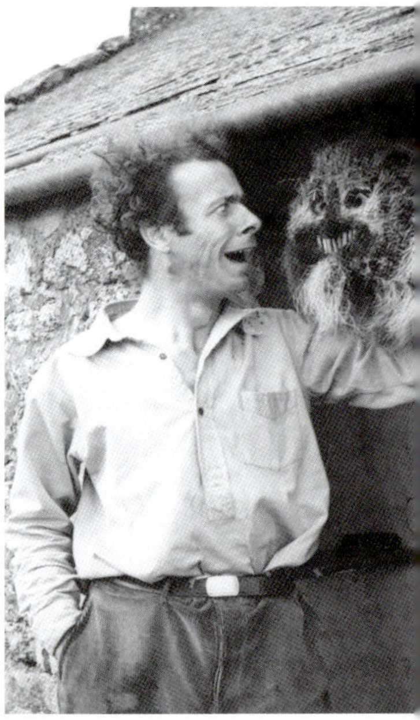

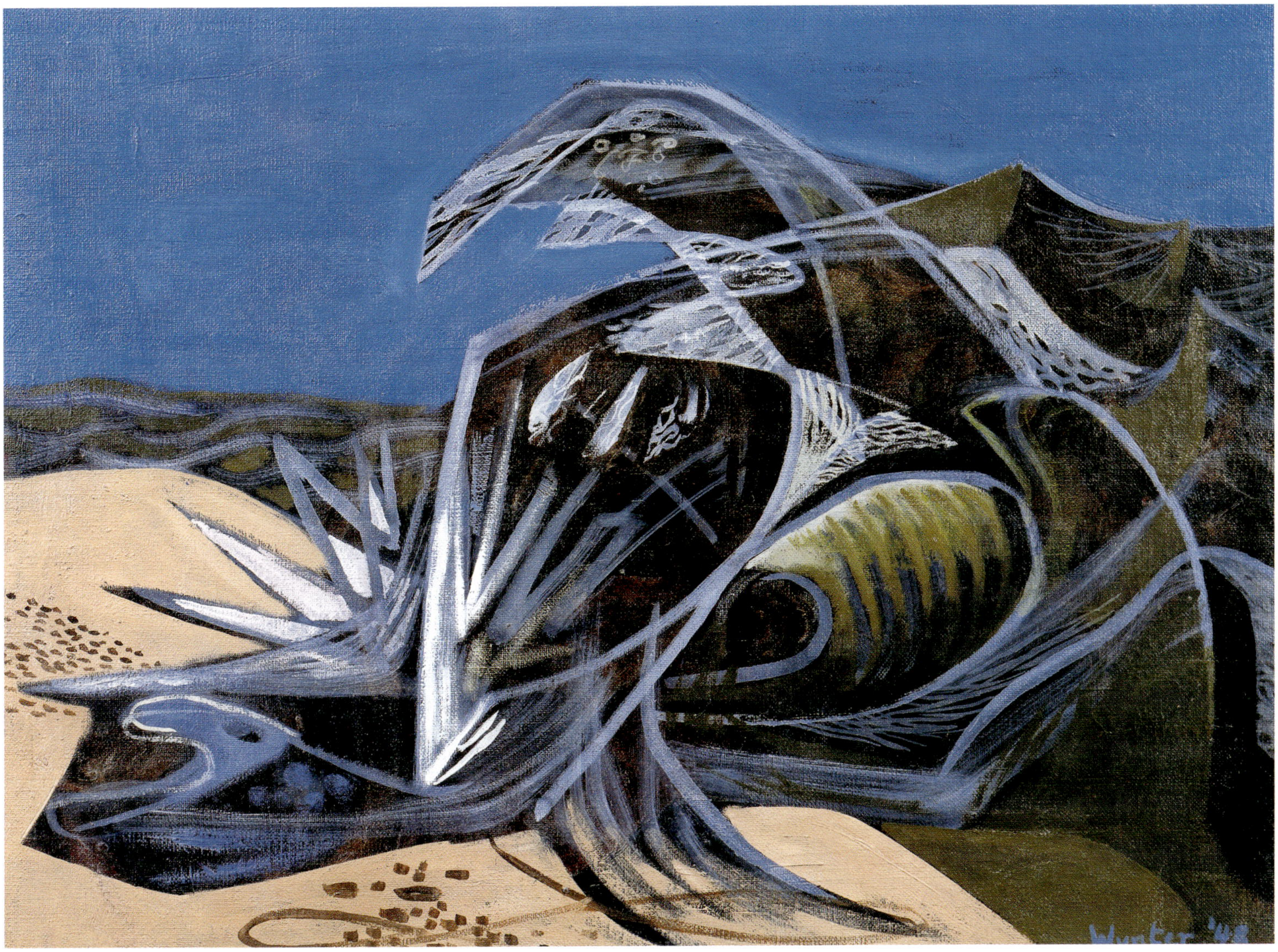

49
Breaking Wave
oil on canvas
46 x 61 cm (18 x 24 in)
1948
Private collection

flying through the dark air beyond the Carn. There's a similar moonlit effect in another gouache from 1948, *Cornish Farm* (fig. 52), where the role of spectral visitant is taken by two gaunt trees. The patterns of stonework, farm track, slate roofs and other 'figurative' elements in the image are painted with a kind of somnambulistic absorption, as though Wynter were intent on something quite other than the picture's literal subject.

Always wary of being drawn in to the 'arty town' on his doorstep, Wynter was nevertheless putting down roots in Cornwall. Paintings such as *Breaking Wave* have something, however superficial, of a shared 'St Ives' idiom. The freeze-frame arcs of water, like the involuted, icy geometries of Wilhelmina Barns-Graham's slightly later 'Glacier' paintings, relate to the cool, clean lines of Gabo's Constructivism as well as Hepworth and Nicholson's humanist softening of his abstract principles. However much Wynter preferred to maintain his physical isolation and artistic independence, there seemed to be no avoiding a degree of either identification with or influence by what other artists in and around St Ives were doing, not least because of the unavoidable fact of artistic life that individual reputations usually rise faster when they're connected to a perceived group or movement.

By 1948, in any case, Wynter's personal affairs had already become much more deeply enmeshed in St Ives. In 1946, soon after the 23-year-old Sue Lethbridge (fig. 53) arrived in the town to set up a small toy-making business, the Toy Trumpet, she and Wynter began a relationship. Berlin described her as 'a tall, vivid young woman with hair as red as a Russian doll in a ballet'.[37] With a rootless childhood and recent unhappy break-up behind her, Sue didn't burden Wynter with any expectation of a conventional ménage. Their life together

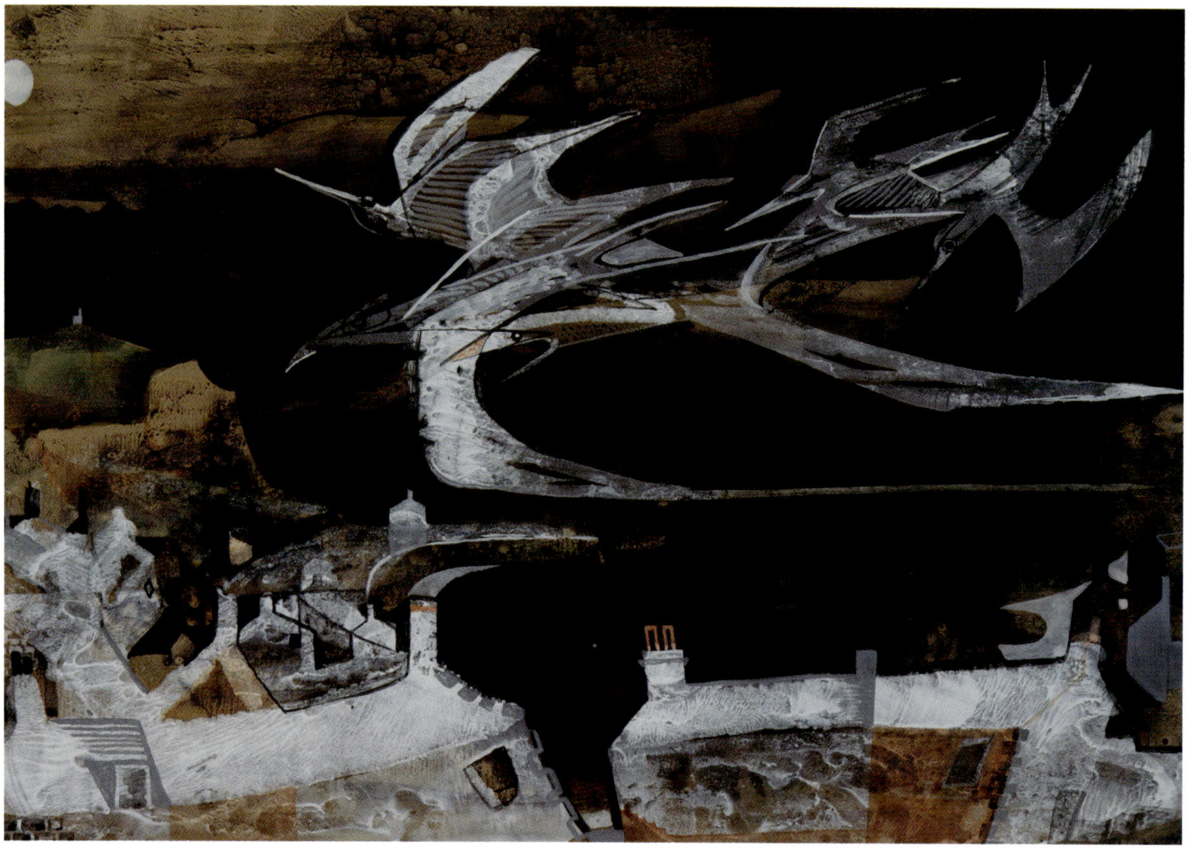

50
Birds Disturbing the Sleep of a Town
monotype and gouache on paper
35.5 x 50.7 cm (14 x 20 in)
1948
Collection of Newlyn Art Gallery and The Exchange

took on a peripatetic rhythm: they would camp out at the Carn for three days at a time, then return to Sue's small house in St Ives. Wynter, she recalled, was 'always leaping around on the moors'.[38] Sometimes he worked up at the Carn alone; sometimes he disappeared to London or elsewhere. Like him, Sue was determinedly independent: in her portrait by Heron this determination can be felt breaking through the decorous homage to Braque. After war work servicing Spitfire engines in Scotland, she had turned to making miniature gypsy caravans and other 'toys'. In the early days of the business these beautifully crafted objects weren't really intended for children, being sold to collectors in Burlington Arcade, Fortnum & Mason, Harrods and other upmarket London outlets.[39]

Despite its isolation, visitors frequently made their way the Carn. For all his rejection of social convention and consumer comforts, Wynter liked to maintain a certain order in his living and working arrangements. When the deaf South African poet David Wright came to stay in March 1949, Wynter wrote exasperatedly to Hedy of his slovenly habits:

He has a passion for leaving large objects such as paraffin cans, rucksacks & on one occasion his trousers, trodden off onto the ground & lying there like a cowpat (he had just got back into bed) right in the centre of the floor ... He also produces stencilled patterns of his chair & feet in cigarette ash, ends, matches & scraps of paper on the carpet.[40]

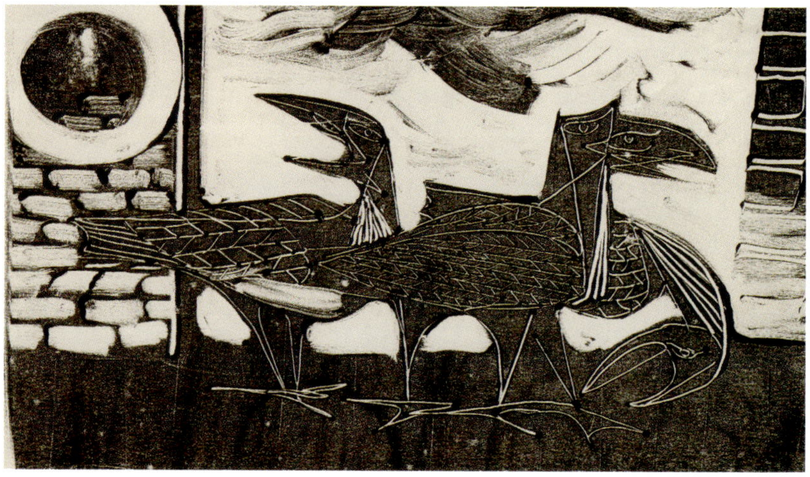

51
Three Birds
monotype on paper
51 x 75 cm (20 x 29½ in)
1949
Artist's estate

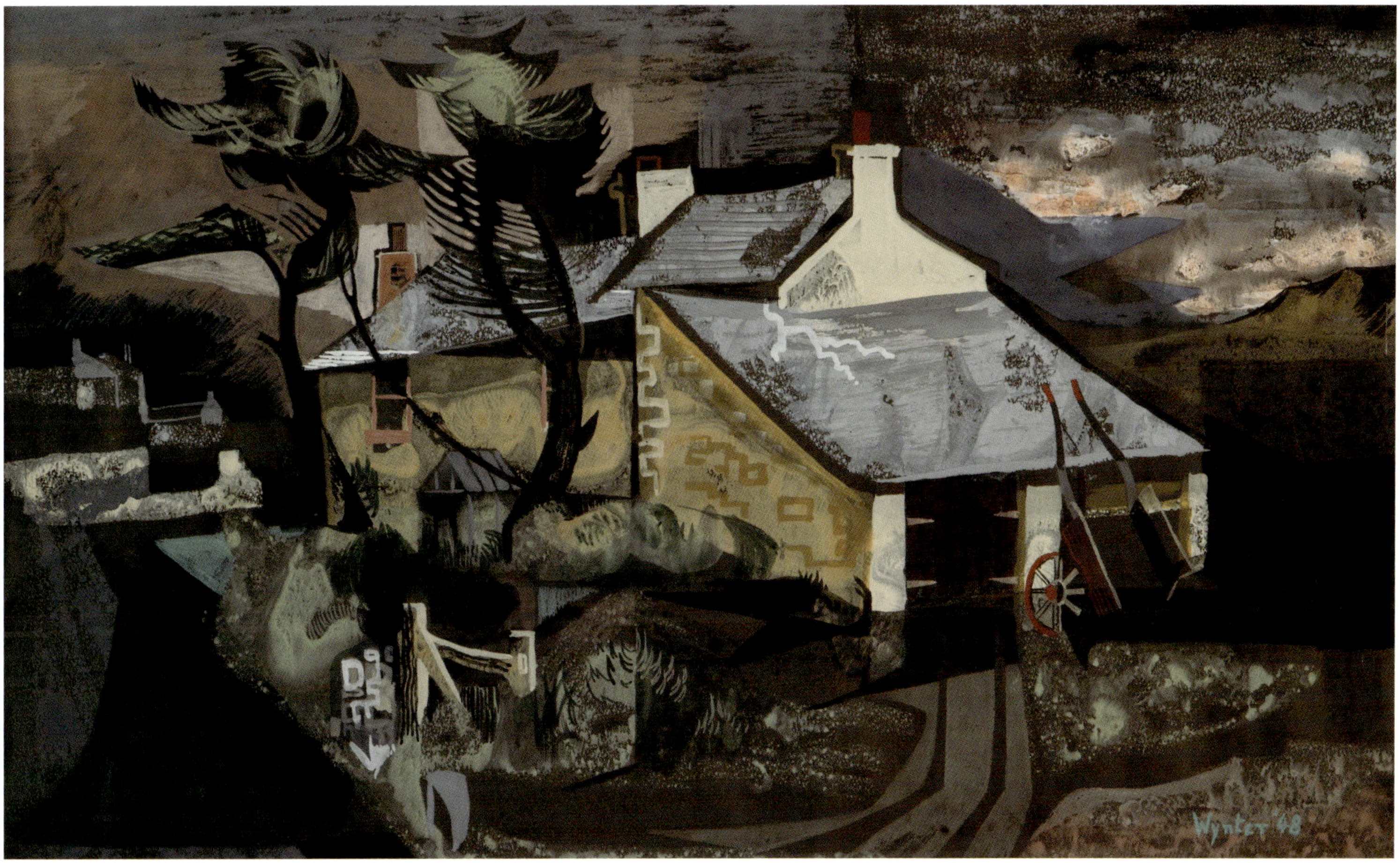

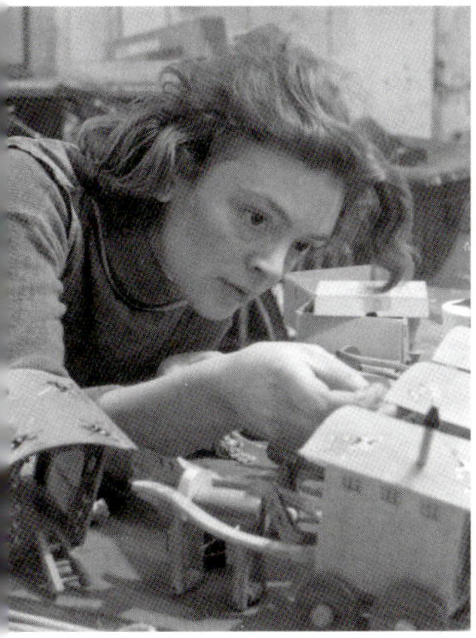

52
Cornish Farm
monotype and gouache on paper
50.8 x 73.6 cm (20 x 29 in)
1948
Artist's estate

53
Sue Lethbridge in the Toy Trumpet workshop, St Ives, c.1947

In the late 1940s Wynter's closest neighbours were the so-called Moor Poets, who formed a small, shifting colony in the Zennor area. Wright was often around, as was Heath-Stubbs, who had left Oxford and was now living in London, and Michael Hamburger, who had apparently been helping Hedy in her search for work as an illustrator. George Barker and John Fairfax rented a house near by. In a valley running inland below the Carn lived Kit Barker, George's brother, with whom Wynter shared an exhibition at Downing's Bookshop in St Ives in the autumn of 1948. It was around this time that Sue became pregnant, and, following Wynter's own, curiously insistent advice to Hedy when she'd found herself in the same situation three years earlier ('If you really want to have a child, why not settle the matter between you & get married'[41]), the couple married early in 1949.

Writing to Hedy in March, Wynter was again proffering advice about life with children: she must arrange some regular childcare for her young son, he told her, so that she could get out and meet people. In his own case he sounded self-pityingly adrift: 'I think I do best on my own. No one will look after me & encourage me in my work without trying to eat out my soul.'[42] There were professional anxieties too: 'How I live & how I paint are so closely linked & how I paint now seems to affect how much money I make & the money again affects how I live – a treadmill very precariously balanced.'[43] A trip to France that April with his brother Eric, who paid their air fares, temporarily cheered him up. They stopped off in Paris, where Wynter found contemporary French art 'tasteful but without force or direction'; he then proceeded to the Riviera and Provence alone. In the south of France, he reported, he had 'drawn & drawn & drawn', and hoped to paint a series of Provençal landscapes on his return. Yet 'the air here is so clear, the sun so hot, & the colour so brilliant that I sometimes doubt whether I will be able to resurrect it in the grey & sombre atmosphere of Cornwall.'[44] There was no mention of impending fatherhood.

Back in Cornwall, the Wynters' first child, Jake, was born in July. At the age of thirty-three Wynter was apparently still far from ready to settle down. Family life didn't mix easily with 'leaping about on the moors' – he seemed more than usually restless and preoccupied.

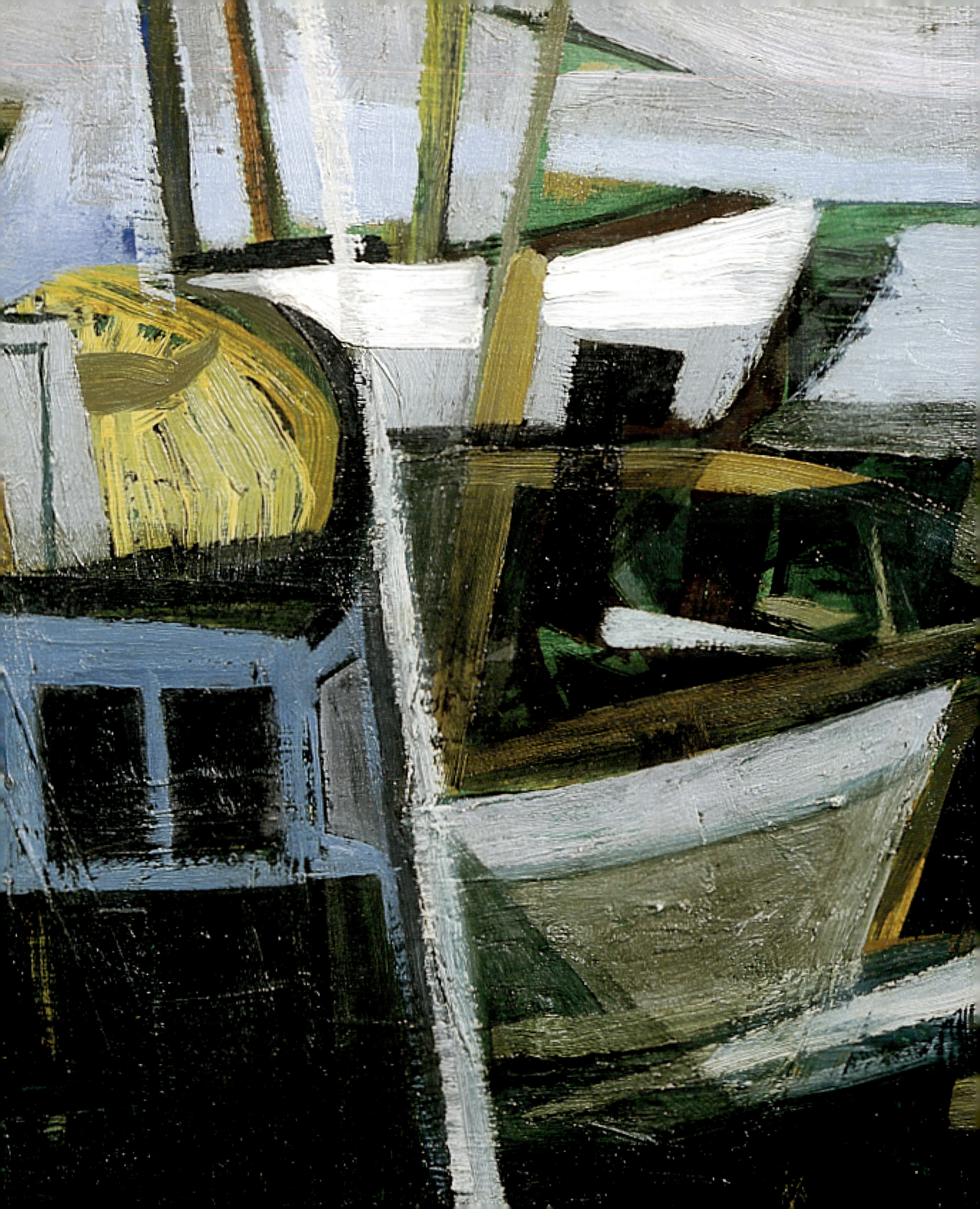

4

'Between Realism and Abstraction': a Time of Transition, 1949–55

Over Christmas 1949 the Wynters and their six-month-old son swapped Sue's cottage in St Ives for a houseboat in Oxford. Crawling across England at an average speed of 25 m.p.h. in Bryan's broken-down old car, they spent two days on the road. When they finally arrived, the boat – a decrepit university pleasure barge – was in no better shape. They had to start each morning by pumping out the several inches of water that had seeped in during the night and caulking fresh leaks with clay. Yet Wynter pronounced it 'a fine change'. There was, he claimed, plenty of room to work, and Jake was 'a well behaved little creature who lets us sleep at night'. Most of all, 'It is a great relief to be clear of St Ives for while. It was really getting me down with it's [*sic*] small-town artistication, & few people whose company I can enjoy.'[1]

This wasn't quite the tone required from a founder member of the Penwith Society of Arts, which had held its first exhibition in St Ives the previous summer. Whereas the Crypt Group, which had staged two further shows in 1947 and 1948,[2] represented an avant-garde minority exhibiting under the aegis of the staunchly traditional St Ives Society of Artists, the Penwith Society was a full-scale breakaway organisation involving almost thirty artists and craftspeople. With Nicholson and Hepworth in a dominant position, it effectively became a vehicle for the modernist faction in St Ives. This was its appeal, at least, to the various grandees of the British art world who were persuaded to take an interest. Herbert Read, now a ubiquitous figure on boards, committees and judging panels involved with the arts, accepted the invitation to become the Society's first president. For him the Penwith was a living demonstration of one of his cherished visions, in which art was to play a leading, even formative, role in post-war community life. Nevertheless, although the Penwith subscribed to the all-pull-together rhetoric of its day – it was, announced the inaugural catalogue, 'entirely opposed to exclusiveness and antagonism' – the small-town tensions and rivalries that so irked Wynter could not be smoothed over for long. Almost exactly a year after the Penwith's formation, a row over proposals to segregate the membership into 'abstract' and 'representational' artists led to a spate of resignations.

Wynter avoided being drawn into this schism. And, in spite of its acrimonious fall-out (Lanyon never forgave either Hepworth or Nicholson for their role in the affair), there remained advantages in being linked to St Ives's expanding network of art world contacts. The Arts Council's director, Philip James, took a close interest in St Ives, and the Council's regional representative, Jack Wood Palmer, had a house near by. In February 1950 Wynter was included in 'Contemporary English Painting', an exhibition organised by Wood Palmer at Bristol City Art Gallery. In this pre-televisual era such exhibitions were the main means of shaping people's ideas as to which contemporary artists mattered. The line-up in Bristol also included Paul Feiler, who had been teaching at the West of England College of Art in the city since 1946 and had originally proposed the show, together with three other former Slade associates: Heron, Adrian Ryan and Robin Treffgarne. Wood Palmer introduced Wynter as 'one of the most distinguished of our younger painters today', adding that 'In steering his middle course between realism and abstraction he has combined the best of both worlds'.[3] Also frequently in St Ives, scouting for talent among the younger artists there, was Hepworth's friend Lilian Somerville, the British Council's formidable director of fine art. Another of the Council's senior officers, Francis Watson, meanwhile, had officiated at the opening of the third Crypt Group show. In January 1951 Wynter was represented in 'Fifteen Artists & Craftsmen from around St Ives' at Heal's department store in London. 'St Ives' was emerging as a versatile brand, encompassing both abstract and landscape idioms, and ranging in ideological temper from Hepworth's high-minded modernism to the marketing of art alongside dining tables and bespoke curtains.

By 1951, some six years into his career, Wynter's

detail of **62**
Boats in Harbour, 1952

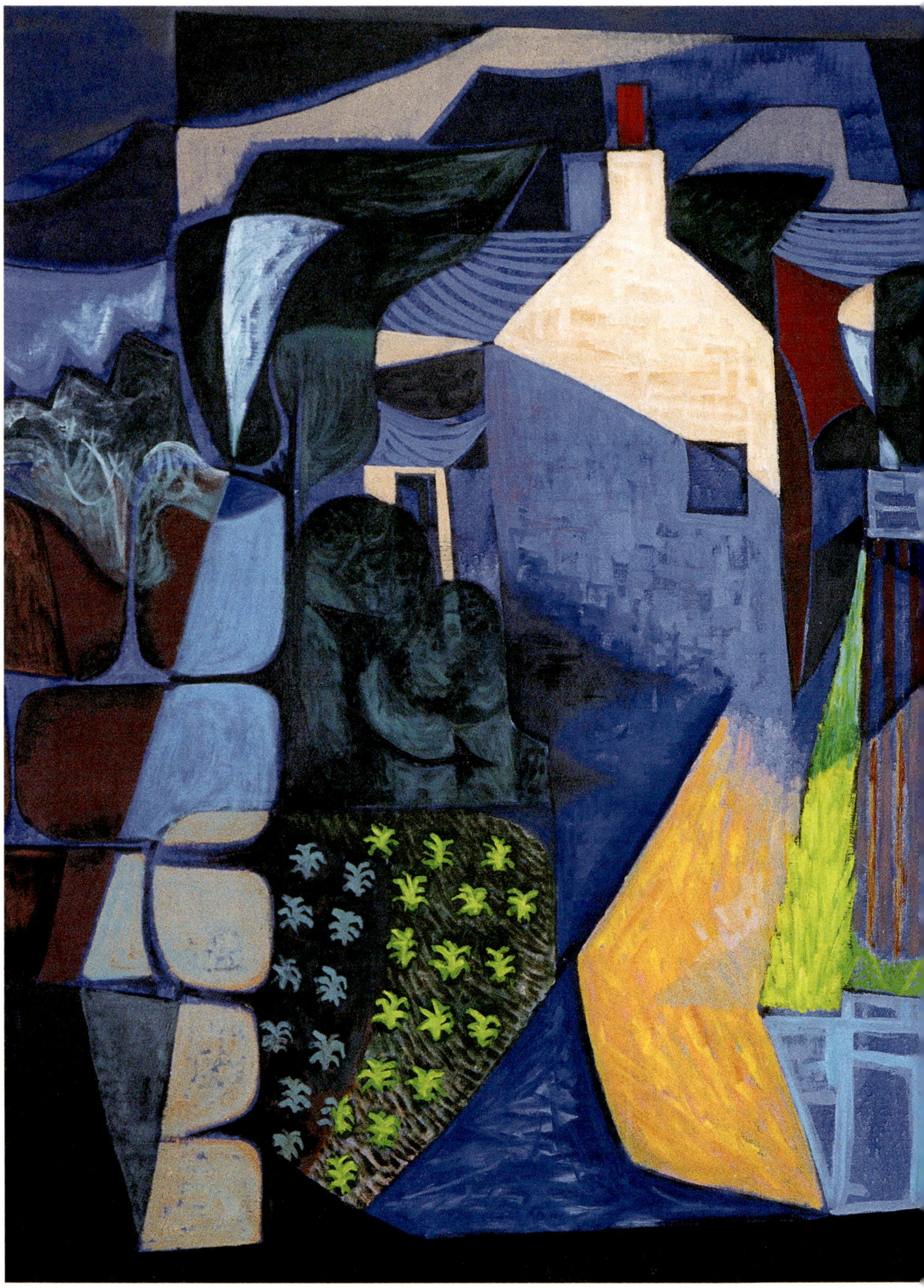

54
Blue Landscape
oil on canvas
122 x 241.5 cm (48 x 95 in)
1951
Collection of the Suter Te Aratoi O Whakatu, Nelson, New Zealand

place in the front ranks of younger British artists seemed assured. He was featured by Herbert Read in *Contemporary British Art*, a mass-market paperback intended to popularise 'the leading artists and sculptors of the modern school'.[4] The painting Read reproduced, *Foreshore with Gull* (see fig. 2), had already been acquired for the British Council's art collection, and Wynter was duly included in a British Council exhibition that toured Germany that year. He was also among the sixty artists commissioned to create work for an exhibition of paintings to accompany the Festival of Britain (this list, for which Nicholson and Heron were among those quietly recommending names, was in effect the Arts Council's definitive take on contemporary talent). Artists were required to produce works of at least 45 x 60 inches (114 x 152.4 cm) in size, for which canvas and stretchers (still an expensive luxury in 1951) were supplied. Before this, Wynter had painted mostly either on paper or, using a common trick of the time, on a canvas-textured support made by gluing butter muslin to hardboard.

For Wynter, as for most artists of his generation, the Festival painting was his first public commission. Lanyon laboured for months in St Ives to complete his towering vertical landscape *Porthleven*, in which realism and abstraction were not so much combined in a 'middle course' as thrown at each other's throats like wrestlers. Wynter, meanwhile, set up studio in Richmond, where he rented premises with his Oxford friend Edward Walton, who had (according to Berlin) 'done a Gauguin on his wife'.[5] Up at the Carn there was room enough to work on gouaches and drawings, but for this commission Wynter needed more space. He could have found a serviceable old sail loft in St Ives; instead, as he was again to do when embarking on a new scale or type of work, he preferred to reinstall himself in London. Like Lanyon's, his submission, titled *Blue Landscape* (fig. 54), had a Cornish landscape theme. But where Lanyon's painting records his furious determination to engage with the nature of a real place while retaining a qualified allegiance to the principles of Constructivist abstraction (he never lost his admiration for Naum Gabo), Wynter's resolution of moorland topography into abstract patterns has a much more detached, reflective effect. Subject and pattern seem to float exactly level with each other: here are fields, cottages and hillsides, but there's no hint of narrative, illustrative bait to draw you in, as there almost always is in Neo-Romantic art such as Craxton's or Minton's. The imaginative movement that Wynter had 'mentioned as a theory of art' to Hedy in 1945 still held

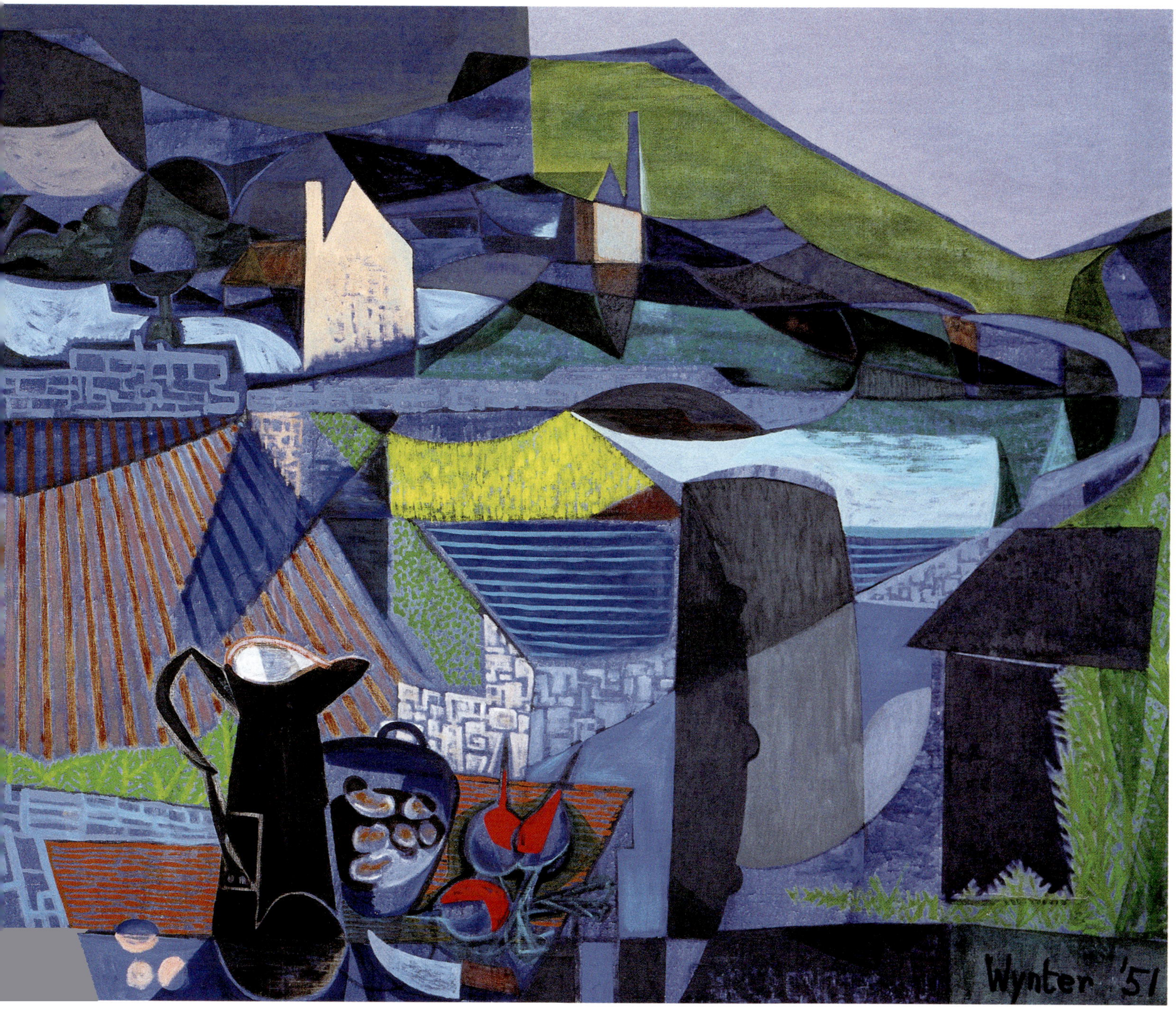

good for him: the picture plane is a threshold across which passes a two-way traffic between mind and material reality.

This was certainly not how Heron saw things. For him a painting's primary function was to create an experience of illusory space. 'What time is to the musical composer,' he wrote, 'space is to the painter.'[6] In his discussions of pictorial space Heron rarely looked behind the image into questions of motivation or meaning. Psychology (or indeed any other scientific or literary discipline) seemed to him barely relevant to the business of visual art. In *Blue Landscape*'s cusped, zigzagging interpenetration of floodlit colour and inky nocturne, Heron probably sensed above all the presence of Braque. What else would have led Wynter to replace the two galvanised milk churns that occupy the foreground of his small preliminary gouache with a table-top still-life in which a Braque-style wine pitcher, bowl of apples and wineglass are thinly disguised as a milk jug, pan of potatoes and bunch of radishes or beetroots? Instead of inviting the viewer into

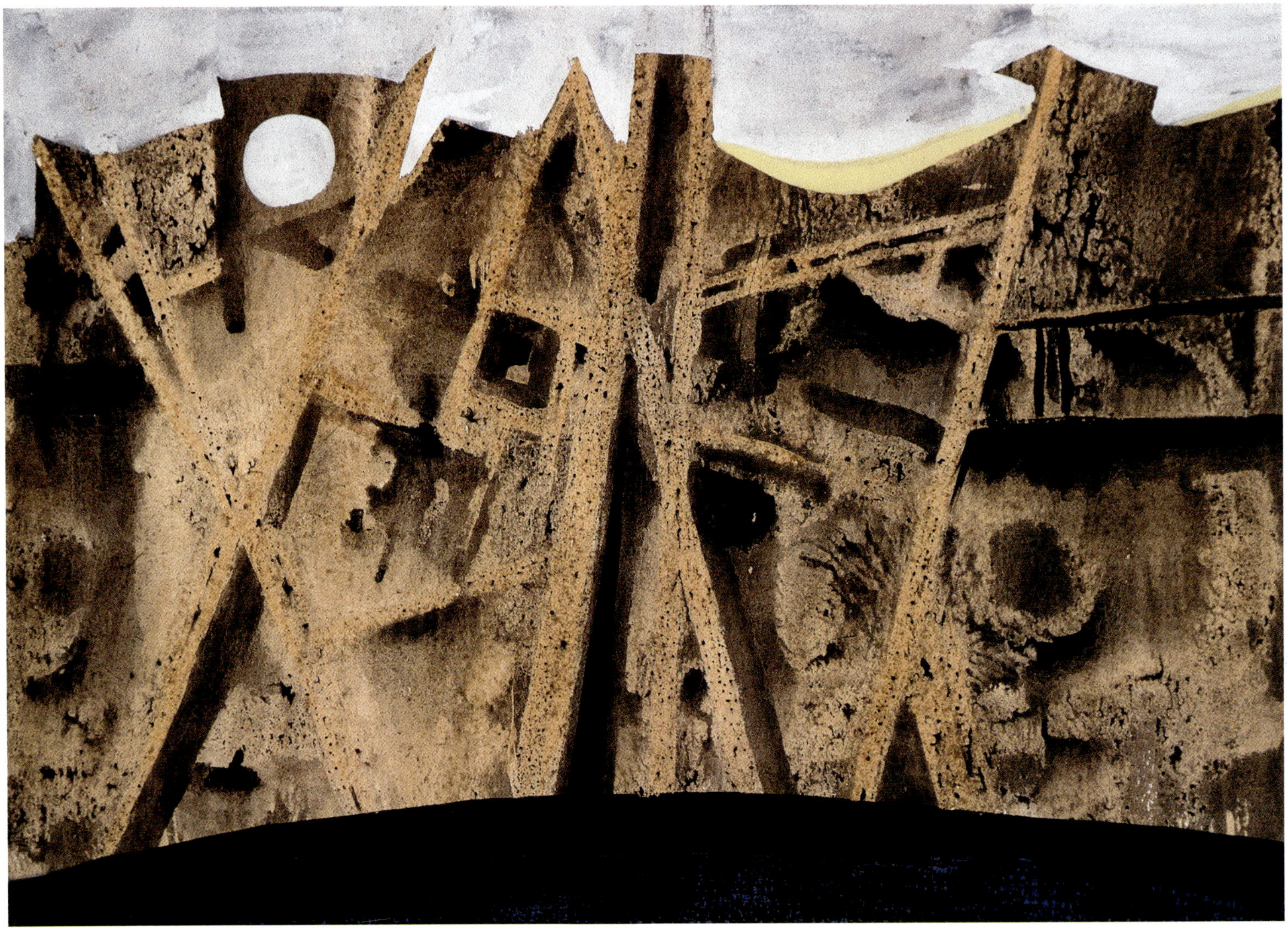

the serene depths of illusory space, however, Wynter's landscape creates a feeling of disjunction. Partly it's the sooty jug, which obtrudes like a head in the next row of cinema seats, somehow stopping us from crossing the threshold of the picture plane. Partly it's the expressionistic intensity of the colour and lighting effects, which, as in Klee, so clearly belong to spaces of the mind rather than, as Heron tended to mean by space, the lucid air through which you imagine reaching for a coffee cup on a Bonnard table.

Around the turn of the decade Wynter was exploring several quite distinct approaches in his work. He continued to treat Cornish landscape subjects in a fairly straightforward manner, as well as in a more surrealistic vein, of which *Levant Cliffs* (fig. 55) is a particularly Ernstian example. His *Breaking Wave* (1951; fig. 57) relates to Lanyon's boldly expressive mark-making and abstract-landscape structures, while *Head in Green* (fig. 56) presents a strange amalgam of geometric abstract elements, caricature and a serious attempt to do something more experimental with oil paint than Wynter had so far attempted. The small gouache *Mousehole Quay* (fig. 59) focuses on the girder-like armature of a harbour crane; this may simply be a literal rendering of an actual piece of machinery, although the fascination with such structural scaffolding detectable in the work of several British painters around 1950 can also be ascribed to the influence of the French abstract artist Pierre Soulages (fig. 58). According to Feiler, similar features in Wynter's work at this time were a result of the drawing expeditions the two of them made in the Bristol docks.

In the contributions from Wynter, Heron, Lanyon and Nicholson, St Ives was well represented in '60 Paintings for '51'. On the main Festival site, a futuristic building complex beside the Thames, Hepworth's monumental *Contrapuntal Forms* was prominently located. The nearby

55
Levant Cliffs
monotype and gouache on paper
35.5 x 49 cm (14 x 19¼ in)
1952
Private collection

56
Head in Green
oil on canvas
76 x 51 cm (30 x 20 in)
1950
Private collection

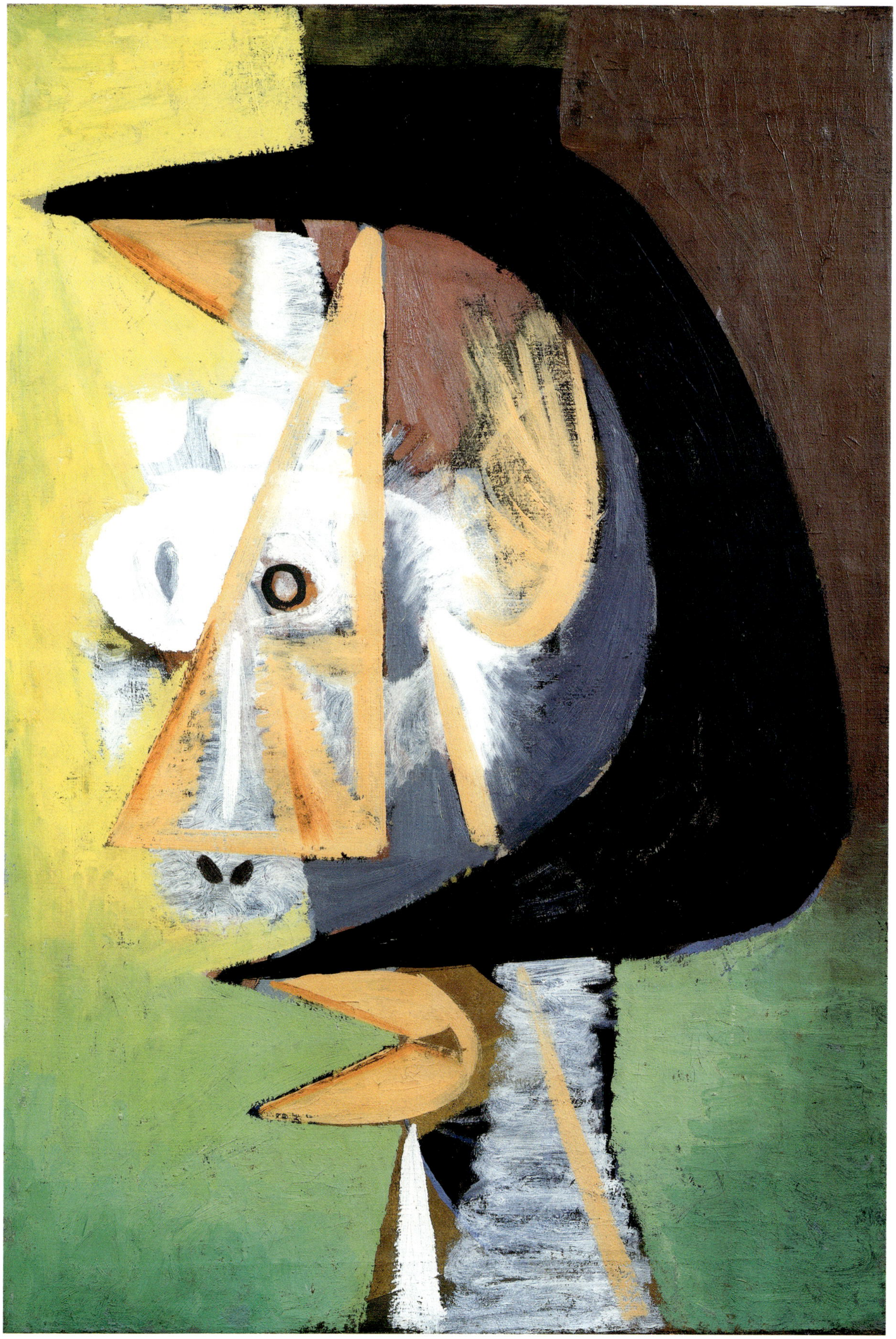

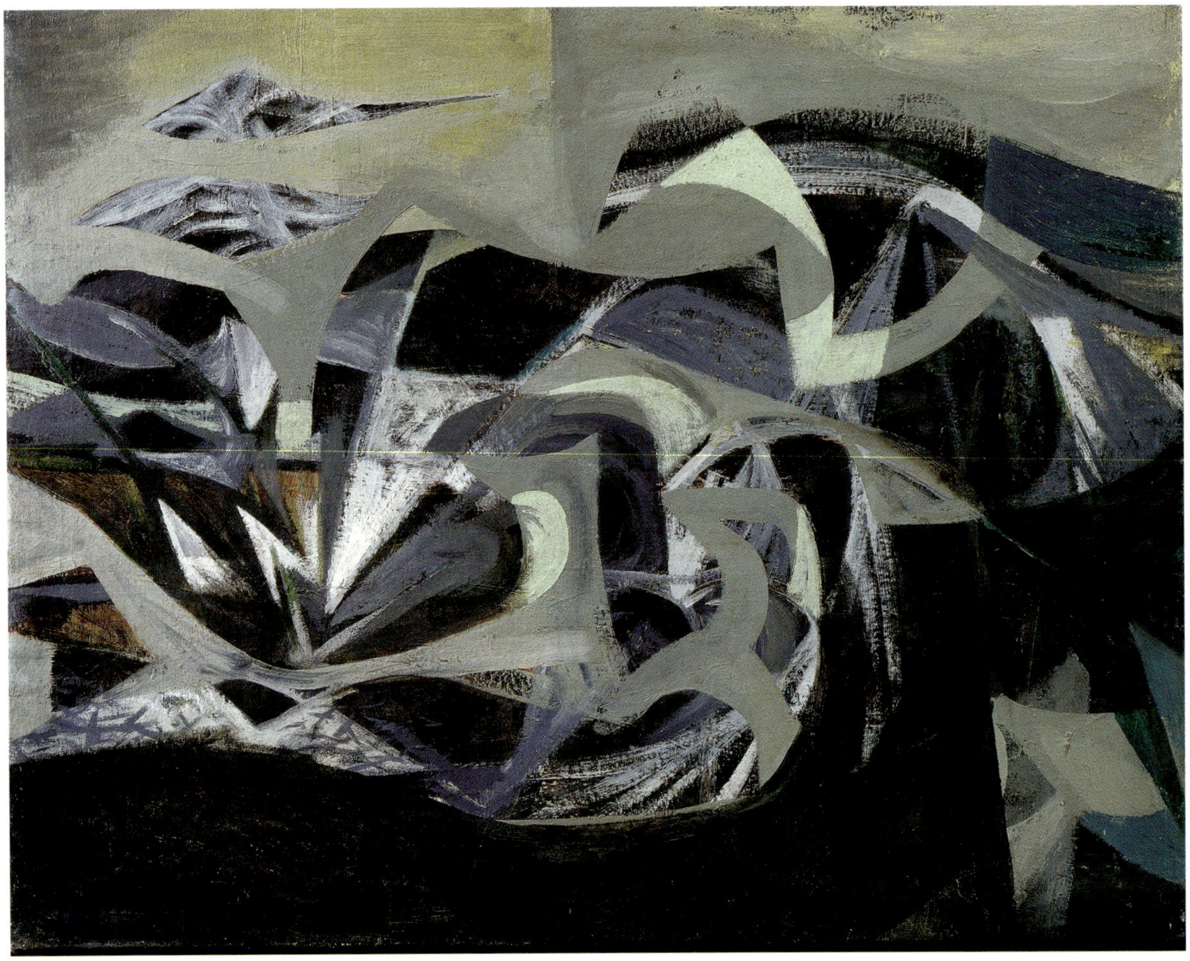

57
Breaking Wave
oil on canvas
61 x 75.5 cm (24 x 29¾ in)
1951
Artist's estate

Riverside Restaurant was decorated with a mural by Nicholson. Altogether, the most ambitious and popular cultural event in Britain since the war provided a high-profile metropolitan platform for artists associated with St Ives. Despite the Festival's upbeat patriotic tone, however, Britain's battered post-war economy was still some years from recovery. For artists, official recognition led to only limited financial rewards. It was to be another government initiative – the provision of grants for ex-services personnel who wanted return to education or retrain – that would indirectly provide an economic lifeline for Wynter and his St Ives contemporaries.

This grant scheme channelled public money into universities, art schools and other educational bodies, which were consequently able to expand their programmes. At Bath Academy of Art the head of painting, William Scott, himself a regular visitor to Cornwall, brought in first Wynter then Lanyon and Terry Frost as visiting tutors. The academy was a new venture that had started life in 1946, when Bath School of Art, a small local institution, reconstituted itself as the first

58
Pierre Soulages,
Peinture 16 Mars
oil on canvas
129.5 x 88.9 cm (51 x 35 in)
1955

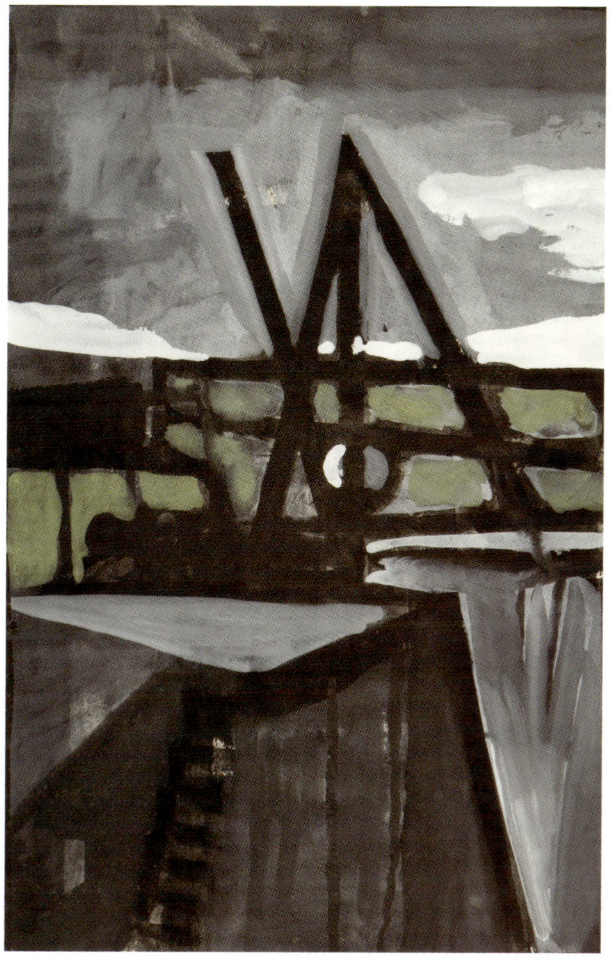

59
Mousehole Quay
gouache on paper
41.5 x 26.5 cm (16¼ x 10½ in)
*c.*1950
Private collection

residential art school in England, where students could take diploma courses in fine art or teaching. The artist and landowner Lord Methuen offered the use of his Elizabethan mansion Corsham Court, a few miles north-east of Bath, which had been commandeered as a military convalescent home during the war but, unlike many such country houses, had emerged more or less intact. In the scuffed grandeur of its interiors still hung the Methuen family collection of Gainsborough portraits and other works of art. Nissen huts in the grounds offered useful extra accommodation and studio space.

Under its principal, Clifford Ellis, Bath Academy of Art (usually known simply as 'Corsham') became a controversial model of progressive, multi-disciplinary educational practice, comparable in some ways to the contemporary Bauhaus-influenced programme at Black Mountain College in North Carolina. Whether students were training as artists or as teachers, Ellis believed that they should learn a variety of creative disciplines. He drafted in specialist staff, who might sometimes be required to teach each other's subjects. Scott and the sculptor Kenneth Armitage joined the Corsham staff straight after demobilisation in 1946. Litz Pisk, who had designed stage sets for Brecht and Weill in the early 1930s, gave classes in movement; Helen Binyon taught puppetry; the flamboyant James Kirkup was poet in residence; and James Tower, an admirer of Picasso's ceramic art, ran a pottery, where the painting tutors as well as their students worked under his supervision. Ellis could be doctrinaire in his promotion of free expression, but to most students in the Austerity-pinched early 1950s, the set-up at Corsham was extraordinarily different from anything they had previously encountered. It was, recalled one, 'inspiringly unique', a kind of British Bauhaus in the Wiltshire countryside.[7]

Visiting tutors such as Wynter generally taught for two or three days a week in six-week blocks. They were never sure whether their appointment would be renewed until the hoped-for postcard from Ellis arrived shortly before the start of term. For painters based in Cornwall, the term-time absences put a strain on family life: by the early 1950s both Frost and Lanyon had several young children, and Lanyon's liaisons with female students, who greatly outnumbered the men at Corsham, were notorious. Frost was employed to pass on the skills in measured drawing he had learned at Camberwell School of Arts and Crafts after the war, although the rigorous observational method developed there by William Coldstream was by now very far from his geometric abstract painting. Wynter, on the other hand, evolved a teaching method more in tune with the Corsham ethos of experimentation. He assembled still-lifes from tree bark, moss, animal skulls and other natural *objets trouvés*, which students were encouraged to paint as landscapes. Students found Wynter, unlike the garrulous Scott, almost taciturn in his reluctance to pass judgement or impose solutions. Recollections of his teaching style have nothing of the prankster boisterousness associated with, for example, Lanyon and Jack Smith, who on one occasion apparently organised an outdoor life-class in which the nude model rode around on a motor bike. Ellis was eventually persuaded that measures should be taken to prevent Corsham's record of innovation from being overshadowed by its egregious reputation for licentiousness. One solution – surrounding the women's accommodation block with barbed wire – seems unlikely to have had much effect.[8]

Though the income was useful, and the social life based at the lodgings he shared with the painter William Brooker enjoyable, Wynter found that the rhythm of teaching interspersed with time in the studio played havoc with his work. Compared with the prolific years between 1945 and 1951, very little survives from between about 1952 and 1955. The Wiltshire countryside – too similar, perhaps, to the arable Hertfordshire of his childhood – failed to excite him. At the same time, the aspect of Cornwall he had made his own – the atmosphere and texture of its western moors, a treeless, semi-abandoned landscape – seems to have lost its piquancy, at least in any representational sense. *Frozen Landscape* (fig. 61), an almost monochromatic oil painting from 1951, which can be seen propped on the mantelpiece in a slightly later photo of the Carn (fig. 60), is markedly different from Wynter's Festival commission, both in tone and in content. The landscape references, such as they are, come solely from branching, stick-like shapes, which suggest the blackthorn thickets that crowd out hundreds of disused stone-walled fields on the Penwith moors.

The title feels like an afterthought. 'Frozen' is less about this painting's subject than about how it feels, whether the actual time of year is winter or spring. With their shorter opposed branches on a long central stem, the stick forms can just about be read as plant-like rather than humanoid. Even so, they echo the shapes of welded steel sculptures that Reg Butler was making at about this time. His description of 'remote inscrutable custodians of a landscape hostile to man',[9] actually applied to the military radar towers at Bawdsey in Suffolk, serves equally well for his own etiolated metal figures, which resemble a sci-fi master race of sinister insects. Butler had been in St Ives visiting the Herons in early 1951; if Wynter didn't meet him then (when he was working much of the time in Richmond), he could have seen Butler's sculpture *Birdcage* at the Festival of Britain that summer. Wynter's fascination with various manifestations of 'remote' or alien presence went back a long way. His *Counterpoint* creatures, and the strange gulls and screaming birds of his Cornish landscape period, were all visitants from some region hostile, if not to humankind in general, then to its ordinary civilised habits. The mood of *Frozen Landscape*, however, seems more autobiographical than Butler's sculptures, which have often been interpreted as embodiments of early Cold War *angst*. Wynter's own tall, lanky figure may feature in *Frozen Landscape* in a quite literal sense,

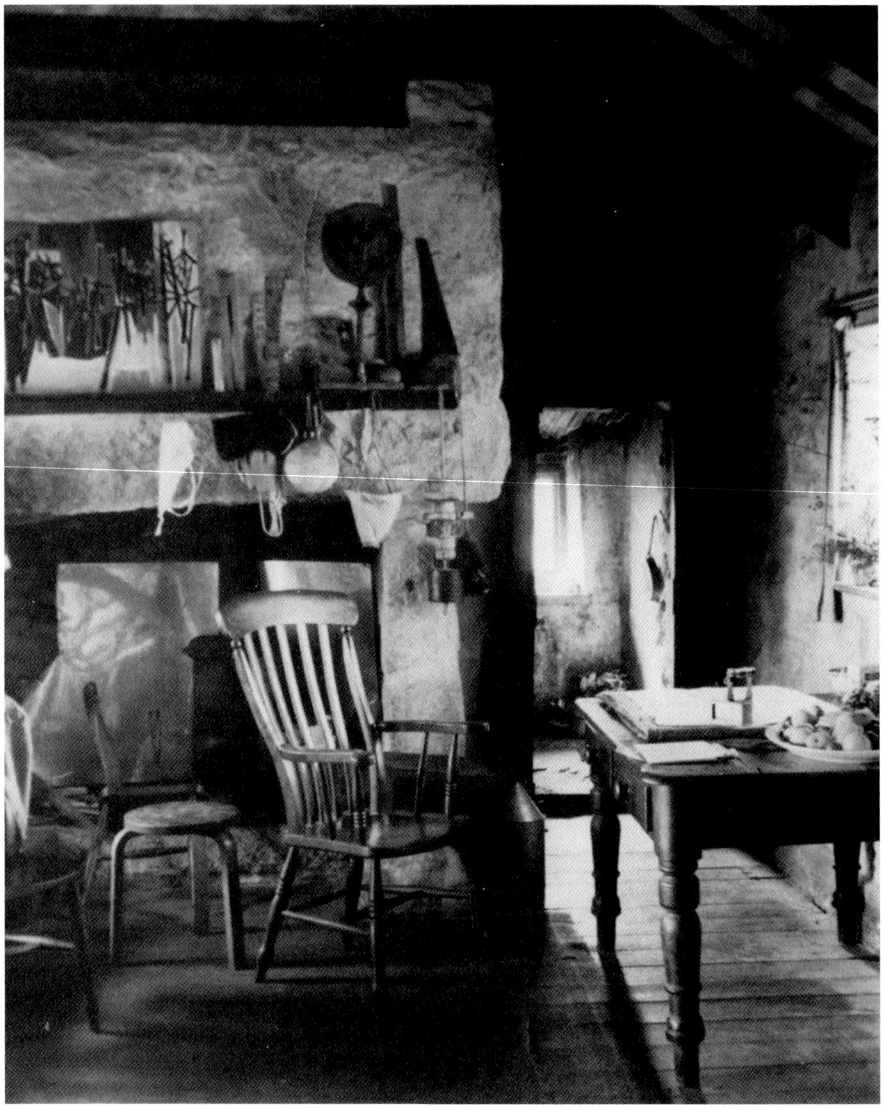

60
Interior of the Carn, 1956

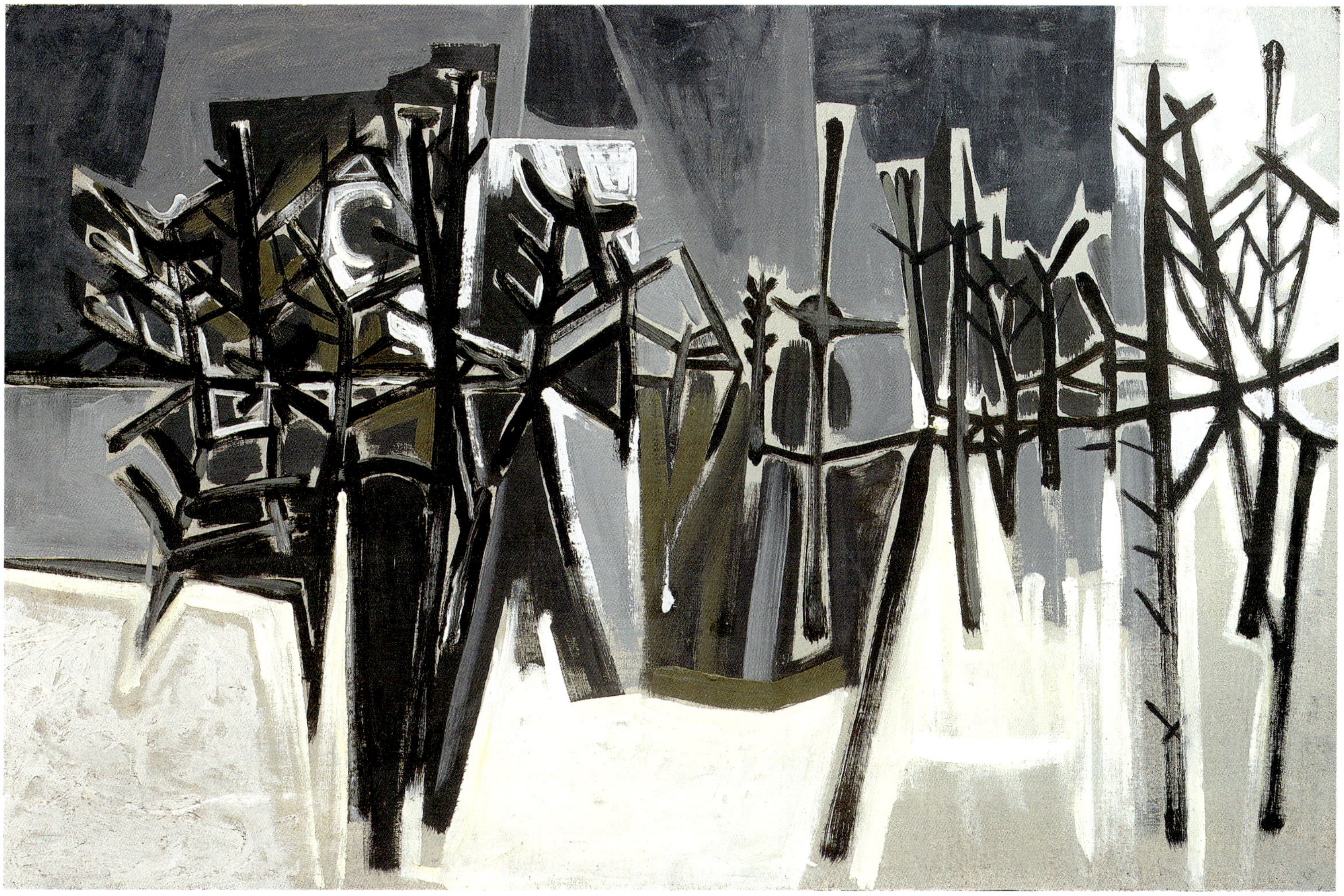

61
Frozen Landscape
oil on muslin laid on board
61 x 91.5 cm (24 x 36 in)
1951
Artist's estate

impaled on a thorny predicament that was proving hostile to any form of resolution.

This may not have been far from the truth. Wynter had apparently declared to Berlin, 'Yes I know family suits you, Sven ... But not for me!'[10] Years earlier he had pleaded with Hedy to understand his need for solitude within their relationship. Now, with a small child, a teaching post that took him away from home for several weeks at a time and, even back in Cornwall, a constant to-and-fro between the Carn and St Ives, he struggled to retain a sense of momentum. There was always, too, a shadow side to Wynter's personality. Berlin may have added his own touch of melodrama to Wynter's account of *Birds Disturbing the Sleep of a Town* – the 'suicidal' feelings assuaged by a curlew's cry in the night air – but the emotional lows could clearly go very deep. Towards the end of 1952 the slow disintegration of his marriage came to a head. Sue, pregnant with their second child, moved away to London, where Jim Wynter, once again assuming the role of provider–controller, installed his daughter-in-law and grandson in a house in the northern suburb of Crouch End.

These circumstances are probably reflected in the uncertainties that dogged Wynter's work in the early 1950s. Though he started increasingly to use oil paint on board and canvas, it took him some time to feel fully at home with the medium. Its thicker consistency seems to have hampered his instinct for a drawn line. When it came to experimenting with grounds and washes, it felt like an altogether clumsier vehicle than ink and gouache on paper. The interruptions caused by bouts of teaching made progress seem slow, but something was changing all the same. Even in the rather joyless clutter that characterises the central area of *Boats in Harbour* (1952; fig. 62) there's a growing conviction in the paint marks simply as marks, rather than as schematic cabins, gunwales or other boat parts. This wasn't exactly Wynter's discovery; he was well aware of contemporary French *tachiste* painting, in particular Nicolas de Staël's adaptation of abstract mark-making to create semi-

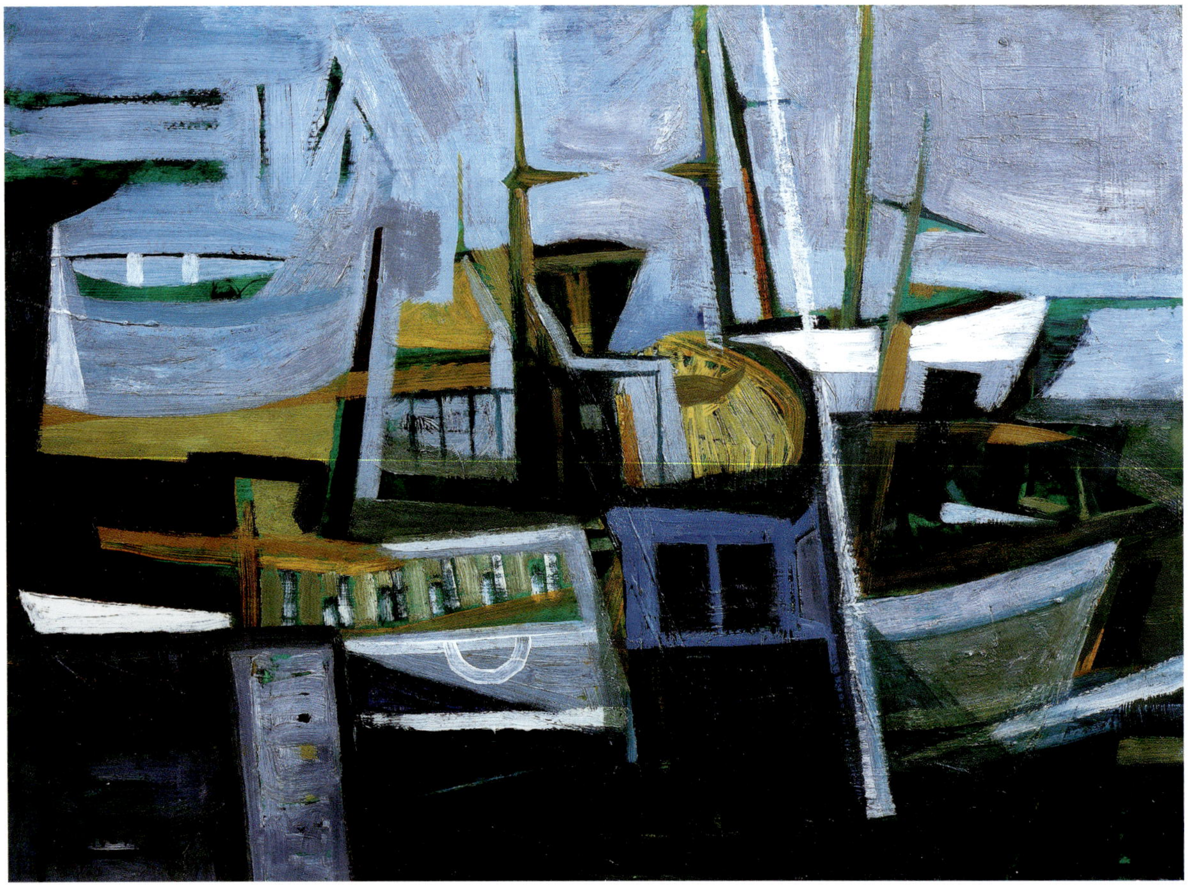

62
Boats in Harbour
oil on canvas
76 x 51 cm (30 x 20 in)
1952
Private collection

63
Bryan Wynter, 1951

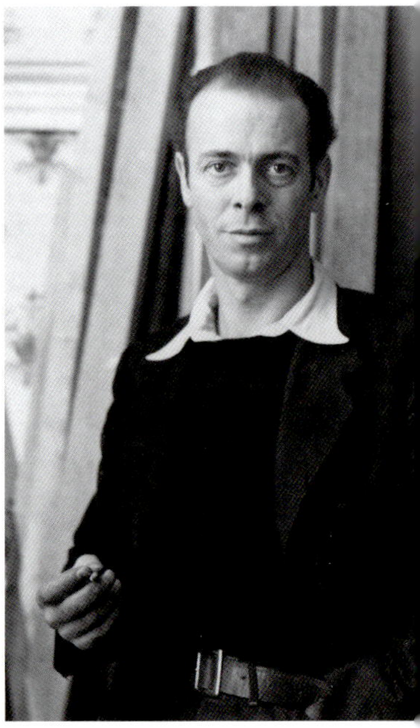

representational landscape and figure images (De Staël had a solo exhibition in London in 1952). An awareness of the French scene is also reflected in a photograph of Wynter in 1951, posed in typical Existentialist manner in dark jumper and open-neck shirt, with pensive cigarette in hand (fig. 63).

Though he had earlier criticised what he saw as a 'tasteful' absence of 'force or direction' in contemporary French art, Wynter's own painting was adopting a more *tachiste* approach. During the previous five or six years he had tended to use something given – for example, the actual forms of a landscape or the accidental patterns created by a monotyped ground – as a theme on which to compose. Now the paint mark itself was becoming the start of the process, the painting's primary material. It took some time for this transition to take effect. *Marshy Landscape* (1952; fig. 64) is another of Wynter's early 1950s' oils that seems uncertain which way to jump. There's the high-definition, rather stolid blocking-in of shapes, reminiscent of the heraldic field patterns he was painting in the late 1940s, but the oily ideograms, overdrawn in thin black flicks, want to get moving and go it alone. In *Offshore Rocks* (fig. 67) from the following year, the paint is handled in a freer, more diluted way. Criss-crossing dribbles of white show that the board has been turned. At some point it may have been intended as a horizontal, landscape-format image that later reared upright into the posture of a standing figure (a duality highly characteristic of Lanyon's landscape art). Other oil paintings from the early 1950s, such as *Untitled Landscape* (1953) and *Hill Landscape* (1954–5; fig. 66), retain a more representational approach, inflected by contemporary French art as well as by the impulsive deliberation and roughshod bravura of Lanyon's manner in such Corsham-era paintings as *Green Mile* (fig. 65).

In terms of the exhibitions in which his work was seen, Wynter sometimes appeared in Neo-Romantic company, sometimes as a 'St Ives' artist. In 1953 at the Redfern he showed both gouaches and oil paintings, including *Offshore Rocks*, with the Neo-Romantic heavyweights Michael Ayrton and Graham Sutherland. In the same year he had a couple of paintings in the Arts Council touring exhibition 'West Country Landscape', an anthology of genres and generations that included Sickert and Nicholson alongside Heron, Lanyon, Frost and Feiler. Hovering around such unpretentious mixed

64
Marshy Landscape
oil on board
40.6 x 30.3 cm (16 x 11¾ in)
1952
Private collection

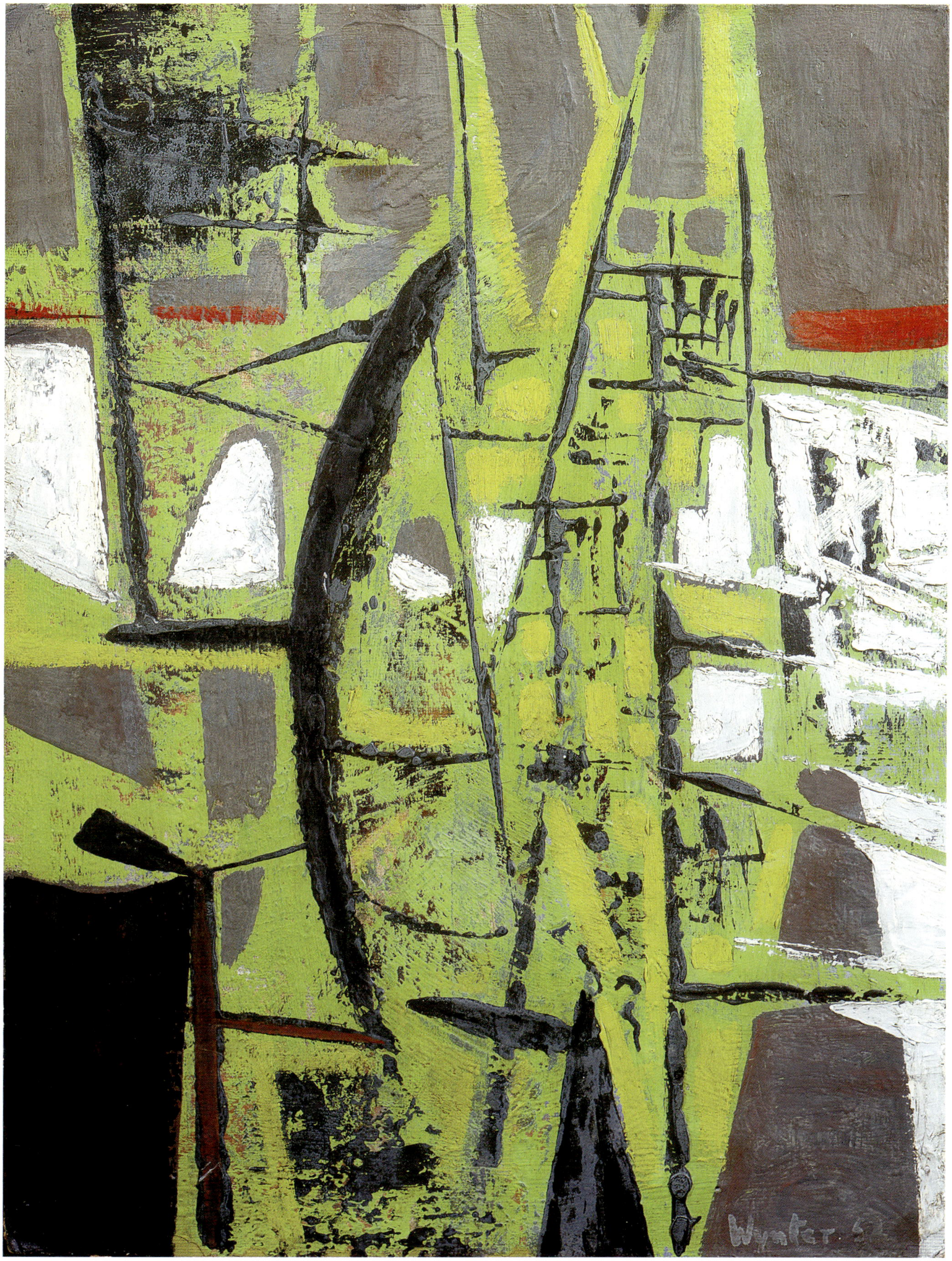

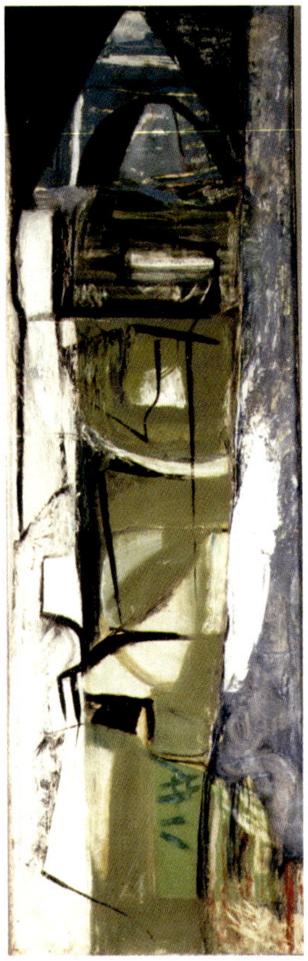

65
Peter Lanyon, *Green Mile*
oil on masonite
161 x 49.5 cm (63½ x 19½ in)
1952
University of Chichester

exhibitions were cultural notions of Britishness that slipped constantly into cliché in their reluctance to tear modernity once and for all out of the embrace of tradition. 'West Country', for example, was really a tourist industry tag, more accurate as a description of artists' home addresses, social circles or holiday habits than as any kind of aesthetic category. Here, as in many other instances, the theme of landscape was treated as a solvent in which otherwise incompatible artistic tendencies could be united in a putative expression of national creative consciousness.

Herbert Read had been propounding this view since the end of the war, insisting at every turn on the essentially Romantic roots of modern British art. As the 1950s wore on, Read's vision came to sound increasingly outdated. A more contemporary measure of the nation's artistic pulse came with 'British Painting and Sculpture' at the Whitechapel Art Gallery in the autumn of 1954. In surveying what he presented as 'a reasonable cross section of British art as it stands at the moment',[11] the gallery's director, Bryan Robertson, discerned a new trend shared by otherwise quite different artists. Their work was, he thought, simply getting larger, perhaps as a result of a new conception in which a painting was seen no longer as an *objet d'art* but rather as a statement, a creation that had no particular duty to fit in with domestic furnishings or rules of taste. Robertson's programme for the Whitechapel, which he had swiftly revitalised after being appointed director in 1952, involved steering British art away from the insularity in which it had taken refuge during the war. If he supported Hepworth, for example, whose retrospective at the Whitechapel in the spring of 1954 was credited with reviving her reputation, it was not because her work was quintessentially British but because it weighed in alongside that of her international contemporaries. In general, Robertson liked abstract art and took the 'St Ives' faction seriously.

Wynter was represented in 'British Painting and Sculpture' by *Dark Landscape* (fig. 68). At under a metre high, this is not a large painting, but it is larger than much of Wynter's earlier work, apart from his Festival commission three years earlier. *Dark Landscape* has little either of *Blue Landscape*'s high-toned colour or of the vestigial plant forms in *Frozen Landscape*. In the absence of identifiable reference points – an engine house here, a blackthorn hedge there – the 'landscape' of the title has crossed the border into mindscape. The dark structural brushwork that holds the painting together – as though this cantilevered nest of girders had been balanced as provisionally as a house of cards – has echoes, on the one hand, of Sutherland's spikiness and, on the other, of Soulages's abstract gantries of blacks and greys. At the same time there is a sense of journeying that belongs to the kinds of landscape often painted and drawn by Wynter: upwards and downwards, along mine adits and through thickets, inwards through fissures in a rock face, whether along the Penwith coast or in his dreams. *Dark Landscape* was the painting that represented Wynter most often in 1953–4. Three months after the Whitechapel show it was seen alongside work by Paul Feiler and Wynter's fellow Corsham tutors Lanyon and Peter Potworowski at a joint exhibition in Bath. Then it was packed off to Canada for 'Six Painters from Cornwall', which also featured Lanyon, Wells, Frost, Heron and Wynter's former Slade contemporary David Haughton.

The critic keeping the closest eye on these developments was Patrick Heron. Since his first piece for the *New English Weekly*, a review of Ben Nicholson in October 1945, Heron's journalism had kept him almost as busy as his painting. In 1954 he was collecting his numerous articles on British and French contemporaries into a book. ('The American scene', he thought, had at this date still 'not yet revealed itself through a visual imagination'.[12]) In 1950 Heron had been summarily dismissed after two and a half years as the *New Statesman and Nation*'s art critic, on the grounds that its readers should 'at last have some respite' from his

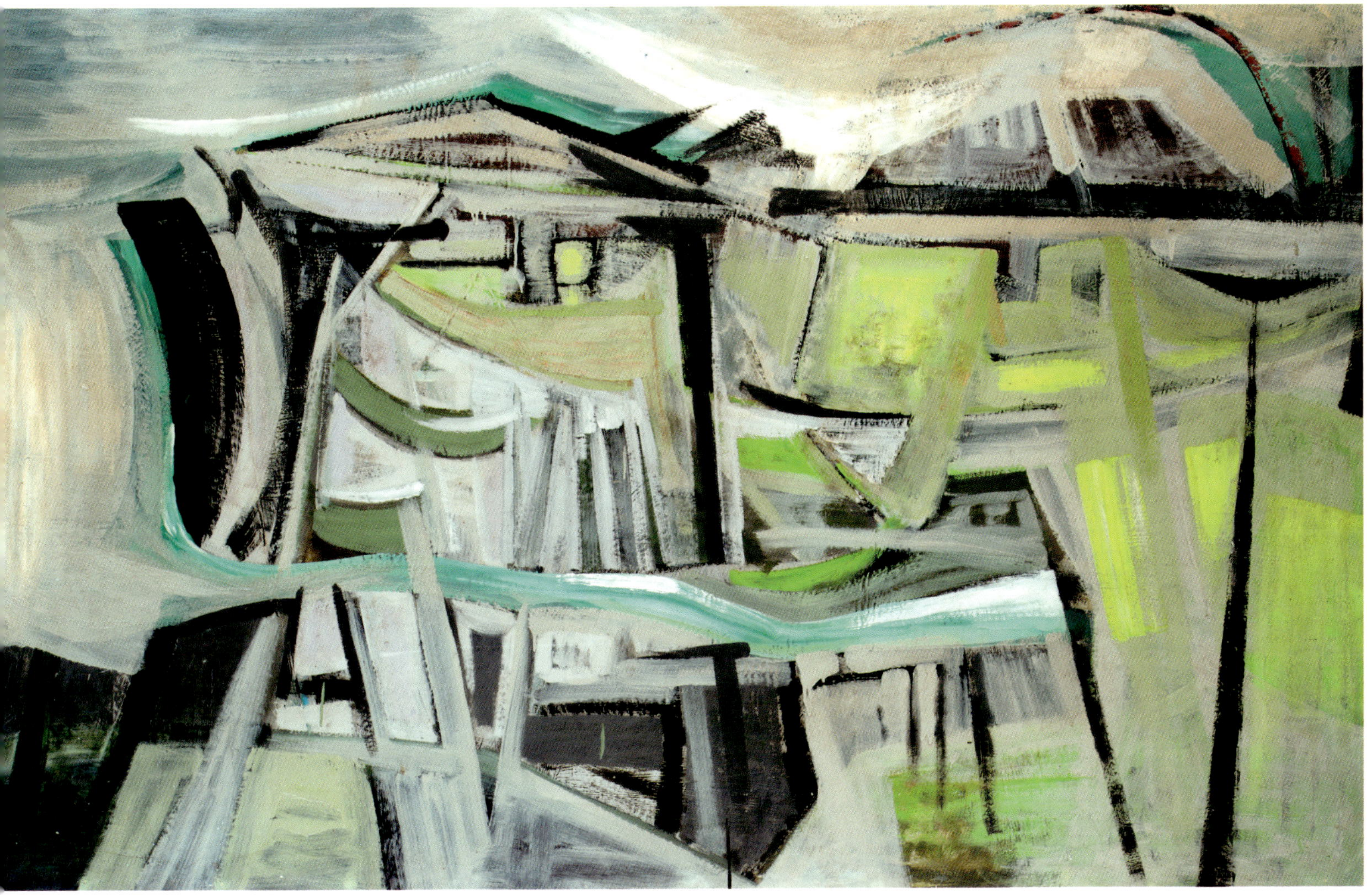

66
Hill Landscape
oil on board
121.9 x 188 cm (48 x 74 in)
1954-5
Private collection

weekly meditations on space in painting.[13] Undaunted, Heron had continued to pursue his 'space' agenda as a writer and guest curator. In July 1953 he organised the exhibition 'Space in Colour' at the Hanover Gallery in London.[14] Though the ten artists he selected did not include Wynter, whose artistic concerns Heron evidently felt lay elsewhere, he made up for this omission by writing a piece on Wynter specially for inclusion in his book. Composed in October 1954, while the Whitechapel exhibition was on, and perhaps prompted by seeing *Dark Landscape* there, the essay was published in 1955 in *The Changing Forms of Art*.

This short profile forms the final section of an essay titled 'Modern English Romantics', which also discusses Sutherland and Keith Vaughan. Despite Heron's unerring eye for Wynter's visual sensibility and the technical approaches this gave rise to, he betrayed an underlying irresolution on the question of where, among the categories of contemporary painting, Wynter should be placed. After asserting that he 'may safely be described as a Romantic Landscape Painter',[15] a species Heron declared to be 'probably extinct outside this country today', he praised Wynter's 'mastery' of a formal vocabulary 'received direct from the Cubism of Gris, Picasso and Braque'. Wynter's 'Cubist-educated eye analyses the chosen Cornish terrain of moor and cliff, cromlech-strewn hill-line, wall-threaded cliff-tops, lane-linked stone cottages with the deft certainty of a brilliant pianist unfolding the patterns of Bach'.[16] In the following description of a typical Wynter painting, Heron was probably thinking of *Blue Landscape* (see fig. 54) or a work very like it: 'Where Braque splits a table-top into a light and a dark half, Wynter splits a whole hillside, or a cottage roof, or the great Atlantic Ocean itself.'[17] In sum, Wynter's 'agile' formal inventiveness allowed him to be simultaneously Romantic and Cubist.

Since to admit as much would have undercut his own notions of space in painting, Heron ignored the possibility

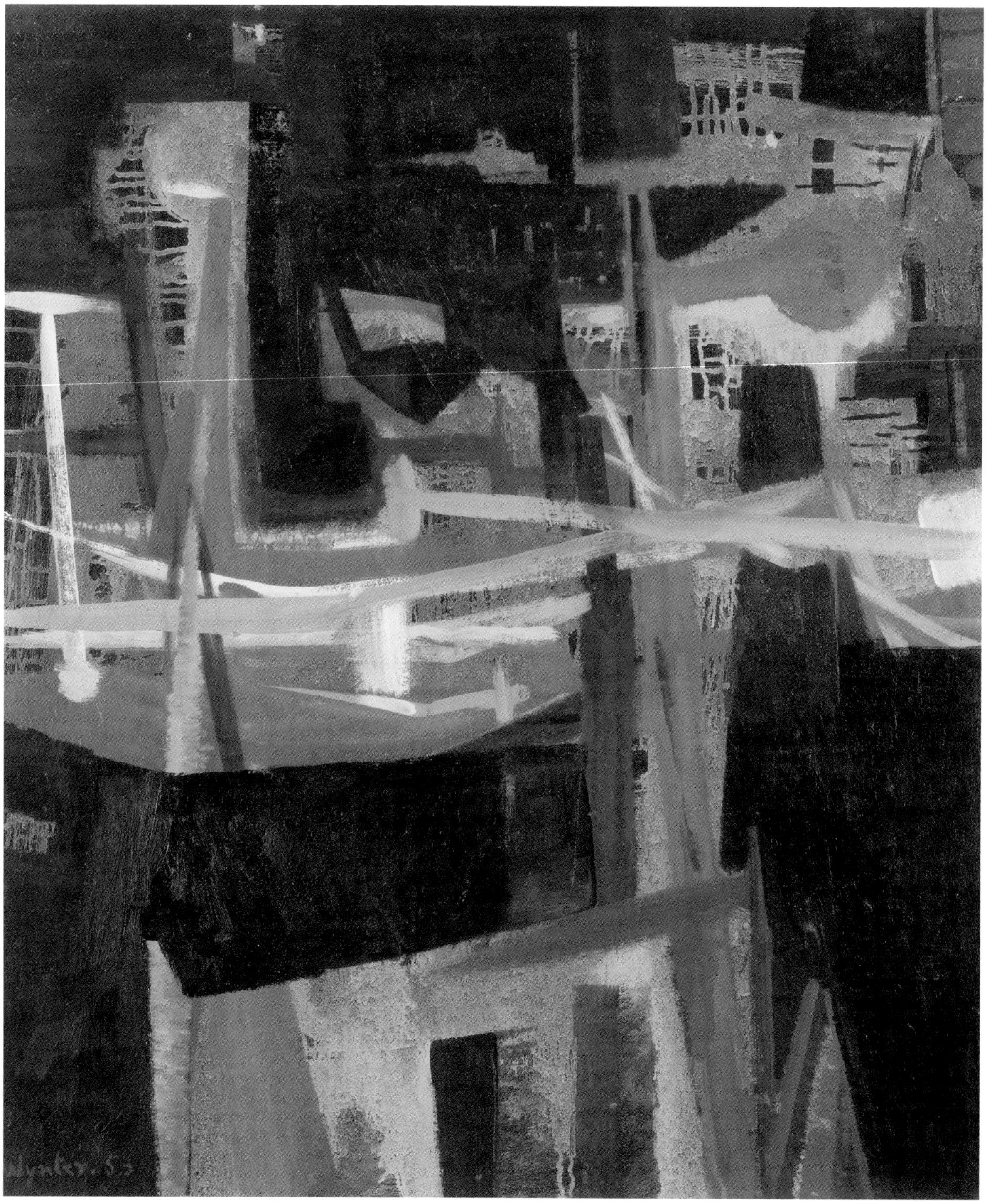

67
Offshore Rocks
oil on board
72.4 x 61 cm (30 x 24 in)
1953
Government Art Collection

that Wynter's 'agility' stemmed from an artistic approach that was at least as cerebral as it was sensual. He either could not or did not want to recognise that Wynter's mark-making, in which expressiveness was always informed by intense deliberation, was closer to handwriting, or calligraphy (a word that was often to be associated with Wynter's later abstract work), than to the intuitive balancing of colour and shape with which Heron himself was deeply engaged. In this sense Wynter was the most literary artist among the contemporaries with whom his name was usually linked in the mid-1950s, through both St Ives and the London gallery circuit. By 'literary' I don't mean based on works of literature (even when Wynter was writing poetry in the 1940s, the correspondence was never quite that direct). Rather, perhaps, Wynter's mark-making in a drawing or painting

68
Dark Landscape
oil on board
91.4 x 71.7 cm (36 x 28¼ in)
1954
Tate

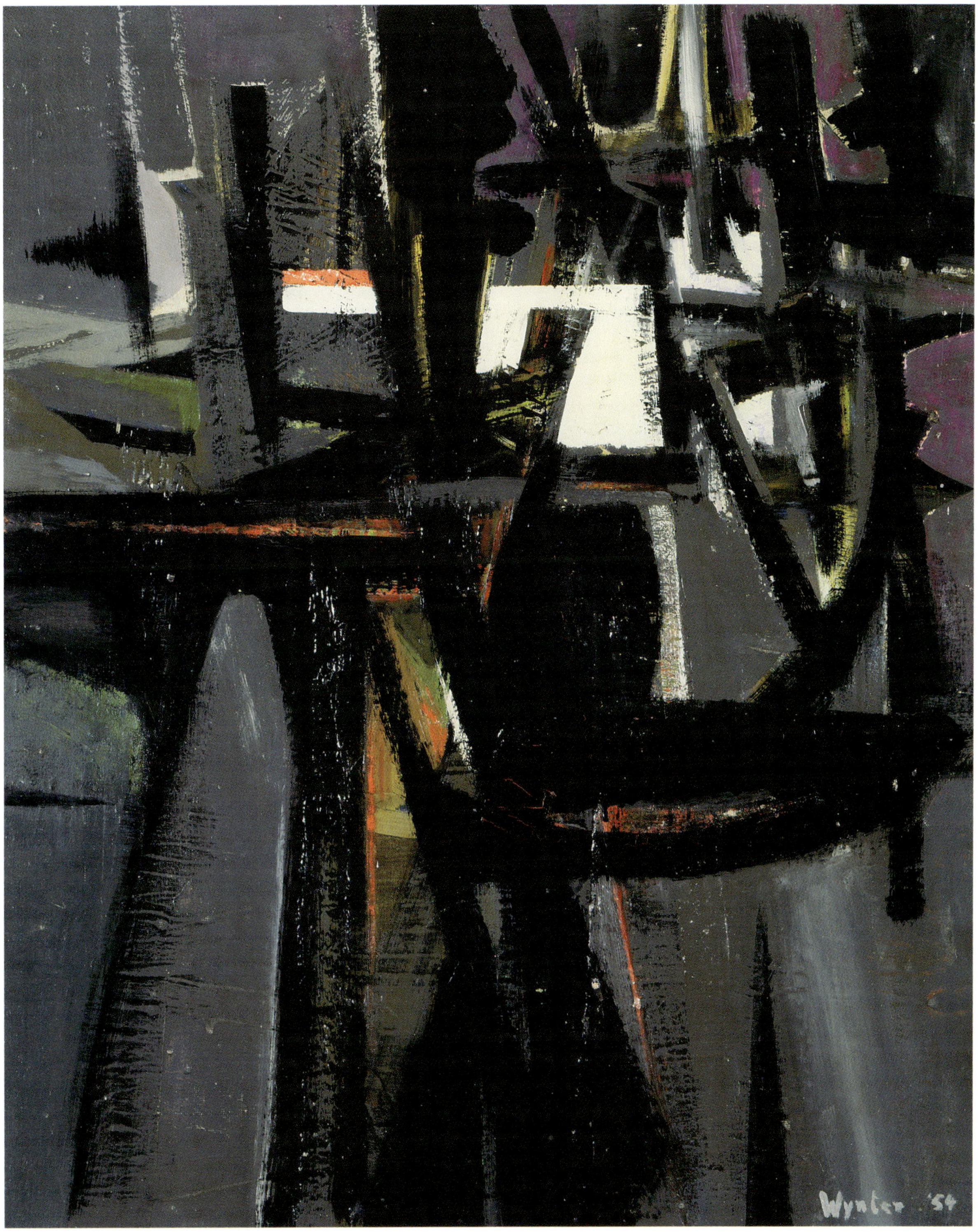

can be seen as a form of writing for expressing non-verbal thoughts. He was certainly interested in the relationship between his art and cognitive processes, describing a few years later how 'I find it helpful to think of that moment at which the eye looks out at the world it has not yet recognised'.[18]

This was written for the catalogue for the exhibition 'Statements: A Review of British Abstract Art in 1956', held at the Institute of Contemporary Arts, London, in early 1957, in which Wynter featured alongside twenty other artists representing a wide range of 'abstract' practice. During the previous three years there had been several changes in Wynter's life. Each had a bearing on his work; collectively they created a watershed. While teaching at Corsham he had started an affair with a student, Monica Harman (fig. 70). Such affairs were a

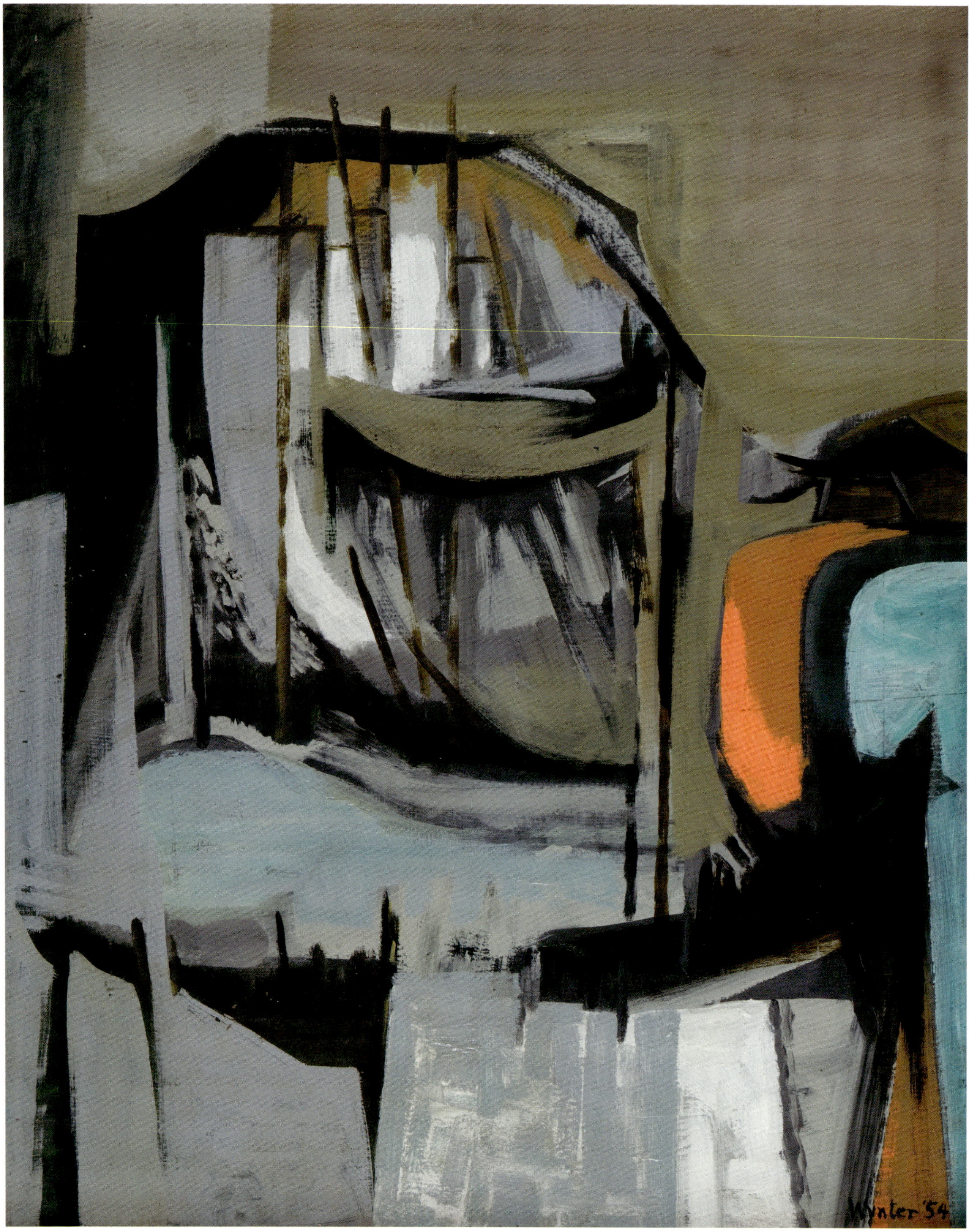
Wynter '54

69
Golden Cap
oil on board
91.4 x 72 cm (36 x 28½ in)
1954
Private collection

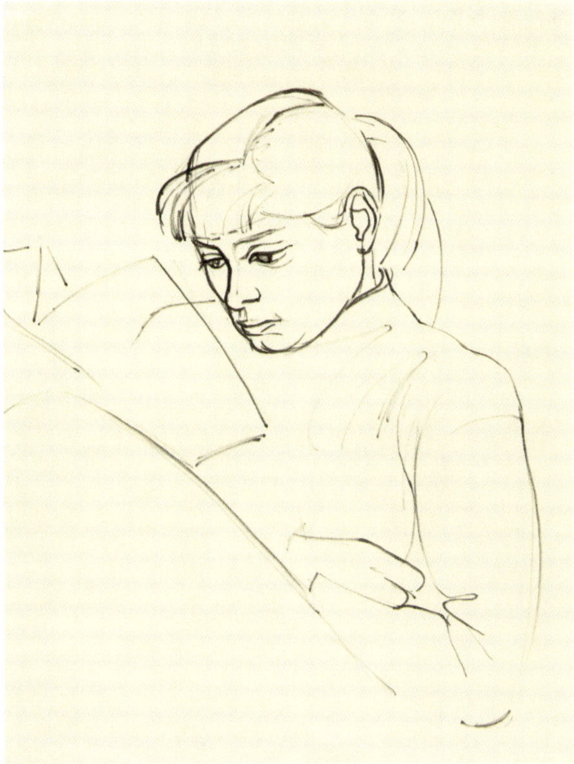

70
Monica Harman
pencil on paper
38.1 x 29.2 cm (15 x 11½ in)
*c.*1955
Private collection

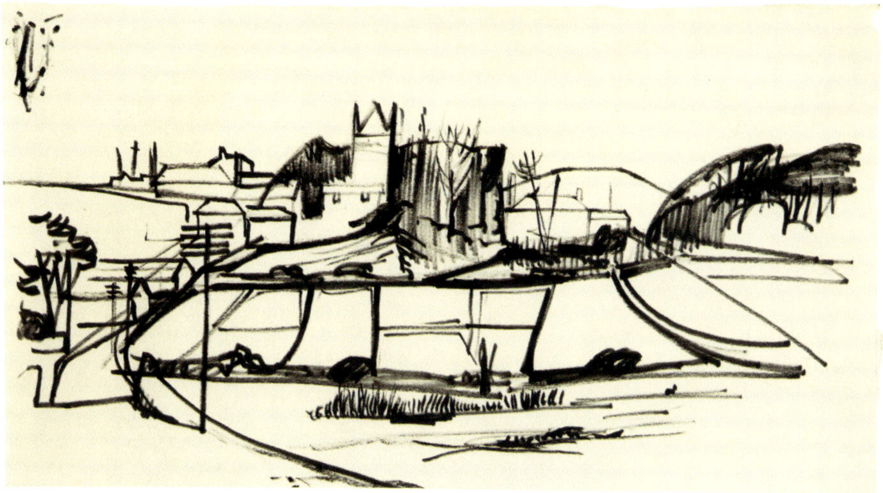

71
Landscape (Phillack)
fibre-tip pen on paper
21.6 x 38.1 cm (8½ x 15 in)
*c.*1954
Private collection

fairly common occurrence among Clifford Ellis's staff, in some ways implicitly encouraged by the principal's insistence that tutors and students should mix socially on equal terms. Monica recalled that her first impression of Wynter was of a sympathetic listener, 'someone I could talk to'. Some seventeen years younger than him, she had first encountered his work in the 1951 Bristol exhibition, where her response had simply been 'He's been looking at too much Picasso'. Coming from a stable, sensible middle-class Quaker family in Buckinghamshire, she was (if Corsham's lurid reputation held any truth) precisely the kind of student that Ellis's liberal regime was designed to lead astray – or rather, in Corsham terms, on to the path of self-discovery. A visit to Dorset early in Wynter and Harman's relationship is commemorated in his painting *Golden Cap* (fig. 69), named after a high sandstone cliff. (Not so far along the coast is Lulworth Cove, a location painted by Lanyon with similar associations in mind.)

In 1954 Wynter came across an article in the *Manchester Guardian*, brought to his attention by his St Ives friend and Corsham colleague Terry Frost. Written by a self-styled psychic researcher, Rosalind Hayward, it discussed her investigations into the use of mescalin in psychiatric therapy. A former prisoner of war, Frost may have encountered fellow inmates in Stalag 383, the huge camp in Germany where he was interned, who drew and painted while experiencing hallucinations caused by hunger. At any rate, he knew how much Hayward's ideas would appeal to Wynter, who apparently wrote to her immediately, offering himself as an experimental subject so that she could include visual artists in her research. In *The Doors of Perception*, published in 1954, Aldous Huxley asserted: 'What the rest of us see only under the influence of mescalin, the artist is congenitally equipped to see all the time.'[19] For his part, Wynter was quickly convinced that his experience of mescalin might prove of even greater import for his own work than for Hayward's research, although, unlike his Belgian contemporary Henri Michaux, he produced few works during actual mescalin trips (see fig. 74). Then, towards the end of 1955, there was a third new development in Wynter's life. His father retired and, denied a willing heir for his empire, sold the laundry business. Relations between father and son must have mellowed slightly by this date, since Wynter received a share of the proceeds from the sale. With this inheritance, he optimistically confided in Sven Berlin, he would have 'more money than I shall ever want'.[20]

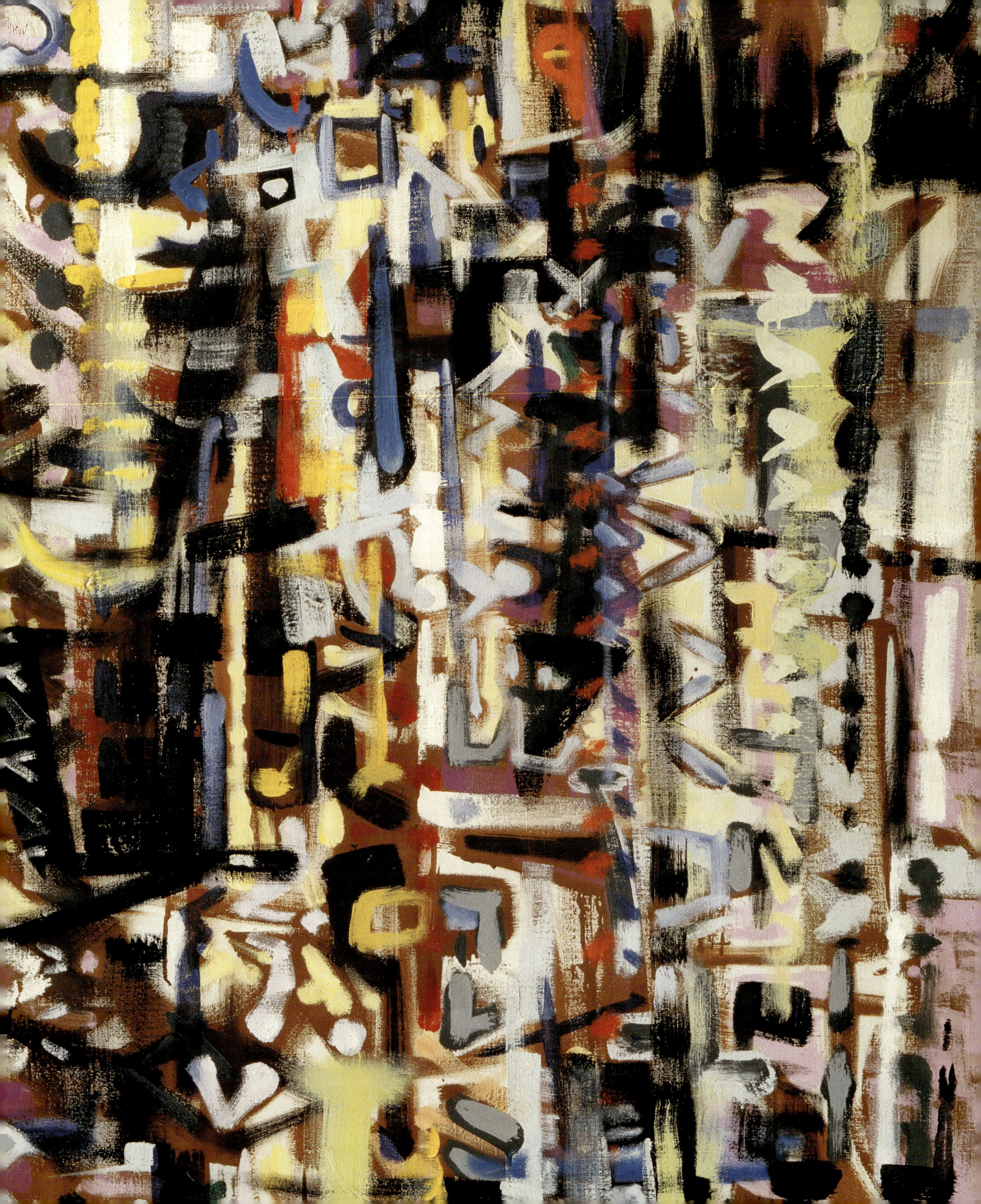

5

'A New Painting Consciousness':
the Abstract High Noon, 1955–9

Wynter's improved financial circumstances in late 1955 coincided with a more widely shared sense of recovery from Britain's protracted post-war economic malaise and the restrictions imposed under the government's Austerity programme. Food rationing had ended the previous summer, and the national mood was more upbeat than at any time since the war. People at last felt they had better job prospects and more disposable income, much of which they dreamed of spending on American imports. For Wynter this moment of relative prosperity had an impact on both his way of life (he acquired the freehold to the Carn and bought a Land Rover) and his art. At the end of the autumn term he was able to give up teaching at Corsham, which he'd never found easy to balance with his own work, and to spend more on materials. He also purchased his first camera.

It seems that for various reasons, including the pressures of teaching and a general uncertainty about the course his work was taking, Wynter almost stopped painting during 1955. His creative energies, recalled Monica, 'had become increasingly stuck'.[1] It was around this time that he produced a plaster sculpture of the angular gull figure that had featured repeatedly in his work throughout the previous decade (fig. 72). This sculpture, never exhibited and later destroyed, had a talismanic importance for Wynter. Rare surviving paintings include a largeish oil on board, *Headland*, which reprises the scaffold structure of *Offshore Rocks* and *Dark Landscape*. It has a similar cantilevered lift towards the sides and corners, the heart-like cavern near the centre. This time, however, Wynter lightened the formal heftiness with touches of faster, lighter brushwork – short, summary marks that have a hieroglyphic energy of their own. The image feels contemporary – fashionable, even – in its semi-abstract landscape references (Sutherland, Lanyon and Frost all come to mind), but it doesn't feel like a breakthrough.

During the mid-1950s Wynter's drawing style had been changing, too, shedding its poetic, surrealistic overtones to become sparer and more formal (see fig. 71). After 1955 photography virtually superseded his earlier practice of drawing in the landscape (fig. 73). Monica observed how he

> made series after series of colour slides recording the landscapes in which he loved to be. These might be both close-up textural studies and more conventional 'views'. I suppose one could say that he was recording what might become the content of paintings without it being a recognisable subject – he was making (photographic) images of what he liked to look at.[2]

The many sets of colour slides Wynter accumulated include distance shots of the line of a hillside or rock formations, close-ups of the undergrowth, of runnels in

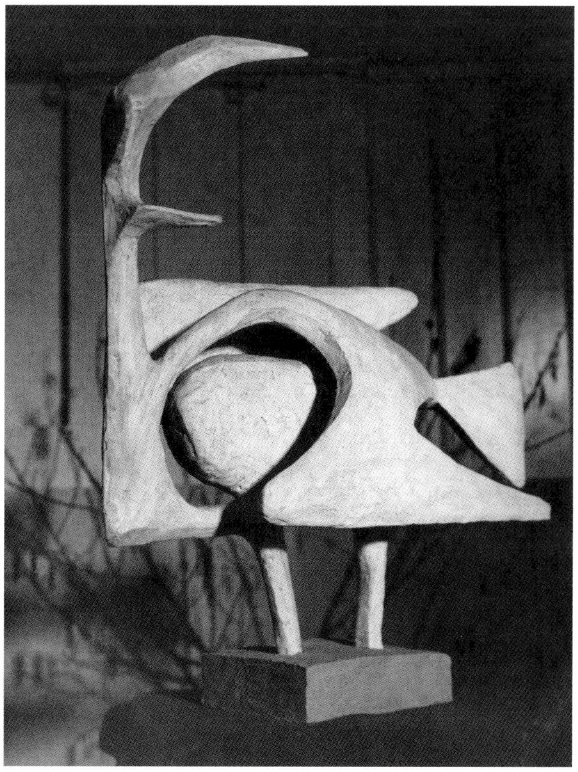

OPPOSITE: detail of **83**
Carnival, 1956

72
Untitled (Bird)
plaster
*c.*1955
Untraced

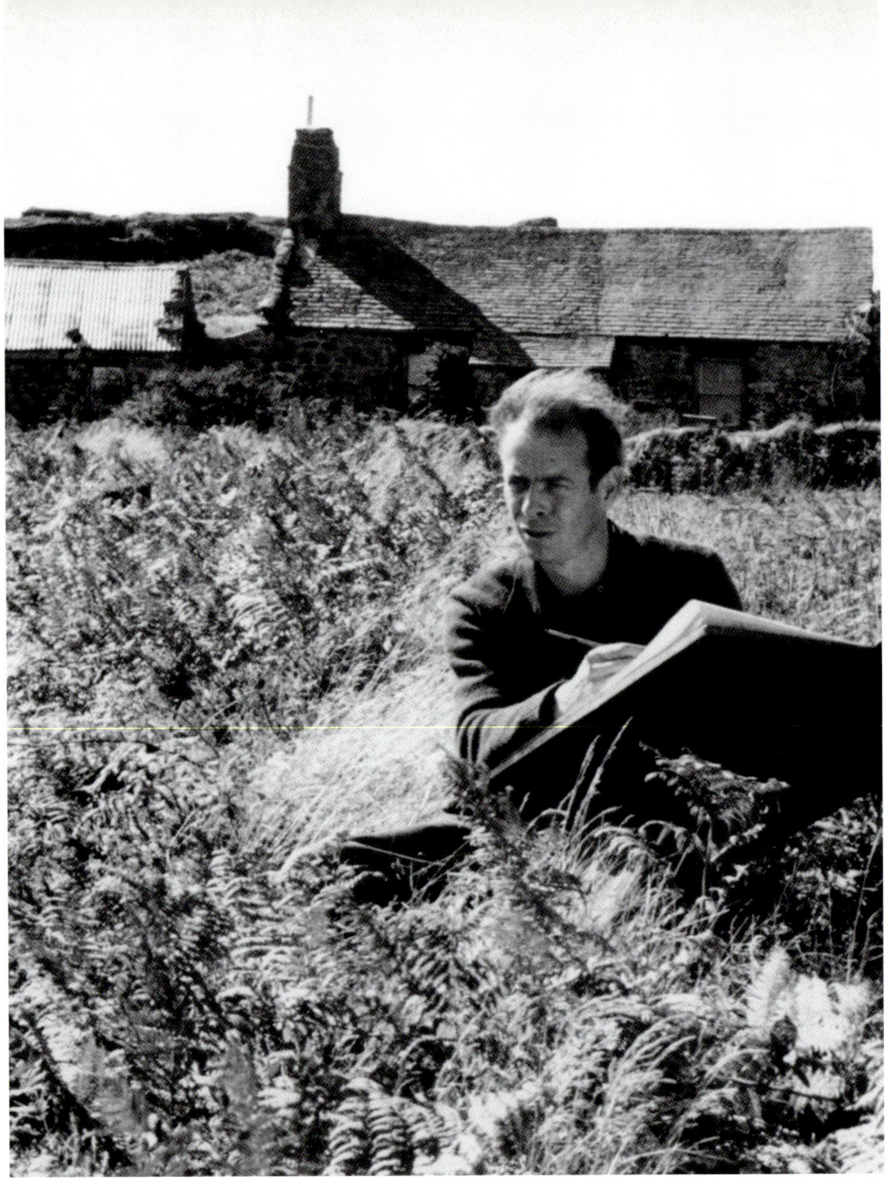

73
Bryan Wynter drawing outside the Carn, 1955–6

sand, ice in puddles, reflections in water – the protean shapes and textures of the Penwith moors and coastline. As drawing had been before, colour photography became both a way of looking and a source of images and ideas to which Wynter devoted much time and energy throughout the rest of his career (see fig. 165).

As late as 1957, Wynter still described himself as being 'intermittently resident in Cornwall'.[3] It was important for his markedly 'restless'[4] nature that his working life should not become too fixed or sedentary. Newly liberated from teaching, for the first three months of 1956 he rented a temporarily vacant studio in London. It was one unit in a long block that ran between the back gardens of The Boltons, two facing nineteenth-century terraces in Chelsea. In the west London *demi-monde* of the time 'studio' was a fairly vague category of accommodation; Wynter often found himself answering the phone to men who, declining to be identified, evidently wanted to speak to one or other of the two women who had previously occupied the place. These interruptions aside, he was free to work. In the new series of canvases he began at The Boltons, all the uncertainties and frustrations of the past three or four years – the end of his first marriage, the on-off routine of teaching at Corsham and the uneasy stalling of momentum in his work – seemed suddenly to be left behind. For the moment, too, he felt able to work without thought of meeting the expectations of dealers or buyers, or any of the old the Austerity-era parsimony with materials. These were productive weeks. Wynter generally worked slowly, revising a painting many times before he considered it finished, but he told his brother that he had completed eleven new paintings during the first half of 1956.[5]

These works are strikingly different from the landscape-themed abstracts that had preceded them. Most obviously, they are painted in an all-over manner, in which traditional compositional structures and points of emphasis are absent, and the painting seems to want to stretch out beyond the confines of the conventional

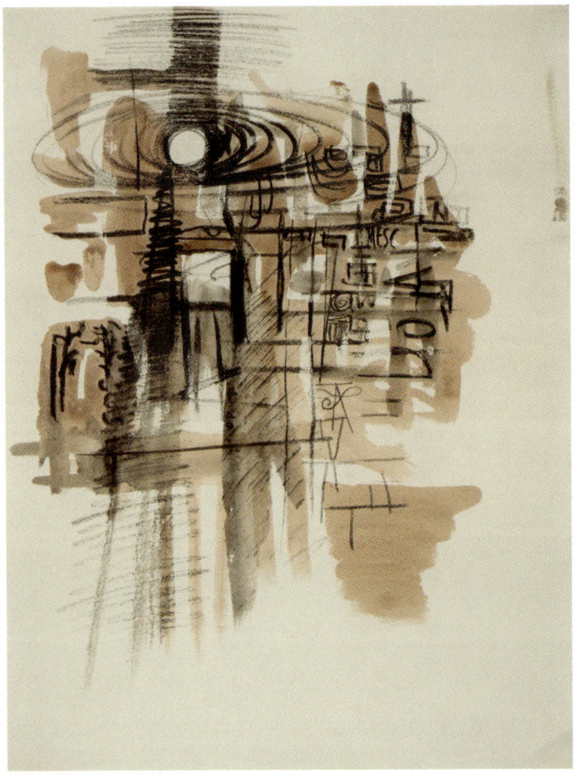

74
Mescalin drawing
charcoal and brown wash
57.3 x 44.6 cm (22½ x 17½ in)
*c.*1955–9
Private collection

75
The Interior (detail)
oil on canvas
127 x 101.6 cm (50 x 40 in)
(overall dimensions)
1956
Private collection

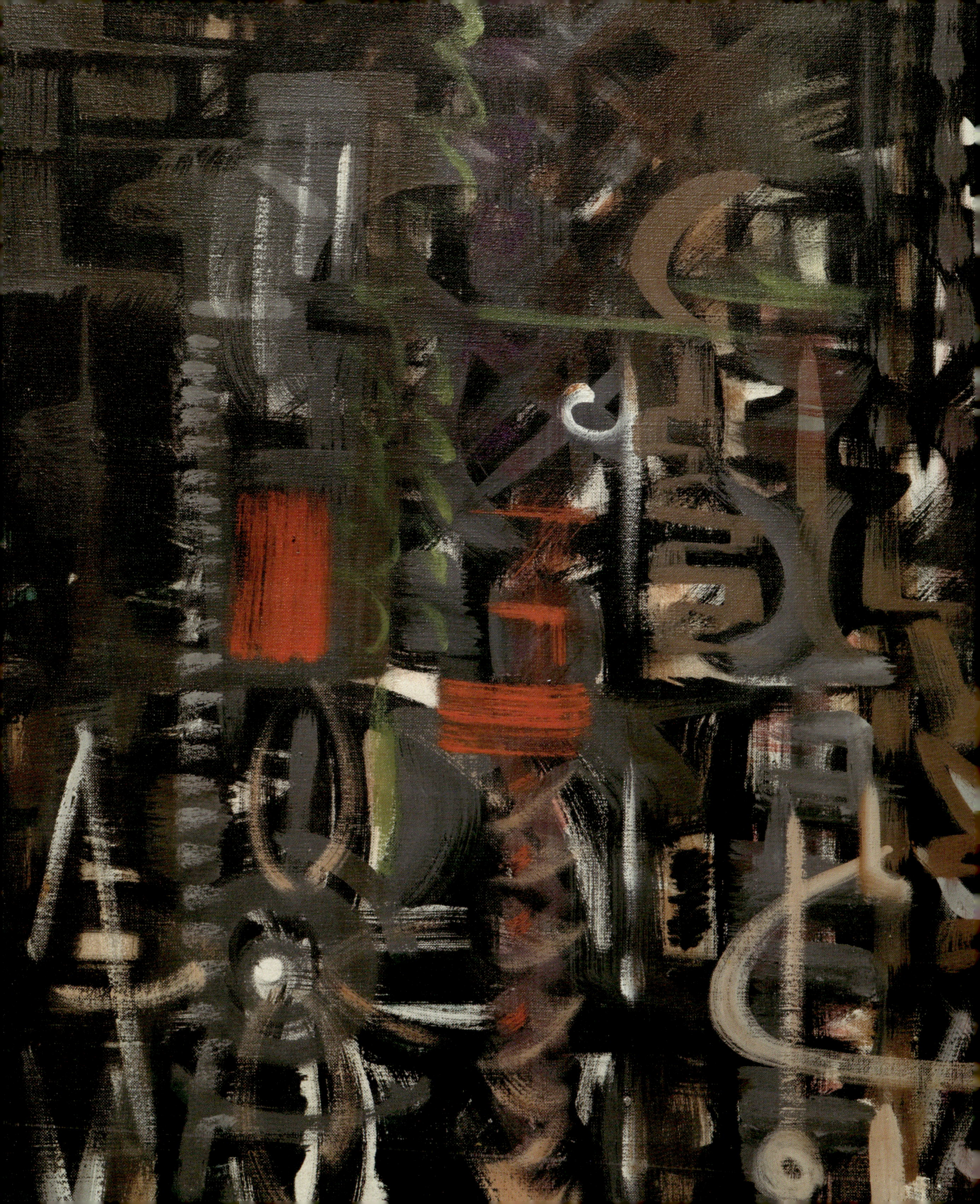

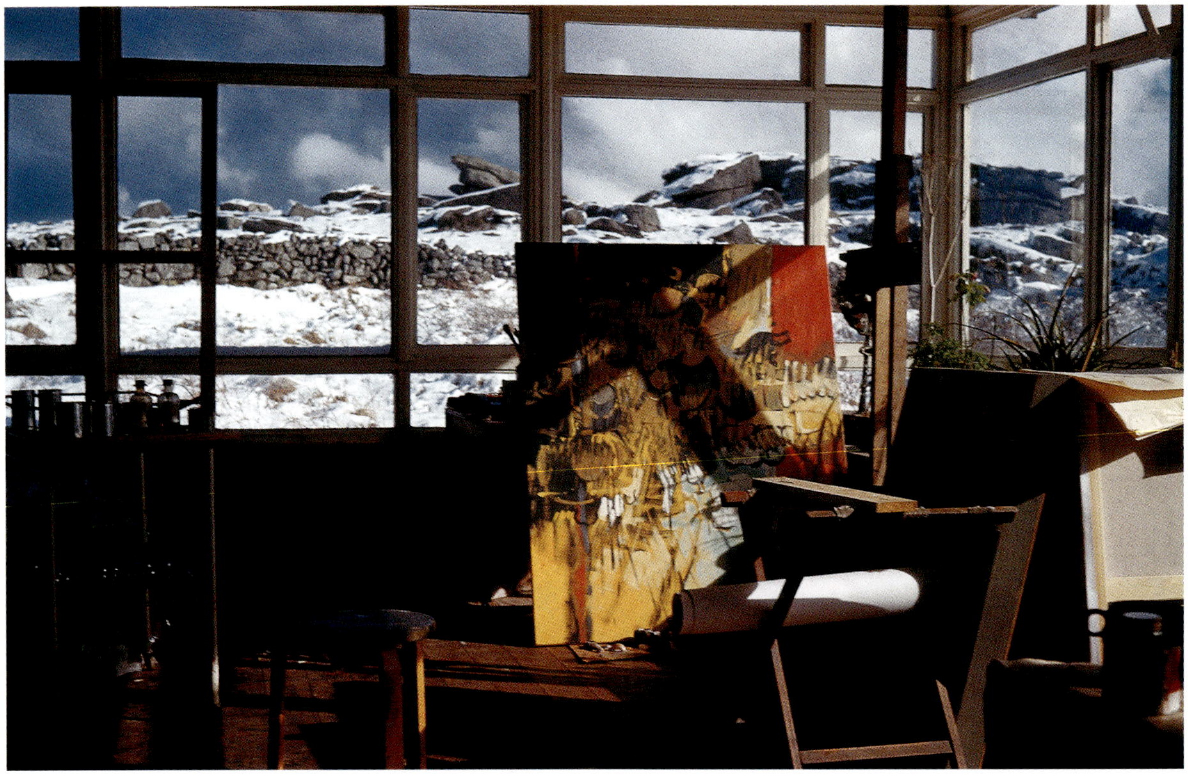

76
The Carn under snow, *c.*1960

rectangular frame. Wynter titled the first of these works to be completed *The Interior* (fig. 75; see also fig. 4). This title (as became Wynter's habit from now on) didn't reflect any pre-existing idea of a subject but arose after subsequent discussions with Monica about the images suggested by the completed work. Reflecting on *The Interior* and the paintings that followed it in quick succession throughout 1956, he wrote towards the end of the year:

> I think of my paintings as a source of imagery, something that generates imagery rather than contains it. Obviously it is I who have put into them what they contain but I have done so with as little conscious interference as possible, allowing them at every stage in their growth to dictate their own necessities.[6]

Wynter had long believed that art could flourish only in the absence of 'conscious interference'. Here he placed a new emphasis on a painting's autonomous generative powers and quasi-organic quality of 'growth'. In his letter of August 1945 to Hedy in which he'd described how landscape 'overflows' while the unconscious 'wells up peopling the real landscape with its own images', Wynter had envisaged his art as a meeting point of inner and outer, psyche and world. His Surrealist techniques mirrored this concept perfectly, as chance textures and patterns generated by frottage or decalcomania both gave rise to and received representational images of mine buildings, cliffs, shorelines, bones. Sheep skulls or coffee pots may have invited a semi-abstract treatment, with a nod to Picasso, Gris or Braque; but at the same time there were actual skulls and pots in the Carn, and it was these objects that 'generated' imagery, rather than the other way round. As Wynter's painting became less representational in the early 1950s, the elements of chance and intention became less easy to separate. It became harder to identify 'the real landscape'. Where, for example, was this to be found in *Dark Landscape* or *Marshy Landscape*? Perhaps these were not places at all but images of the experience of a place, what it made you feel rather than what it looked like. The transition between an art that refers and one that 'generates' can almost be seen taking place in a beautiful small gouache from 1956, *Rockface* (fig. 78), in which delicate, leafy patterns apparently produced by frottage on an embroidered fabric are over-painted with abstract shapes and ruled lines. Even after Wynter ceased to base his oil paintings on detailed preliminary drawings and gouaches, he continued to use gouache in this manner to explore ideas (fig. 79).

77
The Indias
oil on canvas
228.6 x 111.7 cm (90 x 44 in)
1956
Private collection

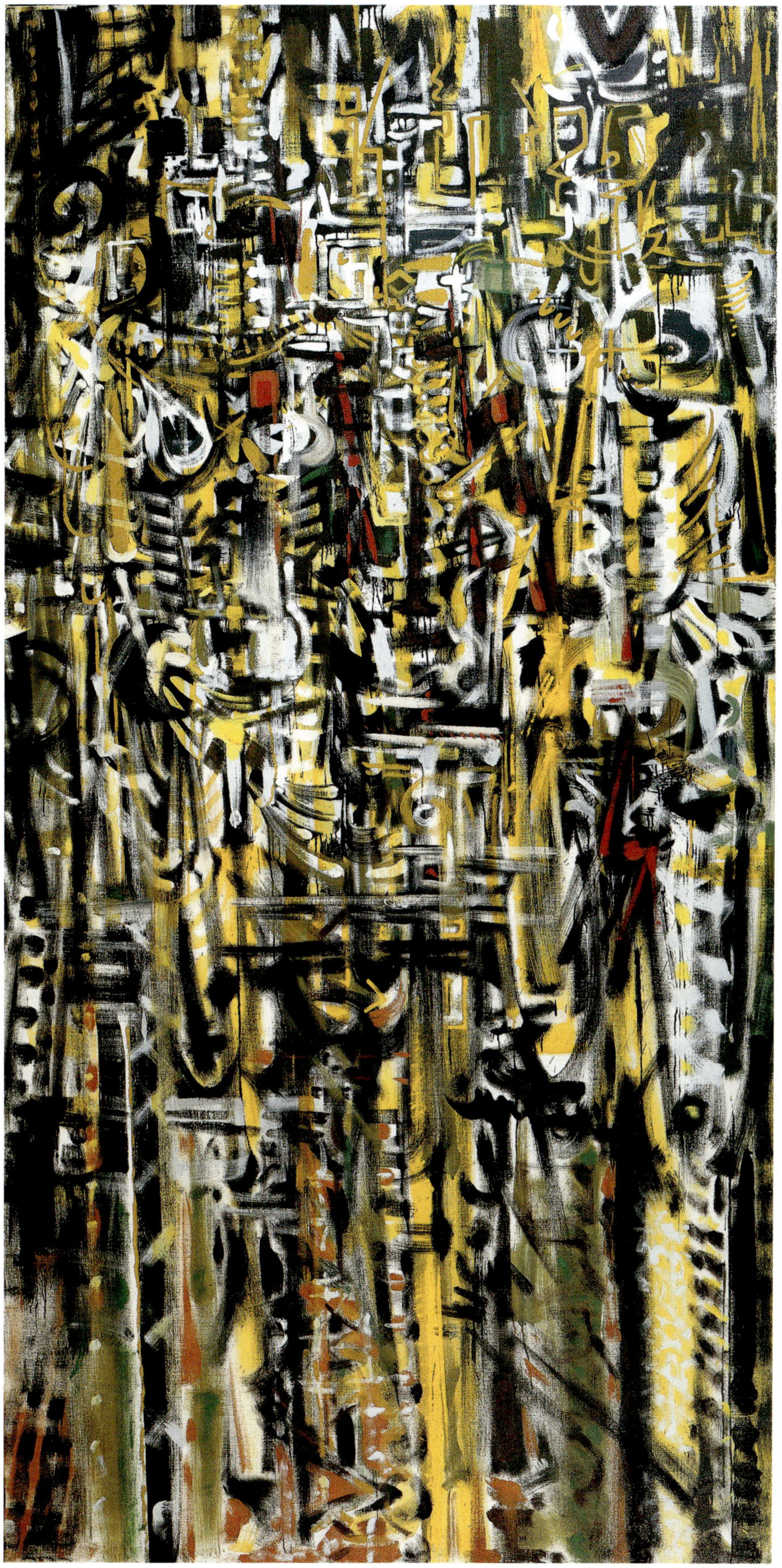

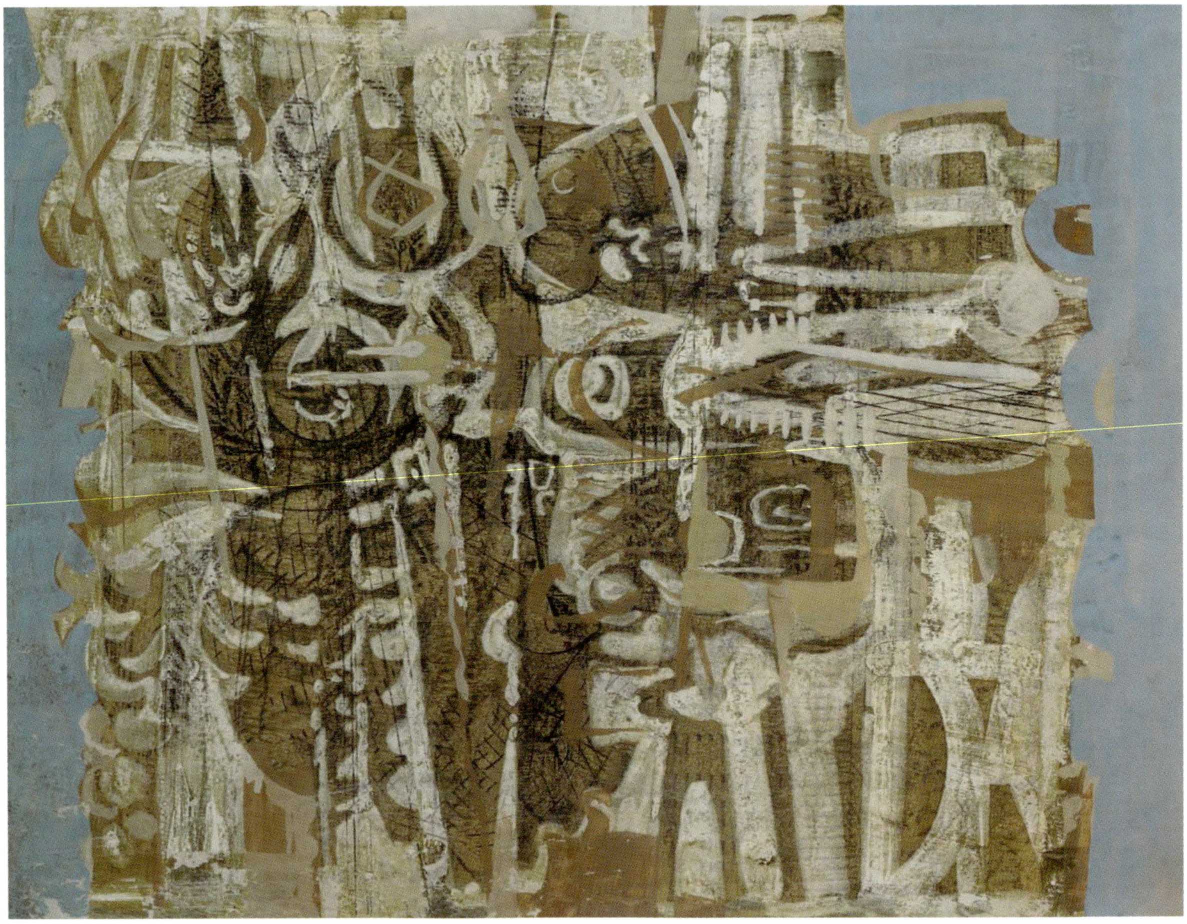

78
Rockface
monotype and gouache on paper
35.5 x 47 cm (14 x 18 ½ in)
1956
Jonathan Clark Fine Art

Although Wynter's 'landscape' paintings of 1953–4 could be called abstract, their forms and colours still seem to refer to something he could touch, somewhere he'd been. Not so with *The Interior*. Now it was the painting that came first, generating the viewer's experience without direct reference to anything else. None of the hundreds, perhaps thousands, of separate paint marks that make up *The Interior* is representational. Braque's 'Atelier' series contained individual passages of paint used in this sort of way (see fig. 44); all the same, you could distinguish birds, tables and other objects in these works. Wynter's new manner provided no clearly defined shapes to latch on to. Yet, while each of the individual marks has an impulsive, momentary vitality, the work as a whole has a complementary feeling of steady poise. It is difficult to explain how such an animated paint surface can create an effect of such lucid stasis. Heron was one of the first to try, describing how a 'grille, or network of brushsigns (I think the word "brushstroke" no longer applies where the stroke is itself become the chief object in the picture) strings itself along either vertical or horizontal lines ... It is as though Wynter were looking into a system of semi-transparent bead-curtains.'[7] But what was this work 'about'? If Heron (and others since) saw in the painting hints of a domestic interior, a depth of pictorial space 'into which you feel you could shoot an arrow',[8] Wynter might have responded that they could well have seen these things, but he hadn't deliberately put them there.

Something like this argument had been current in New York for several years. Wynter would have encountered it in conversation, in art magazines, possibly through accounts from William Scott, who made a teaching trip to North America in 1953, while Wynter was still working with him at Corsham. On this visit Scott had become one of the first British artists to meet Jackson Pollock, Mark Rothko and other painters in New York who had collectively become known as Abstract Expressionists. The term had first been used to describe them in 1946 by *The New Yorker*'s art critic Robert Coates, who appropriated it from its earlier application to European abstract artists such as Kandinsky. Some kind of name was clearly needed for the new American abstract art, which, as Heron slightly huffily remarked in

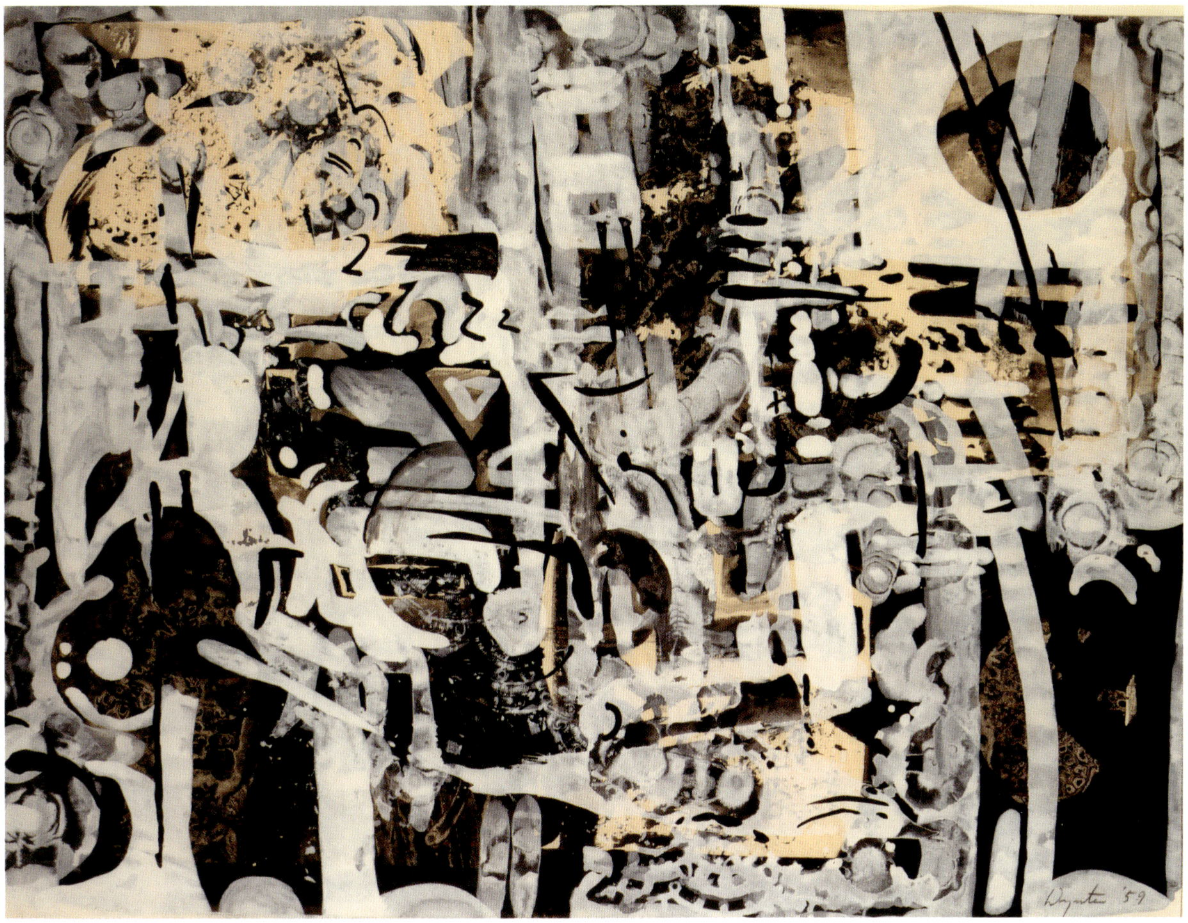

79
Black Summer
gouache on paper
34.3 x 47 cm (13 ½ x 18 ½ in)
1959
British Council Collection

1949, had become 'a movement of immense proportions'. It was not, in his opinion, a very promising development but rather a sign of America's failure to produce 'a genius whose sense of European art, past and present, is capable of white-hot fusion with his sense of America's visual reality'.[9] Five or six years later the Eurocentric certainties that underpinned this judgement had been all but completely overturned.

Of all the American Abstract Expressionists, Pollock was by a wide margin the best-known and most successful. In the October 1947 issue of *Horizon*, which had a dedicated readership among British artists and intellectuals, the New York critic Clement Greenberg had declared Pollock to be 'The most powerful painter in contemporary America ... a Gothic, morbid and extreme disciple of Picasso's Cubism and Miró's post-Cubism, tinctured also with Kandinsky and Surrealist inspiration'.[10] The appeal of phrases such as this to Wynter can be imagined. Indeed, his own brooding gouaches of the late 1940s had been described by critics in not dissimilar terms. Pollock, of course, was up to something very different by 1947. The poured, dripped and spattered paintings for which he became famous were in full flow. There was nothing in British art that remotely compared with Pollock's wild visual rhythms, the lithe, fluid architecture of his madly meshed paint trails or his paintings' expansive scale and physicality.

Had Wynter seen an actual painting by Pollock when he began *The Interior*? Possibly, since three large canvases were included in the Institute of Contemporary Arts' exhibition 'Opposing Forces' in 1953. He had almost certainly seen work by another early practitioner of abstract all-over painting, Mark Tobey, who had a solo show at the ICA in May 1955 and whom Wynter met when he visited St Ives that year. Tobey's style of mark-making and the smaller scale of his paintings were easier on European sensibilities than Pollock's. He had, moreover, spent several years in England. In 1931 he was appointed resident artist and teacher at Dartington Hall in Devon, where he met Bernard Leach. In 1934 he travelled with Leach down to Naples and thence to Hong Kong and Shanghai. Tobey continued alone through China and then to Japan, where a spent a couple of weeks in a Zen monastery, studying poetry and calligraphy. He was

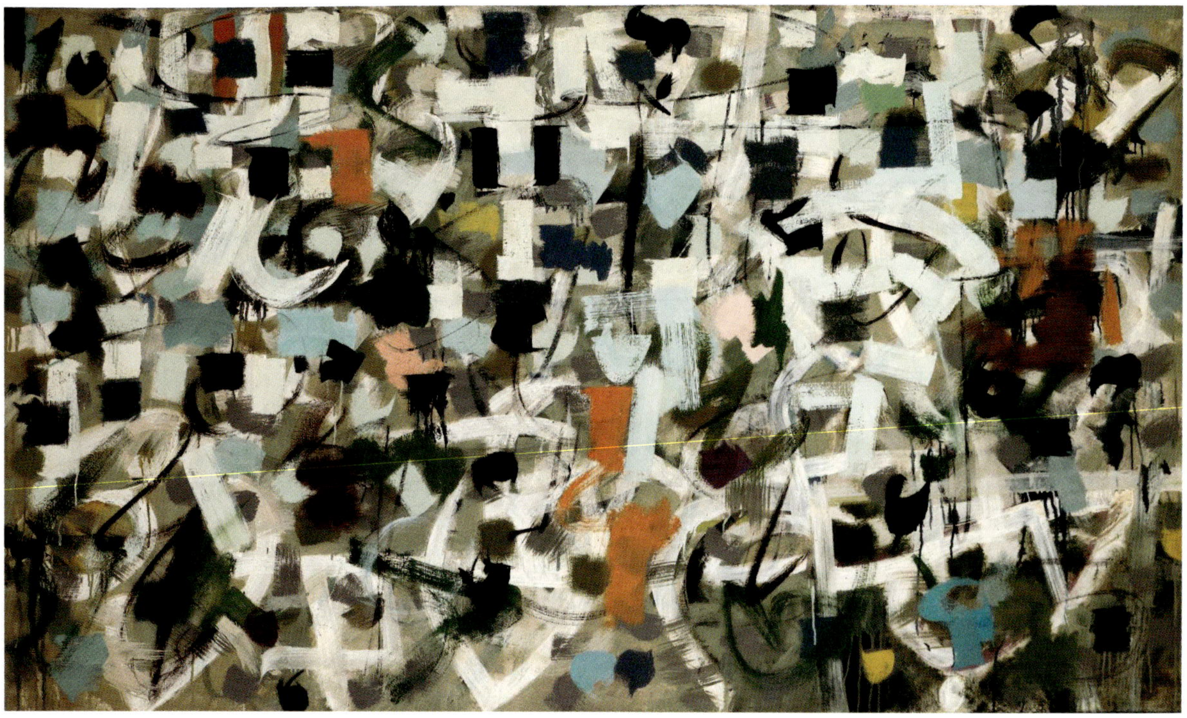

80
Bradley Walker Tomlin,
Number 15
oil on canvas
116.8 x 193 cm (46 x 76 in)
1953
Private collection

credited by some American critics with introducing an 'Oriental influence' to contemporary painting that, together with the Surrealism imported to New York by refugee European artists later in the decade, had given birth to Abstract Expressionism. Tobey was, explained the American curator and critic Holger Cahill, one of the 'old Masters' of this new movement. In particular, Tobey had developed a technique he called 'white writing', in which he worked the whole surface of a painting in a feathery, all-over blizzard of pale dabs of paint, building up a delicate illusion of textural rather than airily spatial depth. The effect could be compared to the broad-brush oriental glazes so dear to Leach. 'White writing' was not, implied Cahill, really writing at all, since it was 'not based on calligraphy but on the free movement of the Chinese brush, looping over layers of interpenetrating space ... holding icons in a shifting web ... The activity of Tobey's painting is a subtle interplay between intangible structures and shadowy background, a poetry of suggested forms and weaving light always on the edge of equivocally determined space.'[11]

'Layers of interpenetrating space', 'icons in a shifting web' – this certainly sounded like Wynter's own explorations in *The Interior*. The phrases come from Cahill's catalogue essay for 'Modern Art in the United States', which was showing at the Tate Gallery (now Tate Britain) while Wynter was working not far away in his temporary studio at The Boltons. The final room of this large survey exhibition contained a tantalisingly selective round-up of Abstract Expressionist painting. There were two paintings by Pollock and four by Tobey. Mark Rothko, Clifford Still, Franz Kline, Willem de Kooning and Robert Motherwell were also represented, as was Bradley Walker Tomlin, whose abstract marks resembled, in a manner often compared to Wynter's, discrete glyphs or symbols (fig. 80).

Altogether there was an extraordinarily compendious range of brushwork and mark-making on display – drips, dabs, swirls, flat strong colour, big-brush gesturalism – paint being used for any and all of the effects that paint could achieve. And from all this Wynter clearly learned. Some of the large canvases that rapidly followed *The Interior*, such as *High Country* (fig. 81), vary the width and length of the brushstrokes to a noticeably greater extent. If Braque's influence could be detected in the first of Wynter's new series, he was at least partly succeeded by the Americans as these works developed throughout 1956 and 1957. Whereas the very title *The Interior* could be taken as a homage to Braque's 'Ateliers', *High Country* echoes Cahill's assertion that Abstract Expressionism owed its energy to the monumentally expansive scale of the American landscape, 'prairies rolling horizon beyond horizon ... boundless high plains' and so on. From the same year, Wynter's title *Mars Ascends* (fig. 82) picks up

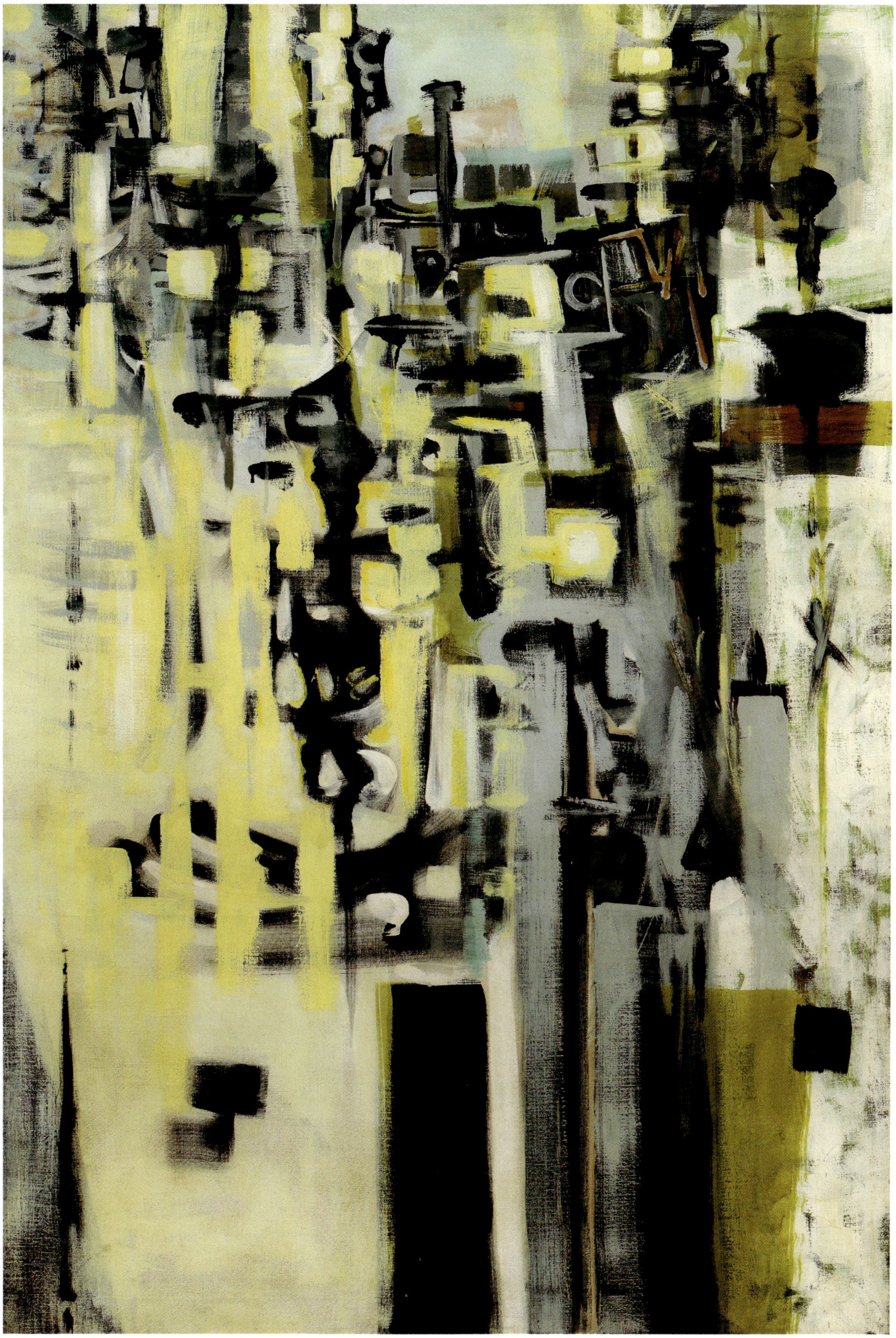

81
High Country
oil on canvas
152.4 x 101.6 cm (60 x 40 in)
1956
Artist's estate

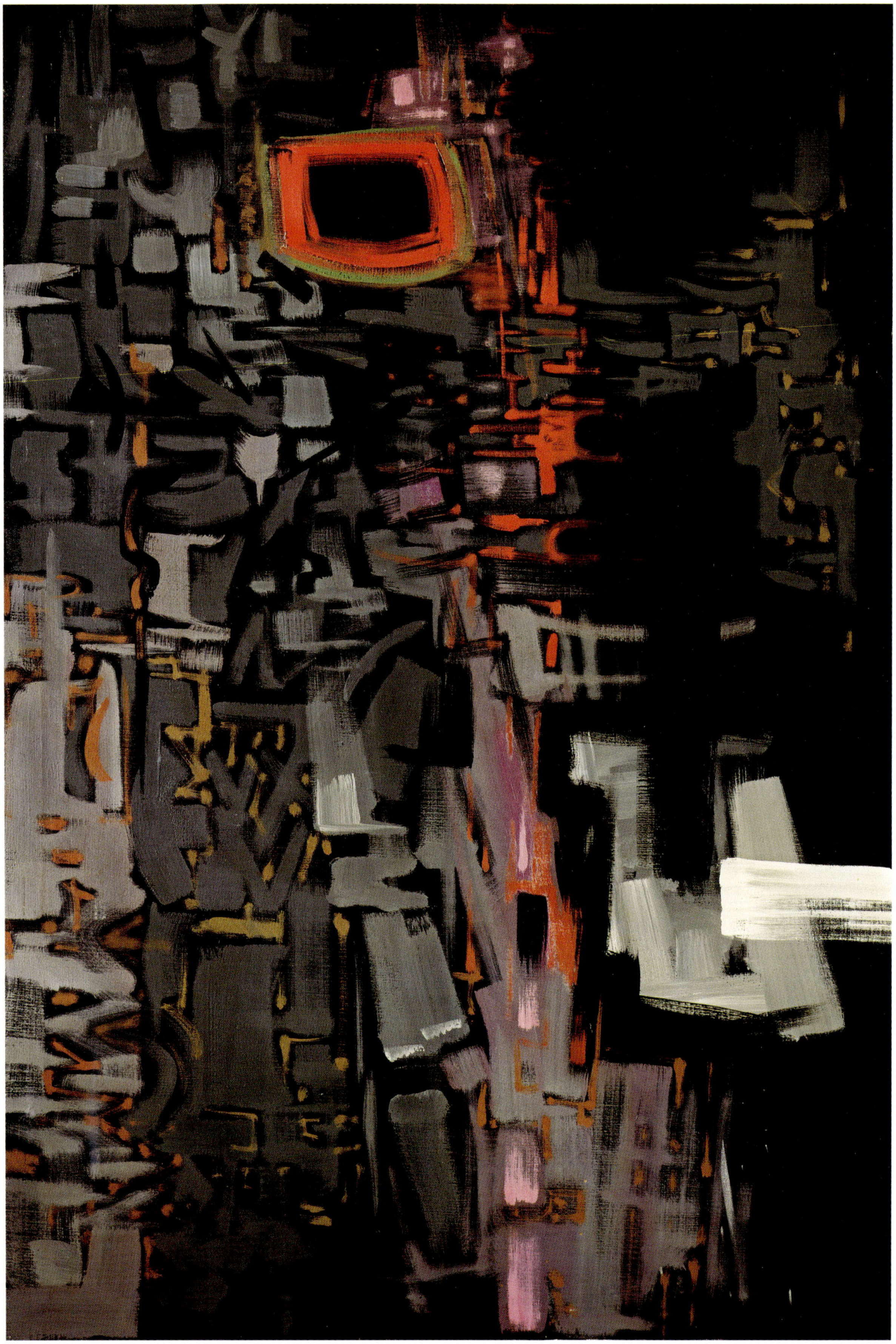

82
Mars Ascends
oil on canvas
152.4 x 101.6 cm (60 x 40 in)
1956
Tate

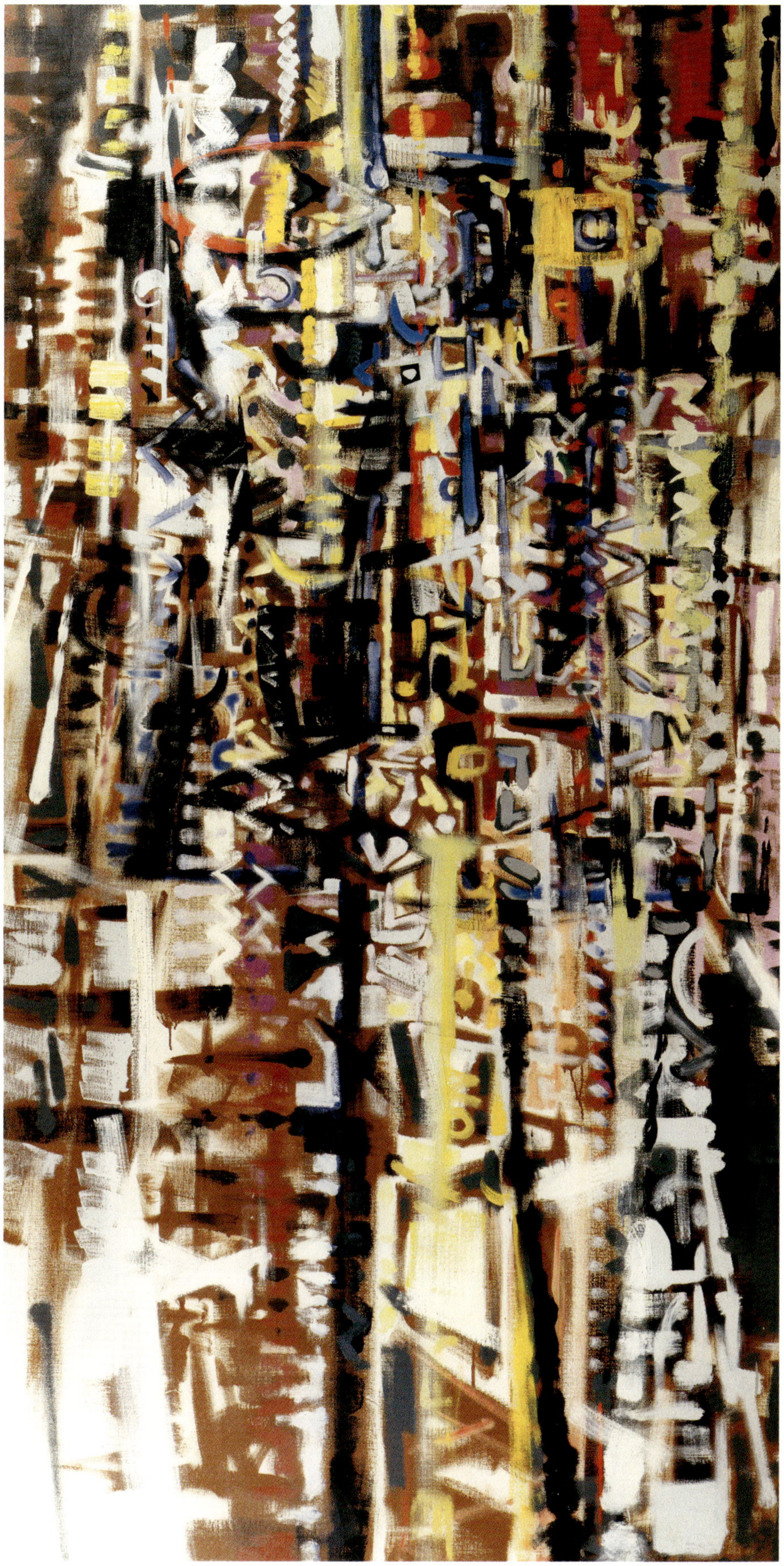

83
Carnival
oil on canvas
223.5 x 113.6 cm (88 x 44¾ in)
1956
Private collection

on the beginnings of the Cold War space race, at a time when both the USA and USSR were redoubling their efforts to get the first satellite into orbit. Like *High Country*, the painting is made of wider brushstrokes, creating an effect quite different from the shimmering intricacy of *The Interior*. A cavernous, squarish shape edged in red is lifted through a cumulative, buoyant movement towards the painting's upper edge. When you compare this with the almost central placing of similar chunks of dark matter in works from a year or two earlier, such as *Dark Landscape* or *Headland*, the sense of uplift in the 1956 series becomes palpable.

If *High Country* and *Mars Ascends* were Wynter's only surviving works from early 1956, it would be fair to conclude that, in technical terms at least, he'd taken his cue from Tomlin's two paintings at the Tate, *Number 20* (1949) and *Number 4* (1952). These consisted of a comparable weave of distinct but interlocking spatulate marks resembling signs or graphemes. Wynter's feeling for paintstrokes as handwriting, a form of gnomic inscription, went deep. The Latin verb *texere* – 'to weave' – gives us both 'text' and 'textile'; in Wynter's, as in Tomlin's, paintings, the meanings of these two nouns fuse at the root. Yet Tomlin's look much flatter and more graphic – altogether more text-like. Maybe, after all, Wynter was closer to the French *tachiste* manner, which Heron was also exploring at this time as he emerged from an even more intense enthralment by Braque. At a certain point, however, it becomes clear that the argument for Wynter's influences leads in too many directions, since what compels our attention is his assimilation of these different sources (and much else besides) in a synthesis that demands to be greeted on its own terms.

Although the magnificent, unbroken succession of large canvases that Wynter painted during 1956, which also includes *Prison*, *Carnival*, *Monumental*, *Deep Current*, *The Indias*, *Hostile Tribe* and *River Boat Blues* (figs 84, 83, 87, 85, 77, 88, 86), clearly forms a series, these works are

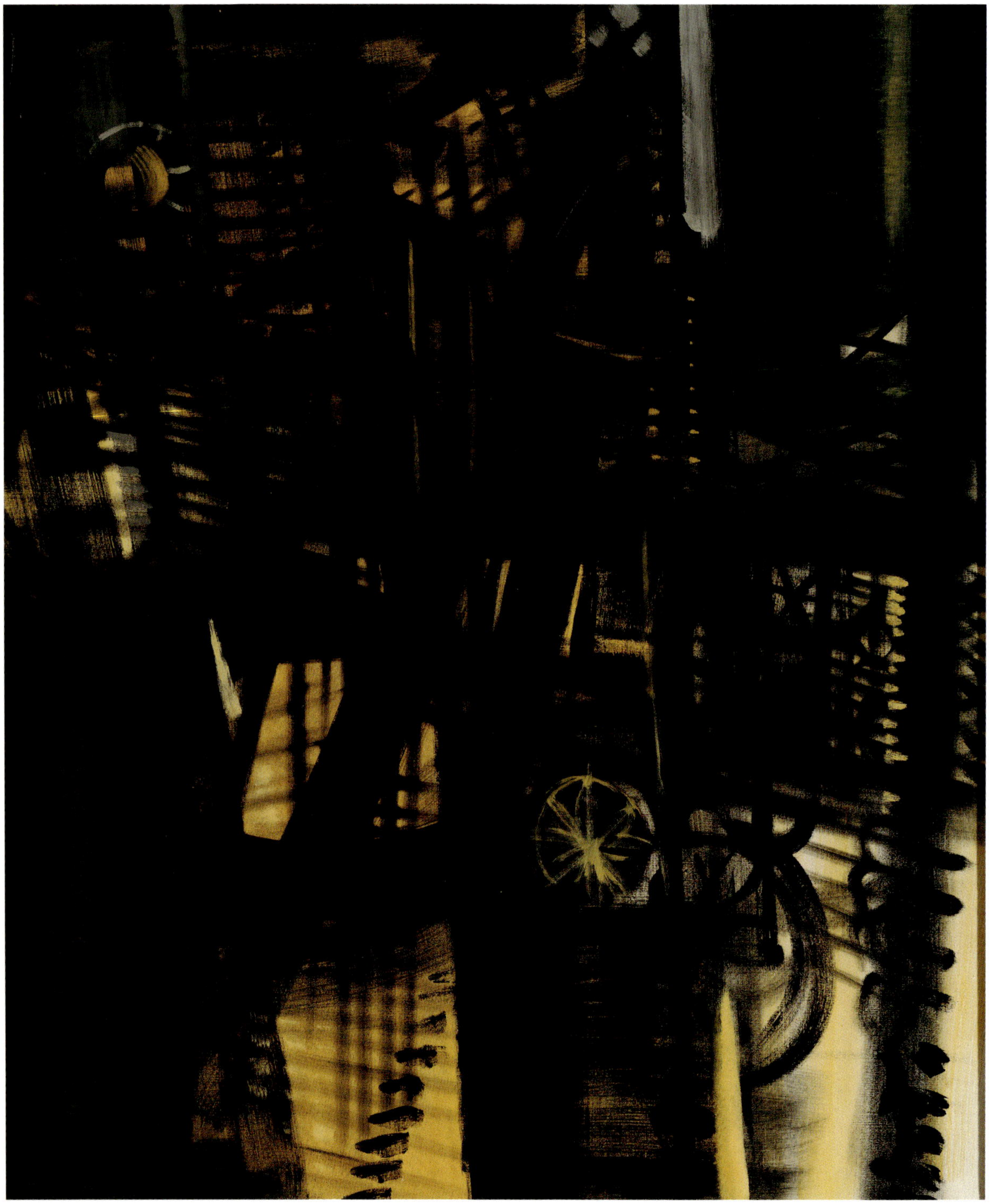

84
Prison
oil on canvas
127 x 101.6 cm (79 ½ x 40 in)
1956
Artist's estate

individually quite distinct. Their differences have tended not to be clearly enough recognised, largely because these paintings have often been shown singly. (It's like trying to hold Pollock's 1950 series in mind after seeing each painting separately.) Take *The Indias*, for example, which at first seems similar to *The Interior* in the balance of different kinds of marks that make up its thickety surface. Yet the 'writing' is much more sharply defined in its abstract penmanship, a debt (perhaps) to Tobey that Wynter has fully assimilated for his own ends. Then there is *Hostile Tribe* (fig. 88), which, unusually for this group of works, has a horizontal or 'landscape' format. The title acknowledges the vestigial presence of the phalanx of primitivistic figures that materialises out of its clustering paintstrokes. Both the term 'hostile' and the angular skeletal armatures of which the (apparent) figures

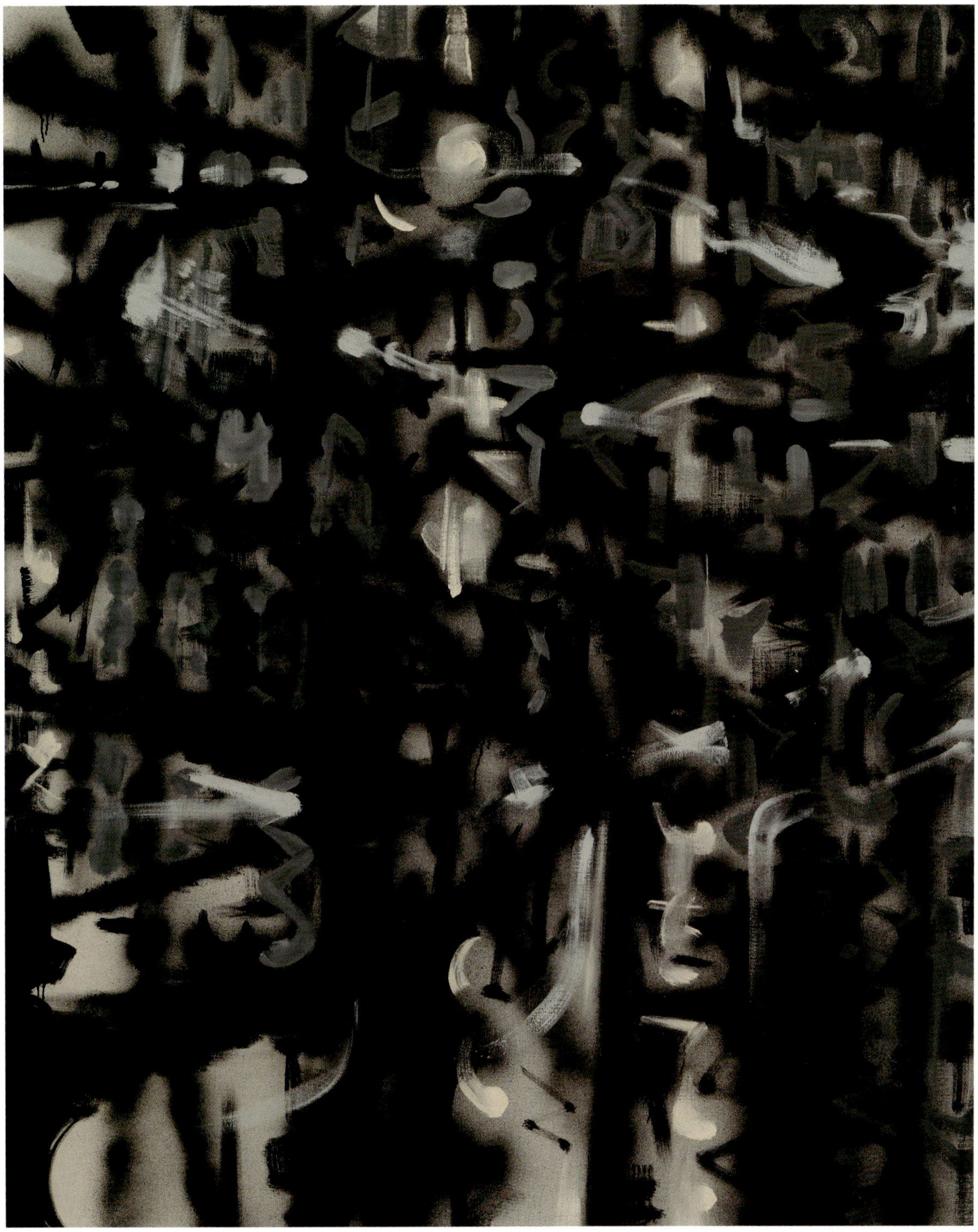

85
Deep Current
oil on canvas
142.3 x 111.8 cm (56¼ x 44¼ in)
1956
Artist's estate

apparently consist recall the phrase Reg Butler had used – 'remote custodians of a landscape hostile to man' – in relation to his early welded steel sculptures. The spontaneous generation of humanoid shapes in *Hostile Tribe* was possibly the result of a process Pollock identified in his own work. Objecting to the term 'Abstract Expressionism', he opined that his painting was 'certainly not "nonobjective" and not "nonrepresentational" either. I'm very representational some of the time, and a little all of the time. But when you're painting out of your unconscious, figures are bound to emerge.'[12]

This statement comes from an interview Pollock gave two months before his death in a car crash in August 1956. Since it was not published until the following year, Wynter could not have read it when he titled *Hostile Tribe*. But of course, the notion that figures and forms could,

86
River Boat Blues
oil on canvas
112 x 142 cm (44 x 56 in)
1956
Private collection

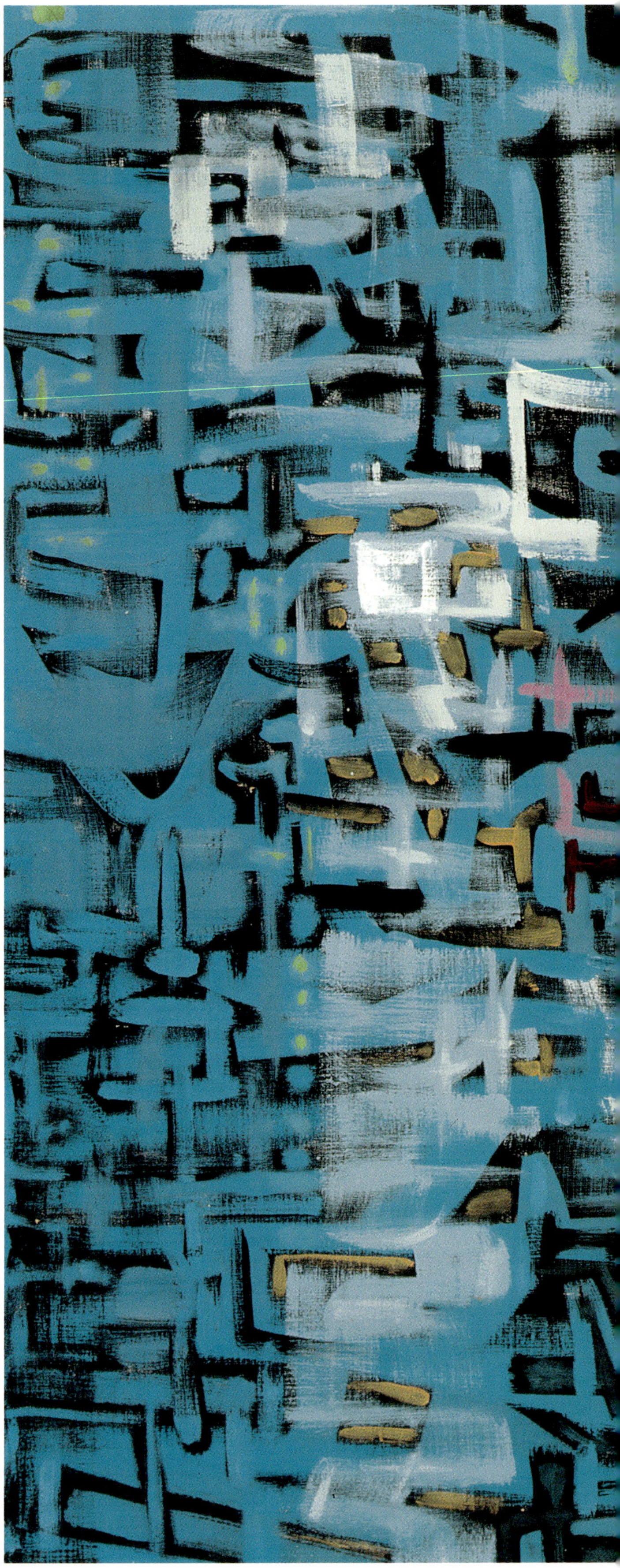

indeed should, emerge unintended from an artist's work was one of the tenets of Surrealist automatism, which, André Breton had insisted, must entail 'the absence of any control exercised by reason'. Pollock, Tomlin and other American Abstract Expressionists had started out as Surrealists; several had been deeply impressed by the exhibition 'Fantastic Art: Dada and Surrealism' at the Museum of Modern Art, New York, in 1936–7, as Wynter had been by the equivalent show in London earlier in the year. Like theirs, Wynter's art had been shaped by Surrealism in both technical and intellectual terms. Other British painters who had to a greater or lesser extent embraced Surrealism – among them Paul Nash, Graham Sutherland, Edward Wadsworth, Ithell Colquhoun and John Tunnard – had tended to stick to a landscape idiom, as Wynter had done until around 1950.

In 1956, however, Wynter was exceptional among British artists in the way his path from Surrealism to Abstract Expressionism paralleled that of the New York artists a decade earlier. This fact has been obscured for two reasons: first, the powerful critical and political interests that, during the Cold War period, promoted as self-evident the idea that America's commitment to individual freedom made it the rightful and only home of Abstract Expressionist art. Second, it was a mixed blessing for Wynter that the British critic most vocal in his support – Patrick Heron – had a profound mistrust of Surrealism and, perhaps even less helpful for Wynter's long-term reputation, was determined to counter the dominance of American Abstract Expressionism by suggesting that British abstract artists of his generation (and often also of his acquaintance) constituted an equally significant movement, united by its desire to explore pictorial space.

If he'd been asked about his most absorbing personal interests in 1956, Wynter might not have mentioned Surrealism or Abstract Expressionism either. Since acquiring a camera, he had been experimenting with stereoscopic photography. It was easy enough to

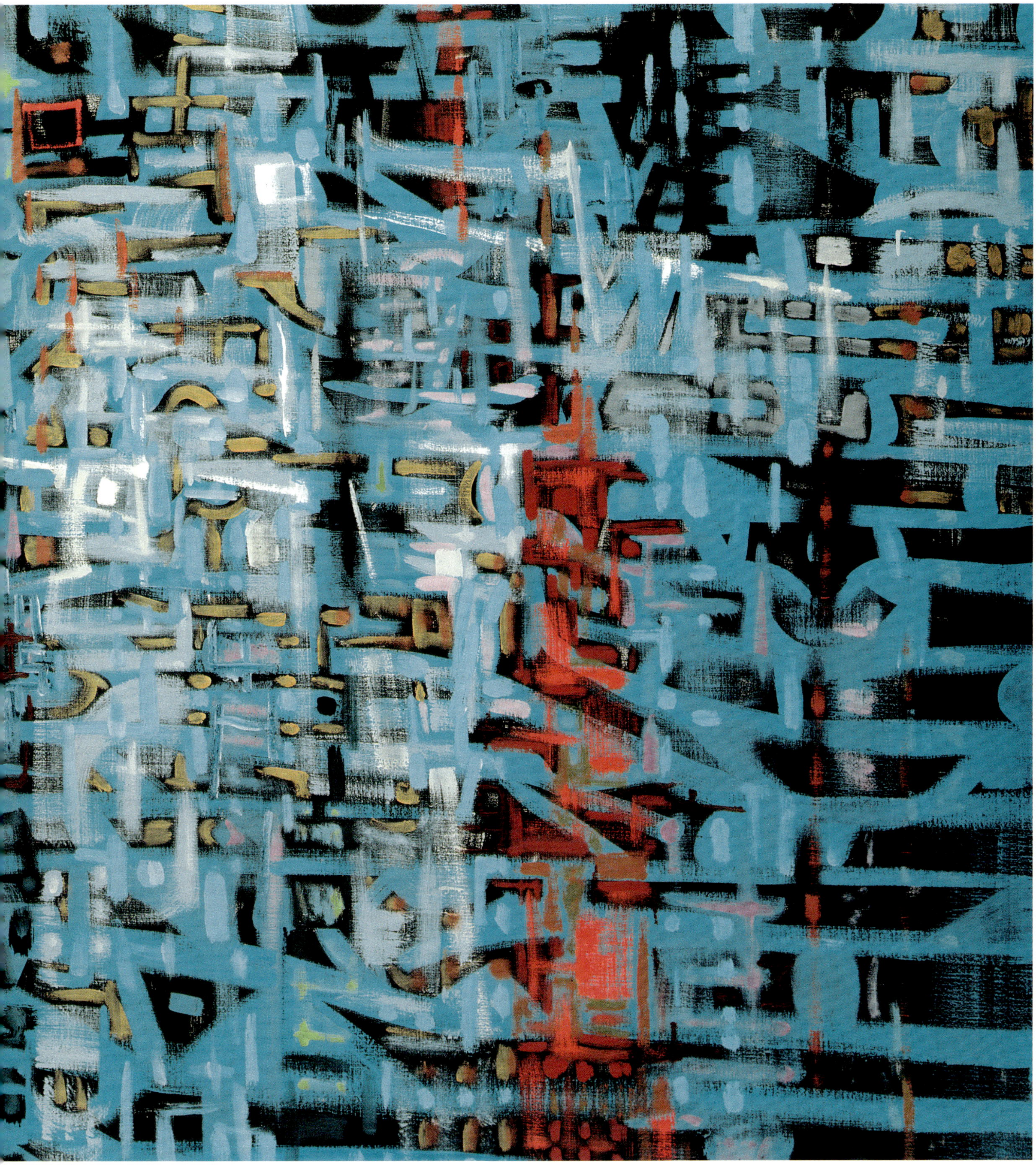

take Kodachrome colour slides that, when looked at through a special viewer, created the illusion of three-dimensionality. Stereoscopes of this sort had been a parlour amusement in Victorian times. Wynter was now attempting to project such images so that they would hover unconfined in space, a form of what came to be termed virtual reality. Mescalin produced its extraordinary visual sensations, Wynter believed, following Huxley, through a chemical liberation of the mind from its conditioning. But how could such sensations be shared? The year 1956 saw another arrival from the USA (alongside Abstract Expressionism and rock 'n' roll), when Cinerama was launched in London. To Monica Harman, who had by now finished at Corsham and was studying at Central School of Art in London and spending a lot of time with Wynter, his enthusiasm for this new kind of cinematic experience seemed at least as intense as his excitement about the Abstract Expressionists at the Tate.

This Is Cinerama – one of the recent releases Bryan and Monica watched together – opened with a rollercoaster ride before whisking the audience off to Niagara Falls, a Spanish bullfight and a bird's-eye tour of 'America the Beautiful' filmed from within the fuselage of a B-25 bomber. These sensational illusions of spatial reality were created by shooting film on three synchronised cameras, which was then projected from three separate projectors on to a vast, curved screen, accompanied by seven-track surround-sound audio. The screen consisted of a multitude of thin vertical strips, each one individually angled towards the audience. This elaborate set-up was highly effective – comparable to the effects later produced with the IMAX system developed in the 1970s. Wynter was fascinated by Cinerama's technical processes, which he emulated in still photography by using a customised camera with three lenses. From this time onwards – and possibly earlier – Wynter was constantly attempting to translate photographic technology into fine-art media. Sven Berlin recalled a visit from Wynter, probably in late 1955 or 1956, when he demonstrated his 'polaroids': 'They were cards of colour which he moved about on the table, creating the first of those poetic sequences for me to see ... These were the prototypes of what I later called his timeless clocks',[13] namely the kinetic constructions, or IMOOS, that Wynter was to develop in the 1960s.

In April 1956 Wynter returned to the Carn with Monica. A mile or so down the stony slope of the moors towards the sea, the view from Wynter's outpost was interrupted by the hulking gables of Eagles Nest, where Patrick Heron had just moved in with his wife, Delia, and two young daughters. Wynter's neighbour here in the early days, Will Arnold-Forster, was a former Labour politician and a gentleman painter who had settled on this naked crag because of its proximity to St Ives's art colony. Wynter had called regularly at Eagles Nest to collect his post (the Carn being off-limits for deliveries) and occasionally to discuss art with Arnold-Forster or share a life model. In 1955, some years after Arnold-Forster's death, Heron had discovered that Eagles Nest was for sale and decided to buy the house. He had an attachment to the place dating back to childhood visits in the 1920s, when his father was managing the Cryséde textile works in St Ives. After the sale had gone through in late 1955, but before the family moved down, Heron had begun a new series of paintings. In these, as in the work Wynter was simultaneously producing in his temporary Chelsea studio, Heron left behind all previous traces of figuration, adopting a *tachiste* manner of broad individual paintstrokes, resembling those of Soulages but much more detached and buoyant. Heron, who had announced just a few months earlier 'I believe in abstract-figuration',[14] was a more unexpected convert to non-figurative painting than Wynter, who had been moving steadily in this direction since around 1952. The two artists certainly discussed these developments, both in London in the early weeks of 1956 and in Cornwall after the Herons' arrival (fig. 89).

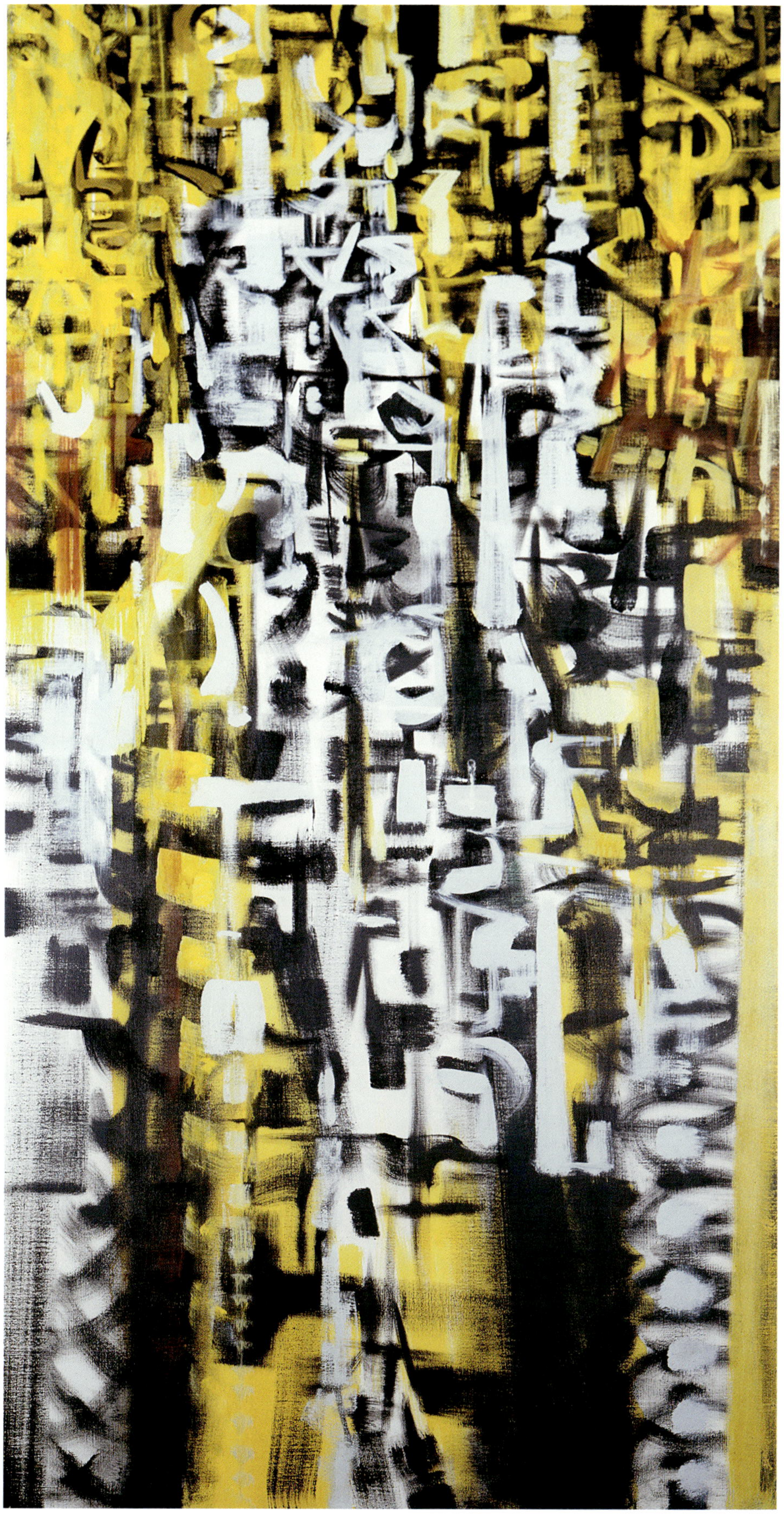

87
Monumental
oil on canvas
202 x 101.6 cm (79½ x 40 in)
1956
Southampton City Art Gallery

Once installed at Eagles Nest, as the azaleas in the sub-tropical garden laid out by Arnold-Forster began to open their blooms in the Easter sea-light, Heron immersed himself in the works that became known as his 'Garden Paintings' (fig. 90). Following his own dictum that 'the major aim of the painter is, and always has been, to organize space in a new and distinctive manner',[15] Heron turned up the colour to produce ensembles of abstract marks much lighter and brighter than Soulages's typically sombre palette. Although these paintings were non-representational, they nevertheless caught precisely the atmosphere of the azalea garden, inviting the eye into their luminescent vernal spaces. To the colourist sensibility informed by his long-standing admiration for Bonnard and Matisse, Heron now added a passion for his new surroundings. Whereas for Wynter the Penwith landscape was 'peopled' by the artist's unconscious, as though it were a projection of the psyche that could be physically encountered and explored, for Heron this same landscape took on the guise of a Celtic Provence. The strong, un-English brilliance of its marine light, and the intensity of colour this gave rise to, seemed to echo his deepest Francophile yearnings.

There are obvious parallels between Wynter's new abstract-calligraphic paintings and Heron's *tachiste* 'Garden Paintings'. During 1956, for example, both artists experimented with vertical double-square format canvases, as a way of responding to the landscape without being drawn into the landscape-style organisation of a painting inevitably suggested by a long horizontal format. The differences between them are, however, just as marked. Heron's fixation on 'space in colour' left no place for painting's intellectual dimension. Not for him Roger Hilton's vision of the artist as 'a man who is struggling with an idea', whose works 'record his thought processes, his outlook'.[16] In a painting such as *Mars Ascends*, Wynter deployed a hanging or floating superimposition of wide vertical brushstrokes not so unlike Heron's. But this work is much closer to American

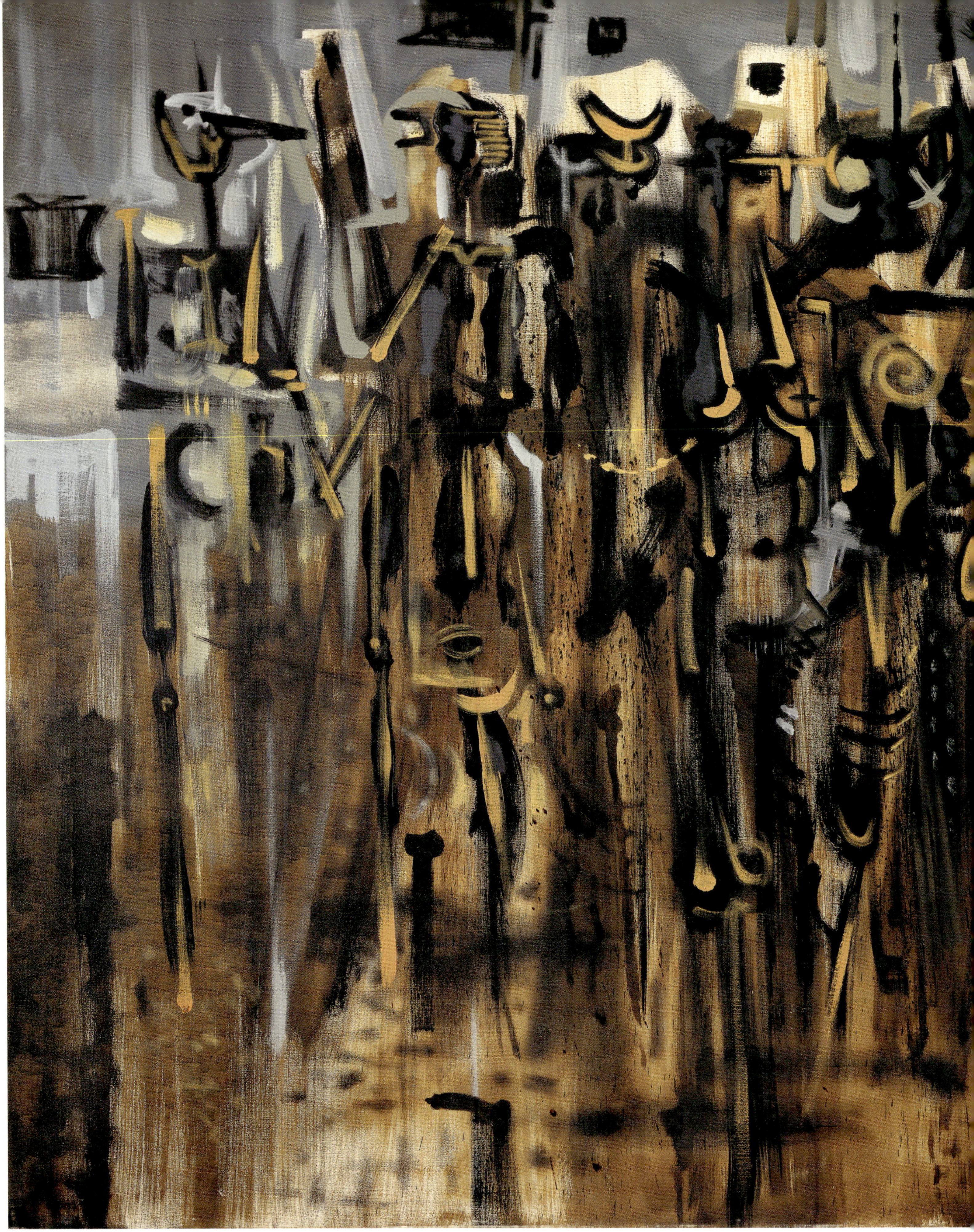

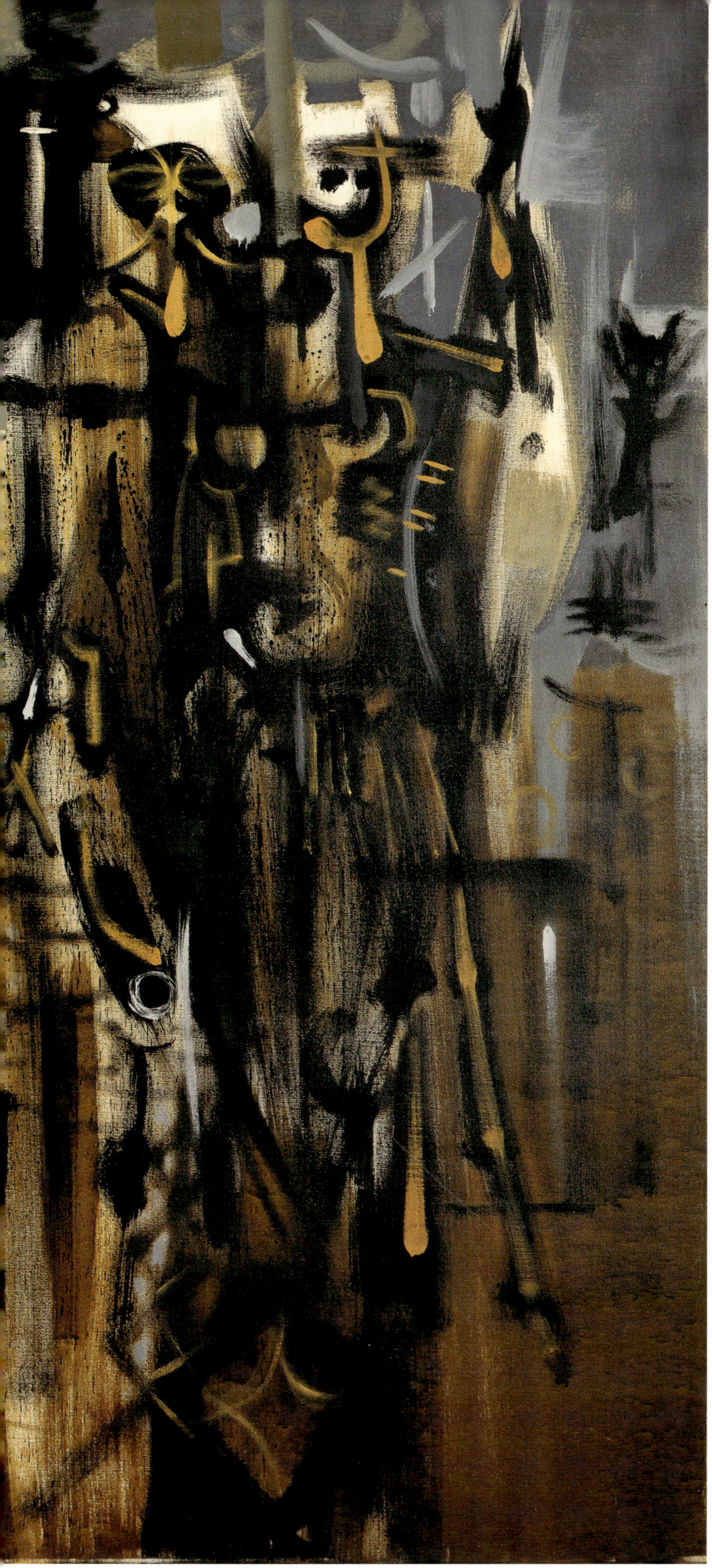

88
Hostile Tribe
oil on canvas
111.7 x 142.2 cm (44¼ x 56¼ in)
1956
Scottish National Gallery of
Modern Art, Edinburgh

Abstract Expressionism in spirit than were Heron's new paintings. You're conscious not so much of being invited to enter an illusory, sensory space as of waiting for meaning to emerge from recesses that feel part-pictorial, part-psychic. And the colours, of course, are much darker and earthier than Heron's. Where Wynter's reds glow like a split ember, Heron's resemble translucent fabric or petals through which the sun shines; it's not just the effect that is different but the whole imaginative ambience.

While Wynter continued to work throughout 1956 and 1957 on the series he'd started at The Boltons, commentators began absorbing his change of manner into a wider debate about the nature of British abstract art that had been under way since the early 1950s, when a new generation of geometric abstract artists had emerged. Now sometimes termed Constructionists, to distinguish them from 1930s' Constructivists, artists such as Victor Pasmore and Kenneth and Mary Martin developed a precise, mathematical approach embodied in three-dimensional, wall-mounted constructions and mobiles. In the catalogue for the exhibition 'Nine Abstract Artists' at the Redfern Gallery in early 1955, the critic Lawrence Alloway had advanced the claims of Pasmore and his associates against the softer, landscape-influenced abstraction that he identified with artists around St Ives (this group, represented in the show by Frost, did not include Wynter, who was still considered a landscape painter). Following the example of the New York art world's kingmaker, Clement Greenberg, Alloway saw himself as setting an agenda for British art rather than simply describing trends. Each of the other three most influential critics of the time – David Sylvester, John Berger and Heron – had his own agenda too. Alloway, however, was more determined even than the resolutely Marxist Berger (who in 1950 had replaced Heron as the *New Statesman*'s art critic) to shift debate about art from its conventional niche into the context of broader social and cultural trends.

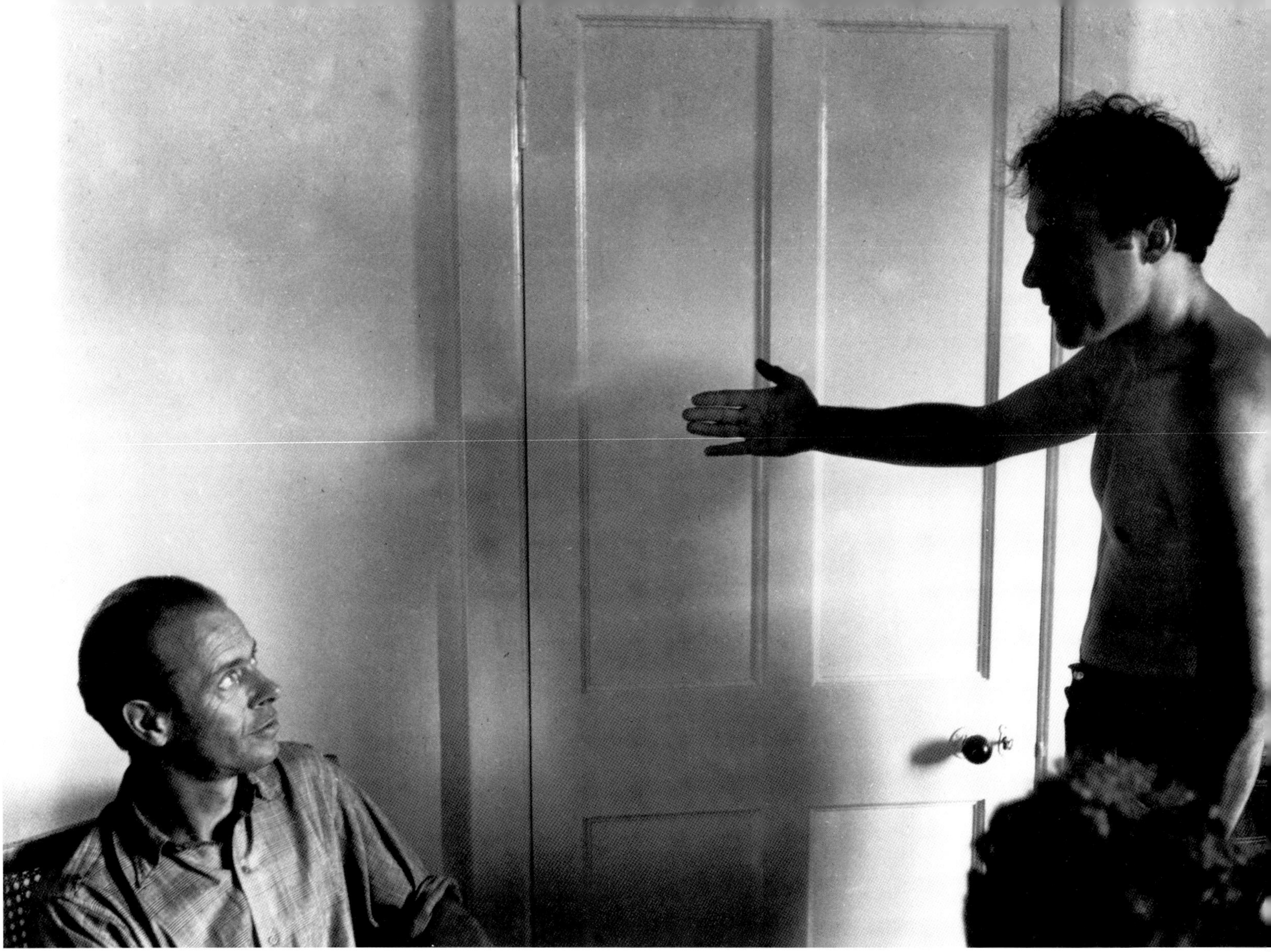

89
Bryan Wynter and Patrick Heron at Eagles Nest, 1956, photograph by Roger Mayne

In August 1956 he had been involved in organising the exhibition 'This Is Tomorrow' at the Whitechapel Gallery, which featured installations conceived and constructed by twelve teams, totalling almost forty contributors, including musicians, designers and architects as well as artists. Among the objects on display were film posters, a model of Robby the Robot from the 1956 sci-fi film *Forbidden Planet*, beer bottles and photomontages. The integration of fine art (Pasmore and fellow Constructionists Adrian Heath, the Martins and Anthony Hill were represented) into a much wider spectrum of contemporary visual culture expressed very clearly the thinking of Alloway and other members of the Independent Group – a discussion forum that had been taking place, on and off, at the ICA since 1952. By the time Alloway came to write the catalogue for 'Statements: A Review of British Abstract Art in 1956', held at the ICA early the following year, his interest in the traditional gallery presentation of paintings in isolation from other visual media had audibly waned: 'British abstract art, which revived after the last war, is still much discussed – buried by some, apotheosised by others'[17] – and so on, as though it were hardly worth taking a partisan stance on such questions any longer.

'Statements' comprised one abstract painting by each of twenty-one artists. Wynter (represented by *The Interior*) and Heron were there, along with a sizeable section of the line-up of 'This Is Tomorrow': Magda Cordell, Robert Adams, James Hull, Pasmore, Heath, Hill and the Martins. Two notable features of the catalogue are the inclusion of statements by all of the artists, several of whom (such Wynter, Hilton and Nicholson) were seldom persuaded to commit themselves in print, and Alloway's assumption that, as far as British abstract painting was concerned, all eyes were now on America. He observed that the 'two St Ives painters' Wynter and Heron were typical of an increasing number of artists in being 'influenced by American art, thus turning away from the once magnetic School of Paris'. Wynter, he thought, was 'influenced by Bradley Walker Tomlin and Mark Tobey', while 'Heron's flat washes derive from the work of Sam Francis'.[18] Such assertions enraged Heron; it became his *cause célèbre* over the following four decades to demonstrate that American Abstract Expressionism was not pre-eminent, that it had developed in parallel to British gestural abstract painting and even stolen the thunder of adventurous British artists outright. Wynter doesn't seem personally to have been too concerned either way, being always more intent on the evolving processes of his work than the critical nuances of its public reception.

In his own catalogue statement Heron emphasised the 'purely pictorial' qualities of his recent paintings, namely 'the architecture of the canvas, the spatial interrelation of each and every touch (or stroke or bar) of colour, the colour-character, the paint-character of a painting – all these I now explore with a sense of freedom quite denied me when I still had to keep half an eye on a "subject".'[19] Wynter characteristically stressed the psychological angle. He spoke of the 'moment of seeing' as 'a fragment of a continuous process which underlies and precedes recognition, a kind of "substance" from which we construct our world of human experience'. 'I think of myself', he concluded, 'as embodying this "substance" in paint.' These reflections were not to be interpreted as a theory of art but were merely 'personal assumptions helpful to me in my work'. Such assumptions were not easy to put into words; in fact, they struck him as being 'strange to language'.[20]

'Strange to language' is an arresting, poetic phrase, carrying intuitions of an entire mental realm for which words provide no, or only limited, access. The phrase could be Wynter's own: he'd written poetry and knew a great deal of verse by heart. But I would also guess that, present in Wynter's creative thinking during 1956–7, as much as anything by Pollock, Tobey or Tomlin that he had heard about or seen at the ICA or the Tate, were the poetry and conversation of Sydney Graham, who had returned to west Cornwall in 1956. After efforts by Wynter, Berlin and others to find them cheap rented accommodation, Graham and Nessie Dunsmuir had been living since March in an old coastguard's cottage at Gurnard's Head, within walking distance of the Carn. In 1955 Graham's volume of poems *The Nightfishing* had been published by Faber and Faber; Wynter must not only have read the book but also heard Graham recite its contents (he took little prompting, either in the company of friends or with whomever he bumped into in the bar of the Gurnard's Head Hotel). The title poem recounts a night at sea as a hired hand on a fishing boat. This episode forms the narrative core of an extended existential meditation:

> So this is the place. This
> Is the place fastened still with movement,
> Movement as calligraphic and formal as
> A music burned on copper.[21]

These lines ('fastened still with movement', 'calligraphic and formal as/ A music burned on copper') seem echoed in the visual texture of Wynter's new abstract paintings, just as, fifteen years earlier, Keyes's poetic imagery could be felt in Wynter's Oxford variations on surrealistic themes. Poetry's combination of time-based rhythmic qualities with visual imagination had a deep hold on him; it fitted his temperament – the compulsive walker and explorer whose mind was alert to images that might 'well up' as he moved through the landscape. Graham, for his part, found that Wynter was someone he could talk to about poetry as he would to a fellow poet. Pub sessions were often followed by the company returning to the Carn or Graham's clifftop cottage for a late night extemporising collaborative poems, reading aloud or reciting from memory. Wynter's rendering of A. E. Housman's poem 'Far in a Western Brookland'[22] became the signature tune of their walks through the Zennor night, with its image of 'starlit fences' where 'The wanderer halts and hears/ My soul that lingers sighing/ About the glimmering weirs'. Graham became increasingly preoccupied with the gap, or 'silence', between words and experiences and their translation into the 'abstract' formal construction of a poem. One November night in 1958, 'fucking about on the edge of silence again in the smallest hours', he wrote in a notebook addressed to Wynter:

> I remember that always somewhere under the live and speaking idiom of the Voice in poetry there is the count, the beats you can count on your fingers. Yes always under the shout and whimper and the quick and the slow of poetry there is the formal construction of time made abstract in the mind's ear. And the strange thing is that that very abstract dimension in the poem is what creates the reader's release into the human world of another.[23]

In painting, as the 'Statements' catalogue makes clear, Wynter too was much concerned with abstract art's capacity to generate a comparable kind of 'release' or 'unfolding':

> One should be able, ideally, to make paintings which throw off imagery of different kinds at different times to different people, continually unfolding different aspects of themselves, ambiguous and paradoxical paintings with no main 'theme', from which the spectator may, by participation, extract his own images.[24]

These reflections belong neither to the Independent Group's modish synthesisation of popular urban visual culture – film posters, abstract paintings, robots, juke-boxes, all jousting for impact – nor to Heron's rather patrician advocacy of a 'purely pictorial' visual art. They do, however, belong very much to the distinctive intellectual context of the Carn–Gurnard's Head axis. Here, in a society of geographically isolated individualists, Wynter and Graham pursued their investigations into the 'ambiguous and paradoxical' ways

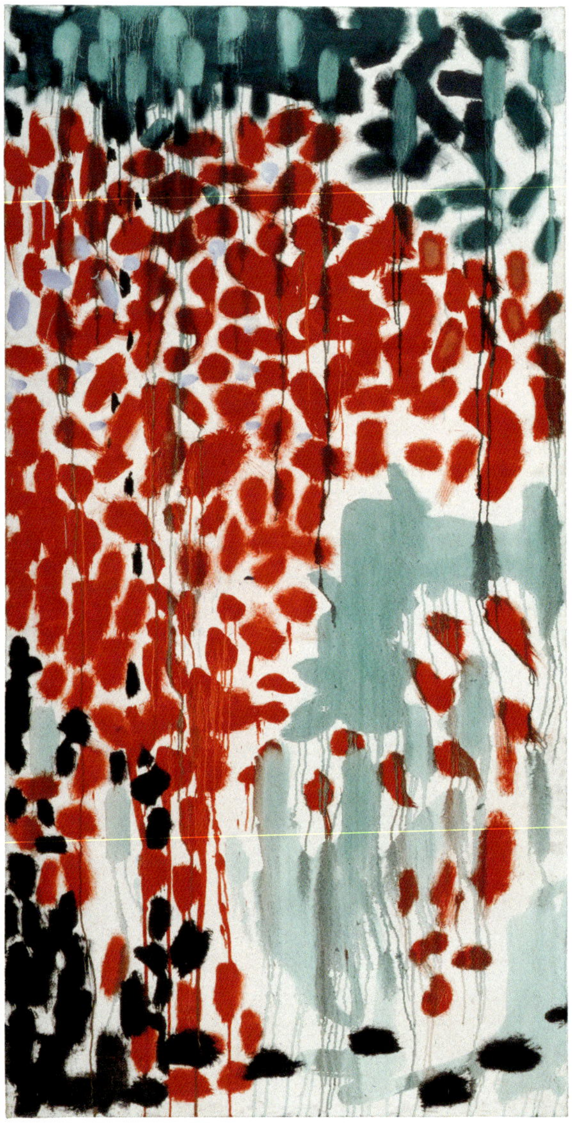

90
Patrick Heron,
Summer Painting, August
oil on canvas
182.8 x 91.4 cm (72 x 36 in)
1956
Private collection

in which poems or paintings invited, or demanded, the reader's or viewer's participation. The ambience was as much verbal as visual. Word-games of all kinds played an important part: as well as the poetry readings and recitations, Wynter and Graham excelled in competitive (often deliberately excruciating) pun-making.

Wynter's enthusiasm for tinkering with new technology, meanwhile, was finding fresh outlets. Although forced to admit defeat in his attempts to create three-dimensional images through the simultaneous projection of colour transparencies, he had become fascinated by the medium of underwater cinematography pioneered by the former French naval diver and explorer Jacques Cousteau. At the Bath Festival, some time while

91
Impenetrable Country
oil on canvas
203.2 x 101.6 cm (80 x 40 in)
1957
Artist's estate

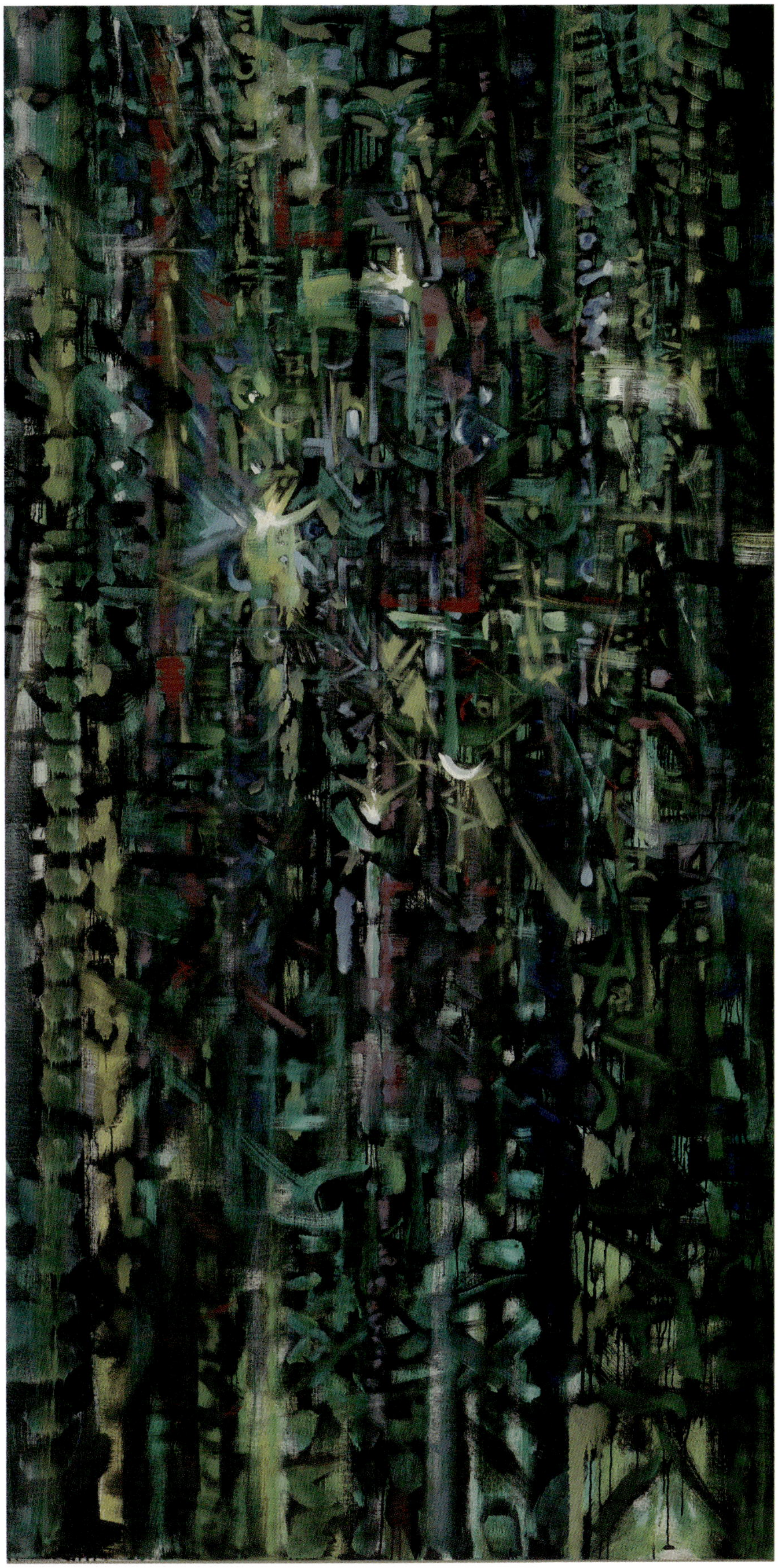

Wynter was still teaching at Corsham, he and Monica saw one of short underwater films Cousteau had been making since the mid-1940s. Wynter had already constructed a basic diving apparatus, involving an air-line supported on the surface by a float. His imagination was seized by Cousteau's beautiful, alien images of the marine world and, in particular, by the divers' complete freedom of movement, made possible by aqualung technology. During the war Cousteau had been responsible for developing the 'demand valve', a device that regulated the supply of compressed air from aqualung cylinders so that divers could breathe normally at whatever depth they were swimming. Although commercially produced aqualungs had been available in France and Britain since the late 1940s, Cousteau's films turned scuba-diving into a popular pursuit.[25] As usual, Wynter preferred to make his own kit, using cheap government-surplus materials (RAF pilots, for example, were equipped with oxygen cylinders). Once again, a large investment of time and ingenuity met with only limited success when Wynter entered the bracing Cornish waters to test his new equipment (fig. 92).

In 1956 Cousteau released a full-length film, *The Silent World* (*Le Monde du silence*). Directed by the young Louis Malle and shot over two years as Cousteau's research boat *Calypso* explored the Mediterranean, the Red Sea, the Indian Ocean and other warm waters, the film was a sensation. Thousands of nature documentaries have followed, but most cinema audiences had never before been able to view the life forms of tropical seas in such intense, abundant colour and lingering detail. Between them, Malle and Cousteau worked the submarine drama for all it was worth, shaking up the dreamy oceanic rhythms with harpoons and explosives when the occasion seemed to demand it. In the memorable opening sequence a team of divers descends as though choreographed through milky blue waters threaded by lithe smoke trails from their glowing flares and the bubble necklaces that flower from their

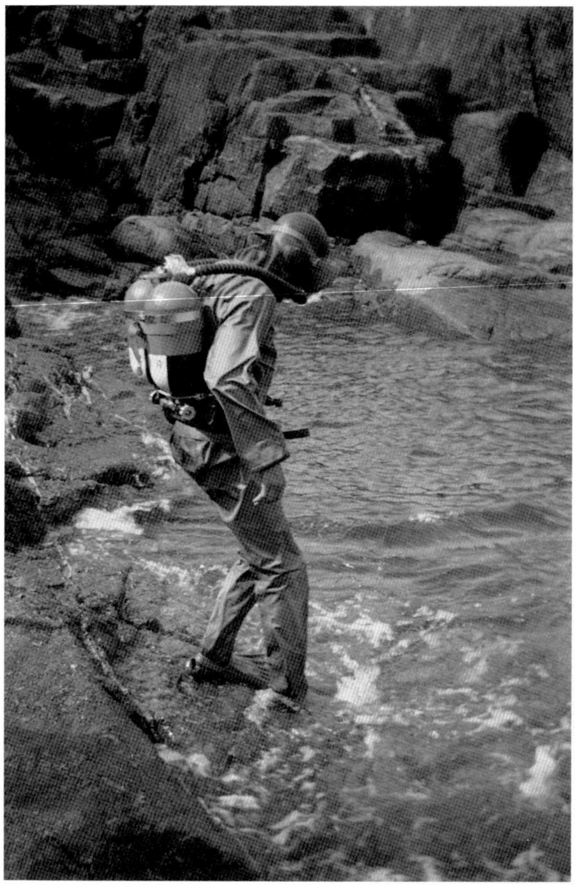

92
Bryan Wynter entering the sea with homemade aqualung, early 1950s

bright yellow aqualung cylinders. The camera zooms until the shapes and colours swirling in the movement of the water become a luminous abstract image, whose strangeness is emphasised by the soundtrack's unearthly gurgling.

In its combination of serious scientific enquiry and mind-expanding visual sensation, *The Silent World* held a powerful fascination for Wynter. Indeed, the peak of his enthusiasm for Cousteau's discoveries coincided with the rapid developments in his own work during 1956. Before this, his thinking had focused on the mind's role in shaping, or editing, human perception. In Oxford he'd read Jung and Freud; later *The Doors of Perception* had provided a bridge between Wynter's youthful ideas of freedom and non-attachment, which had owed so much to Huxley, and his psychedelic experiments. Liberate the mind, ran Huxley's mescalin mantra, and the world will appear as strange and wonderful as it actually is. The aqualung, by contrast, freed the body, so that the diver was able to move at will through a medium where such visual wonder could be experienced without the aid of drugs.

Wynter had always felt both a physical and an emotional need to explore his surroundings, to climb

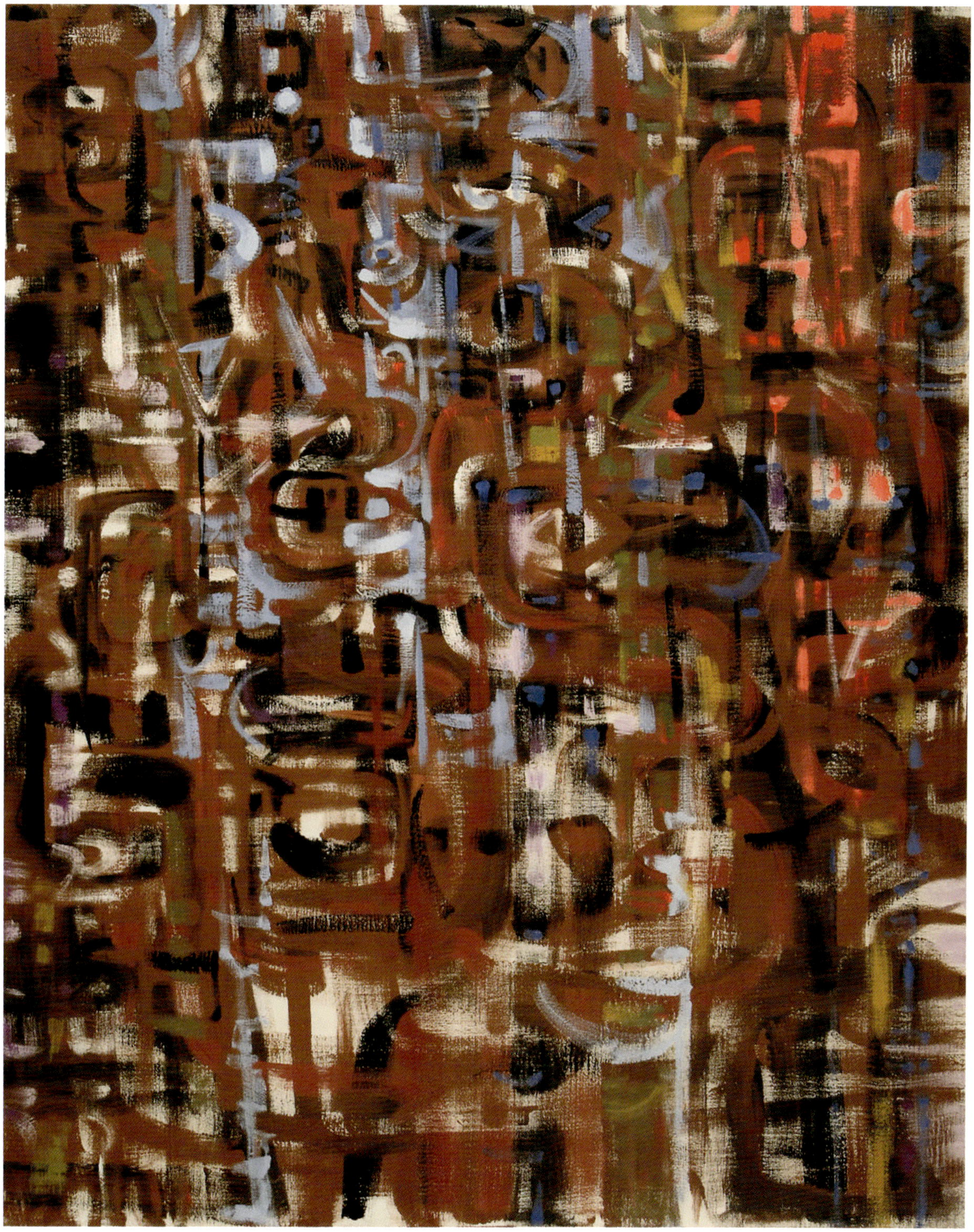

93
Source
oil on canvas
142.2 x 111.7 cm (56 x 44 in)
1957
Artist's estate

rocks, to ramble for miles across the landscape. All the same, from around 1956 onwards, the methods he used in such physical explorations – diving, canoeing, kite-flying and so on – assumed increasing importance in relation to his art. It's not that he engaged in these pursuits in order to discover motifs for paintings; rather, they fed his imagination, much as he believed that mescalin freed his perceptions. 'These divers are true spacemen', announced Cousteau, introducing his team in *The Silent World*. The scuba-diver's experience of space, swimming amid quick shoals of fish in the multicoloured canyons of a coral reef, wasn't quite what

Heron had in mind when he spoke of the 'new conception of space' that, in his view, was the mark of every great painter. In 1958, some years after Cousteau had entered Wynter's life, Sylvester described the effect of Abstract Expressionist all-over painting in the following terms: 'We are as much part of it as we are of the sea when we go swimming. We plough our way through it and in turn are buffeted by the waves ... The space is a fluid space defined and redefined by our movement.'[26] He was, of course, talking about Pollock, but the thought could have been Wynter's own.

By early 1957, just a year after *The Interior*, Wynter had found a firm place in what seemed at the time to be a thriving abstract movement in British art. To the intellectual clarity of pioneers such as Nicholson had been added the full-arm vigour of contemporary 'action painting', which, observed the critic Denys Sutton in his introduction to an exhibition at the Redfern Gallery in April 1957, 'has now become an international style'. During the mid-1950s the Redfern had been one of only a handful of West End galleries showing abstract, or in any way 'advanced' painting (the others were Gimpel Fils, the Mayor Gallery and the Leicester Galleries). This show presented a confident statement of British abstract painters' equal claim to eminence alongside the Americans and the French. Titled 'Metavisual, Tachiste, Abstract', it included Wynter alongside Heron, Frost, Hilton, Lanyon and Feiler. Also featured were: the Constructionists Pasmore and Heath; Sandra Blow, whose abstract idiom derived jointly from her early contact with the Italian Alberto Burri and the American Nicolas Carone; and the out-and-out gesturalism of Gillian Ayres and Alan Davie. The twenty-nine artists in 'Metavisual' were a mixed bunch. What united them, hazarded Sutton, was their determination 'regardless of the consequences ... to press ahead into little-charted territories', their 'refusal to be slaves of the object'. Their work was 'vivid, dazzling, amusing, teasing even'; above all, it possessed 'one single and irresistible quality: that of life-enhancement'.[27] Abstract painting, on this assessment, was a heroic, exploratory endeavour, comparable to taking a torch into the depths of the ocean or penetrating the inner workings of the mind.

Wynter was represented by ten paintings produced during the previous year. Since some these had been among the twenty-three works he had shown at the Redfern in March – his first true solo show there (all the previous exhibitions had been two-, three- or four-person shows) – it must be assumed that excitement, critical interest and market confidence in contemporary abstract art was not (for the time being, at least) matched by particularly strong sales. A beautiful work from the 1956–7 series, *Impenetrable Country* (fig.91), offers a counterpart to Heron's 'Garden Paintings' (also represented in 'Metavisual') in its palette of sappy, translucent greens. The depths here seem especially sensuous, and it's tempting to date this work to the early summer of 1956, when Wynter and Monica had returned to Cornwall. The bracken around the Carn would have been at its most vivid, uncurling and deepening in colour by the day, becoming more and more impenetrable. There is a feeling of total immersion too, a frond-like aura reminiscent of *The Silent World*. And the mescalin: Monica recalled how her first sight of *The Interior* in Bryan's London studio immediately suggested the world as seen under the influence of the drug (which he had already persuaded her to sample), and also how, on some later occasion, it transformed the fresh growth of bracken around the Carn into a jewelled sea whose shimmering depths contained an extraordinary fauna. There are hints of such all-encompassing perceptual ecosystems in the titles of other works that Wynter contributed to 'Metavisual', such as *Flowering Monolith*, *Mineral World* and *Coral City*.

Commercially, 'Metavisual, Tachiste, Abstract' was an egregious flop. Its failure, reflected Paul Feiler, temporarily 'killed the whole of modern art at the Redfern'.[28] Where institutions and critics were

94
Forest Journey
oil on canvas
00 x 00 cm (00 x 00 in)
1957
Bristol City Museum and Art Gallery

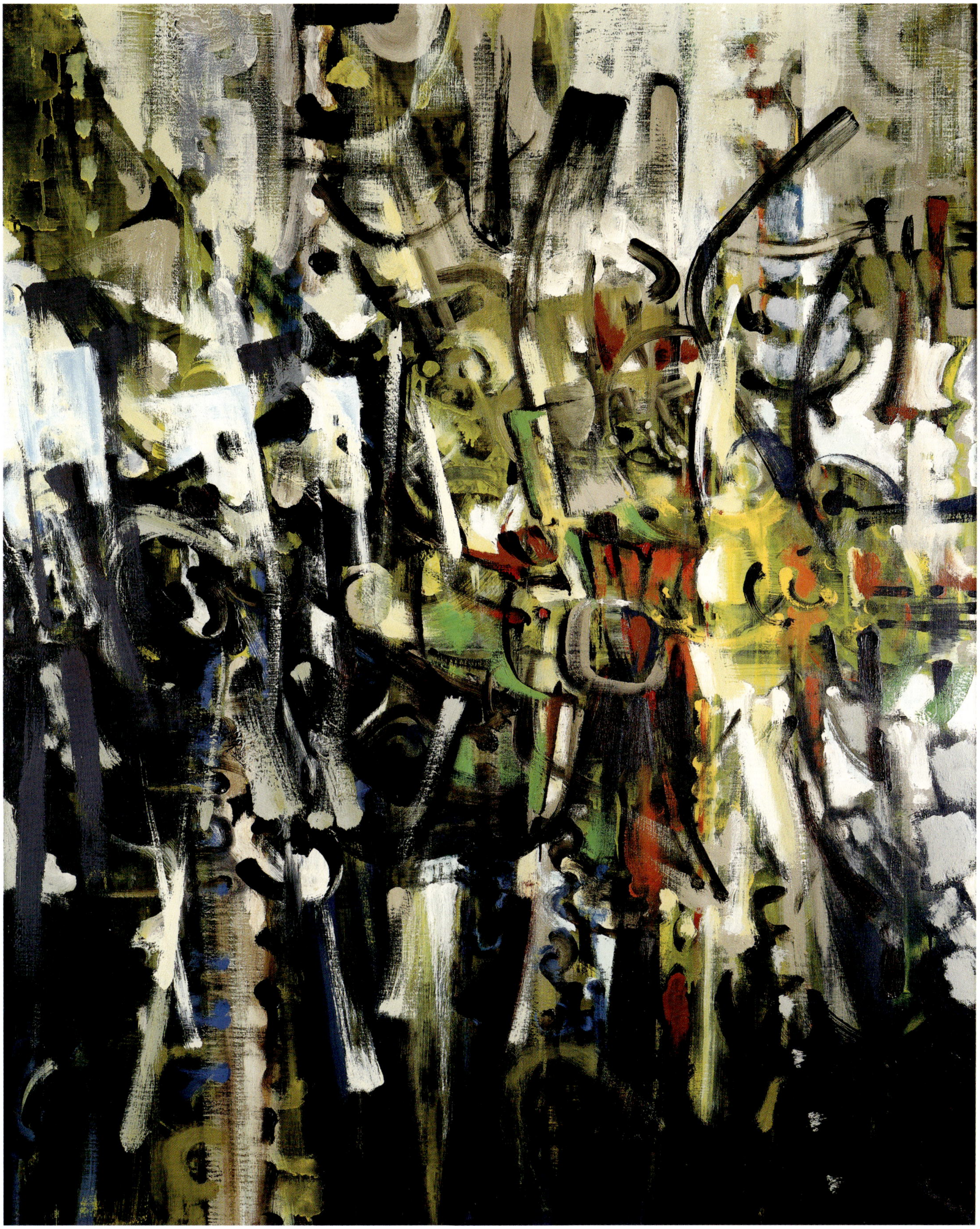

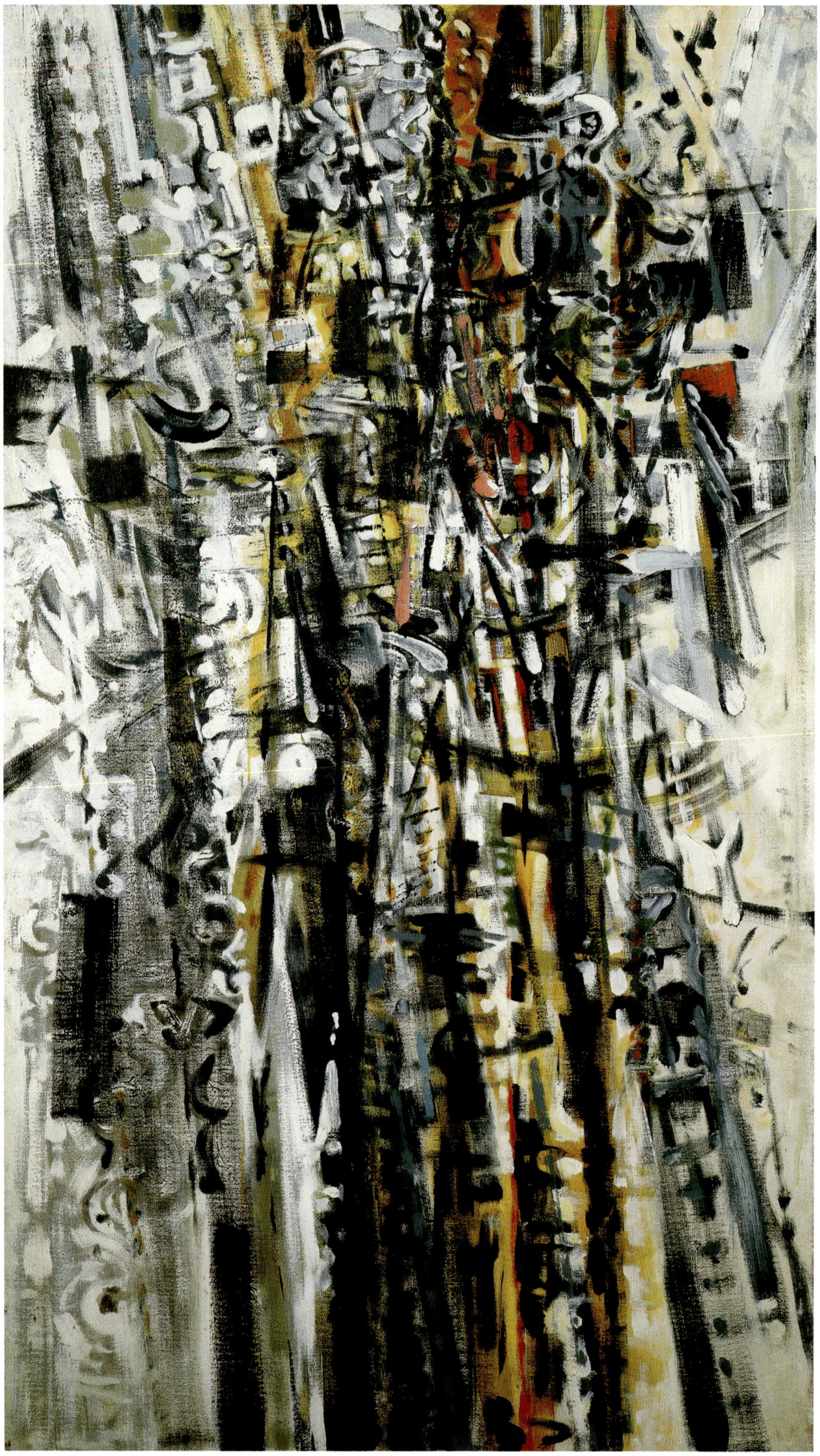

95
Unsettled Country
oil on canvas
152.5 x 89 cm (60 x 35 in)
1957
Private collection

96
Meeting Place
oil on canvas
142.2 x 111.7 cm (56¼ x 44¼ in)
1957
Museum of Modern Art,
New York

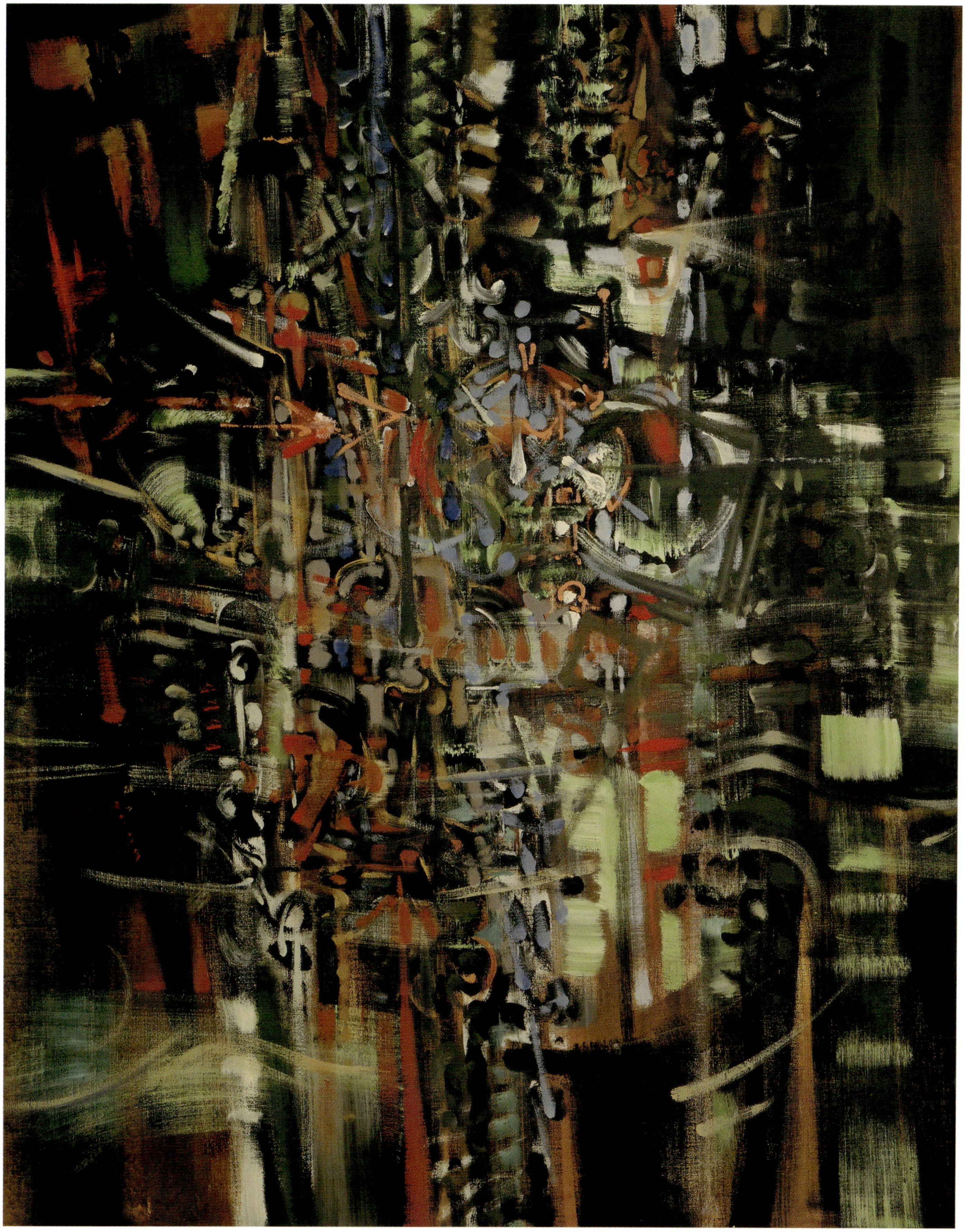

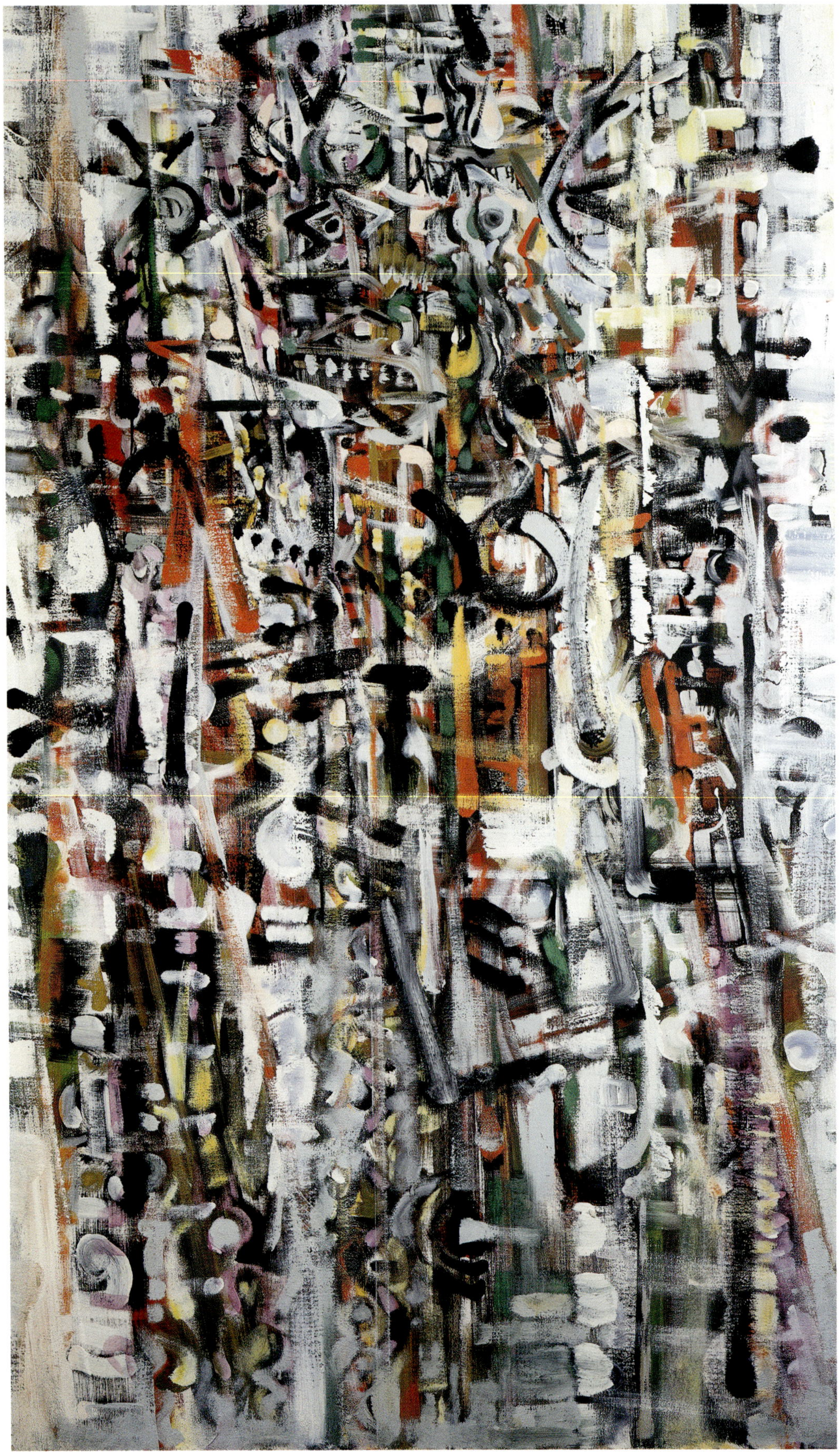

97
Thicket
oil on canvas
152.3 x 88.6 cm (60 x 35 in)
1958
Private collection

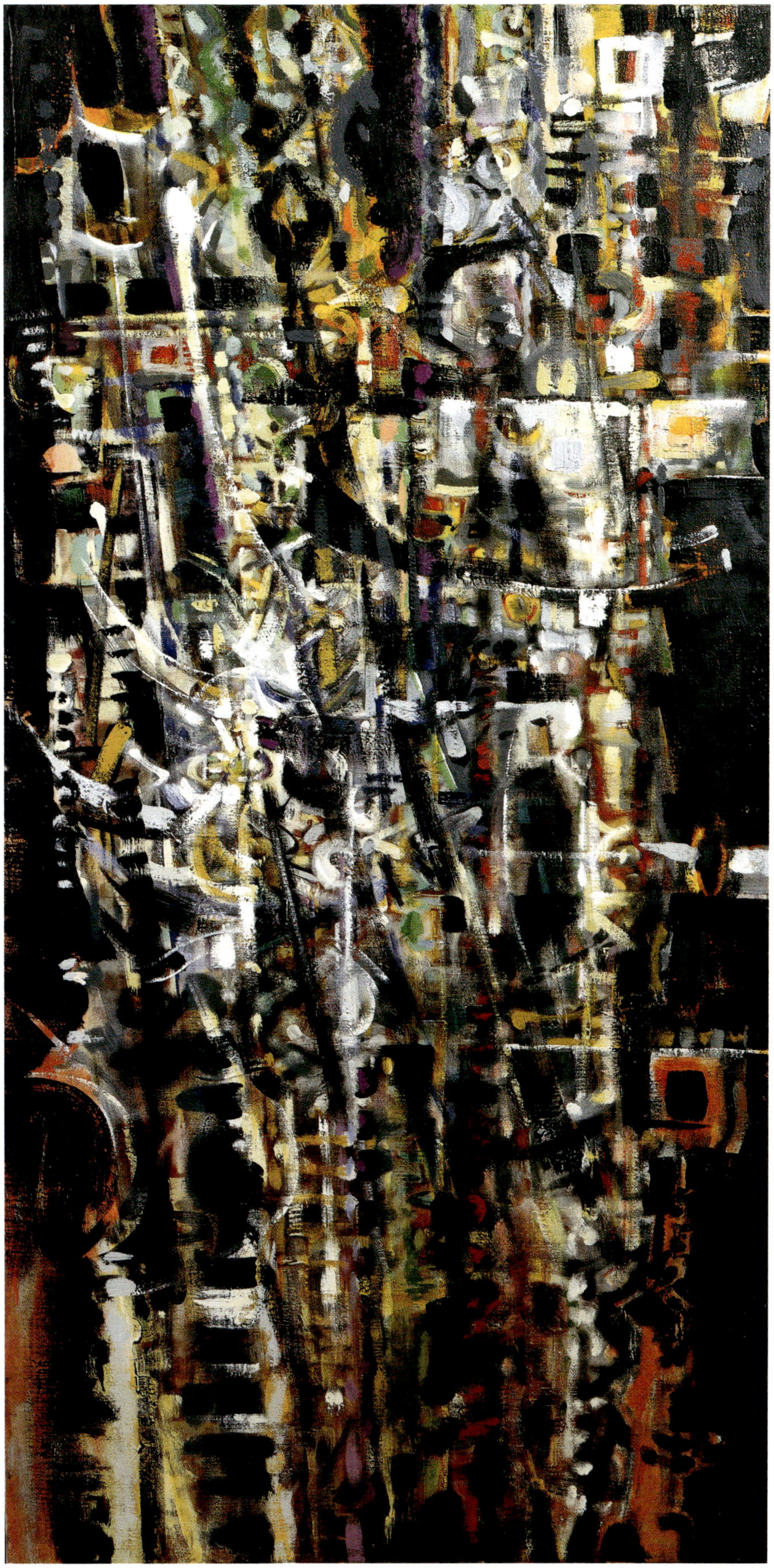

98
North
oil on canvas
151.8 x 76.2 cm (59¾ x 30 in)
1957–8
Private collection

99
Earth's Riches
oil on canvas
91.2 x 61.1 cm (36 x 24½ in)
1958
Whitworth Art Gallery, University of Manchester

100
Earth Tremor
oil on canvas
142.2 x 111.8 cm (56 x 44 in)
1958
Artist's estate

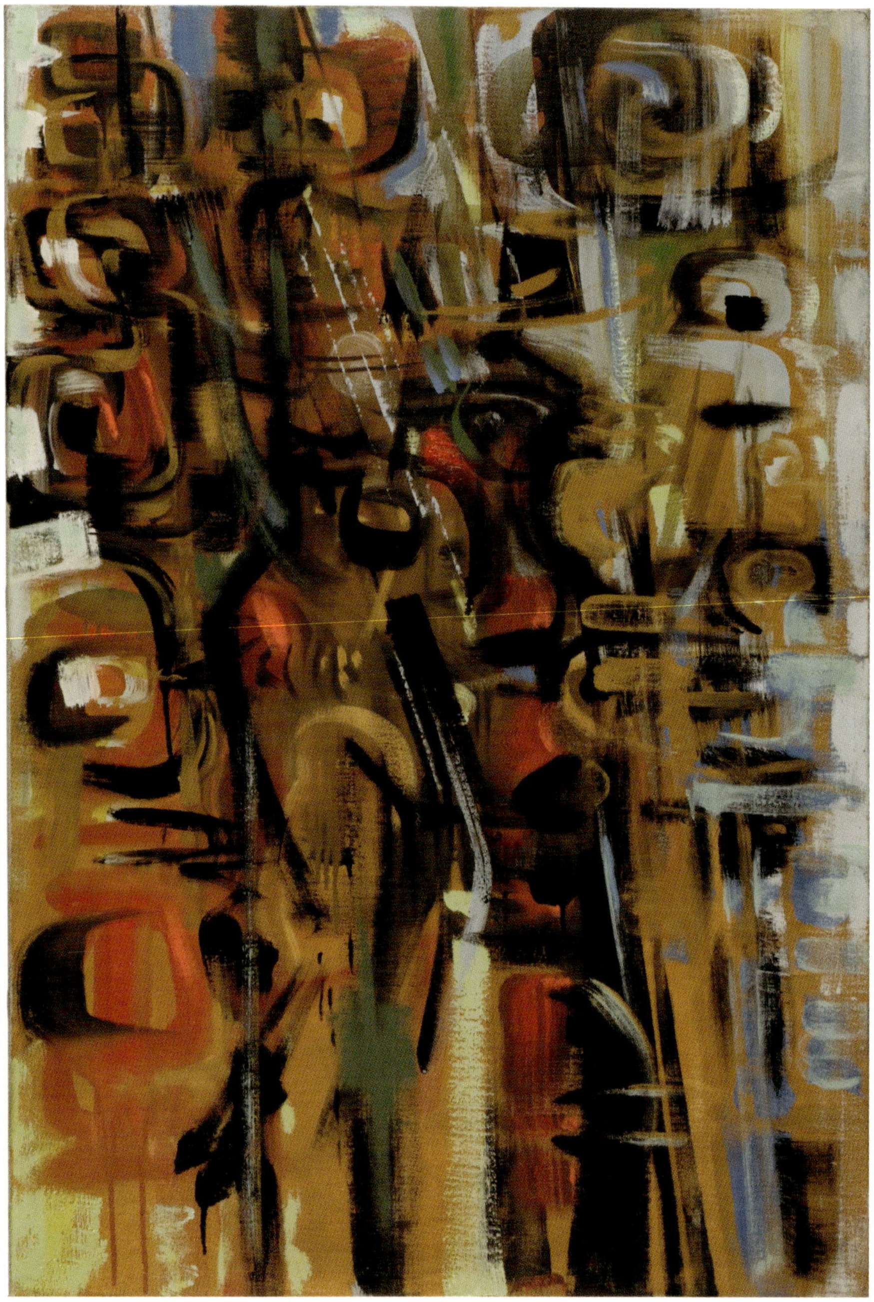

concerned, however, it was a different story. Abstract Expressionism, action painting, *tachisme* or just abstract painting – whatever this movement (if it could be defined as a movement) was called, it was, for a brief period in the later 1950s, genuinely international in the scope of both its rhetoric and its public exposure. The momentum in Wynter's work continued unfalteringly throughout 1957, including such works as *Forest Journey*, *Source* and *Unsettled Country* (figs 94, 93, 95). He was not only well represented in London exhibitions ('Metavisual' was followed by 'Dimensions', curated by Alloway at the O'Hana Gallery, in December) but was also selected for a string of international survey shows, in Tokyo, Liège, Chicago and Rome. In New York, the Museum of Modern Art's curator of collections, Dorothy C. Miller, was eager to acquire representative works by younger British abstract painters that would confirm the ascendancy of American Abstract Expressionism – one of which was Wynter's *Meeting Place* (fig. 96). Institutional acquisitions of this kind marked his arrival as an international abstract artist. The American collector Howard Wise bought two paintings, *Dry Spring* and *White World* (both untraced) and, in 1958, included Wynter in the show 'Contemporary British Painting' at his gallery in Cleveland, Ohio.

It was *White World* that Heron chose as an example in a carefully pitched analysis of British, American and French abstract painting, represented by Wynter, Tobey and César respectively, that appeared in the New York magazine *Arts* in January 1958. Describing Wynter as 'one of the most significant English painters of the present time', Heron returned to a theme close to his heart (and to the development of his own painting in the mid-1950s), namely that abstract painting was not representational painting's opposite but was, rather, the next (that is, more highly developed) stage in painting's evolution. Wynter confirmed this theory, since he had taken 'single typical brush strokes out of the context of his earlier figurative painting and built them into ... new

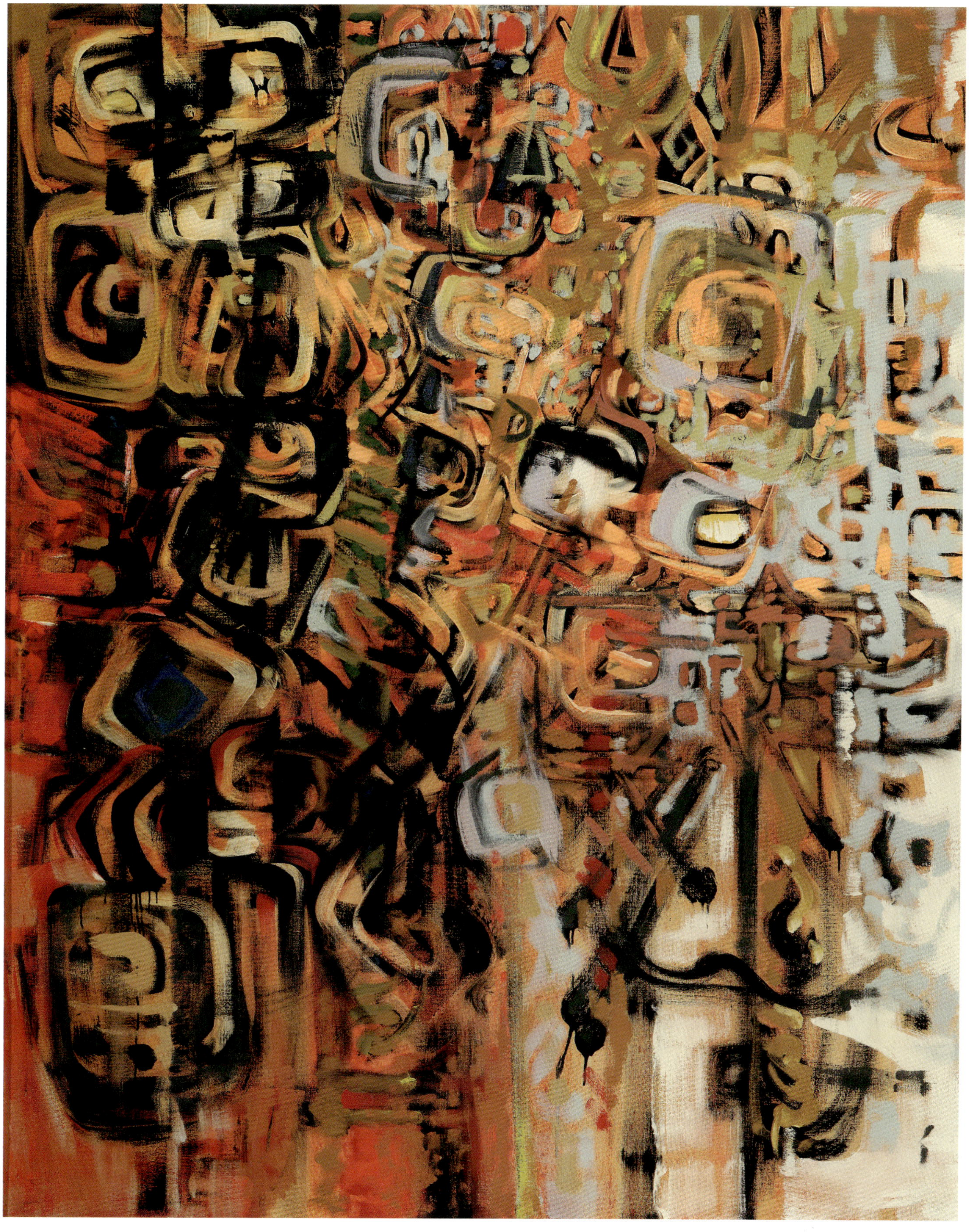

101
Tumult
oil on canvas
137.2 x 91.4 cm (54 x 36 in)
1958
Private collection

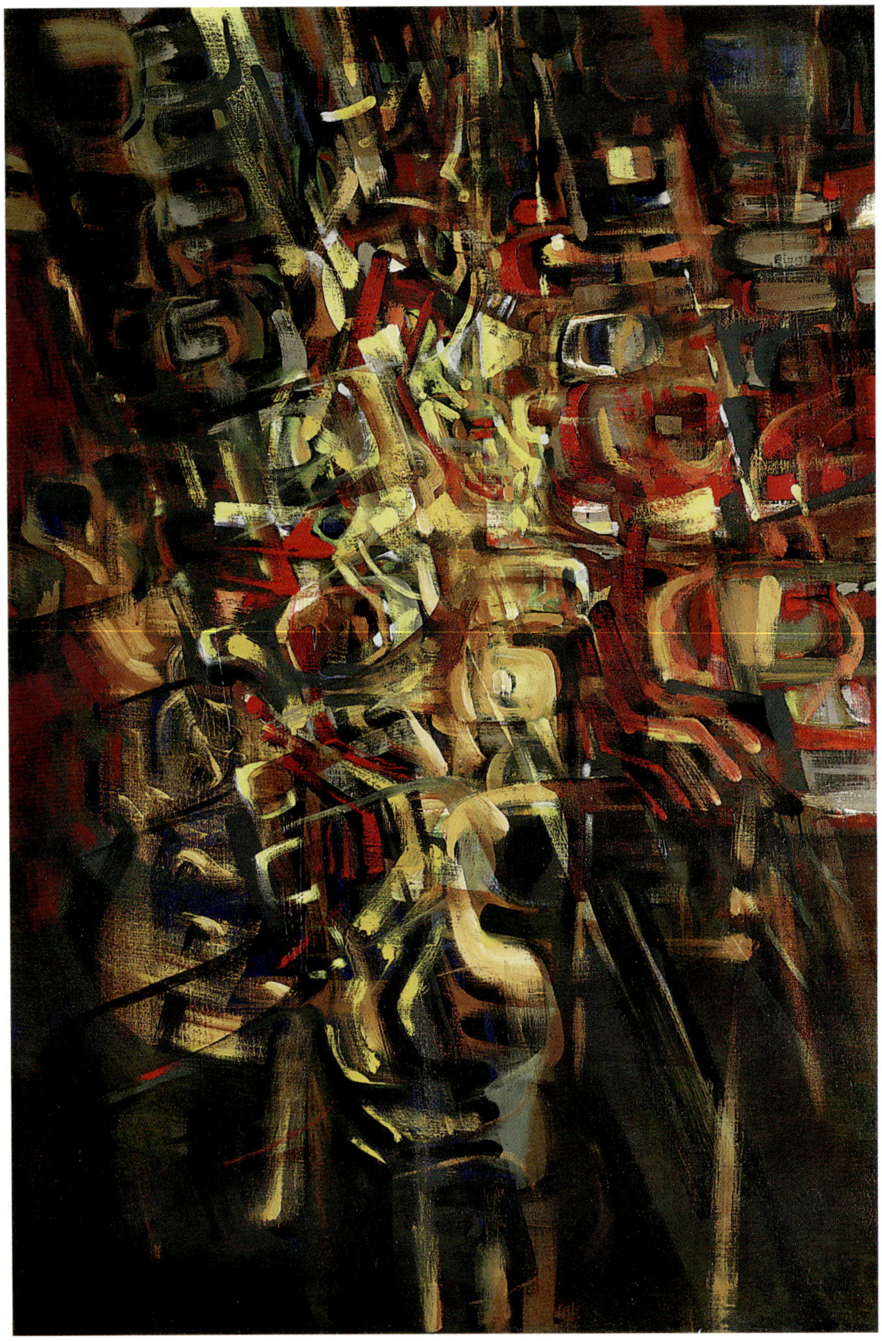

images of space, which, once arrived at, instantly connect with Tobey's'. In this manner, continued Heron,

> the vital underlying patterns of abstract pictorial statement are transmitted from continent to continent today. The colours change, the textures and the handwriting change, from place to place and from artist to artist; but a similar energy and a similar 'armature' of pictorial design persists. In *Aerial City* (1950) by Tobey; in *White World* (1957), by Wynter; and in *Sculpture Murale* (1957) by César, there are extraordinary similarities in the way in which space is so to speak *refracted* by a multitude of shallow facets or planes.[29]

Life-enhancing, freedom-embracing their work might be, but abstract artists in Britain had a problem in the absence of those rich corporate and private collectors who, fired up by collector–dealers such as Peggy Guggenheim and critics such as Clement Greenberg, had enabled American Abstract Expressionists to open up 'little-charted territories' on a grand scale. Heron's 1958 exhibition (his last at the Redfern) of the 'Stripe' paintings that had followed his 'Garden' series marked one of the lowest points of his career. Midway through its run the entire show was removed from the walls so that the gallery could be redecorated. For the time being, Wynter's output seemed completely unaffected by such uncertainties in the market; 1958 was another highly productive year, during which he completed *Thicket*, *Earth's Riches*, *Earth Tremor*, *Tumult* and *Night Journey* (figs 97, 99, 100, 101, 102), whose titles alone strike a resonant note, as though charting an epic progress through some monumental landscape. There's a palpable confidence, too, in the freer, slicing brushmarks of works such as *North* (fig. 98). Yet at the same time Wynter had evidently read the signs at the Redfern and was looking around for a change of gallery.

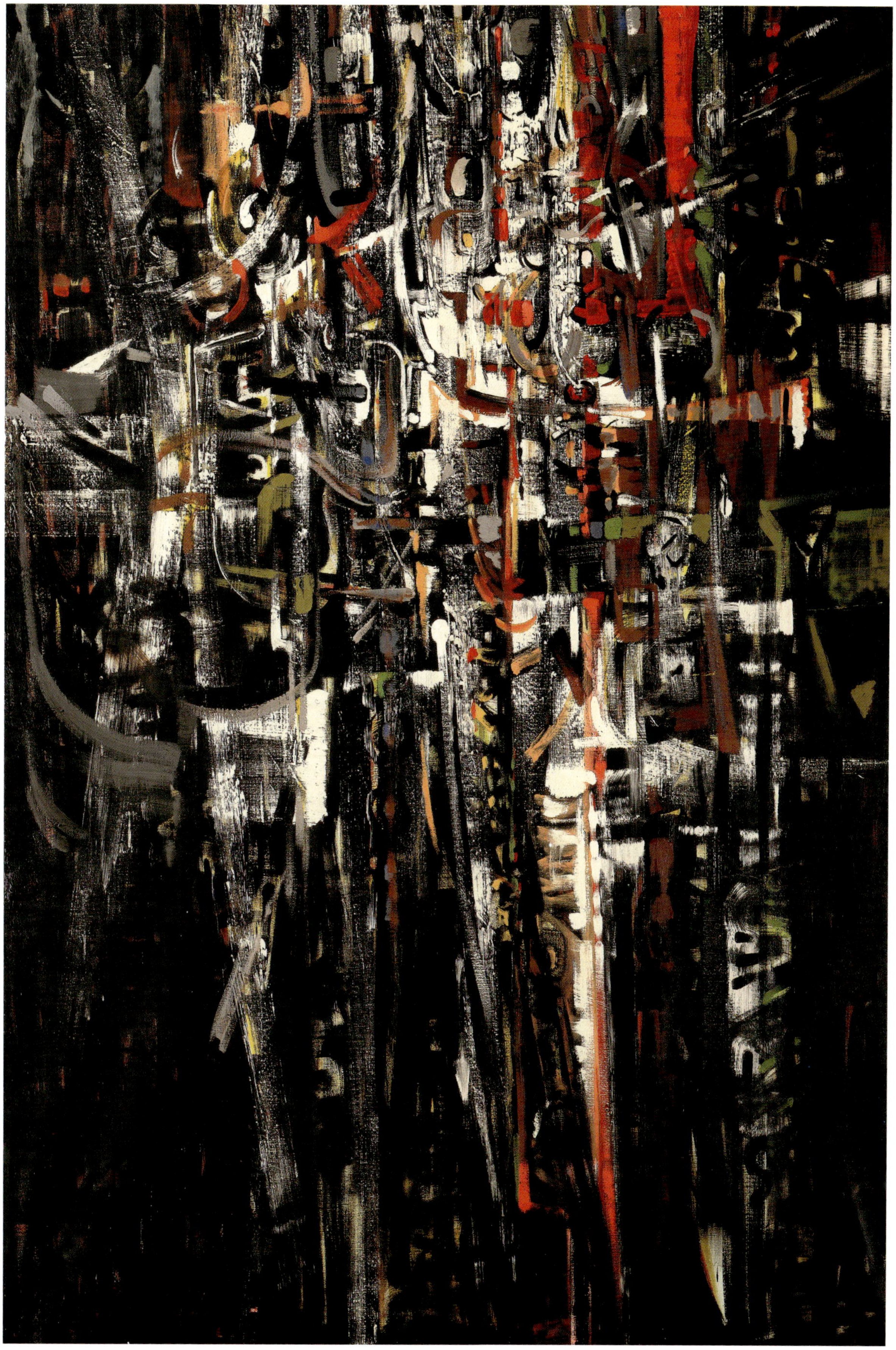

102
Night Journey
oil on canvas
214.1 x 167.9 cm (84¼ x 66 in)
1958
Private collection

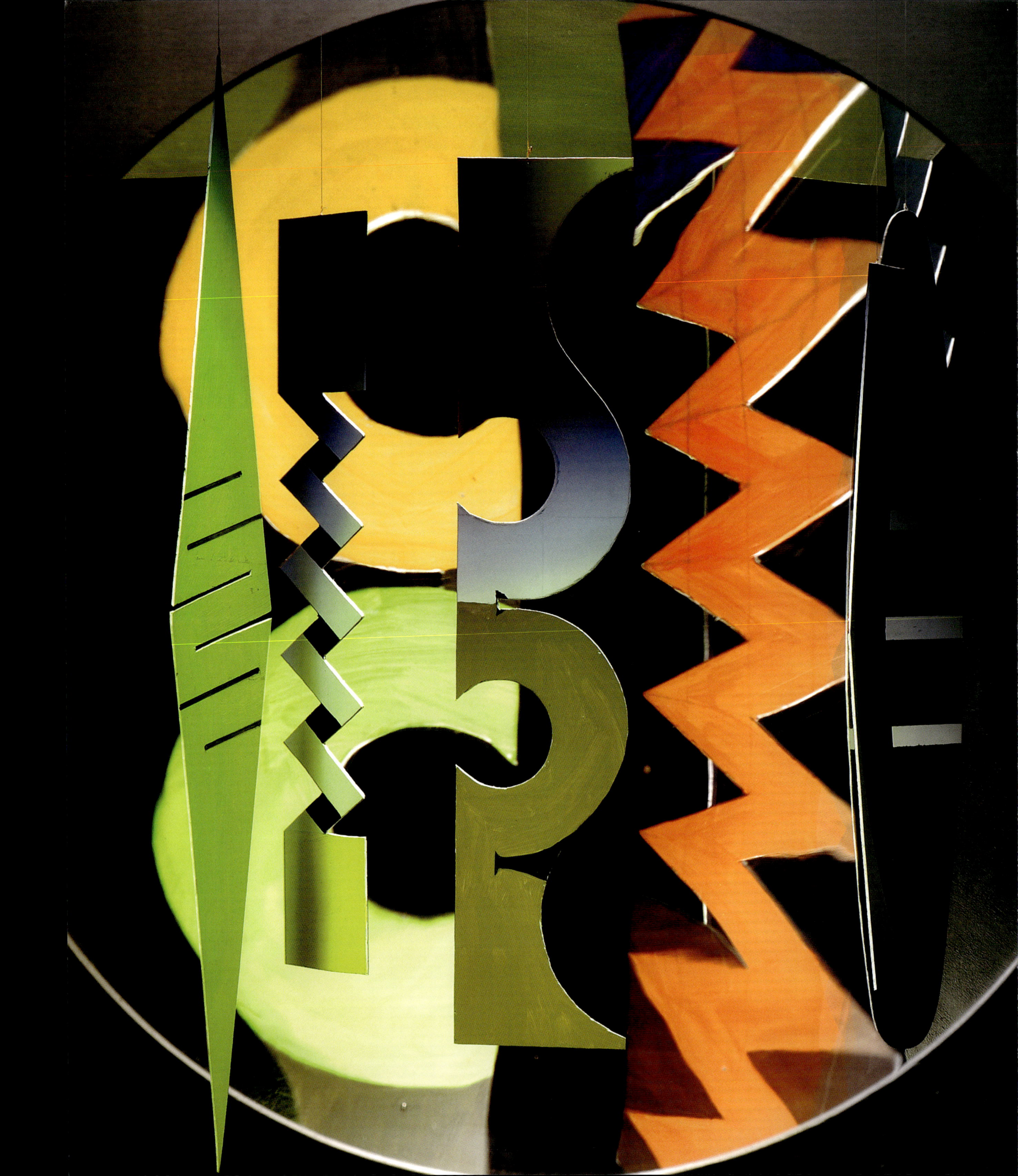

6

'Dynamic Versus Static': an Art of Movement, 1959–64

By the early months of 1959 Wynter was being represented by a new dealer on the West End scene, Victor Waddington, who had opened premises in Cork Street, along the road from the Redfern. Waddington had been running a gallery in Dublin representing Irish artists, notably the prolific Jack Yeats (younger brother of the poet W. B. Yeats), whose semi-illustrative scenes of Irish life had an expressionistic fervour all their own. Arriving in London with a large stock of paintings by Yeats (who had died in March 1957), Waddington quickly identified a group of artists who were loosely united by their association with St Ives as a suitable English addition to his stable. His reasoning may have been that, in the current internationalist buzz surrounding abstract painting, their work, like Yeats's, might go down well in the USA. He also drew on the advice of the young Arts Council administrator Alan Bowness, who had recently married Hepworth and Nicholson's daughter Sarah and had extensive personal contacts among the artists of St Ives.

First to be given a solo show was Trevor Bell, whom Frost had met while in Leeds on a Gregory Fellowship and persuaded to come to west Cornwall. Wynter's exhibition, comprising twenty-eight paintings, followed in March 1959. It coincided with 'New American Painting' at the Tate, where, once again courtesy of the Museum of Modern Art, the American Abstract Expressionists were in town, this time represented by many more works than in 1956. Heron and others might debate the sources of contemporary abstract painting, but this was no mere subject for academic dispute, since there was considerable political investment in the promotion of American primacy. Typical of the hectoring, propagandistic tone that became standard in the artistic arena, as in any other field of Cold War competition, was the announcement by the London correspondent for *Art and Artists* that 'American "Action" paintings at the Tate stood as solid as the Rockies in the face of a score of mediocre London imitators'.[1] There was, the reviewer conceded, just 'one serious challenge' to American dominance of the London scene – namely, Bryan Wynter.

This view was echoed by Bowness in a long piece on Wynter that appeared in *Art News and Review* the same month.[2] 'Bryan Wynter', he asserted, 'is now among the few English painters of unquestionable international status.' In this 'USA Special' edition of the magazine, Bowness's article, illustrated by the two large paintings *Carnival* (1956) and *Wilderness* (1958; fig. 104), was strategically sandwiched between Alloway's 'Paintings from the Big Country', which extolled the 'power and vitality' of American Abstract Expressionism,[3] and three double-page spreads devoted to the subject of his encomium, the current exhibition at the Tate. The message was clear: Wynter was both Britain's answer to the New York School and (as you turned the pages from *Carnival* and *Wilderness* to works by Adolph Gottlieb, Philip Guston, Franz Kline and the rest) an equal member of this international movement. The fact that all these paintings were reproduced in the standard foggy monochrome of 1950s' art magazines somehow emphasised their shared characteristics.

By this stage of the game numerous British artists had adopted an all-over, Abstract-Expressionistic manner of painting. For the general public and the press, who found it hard to distinguish one splash-and-drip canvas from another, the 'action-painting' maelstrom became 'the biggest joke since Moore's holes'.[4] Where artists themselves were concerned, however, beyond a certain common ground lay distinct and even divergent tendencies. For example, there was broad agreement that an artist's 'gestures' in paint should be made with an automatistic suspension of conscious control, although degrees of automatism varied. 'The artist seeks to eliminate his personality in his work', wrote the young abstract artist Ralph Rumney in 1956.[5] Wynter, who declared that he wished to impose 'as little conscious interference as possible', would probably have agreed. Yet Rumney was soon taking a different tack altogether,

detail of
IMOOS 18/1, 1972-3

announcing that 'We (artists) have no intrinsic concern with drawing, colour, *matière*, surface or finish' – more or less the opposite of Wynter's position.

Whereas he revelled in living amid a landscape of rough, exposed, unfinished surfaces, in his work Wynter always retained the high level of technical professionalism that early reviewers had noted. It was important to him that, however obscurely instinctual its origins, a painting or drawing was well made in terms of its fabrication – so that, whatever Wynter's success in keeping conscious intention at bay while he worked, an element of skilful construction was always present. Although his late 1950s' abstracts convey a strong feeling of limber physical engagement in the act of painting, he was never an action painter as the term was popularly understood, conjuring up images from Hans Namuth's legendary (and legend-making) film from 1950 of Pollock at work, in which the artist dances around and above his painting (executed on glass for the camera) like a Native American shaman in a trance.

Wynter approached a new painting with a comparable absence of plan or preconception, but his working practice was methodical rather than impulsively open-ended. He often began with a dense under-painting of black strokes. The next stage involved simplifying this complex all-over design, either by over-painting certain areas with household undercoat or applying a coloured glaze, such as Indian yellow, which might then suggest further possibilities. Subsequent layers of larger or smaller paintstrokes (or 'brushsigns') were added, often with weeks or months between each stage.[6] *Wolf Country* (fig. 103), for example, which he started in 1957, was not finished until 1961. Wynter's working method placed him exactly on the cusp between Abstract Expressionism, with its emphasis on what William Baziotes called 'unpredictable and surprising'[7] paint-events, and the much more systematic creation of optical effects (that is, effects that play on the ways in which the mind processes visual information) later called Op art, on which Victor Vasarely was engaged in the 1950s (Vasarely's term for such effects was *cinétisme*).

There is a parallel here with jazz, in which successful improvisation combines technical virtuosity with exploratory openness ('When you see me smiling', said the pianist and band leader Earl Hines, 'you know I'm lost!'). Since his schooldays Wynter had shared in the craze for American jazz that fired so many artists of his generation (even the dapper and formal Ben Nicholson worked to the strains of American Big Band music). The jazz writer and discographer Albert McCarthy lived for a time in St Ives while editing *Jazz Monthly* magazine and compiling his multi-volume *Jazz Directory*, a dictionary of every known jazz musician, which finally proved

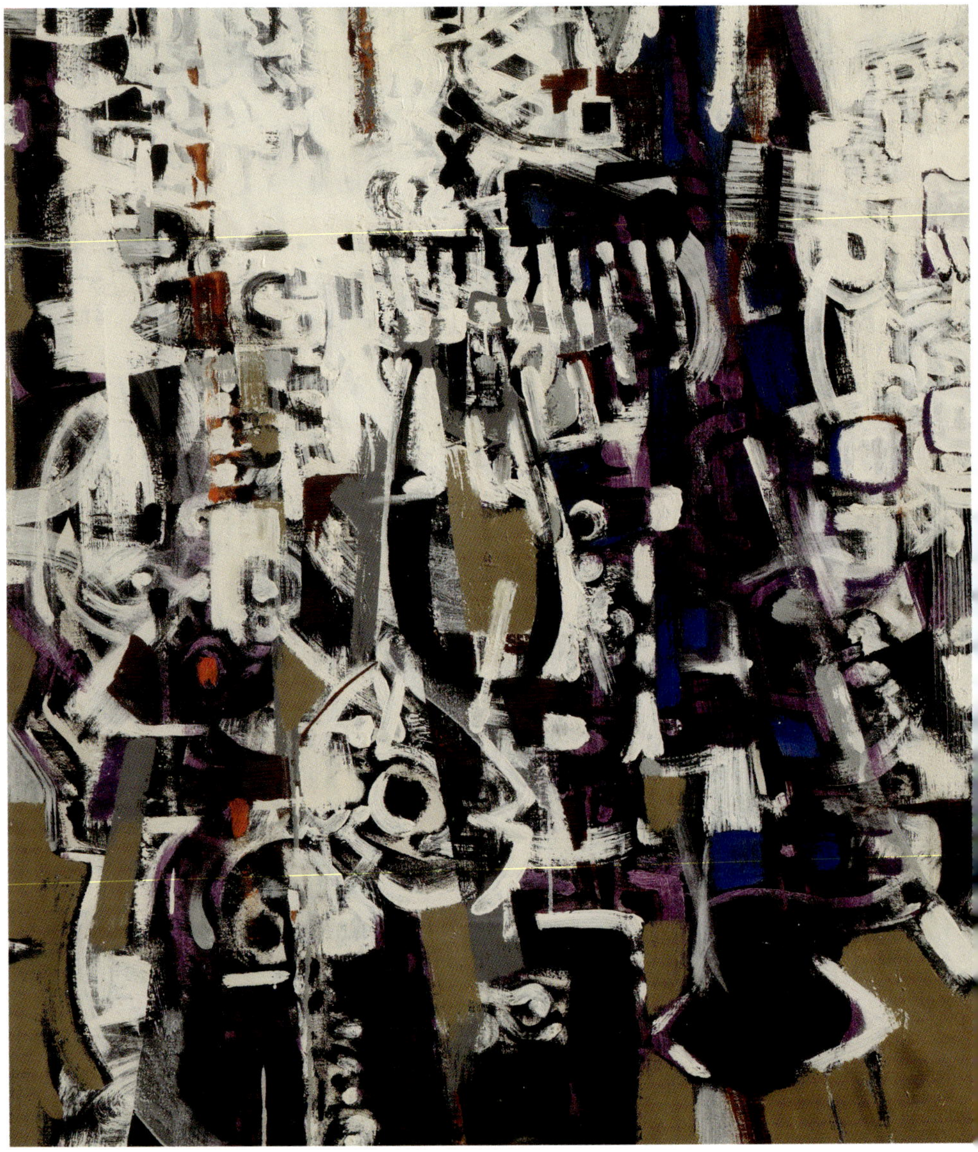

103
Wolf Country
oil on canvas
76 x 63.5 cm (30 x 25 in)
1957-61
Private collection

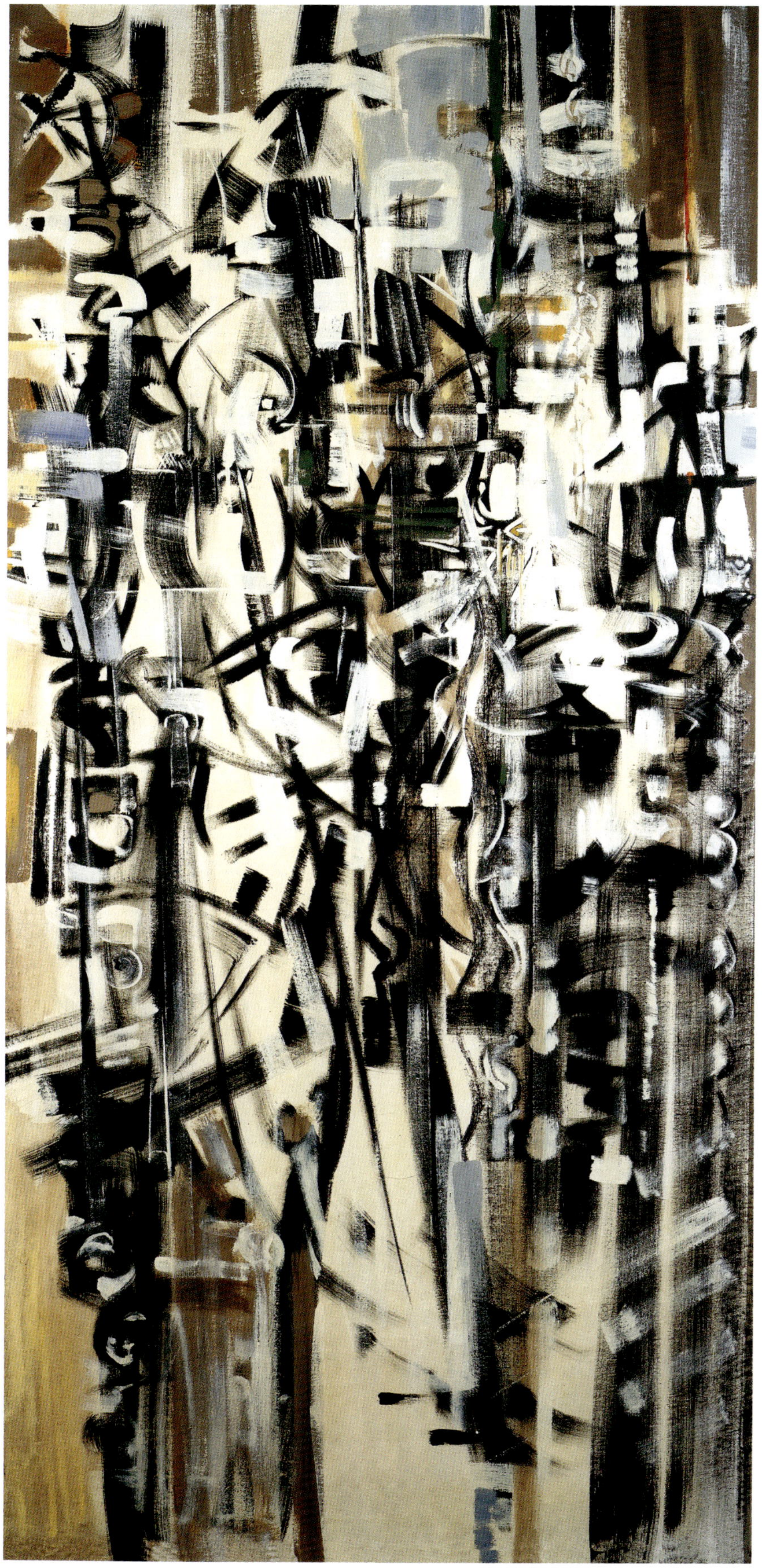

104
Wilderness
oil on canvas
213.3 x 106.3 cm (84 x 41⅞ in)
1958
Private collection

impossible to complete. McCarthy passed on the new releases sent to him for review to Wynter, who recorded them at the Carn on his reel-to-reel tape recorder, powered by wind generator. Duke Ellington and Louis Armstrong were favourites, and later Miles Davies and Charles Mingus;[8] he introduced Monica to Bessie Smith's 'Empty Bed Blues' ('He's a deep sea diver/ With a stroke that can't go wrong').

If Wynter wanted to 'eliminate his personality' from his painting, or at least his conscious personality, he was quite deliberate about the approach he was using and the response he sought. As he later wrote:

> About 1956 I was trying to create a kind of visual flux, a surface on which the eye found it difficult to rest so that, if it were not rebuffed, it would be compelled to push deeper and come to terms with the forces underlying the painting. This demanded an act of imagination from the spectator.[9]

His show at the Waddington Galleries in 1959 contained a series of virtuoso all-over paintings in which this manner of working, popularly believed to be a chance-governed affair, attained classic status. The work still felt exploratory, but there was now an added sense of continuity and assurance. In his piece on Wynter in *Art News and Review*, Bowness discerned 'a new kind of pictorial architecture ... one begins to see that there is more structure than one had suspected.'[10] Here were paintings such as *Journey North* and *Red Moves In* (fig. 105), in which the meticulous superimposition of 'brushsigns' in the 1956–7 all-over paintings had begun to loosen into freer, broader brushwork. In *Riverbed* (fig. 106) and *Seedtime* (fig. 107) the tight weave that characterised earlier canvases softens into more sinuous, organic shapes, as though these cusped hieroglyphs felt the force of wind or gravity – the laws of nature that seem suspended in such earlier paintings as

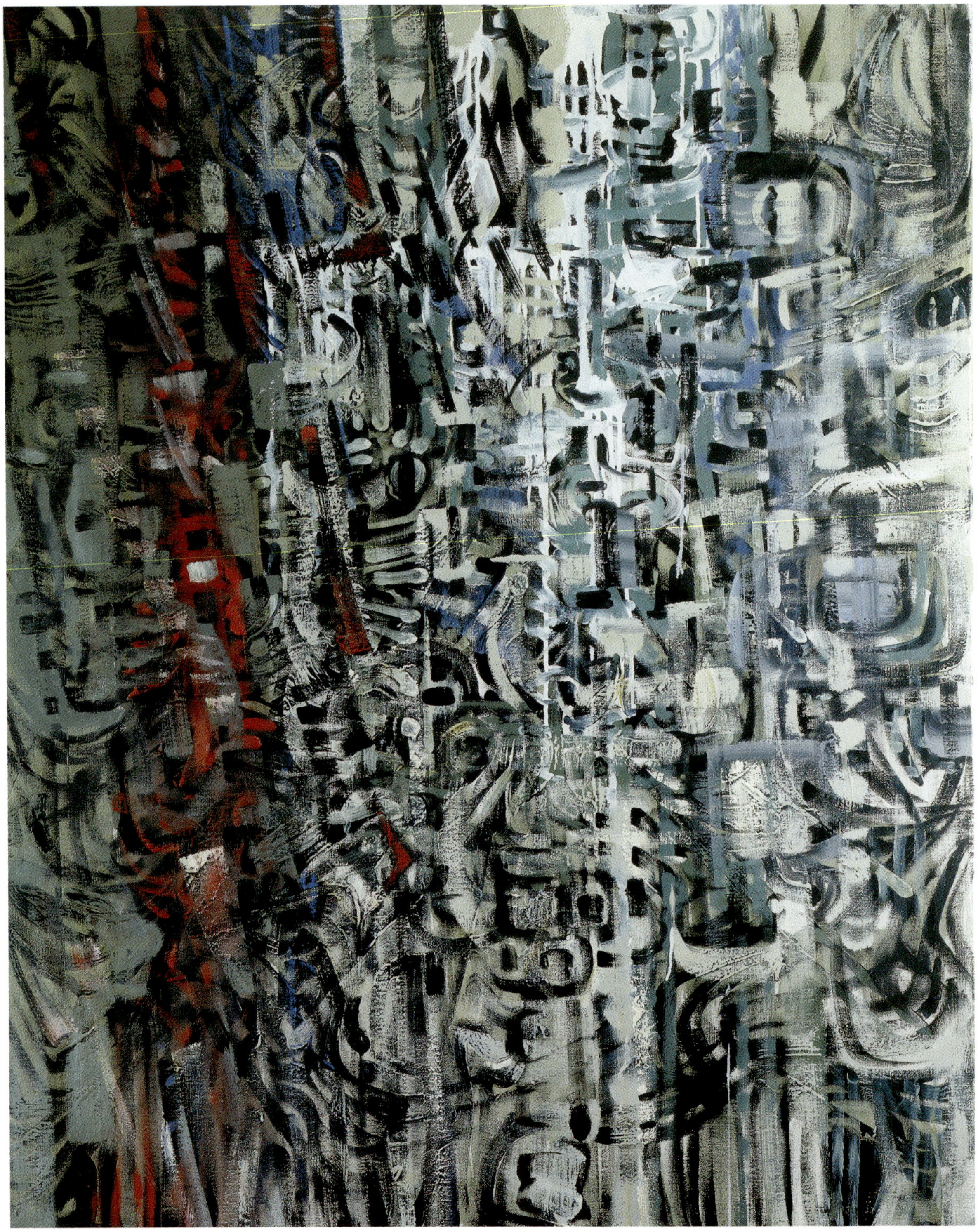

105
Red Moves In
oil on canvas
141 x 110.5 cm (55½ x 43½ in)
1958
Private collection

106
Riverbed
oil on canvas
152.4 x 122 cm (60 x 48¼ in)
1959
Private collection

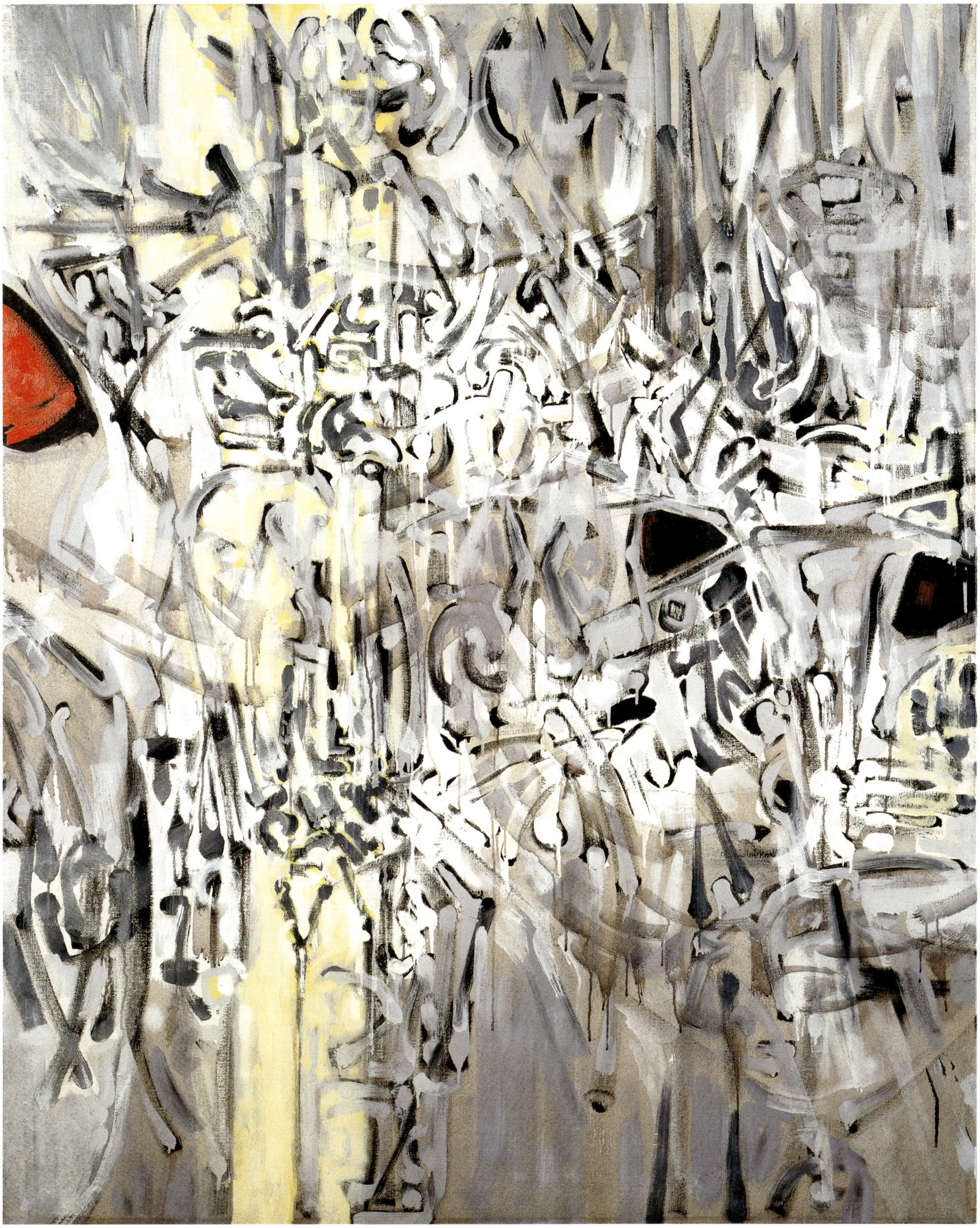

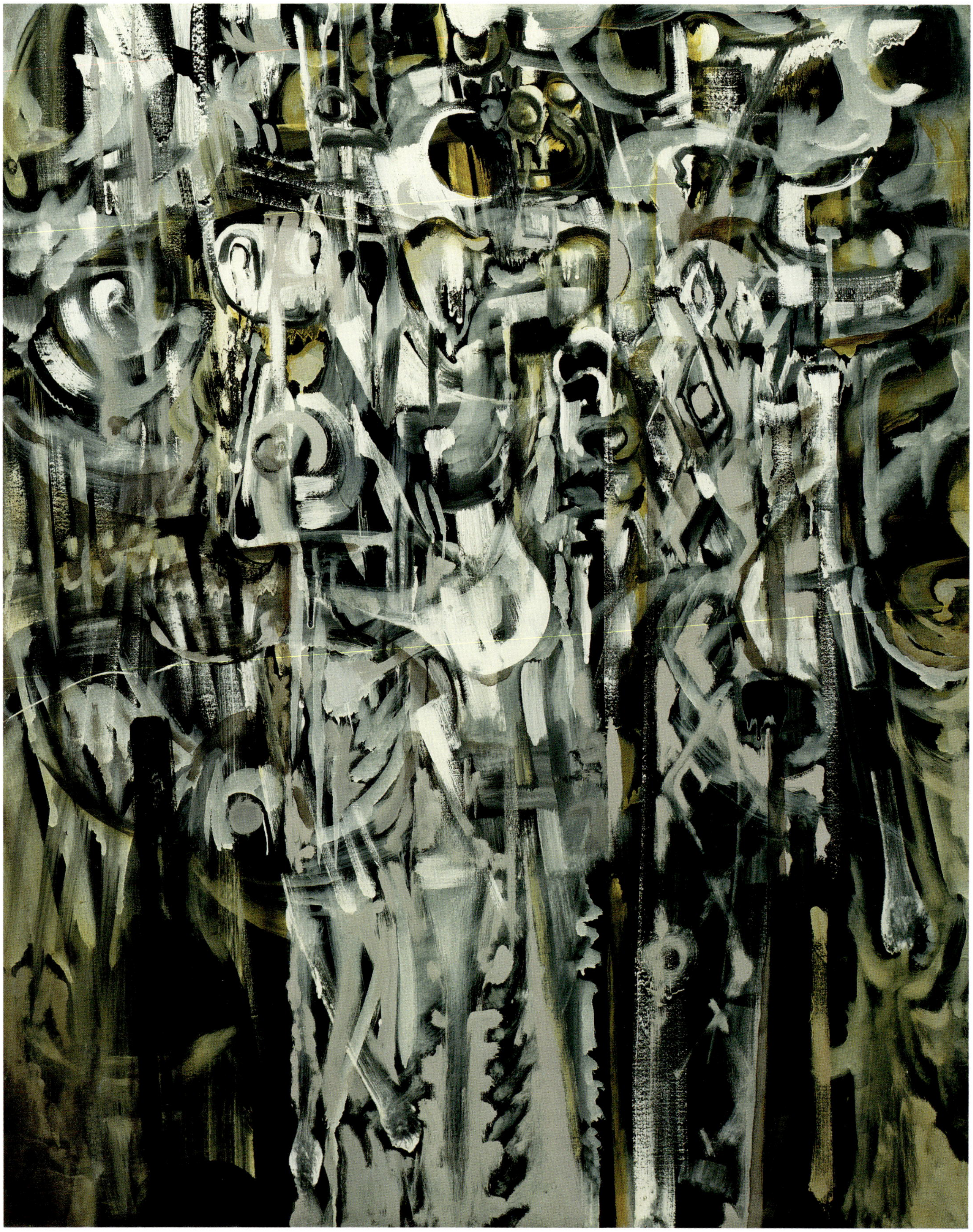

107
Seedtime
oil on canvas
142.2 x 111.7 cm (56 x 44 in)
1958–9
Tate

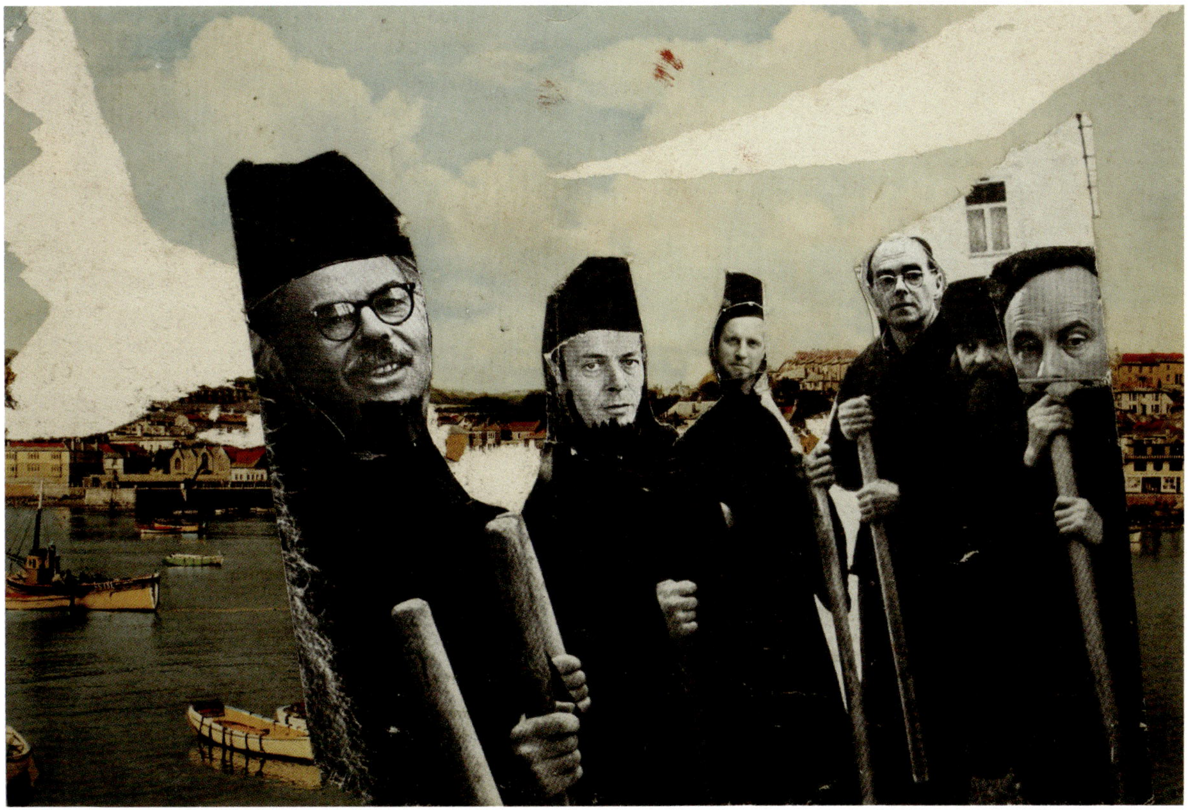

108
Peter Lanyon, collage Christmas card to Terry Frost, *c.*1959 (L to R: Terry Frost, Bryan Wynter, Peter Lanyon, Roger Hilton, unidentified Greek Orthodox monk, Patrick Heron)

The Indias or *Meeting Place*. Also clearly detectable by 1959 is a movement away from the more thoroughgoing all-over approach of the canvases of 1956–7. In *Seedtime*, for example, Wynter's tendency to locate a slightly offset centre of gravity in the upper third of a painting (at about the point where the heart would be in a standing figure) becomes quite marked, as does the correspondingly summary treatment of the lower third of the canvas.

In May 1959, straight after Wynter's solo exhibition, came a four-person show in which he was joined by Heron, Frost and Hilton . This group was billed by Waddington as the 'Middle Generation'[11] – that is, artists who were younger than Nicholson but older than others in the gallery's new intake, such as Trevor Bell or Alexander Mackenzie. All were known for their association with St Ives (fig. 108): the first three lived in the area, and Hilton made regular extended visits, working in rented studios. Heron, meanwhile, had been systematically promoting the idea of St Ives in his art journalism as the British centre of international abstract art. Throughout the 1950s, however, these artists' reputations had been unequivocally based in London, where Heron and Wynter showed at the Redfern, Hilton at Gimpel Fils (who also represented Lanyon) and Frost at the Leicester Galleries. These West End dealers generally discouraged their artists from exhibiting more than occasionally in Cornwall.

Beyond their social ties, these four artists were connected by their commitment (supported, except in Frost's case, by private means) to painting as an art form in which personal integrity and a spirit of discovery were paramount. Such a painter was, in Hilton's words, a 'seeker after truth', 'a man swinging out into the void'.[12] Nevertheless, by 1959 their work was moving along quite different trajectories. Hilton's paintings featured bulky biomorphic shapes, tugged at and balanced by charcoal over-drawing in a manner that seemed increasingly infused with a frank, mesmerised eroticism. Heron was into a new phase – his 'atmosphere' paintings, in which soft-focus, fuzzily regular and intensely coloured shapes appeared to float in a medium thinly brushed and luminous as the sea or foliage in a Bonnard painting. Frost was experimenting with the effect, sometimes quite minimal, of clusters of short lines detached from the more solid semi-geometric structures he had used in much of his work before then. None of this had much in common with Wynter's output during 1959, in which he continued to explore an all-over method using the increasingly summary, free-flowing marks to be found in canvases such as *Coastal Journey*, *Dark Spoor*, *Dispersal*

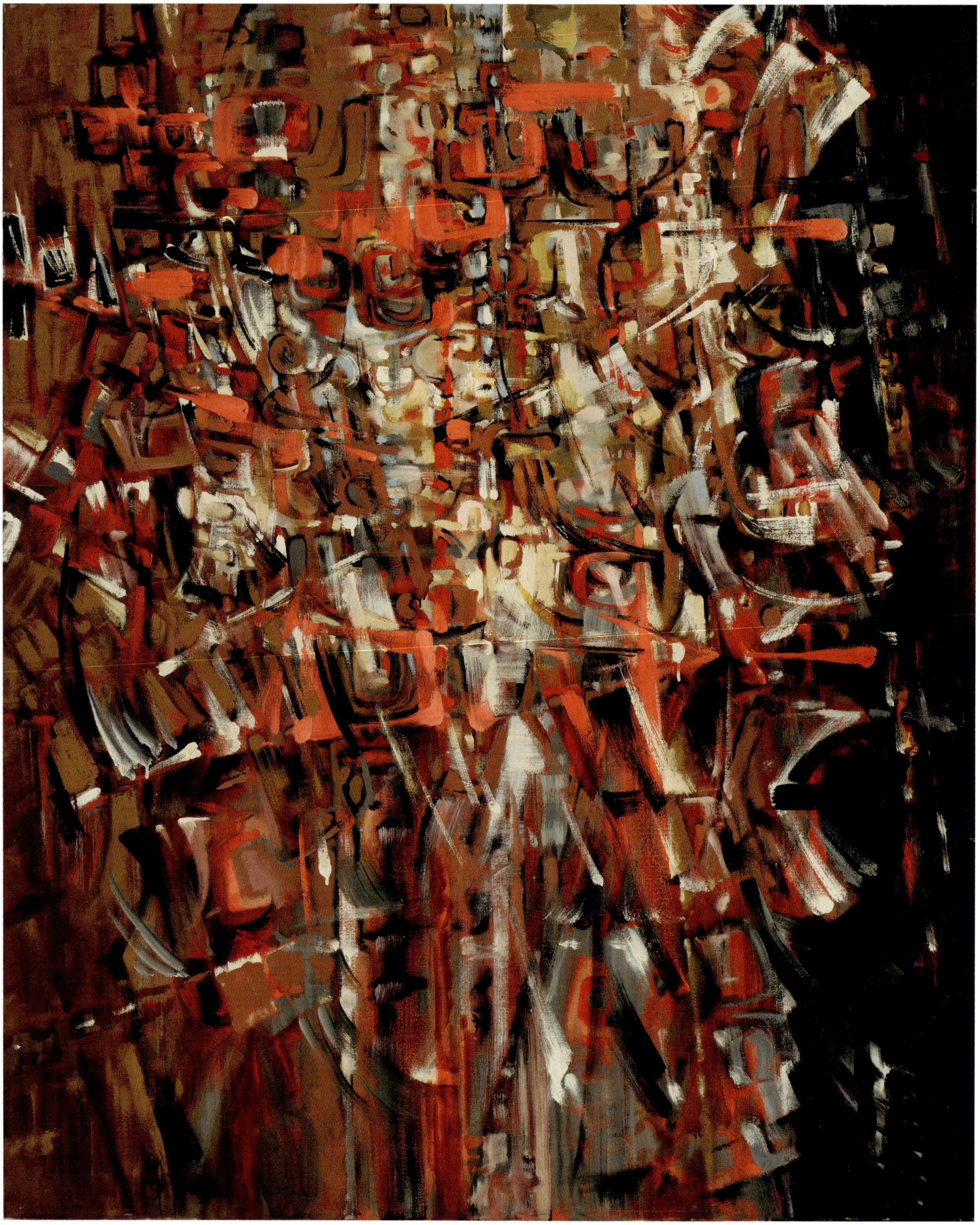

109
Coastal Journey
oil on canvas
152.4 x 122 cm (60 x 48 in)
1958-9
Artist's estate

110
Dark Spoor
oil on canvas
142.2 x 112.1 cm (56 x 44¼ in)
1959
Private collection

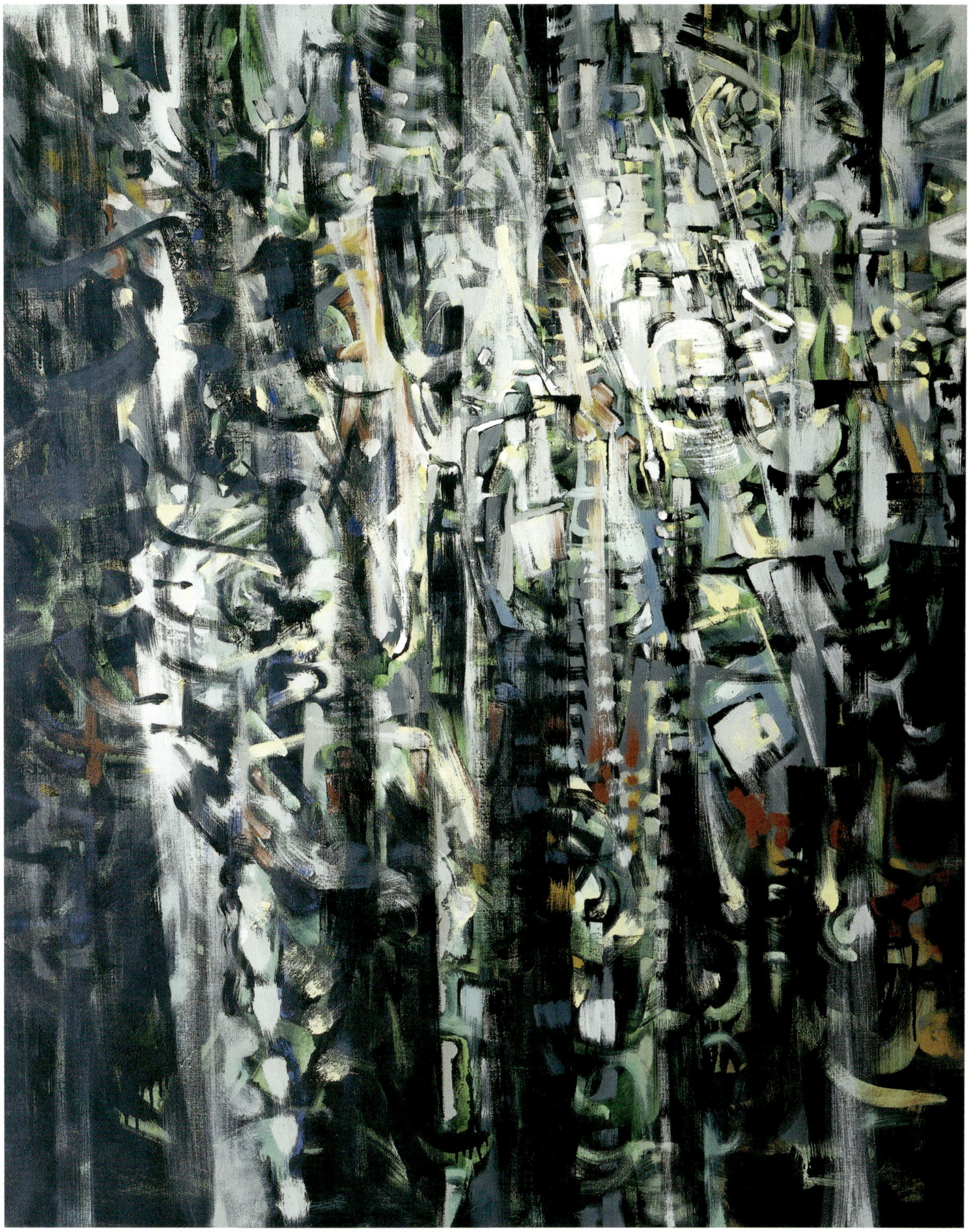

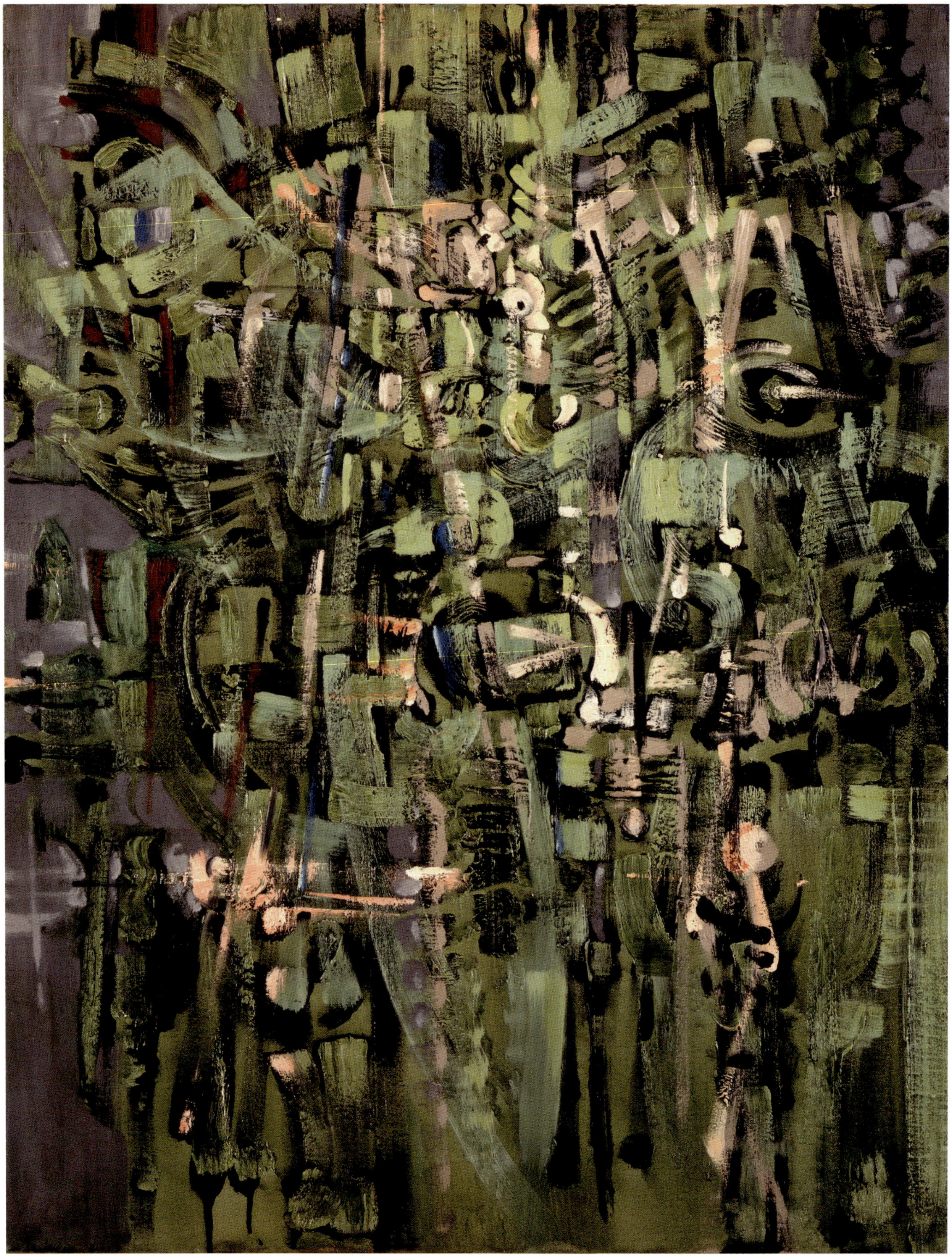

111
Dispersal Point
oil on canvas
101.5 x 76.3 cm (40 x 30 in)
1959
British Council Collection

112
Manresa
oil on canvas
152.4 x 76.2 cm (60 x 30 in)
1959
Private collection

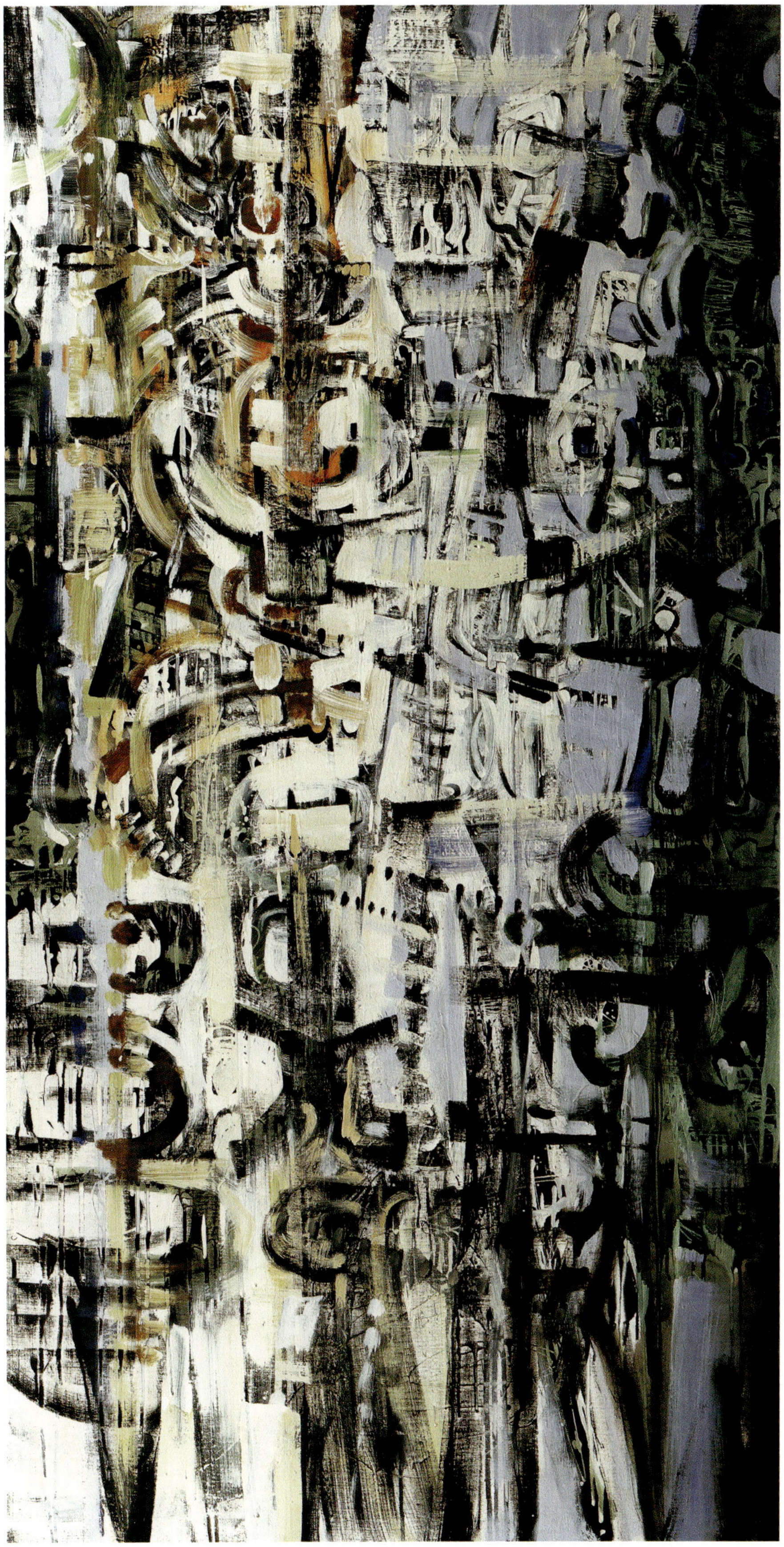

Point, *Manresa* and, at their grandest, most expansive scale, in *The Hunters* (figs 109, 110, 111, 112, 113, 114).

The Middle Generation quartet did, however, share the fact that all their careers had been delayed or interrupted by six years of war. By now they were at or over the threshold of middle age: Hilton was forty-eight, Wynter and Frost forty-three and Heron thirty-nine. It is, in general, young artists who form movements; then, as their work individually develops, the collective notion becomes less tenable. Despite Bowness's assertion that this crew represented 'the spearhead of what one might call the New British Painting',[13] it was hard to make such metaphors of youthful avant-gardism stick. And if these four artists ever were, or could have been plausibly presented as, a Middle Generation movement, that movement's fortunes were not helped by Heron's decision to abandon criticism for good. 'I don't want, any more, to *explain*; or to analyse; or to persuade', he had written to Herbert Read in February 1959: 'I want only to go on creating my images of atmospheric colour.'[14] And that was it (at least, for five years or so) from Heron, the Middle Generation's chief advocate and critical voice.

It was difficult, as Bowness conceded, to tell where these painters might collectively be heading; instead 'one must concentrate on the realities of colour and form and space and design, and trust that something will happen.'[15] 'Trust', perhaps, demanded a more patient approach to artistic development than the market was likely to tolerate. The late 1950s were, recalled Bowness, 'the Sylvester moment' in British art,[16] when the critic David Sylvester's interest in Francis Bacon, in particular, began to shift the balance of educated taste firmly in favour of figurative painting. Sylvester had written approvingly of Pasmore and the Constructionists but had been scathing about the British gestural abstract contingent in the 1957 show 'Dimensions'. In his view, 'whereas the Americans have improvised on their canvases with the positive and unafraid intention of turning those canvases into live *things*, for these British

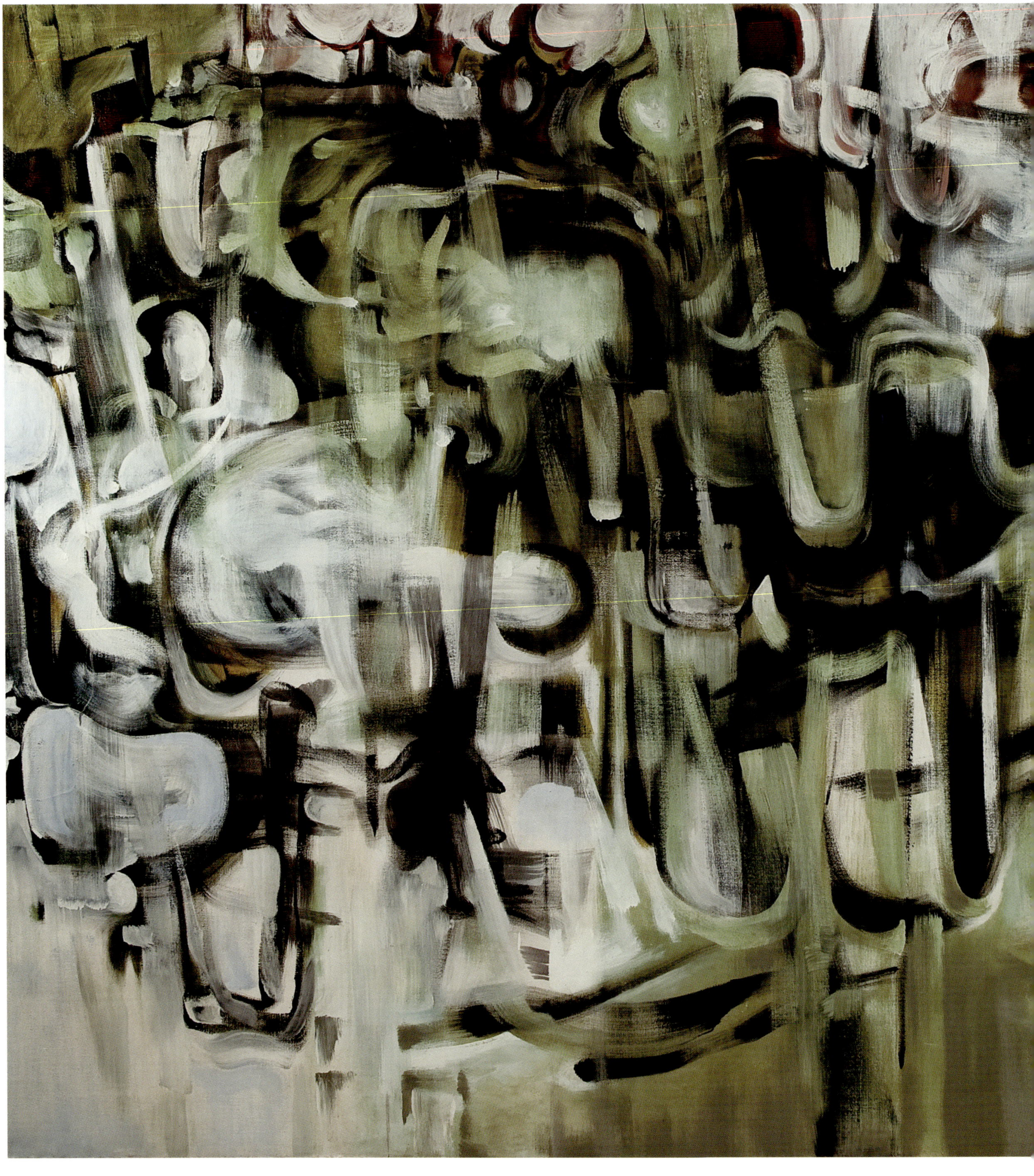

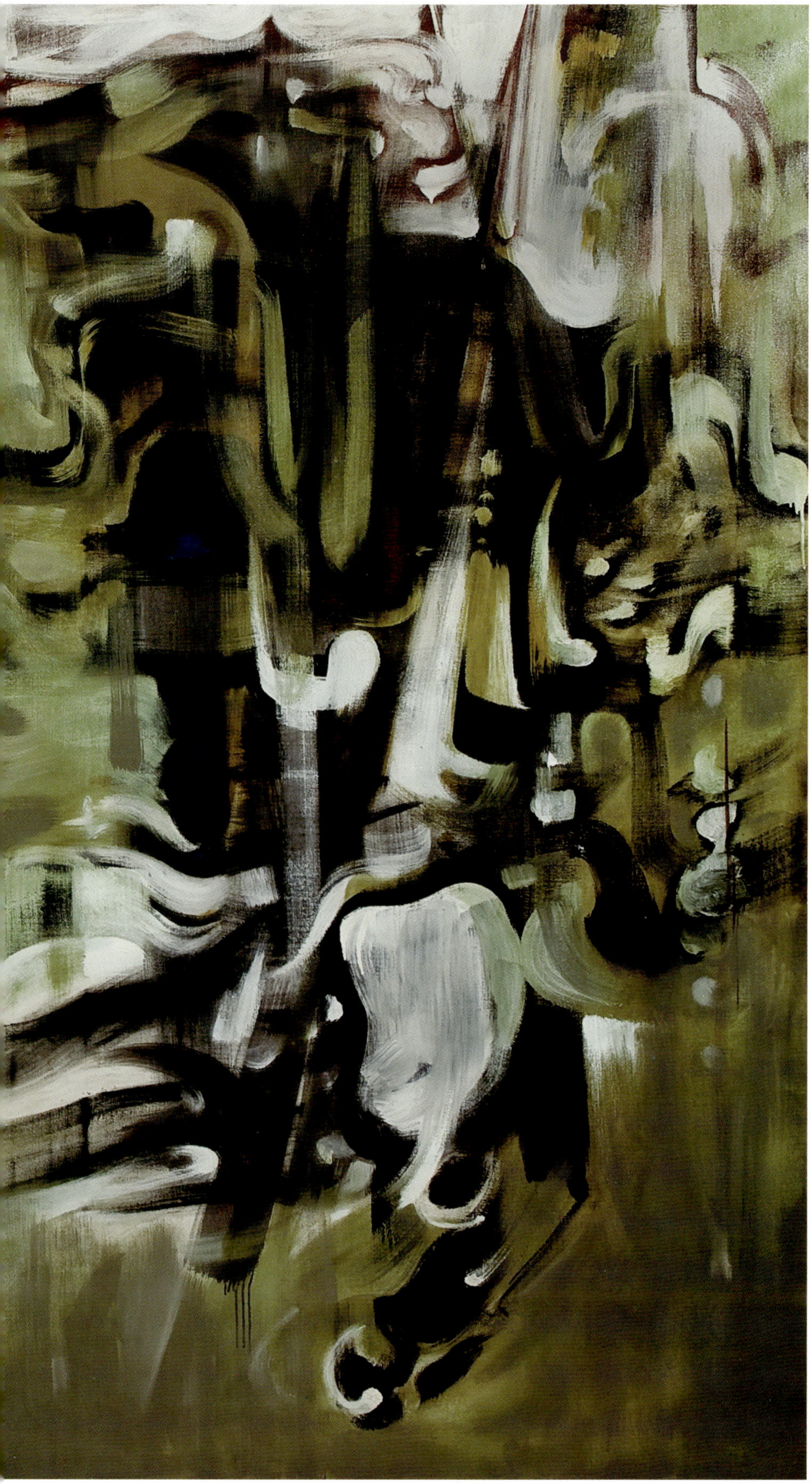

113
The Hunters
oil on canvas
183 x 274.4 cm (72 x 108 in)
1959
Private collection

painters improvisation has meant playing about with paint on the assumption that if they go on long enough something is bound to turn up.'[17]

What turned up just a year or two later spelled the end of any hope that the Middle Generation would be seen as the 'spearhead' of contemporary British painting. While the figurative *gravitas* of painters such as Bacon and Lucian Freud climbed in critical esteem, there were attempts to promote a new kind of abstract painting: huge canvases painted with hard-edged designs in flat, strong colour, as featured in the 'Situation' exhibitions organised by Alloway, which explicitly excluded any artist suspected of 'St Ives' affinities. At the same time, younger artists emerging from the Royal College of Art in the early 1960s were turning the Independent Group's earlier, earnest vision of a marriage between fine art and mass media into the lighter, brighter reality of Pop. David Hockney and his generation had no time for the Abstract Expressionist notion that painting should equate, in Robert Motherwell's sonorous phrases, to 'voyaging into the night', or the idea that 'the function of the artist is to make the spiritual so that it is there to be possessed'.[18] Why shouldn't painting, instead, be witty, illustrative, fashion-conscious and at ease with consumer culture and the mass media? This spirit touched even west Cornwall. In July 1961 *The Tatler* fashion magazine ran a feature titled 'Le Quartier St Ives'; Lanyon, Heron, Frost and other artists posed with varying degrees of cool for the photographer Ida Kar. Wynter was unavailable, although Monica Wynter (the couple had married in 1959) appears with their young son Tom.

Never much concerned with art world fashions, yet somehow infallibly tuned in to new developments, Wynter was in 1960 already on to the next thing. It had appeared in the form of circular mirror, originally part of a Second World War searchlight, given to Wynter by the artist Bill Redgrave, who for some years ran a summer painting school in St Ives with Lanyon and Frost. The convex, or

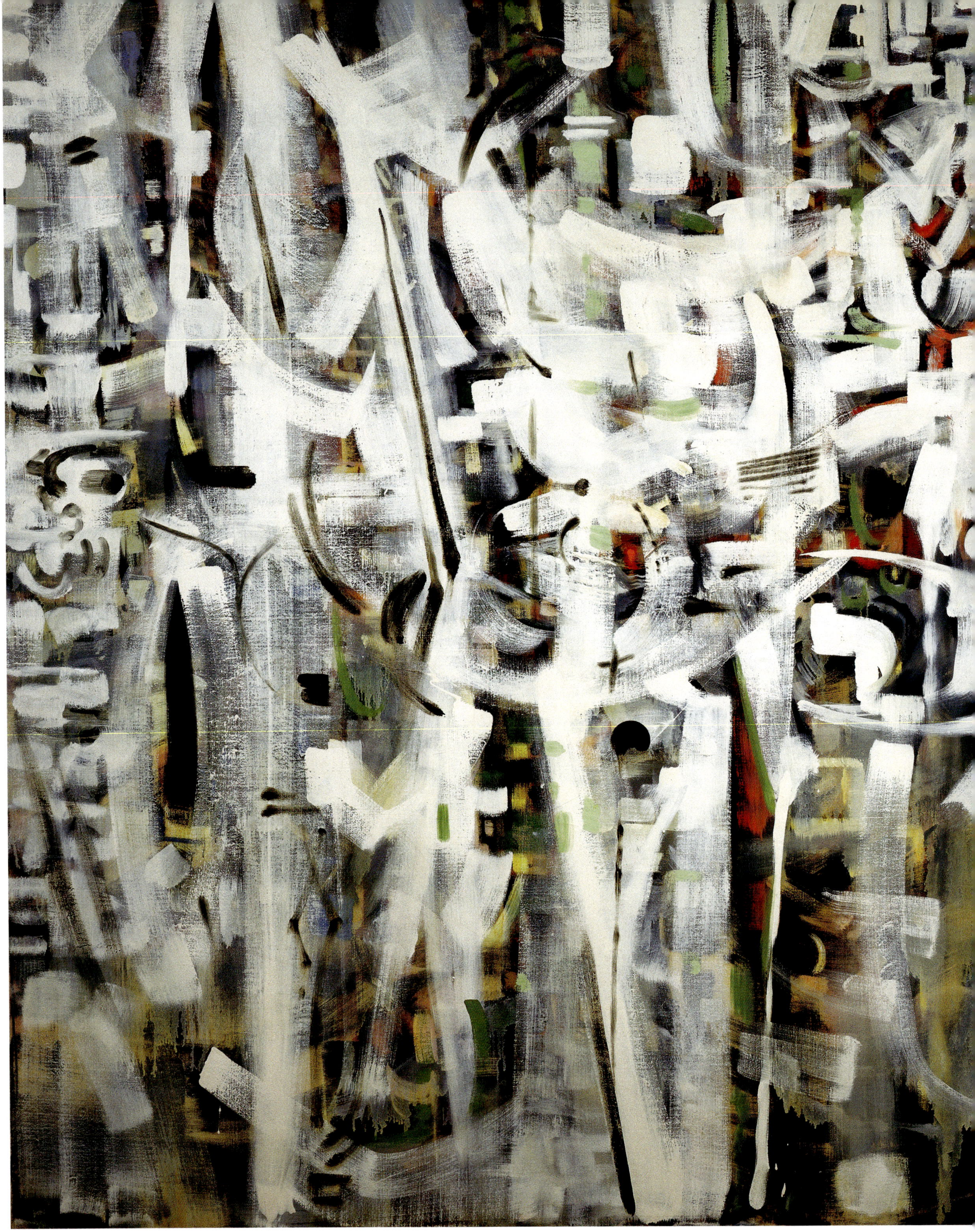

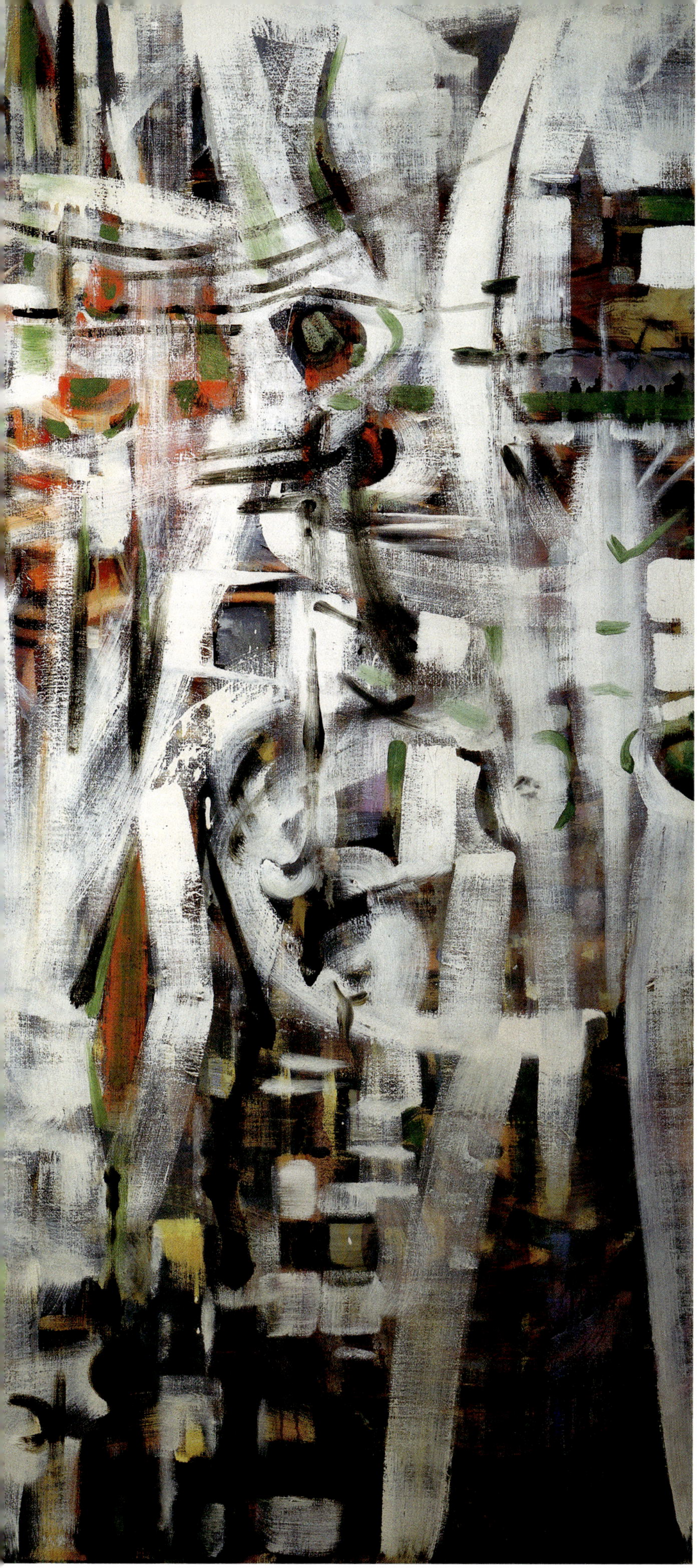

114
Untitled
oil on canvas
167.6 x 213.3 cm (66 x 84 in)
c.1959
Private collection

parabolic, searchlight mirror had the property of making reflections seem to hover in front of the glass rather than, as in flat mirrors, behind it. For a while it stayed propped up in the studio at the Carn, a visual curio whose purpose was yet to be defined. Once again Wynter's domestic surroundings became the starting point for a fresh departure in his art. Over the years, inspired by Alexander Calder's mobiles (one of which had hung in the Abstract Expressionist room at the Tate in 1956), Wynter had made several mobiles and had observed the effects created by suspending one in front of an ordinary mirror. The constant, leisurely rotation of a mobile's facets in relation to each other and to the viewer evoked certain qualities in Wynter's all-over paintings, in which 'deep' marks seem constantly to rise to the surface and vice versa. At the same time, the physical movement of a mobile's parts supplied a dynamic element that was absent from a painting. Wynter discovered that, by placing the searchlight mirror beneath or behind a mobile, the range of visual effects was hugely multiplied. Shapes swung out, shrinking and swelling as they moved, emerging into full, sharp focus as other shapes dissolved behind them. Some time in late 1959 or early 1960 he took these observations a stage further and constructed the first of the kinetic works he would eventually term Images Moving Out Onto Space, or IMOOS (fig. 115).

Within a cubic wooden box, painted black inside, he installed the parabolic mirror on one side, opposite a large round aperture through which the viewer looked. In between, suspended on steel wires, which hung parallel to the roof of the box, was an abstract mobile consisting of several 'elements' cut with great precision from card and decorated with simple, colourful geometric designs in acrylic paint – a different design on each side. Set atop the box was a small electric motor (one of Wynter's huge collection of finds from government surplus stores) to which magnets were attached on rods. As the magnets swung round, they moved the steel wires beneath with

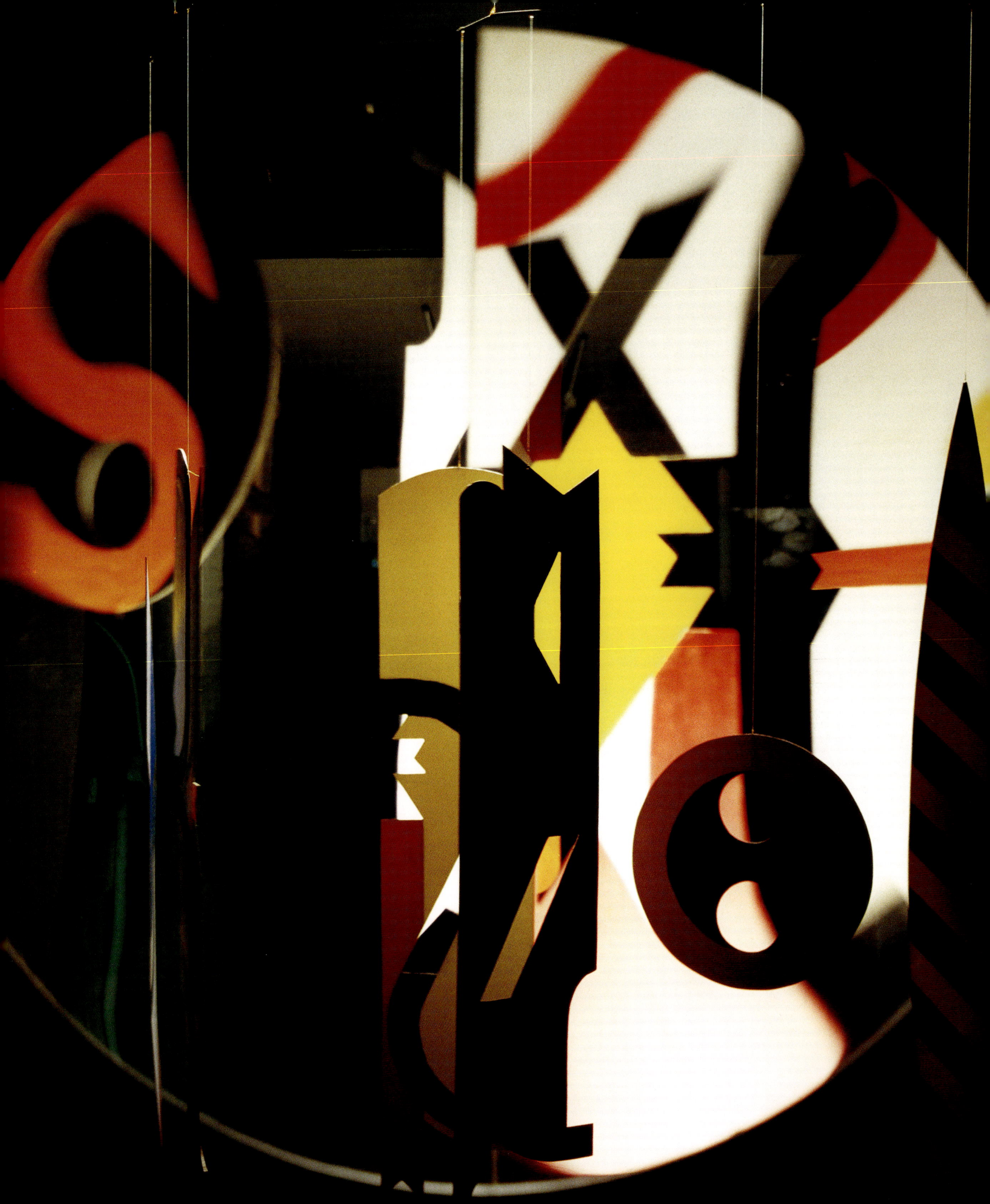

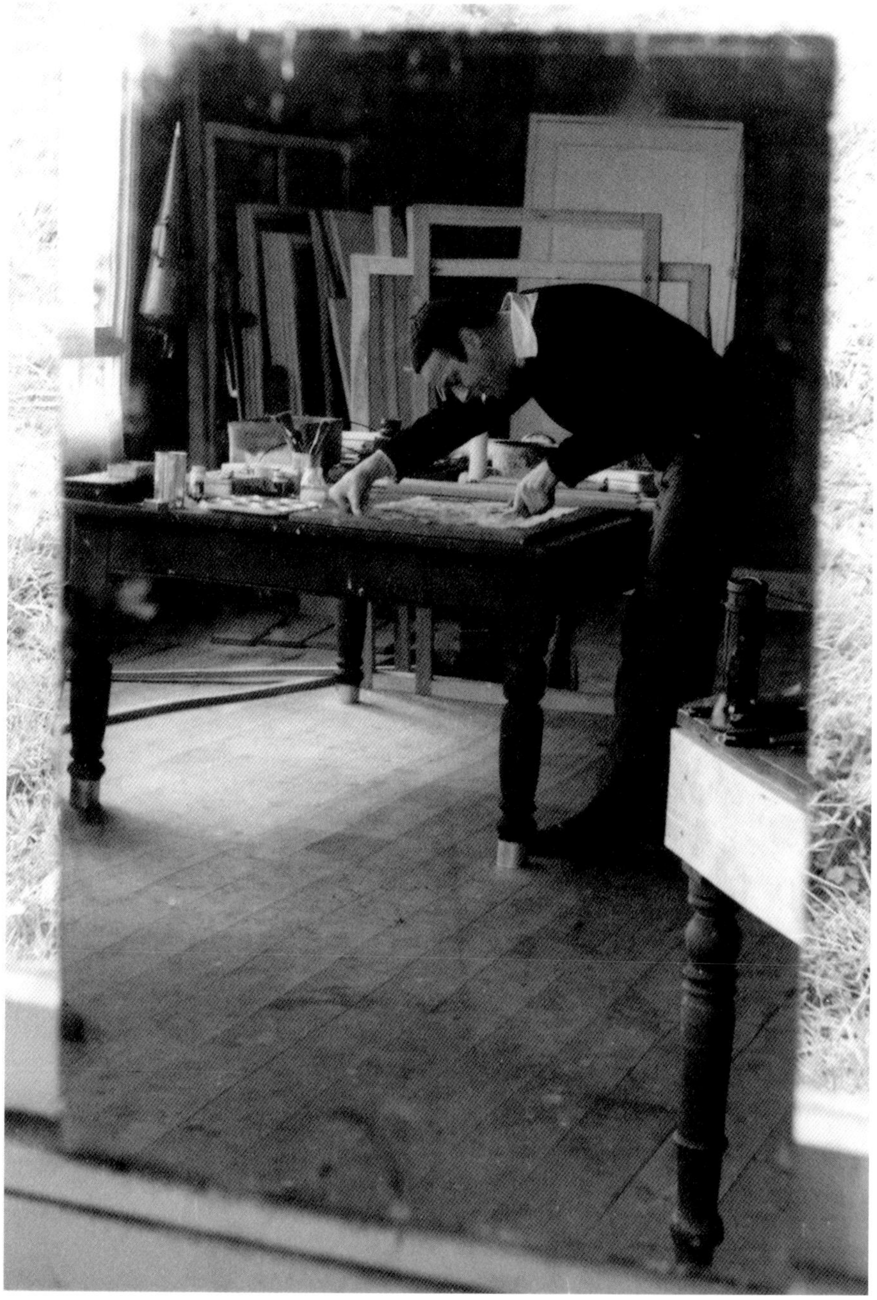

116
Bryan Wynter in his studio at the Carn early 1960s

intricate interweaving and over-painting to be seen in his recent canvases.

When disconnected and stationary, the mirror box looked like a Constructivist toy theatre, an eccentric parlour game. Once the mobile began to turn, however, it created an extraordinary optical illusion, in which the moving coloured elements appeared to mingle with their reflections and to leap out of the porthole-proscenium into the space behind the viewer's back. As an object, an IMOOS – described by one reviewer as 'a cross between a television set and a washing machine'[20] – was an ingenious mechanism. As an experience, it came closer to psychedelic rediscovery of the visible world than a static painting could ever be. It was also a means of bringing physical movement – so integral and essential to Wynter's sense of his environment – into his art. In a much later overview of Wynter's career Heron saw the IMOOS as evidence of his 'passion for exploring pictorial space'. They had, he thought, 'never ... been approached, in the entire field of kinetic art, for their radical innovation, the range of possible areas for discovery they open up, not to mention the sheer beauty of their configuration'.[21]

As early as 1920 Naum Gabo had devised a kinetic construction, *Standing Wave*, in which the motorised oscillation of a single vertical filament created the illusion of a three-dimensional form. László Moholy-Nagy, too, was an early experimenter with kinetic art. His machine *Light Prop for an Electric Stage* (1930) created an effect of abstract cinema as light projected the shadows of its complex and elegant moving parts on to the walls of the space where it was installed. Colour played no role in either of these antecedents, however, which suggests that Wynter had Calder's mobiles very much in mind. Behind Calder, who had shown his first mobiles in Paris in 1932, lay the Surrealist endeavour to liberate art from conscious control. This was one of the main differences between Surrealist theory and the rational idealism of the Constructivist approach. Rather as in Gabo's Constructive method, however, the process of making

115
IMOOS VII
gouache on card, wire, mirror and light set within a painted wooden box
101.5 x 97.8 x 108.6 cm
(40 x 38.5 x 42¾ in)
c.1967
Bristol City Museum and Art Gallery

variable force, activating the mobile. 'The elements were planned, cut out, painted, reversed & juxtaposed all together on the drawing board', he later explained. 'They were then set free to move before the reflector. However carefully each work was planned there were always unexpected "free" developments.'[19] The flat, bright, contrasting colours with which Wynter painted his mobile 'elements' have distant echoes in much earlier paintings of his such as *Blue Landscape* of 1951; but the neat, sharp-edged shapes he used are in effect a miniature equivalent of the vast hard-edge abstract paintings then in vogue in London. There was no sign here of the and setting up IMOOS, on which Wynter was engaged concurrently with his painting during the early 1960s, involved the sort of precise measurement and detailed fabrication in which he readily became completely absorbed (fig. 116).

Few things could be further from the spirit of action painting than constructing an IMOOS. And, once activated, these kinetic works were not visual events orchestrated by the artist, *à la* Pollock, but impersonal performances from which the artist's (self-dramatising) presence was entirely removed. The IMOOS concept also embodied another of Wynter's long-standing preoccupations: the desire to share experiences. These contraptions, he discovered, created a palpable sense of visual embrace. You could glance at a painting and walk away, but the IMOOS projected an ambient visual sensation in which the spectator could not help but feel included. Unlike a painting, too, it worked on purely optical principles, requiring no answering effort of imagination on the part of the viewer.

Wynter had always been more interested in cinema than in theatre, yet his wartime contact with the Oxford Playhouse crowd must have given him a sense of how theatre worked. The director Peter Brook, who had directed his first production at the Playhouse in 1945, was later to formulate a description of dramatic 'gesture' that relates to Wynter's concerns in both painting and kinetics around 1960. A gesture, wrote Brook, 'is statement, expression, communication and a private manifestation of loneliness – it is always what Artaud calls *a signal through the flames* – yet this implies a sharing of experience, once contact is made'.[22] One curious IMOOS effect is that, from time to time as the flame-like, insubstantial reflections bulge and part, the viewer sees him or herself reflected upside down, as though on the far side of a stage.

In his painting, meanwhile, around 1960 Wynter began to renew his interest in 'reading' the physical environment, a process that had fascinated him during his early years in Cornwall in the 1940s. He started to translate all-over, calligraphic mark-making back into a form of landscape or environmental notation. The works that resulted represent a rural form of psychogeography. This was not a term that Wynter is known to have used, but it was current among artists he'd met, including Ralph Rumney, the founder (and possibly sole member) of the London Psychogeographical Association. Psychogeography had been defined in 1955 by the French writer and theorist Guy Debord (briefly an associate of Rumney's during the latter's short-lived membership of the Situationist International) as follows:

> *Psychogeography* could set for itself the study of the precise laws and specific effects of the

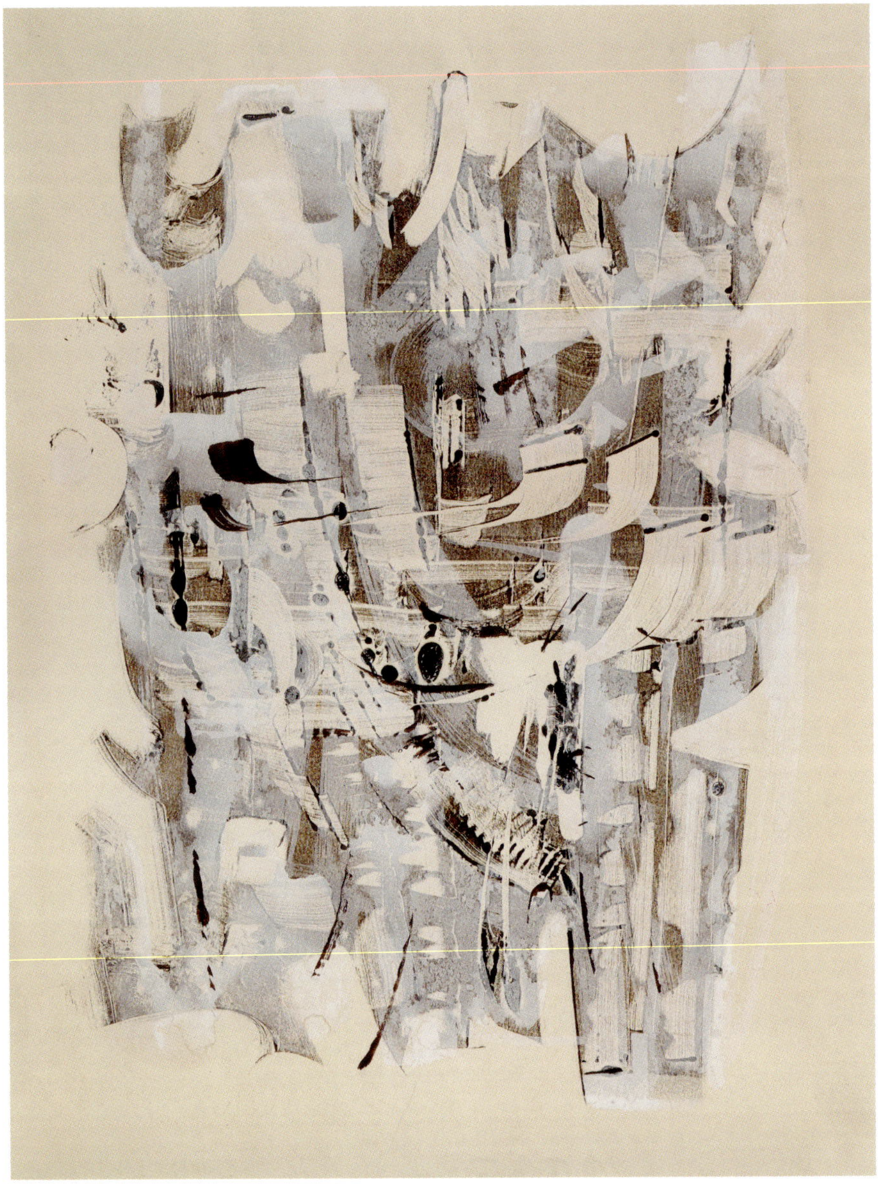

117
Untitled
monotype and gouache on paper
66 x 48.3 cm (26 x 19 in)
c.1958
Jonathan Clark Fine Art

118
Little Odalisque
oil on masonite
20.3 x 20.3 cm (8 x 8 in)
1960
Private collection

119
Summer Garden
oil on board
28.3 x 30.2 cm (11 x 12½ in)
*c.*1960–61
Private collection

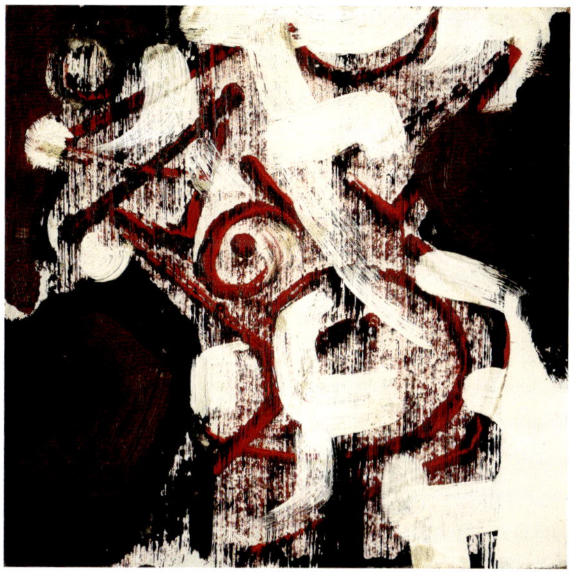

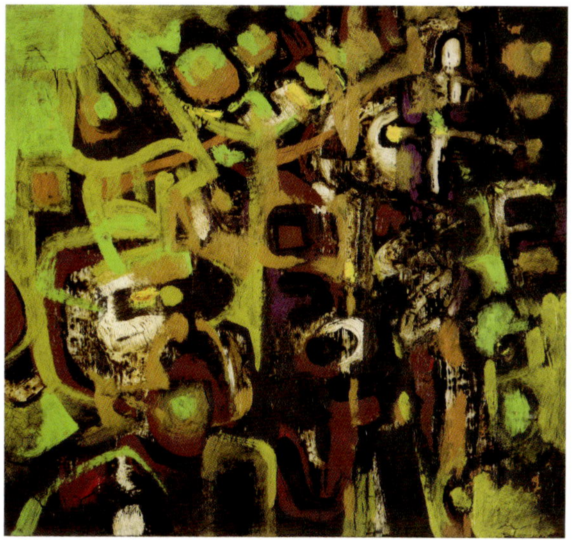

> geographical environment, consciously organised or not, on the emotions and behaviour of individuals. The adjective *psychogeographical* ... can thus be applied to the findings arrived at by this type of investigation, to their influence on human feelings, and even more generally to any situation or conduct that seems to reflect the same spirit of discovery.[23]

Wynter's titles had for some time had a distinctly psychogeographical quality. His 1959 show, for example, had featured *Dark Journey*, *Torrid Region*, *Green Spoor*, *Red Moves In* and *Unsettled Country*. Now the paintings became more closely identified with particular natural processes and ways of experiencing the natural environment.

There were personal factors at work here too. From 1956, when Wynter returned from London with Monica, life at the Carn became a more settled affair, the comings and goings less frequent and impulsive. In 1957 Wynter constructed a new studio next to the cottage. Made from prefabricated wooden sections, it provided a spacious, light-filled working environment where he was able to continue painting on a large scale (as always, he also tried out ideas in smaller paintings and gouaches; figs 117, 118, 119). After Monica and he married in 1959 and their first child, Tom, was born in January 1961, Wynter's 'mountain retreat' became a family home. His first wife, Sue, and their two children visited fairly regularly, as did Eric Wynter, who was now farming in Gloucestershire and firing Bryan's imagination with tales of kayaking on the Severn Bore (a solitary, rapidly travelling wave that periodically forms in the river's lower reaches).

The Carn's other inhabitants included the entourage of wild and semi-tame animals with which Wynter had since childhood liked to surround himself and with which he had, it was often observed, a remarkable natural rapport (fig. 120). In addition to dogs, which Wynter refused to train on the grounds that it would compromise their freedom, there was a raven that he and Eric rescued from the cliffs as a fledgling in 1956. As the bird grew, Wynter taught it to fly, a routine that involved the repeated exhortation 'Come on!' as the young raven was thrown again and again into the air. In the process it learned to repeat this phrase in a perfect imitation of

Wynter's baritone. Monica christened the raven Doom (fig. 121), an allusion to the ill-omened birds of myth and Romantic Gothic literature. Anecdotes about partying at the Carn during the late 1950s almost invariably feature Doom – standing on an unconscious Hilton's chest, admonishing a disoriented and hungover Frost, frightening Sandra Blow away. For Wynter, whose social demeanour was usually described as quietly spoken, the raven was a mischievous familiar, a raucous and transgressive *alter ego*.

With a more settled way of life came a consolidation of Wynter's social circle in west Cornwall. Across the road at Eagles Nest, the Herons, who had been friends of Wynter's since long before their move to Cornwall, were generous hosts with a constant influx of guests – artists, critics, writers, broadcasters. The house often resembled an outstation for the urban cultural elite. Further west along the coast, the ever-penurious Sydney Graham appeared determined to hang on in his cottage at Gurnard's Head, barely scraping a living but always on hand for conversation, poetry and anything that was going in the way of drink or 'uppers' (adrenaline-mimicking amphetamines, or 'speed'). In London, Wynter had met Karl Weschke, a young artist and former German prisoner of war, who had been earning a living as an assistant lion feeder in Bertram Mills circus at Olympia. Although his painting shared almost nothing with the different gestural idioms that Wynter, Lanyon, Heron, Hilton and Frost were variously pursuing, Weschke moved down to Cornwall, renting one of the Tregerthen cottages. Next door was Trevor Bell, who had been living there since motor-biking down from Leeds in 1955. When Bell moved out in the spring of 1957, the new tenant was Sandra Blow, one of the few women artists who were getting anywhere on the London gallery scene at that time. A friend of Hilton's, she had accompanied him to the Easter house party at Eagles Nest. And so the wheels turned and the threads connected. Artistic life in west Cornwall, which had seemed so inspirationally remote and primitive when Wynter arrived in 1945, had acquired an almost metropolitan confidence in its own connectedness. Between September 1959 and January 1960 even Francis Bacon was in St Ives, working in Porthmeor Studios and scandalising fellow residents at Curnow's Hotel by his succession of young boyfriends and the unmistakable sounds of sex emanating from his bedroom.[24]

An interior shot of the Carn taken in 1959 by the photographer Roger Mayne (another regular visitor) shows a group gathered round Wynter's table as the

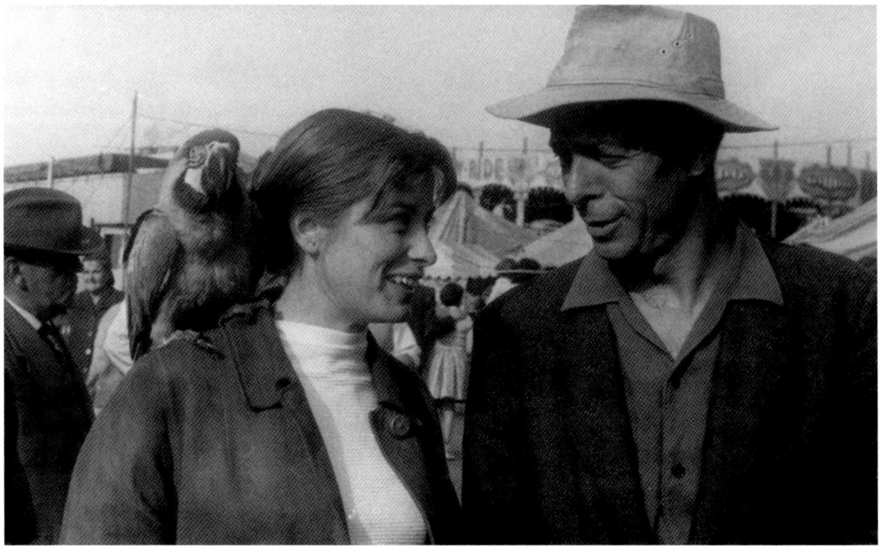

120
Bryan Wynter and Monica Harman at Corpus Christi Fair, Penzance, mid-1950s

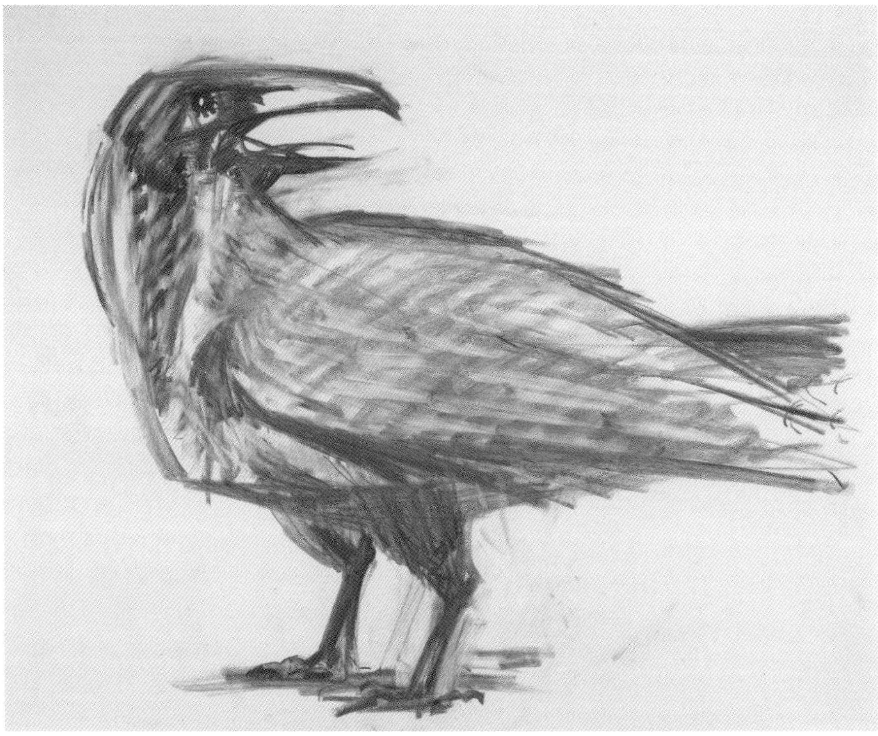

121
Raven
charcoal on paper
42 x 49.5 cm (16½ x 19½ in)
c.1956
Private collection

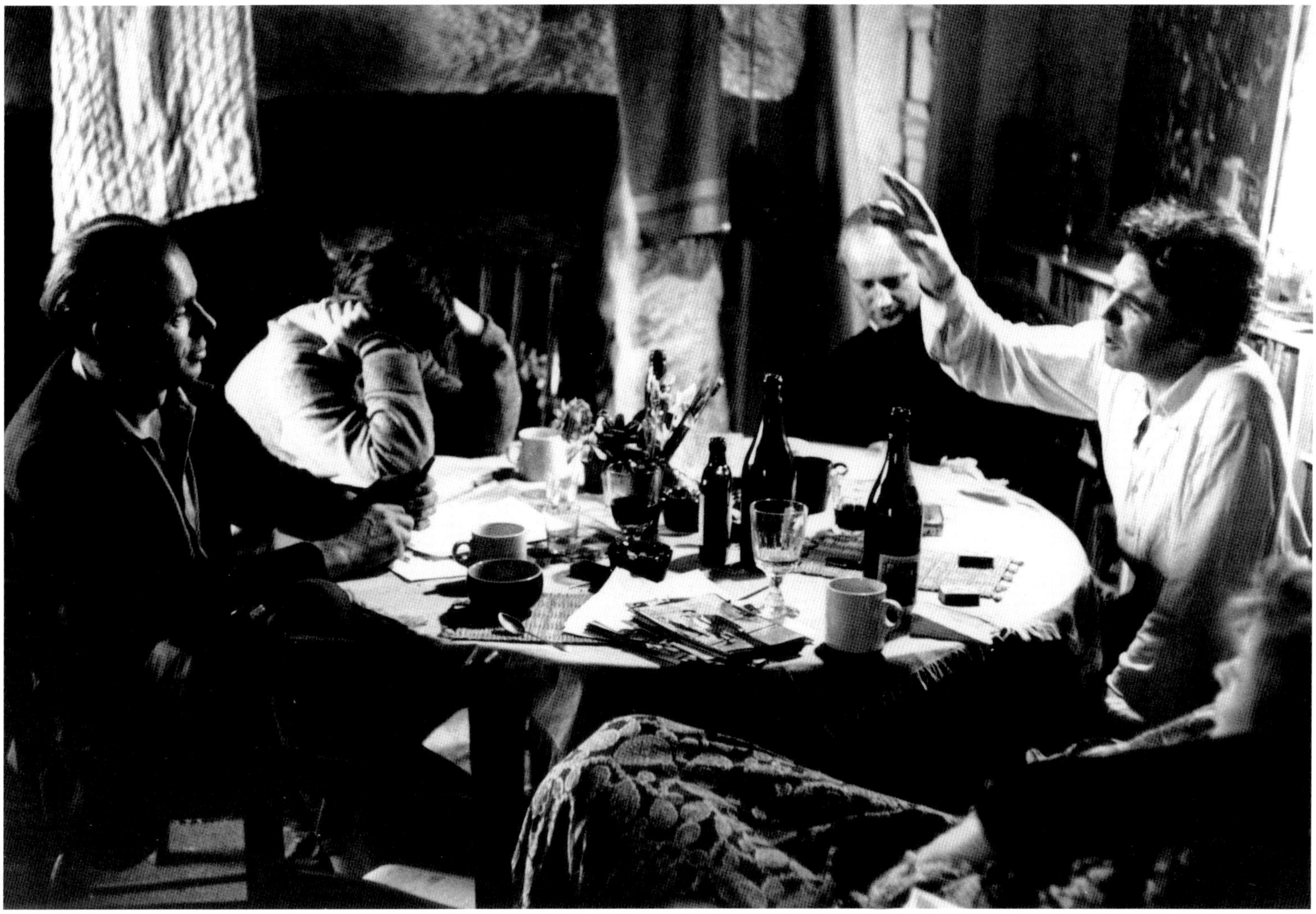

122
All-Night Talk at the Carn, 1959 (L to R: Bryan Wynter, Valerie Fabian, Karl Weschke, W. S. Graham, Monica Wynter), photograph by Roger Mayne

morning light floods in after a night of talk and booze (fig. 122). Graham, one hand raised in his characteristic, oddly Presbyterian gesture of declamation, is unstoppable. Wynter looks on, glazen-eyed but attentive, while Weschke seems about to nod off, and a fourth member of the group (Mayne's friend Valerie Fabian) could be fast asleep. Seated with her back to the camera, Monica Wynter had (as she recalls) retired late to bed and come down in the morning to find the party not yet over. This kind of occasion, typical of the Wynters' life at that time, does not present a scene of the 'small town artistication' that had so exasperated Wynter in 1949. There are undercurrents that prevent us seeing this as an image of camaraderie (Mayne found Graham socially 'prickly'[25]), but it nevertheless expresses a social, intellectual and professional nucleus that, for all the rivalry and hangovers, provided genuine stimulus for work and thought. Away from London, where American art and culture dominated the debate, this circle preserved an unmodish idealism in its considerations of art – especially the philosophical, rather than formal, nature of abstraction. Take poetry: we all use words, all the time, reasoned Graham to Wynter, and hence 'we are sometimes led into the belief that literature is more literary than the other arts'. But, he continued in forthright vein, 'This is not so'.

> In the same way as we don't expect music to tell us about horsemen or unrequited love or painting to illustrate the behaviour of a molecule we should not expect poetry (even although it is an object of words which we might use every day) to hand us out a little nutshell truth which we have pleasure in agreeing with.[26]

However ordinary the materials out of which paintings or poems are made, he seems to be saying, true art possesses a property of strangeness. To put it another

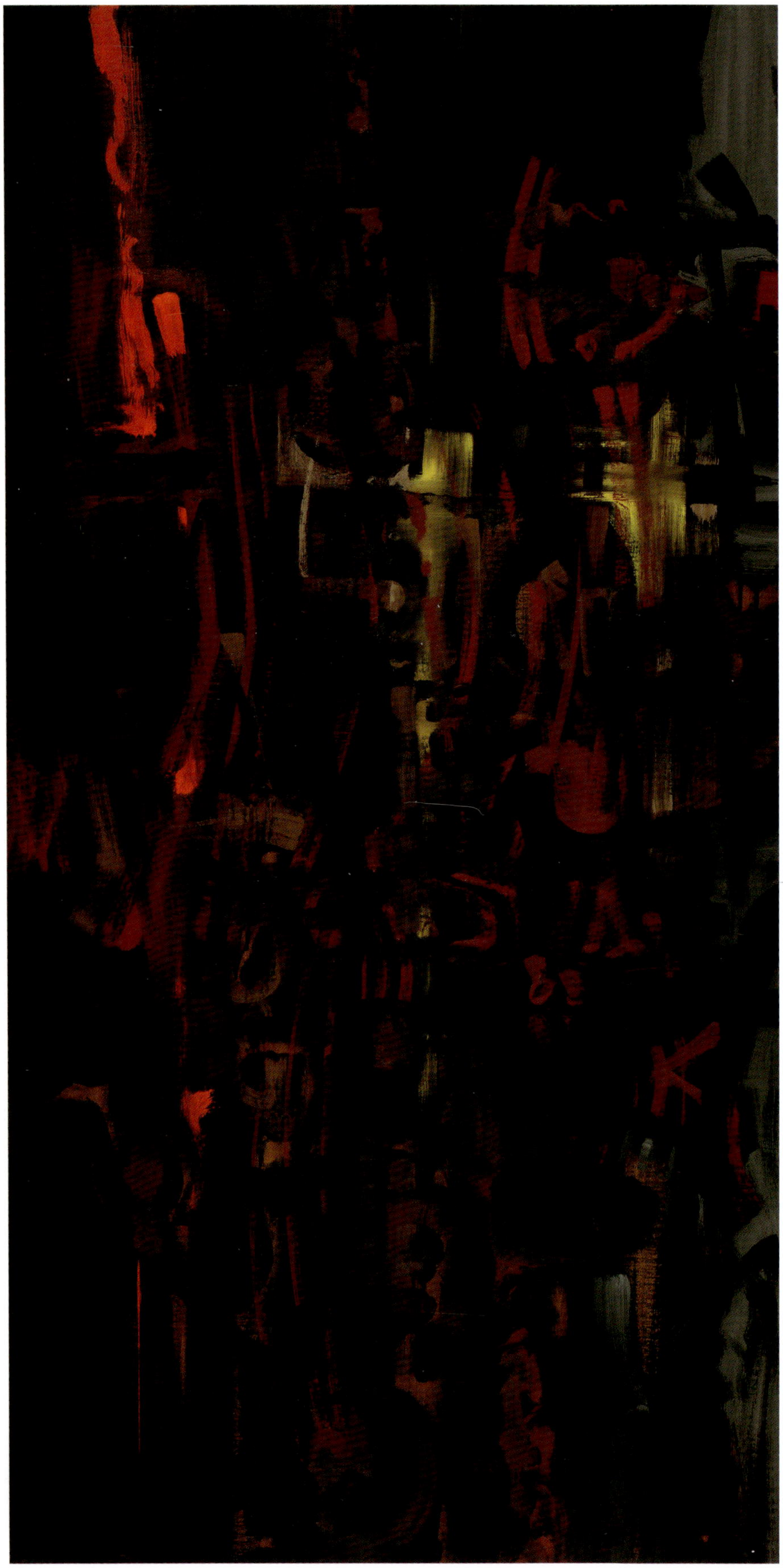

123
Dark Escarpment
oil on canvas
152.4 x 121.9 cm (60 x 48 in)
1961
Artist's estate

124
Firestreak II
oil on canvas
182.8 x 142.2 cm (72 x 56 in)
1960
Private collection

way, the experience of recognition to which art gives rise is altogether different from ordinary familiarity. A work of art, Heron had insisted in 'Art is Autonomous', his counterblast of 1955 to the realist painter–critic John Berger, 'is not just a telephone exchange which facilitates straightforward communication'. Art, in fact, 'is not created in a state of mind which primarily seeks to communicate'. On the contrary, it is 'an act of discovery', 'a revelation to be contemplated'.[27] It's all very well, you might say, for men such as Heron, or Wynter, Hilton and Lanyon, who each enjoyed some form of private income, to attach such values to art. It may also be the case that life in Cornwall was more conducive to thinking about the production of art than its reception. '"To hell with any audience" is the only attitude for a painter at work', fulminated Heron. There's a great deal of daylight visible between this stance and that of the Independent Group, for example, who had developed a vision in which it was the audience, in the form of mass-market consumers, that defined art's proper arena.

For a time, however, it seemed as though what Heron was later to call 'the St Ives–New York axis' was becoming a startling new phenomenon of the British art scene. In July 1959 Heron hosted a six-day visit to Cornwall by the most influential American critic, Clement Greenberg, whom he'd first met in London five years earlier. It was on Greenberg's recommendation that Heron had been writing since 1954 for the New York magazine *Arts*, where he had taken every opportunity to promote the work of his associates, with articles on Lanyon, Davie, Frost, Hilton, Wells and Wynter, among others. The following month Rothko was in west Cornwall as Lanyon's guest. New York galleries, in their turn, were taking an active interest in these British abstract painters. Lanyon was shown by Catherine Viviano, and Heron and Frost by Bertha Schaffer. Wynter, whose work (as was often observed at the time) seemed closest of all to the spirit of Abstract Expressionism, kept at a distance from the rather frenetic social-professional

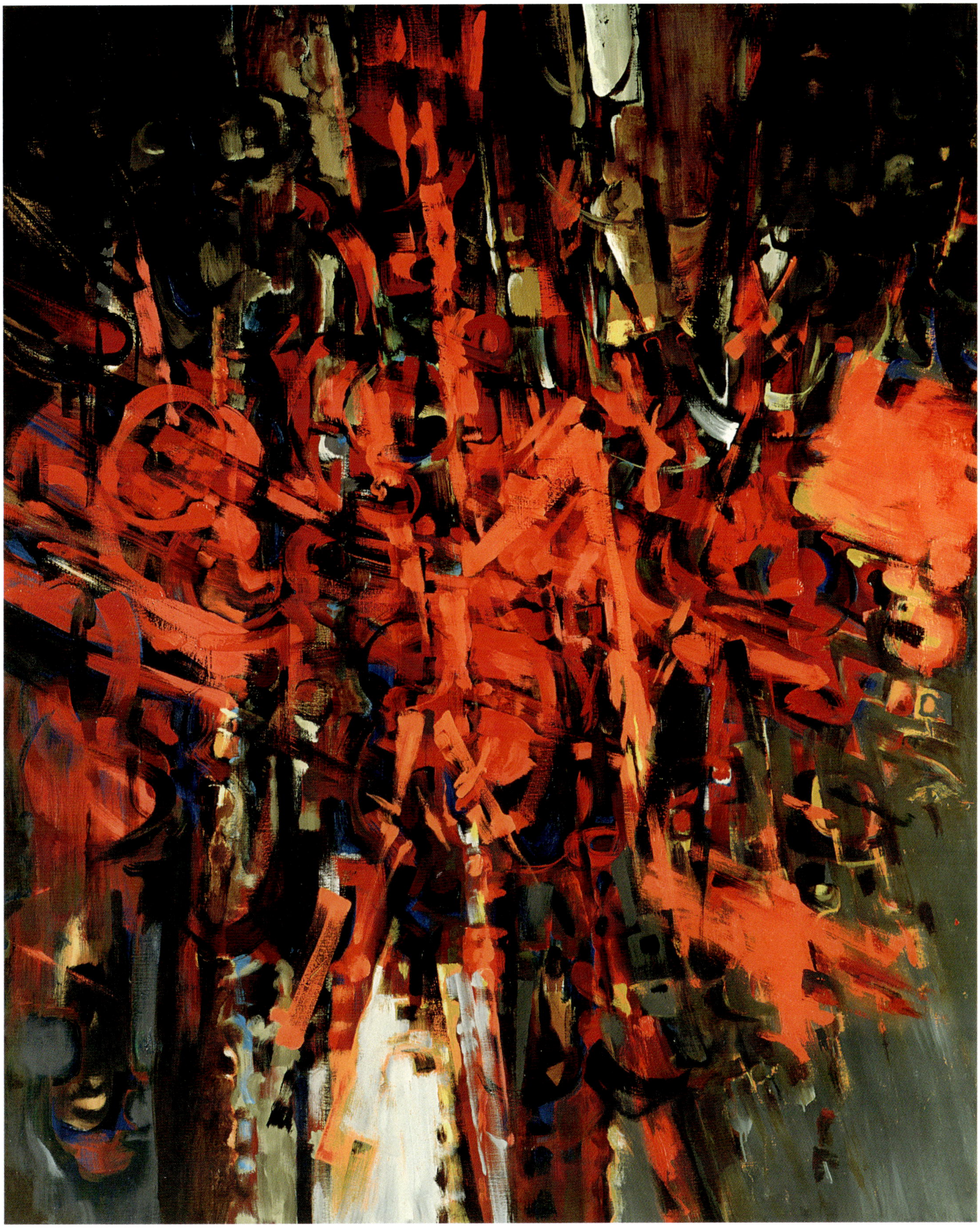

tempo of these times. His attitude can be gauged from a practical joke he played on Hilton in the summer of 1962, while the young American critic Michael Fried was London correspondent for *Arts*. A skilful mimic, Wynter phoned Hilton, posing as Fried's secretary and explaining that the critic was a great admirer of his work and would like to arrange a meeting. Hilton (as Wynter well knew) would have torn to pieces the self-esteem of any artist so vain as to be taken in by critical approval. On this occasion, however, completely deceived by Wynter's cod American accent, Hilton seemed keen to go along. When he duly turned up for the appointment, the puzzled secretary announced 'Roger Hilton's here to see you', to which Fried responded simply 'Who the hell is Roger Hilton?'[28]

During the early 1960s, while the new urban imagery of Pop drew a response from Lanyon, Frost and other abstract painters, Wynter's work became, if anything, more firmly intertwined with his physical environment. His 'Firestreak' series (1960–62) was in part a response to the effect on the land of the routine burning, or swaling, of fields and moorland grazing by farmers, which usually took place in March, just before the growing season. The aim was to remove the rampant overgrowth of gorse and bracken, but the swaling sometimes got out of hand and turned into a fast-moving conflagration. Another time, in September 1959, a bushfire – possibly the result of arson – burnt so fiercely that it threatened to take the Carn in its stride and laid waste the moorland all around, where the peaty soil was incinerated down to bare rock. Wynter photographed the scorched landscape, the shapes of low boulders revealed in the charred soil, the sooty calligraphy of cindered gorse and heather. In *Firestreak II* (fig. 124) intense strokes and patches of red hold attention on the surface rather than, as in many of Wynter's paintings from the previous four years, letting the eye be drawn through the highlights into the illusion of layered depths beneath and beyond.

In January 1960, in response to a request from Alan Bowness (probably in connection with a projected exhibition), Wynter composed a short note about his current work. In place of the desire to 'fox' the conscious mind, and the subjectivity of the viewer's perceptions, both of which he had emphasised in his *Statements* note three years earlier, Wynter offered a concise but eloquent celebration of natural processes as a metaphor for his art:

> My paintings are non-representational but linked to the products of nature in as much as they are developed according to laws within themselves and are a static record of the processes that have brought them about.
>
> A stream finds its way over rocks. The force of the stream, and the quality of the rocks determine the stream's bed. This in turn modifies the course of the stream, channelling out new sluices and hollows. The stream erodes the rock, the rock deflects the stream, until, at some high point, the stream bursts its banks and falls into a ravine. The dry stream bed, carved and hollowed, remains. Its form contains its history.
>
> There are no rocks or streams in my paintings but a comparable process of dynamic versus static elements has attended their development and brought about their final form.[29]

This sounds not unlike Debord's definition of psychogeography ('the study of the precise laws and specific effects of the geographical environment' and 'their influence on human feelings'). But it's doubtful that any such reference was intended by Wynter, since, in contrast to Debord's almost exclusively urban context, his stream metaphor derived (as most of his reflections on artistic process ultimately did) from his physical experiences of a wild coastal landscape. In the early

125
Oceanic
oil on canvas
122 x 96.5 cm (48 x 38 in)
1959
Artist's estate

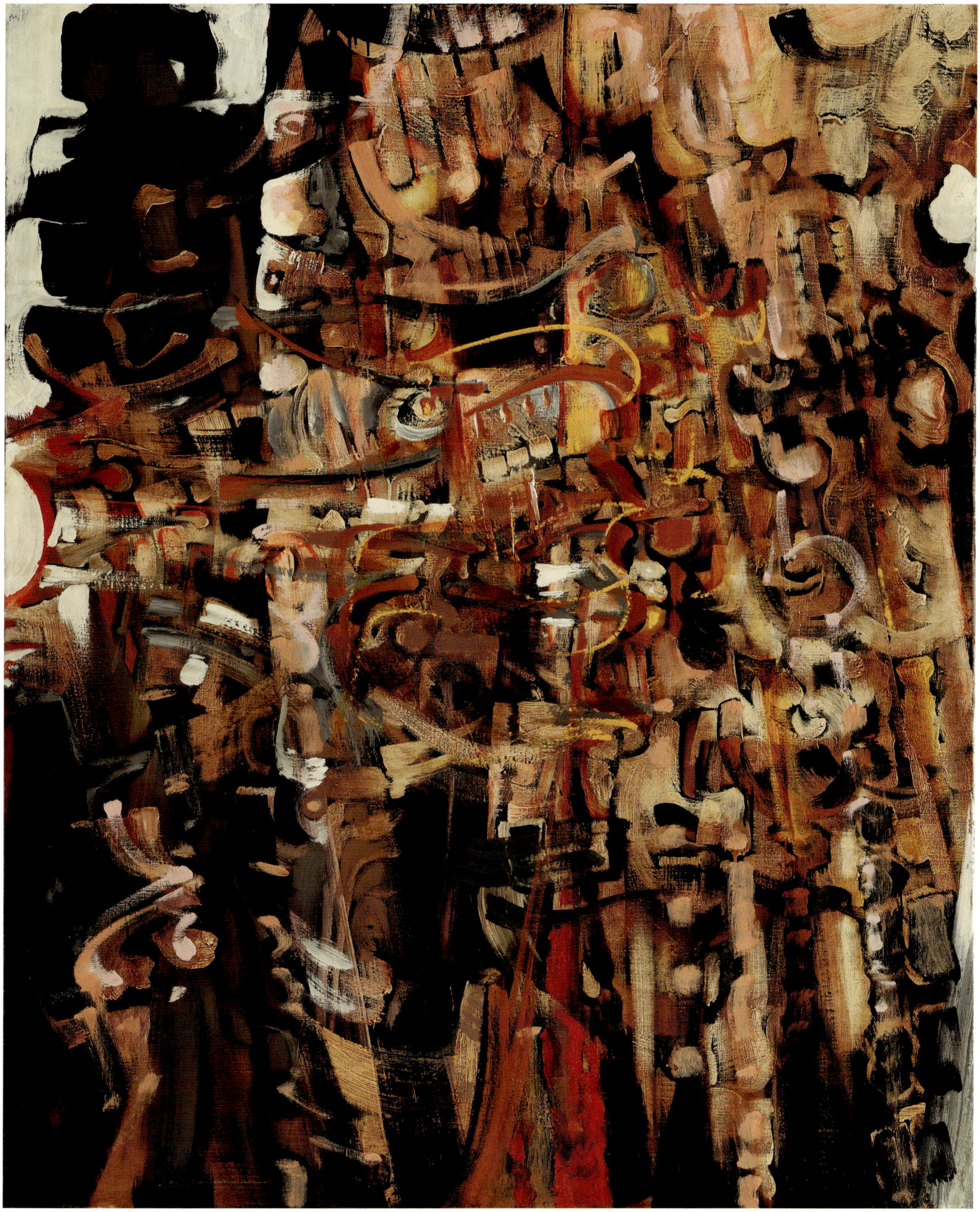

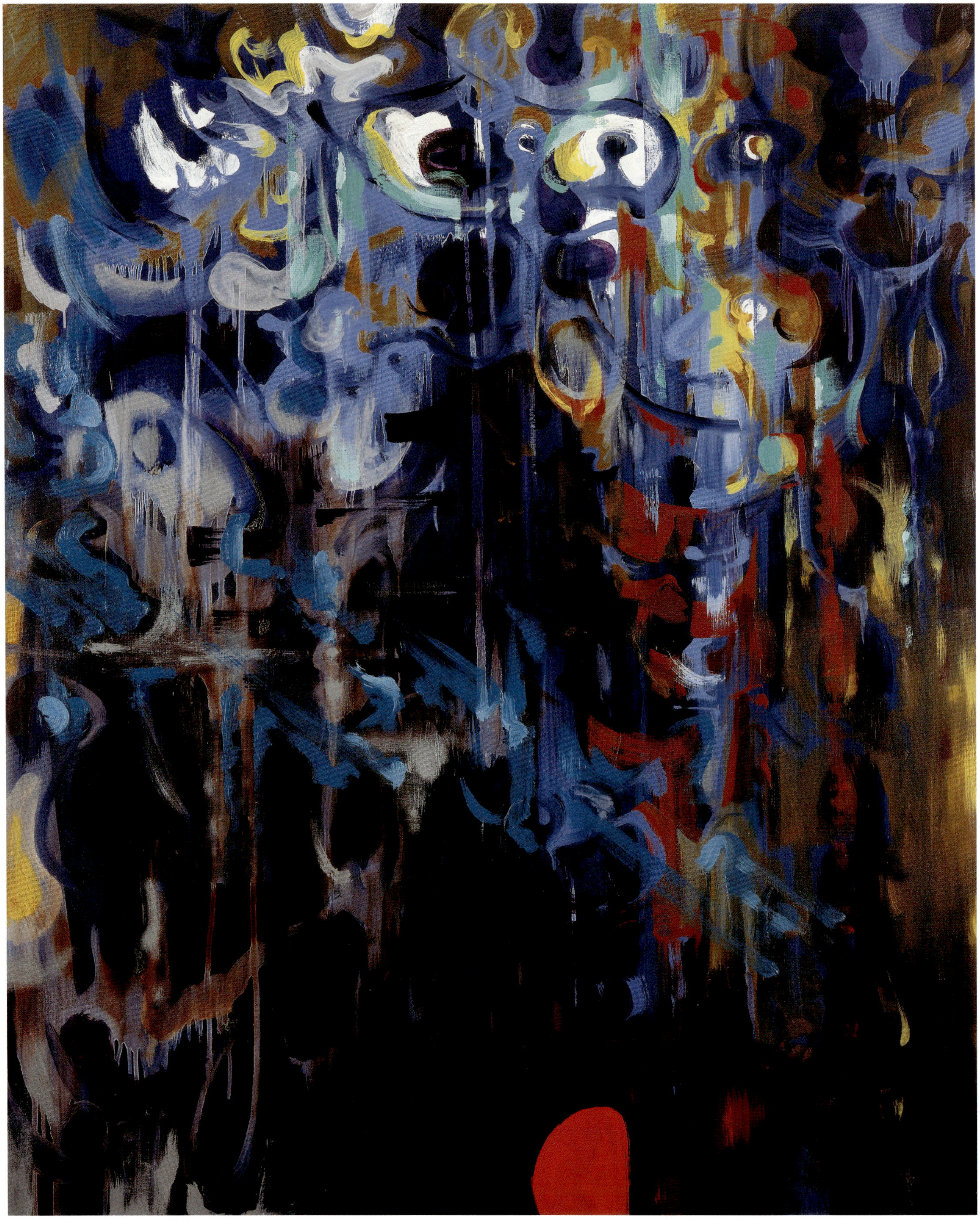

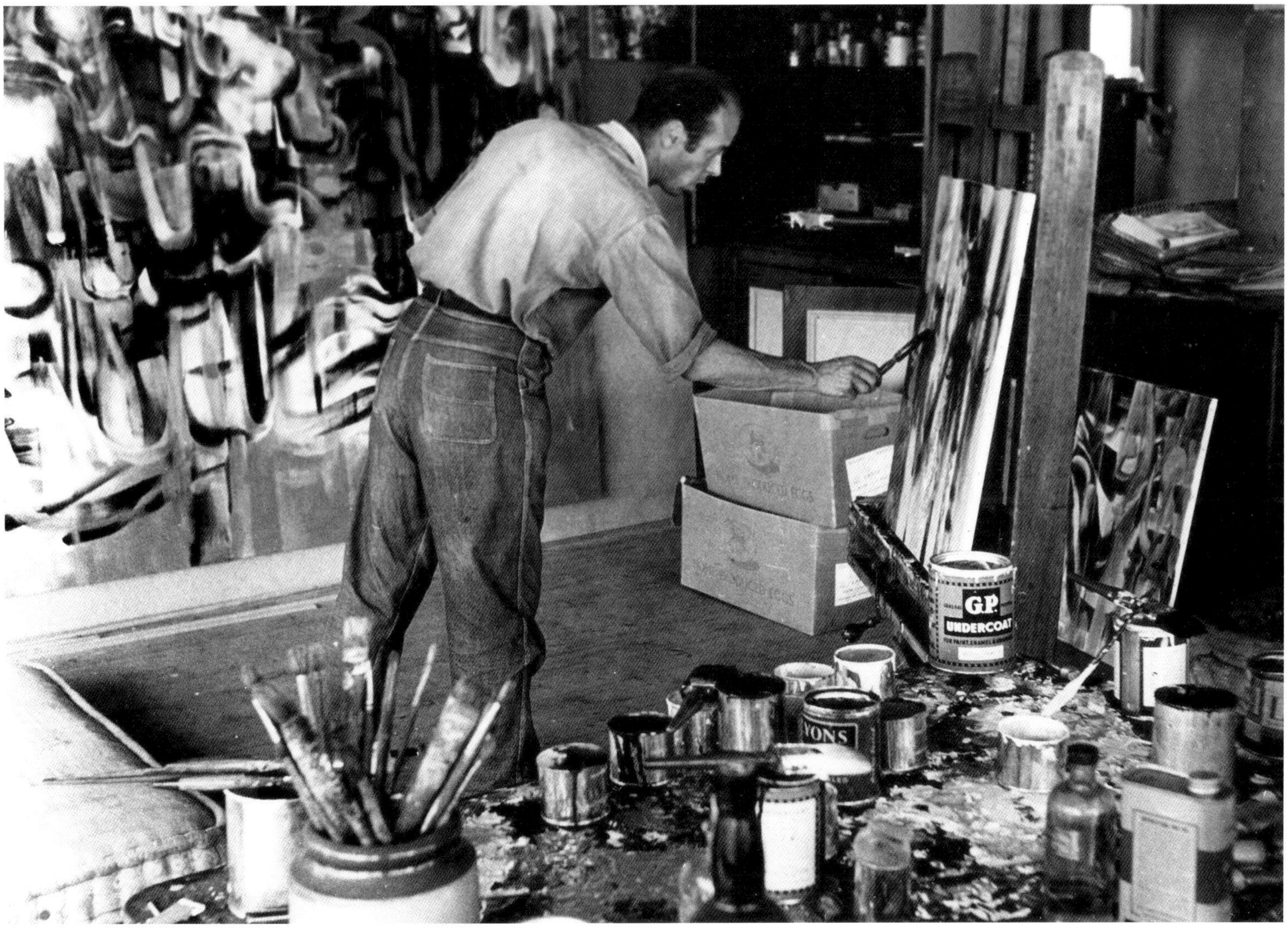

126
Untitled
oil on canvas
142.2 x 111.8 cm (56 x 44 in)
1960
Artist's estate

127
Bryan Wynter in his studio (*The Hunters* in the background), *c.*1960 photograph by Roger Mayne

1960s these experiences centred on Wynter's enthusiasm for canoeing and kayaking (a canoe being an open boat, while a kayak has a closed-in deck with the cockpit sealed by a splash-deck). Despite the limited success of his aqualung experiments, Wynter swam and snorkeled, and altogether 'spent much time exploring below the surface of rock-pools', as Eric Wynter recalled. Indeed, in Eric's view, his brother's entire artistic output during the 1950s could be seen as a submarine continuation of the terrestrial themes in his Cornish landscapes of the 1940s, as Bryan's work 'moved away from recognizable landscape into a kind of abstraction lit up by dimensions underwater'.[30]

It was true that Wynter had a lifelong enjoyment of sports, pastimes and explorations to do with water. In the 1940s he and Eric had canoed down the River Lea in London. In the early 1950s, while still teaching at Corsham, Wynter had constructed a boat with a glass viewing panel in the hull. Yet Wynter's own acknowledgement of the centrality of water imagery in his work seems to date a bit later, to around 1959–60, when titles such as *River Bed* and *Oceanic* (fig. 125) became common. An untitled oil painting from 1960 (fig. 126) shows Wynter's earlier staccato calligraphic strokes modulating to softer, curving marks that suggest fruit-like or frond-like shapes. The colours too – including high-toned blues, reds and yellows – suggest the play of light through a semi-transparent, watery medium.

In *Sea Change I*, a small gouache from 1959, the all-over vertical 'grille' effect is interwoven with a sinuous fluvial musculature – water as the body feels, rather than as the eye perceives, its movement. On a much larger scale, this effect is also present in *The Hunters* (see fig. 113), a 9-foot-long canvas Wynter completed the following year, which can be seen in the background of Roger Mayne's photo of Wynter in his studio, poised (and

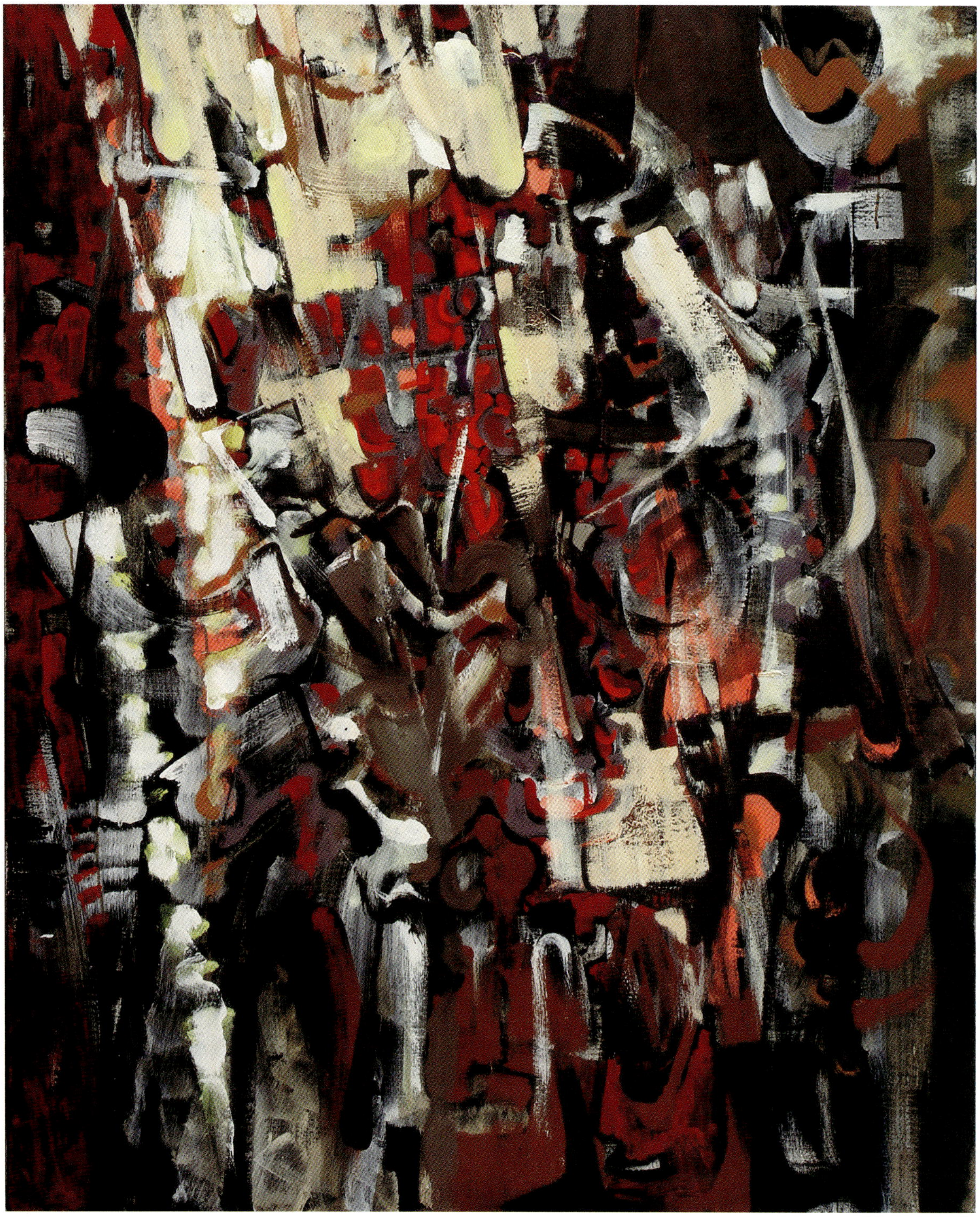

128
Ironstone Journey
oil on canvas
122 x 96.5 cm (48 x 38 in)
1959
Private collection

129
Saga I
oil on canvas
140 x 110 cm (55 x 43 ¼ in)
1960
Artist's estate

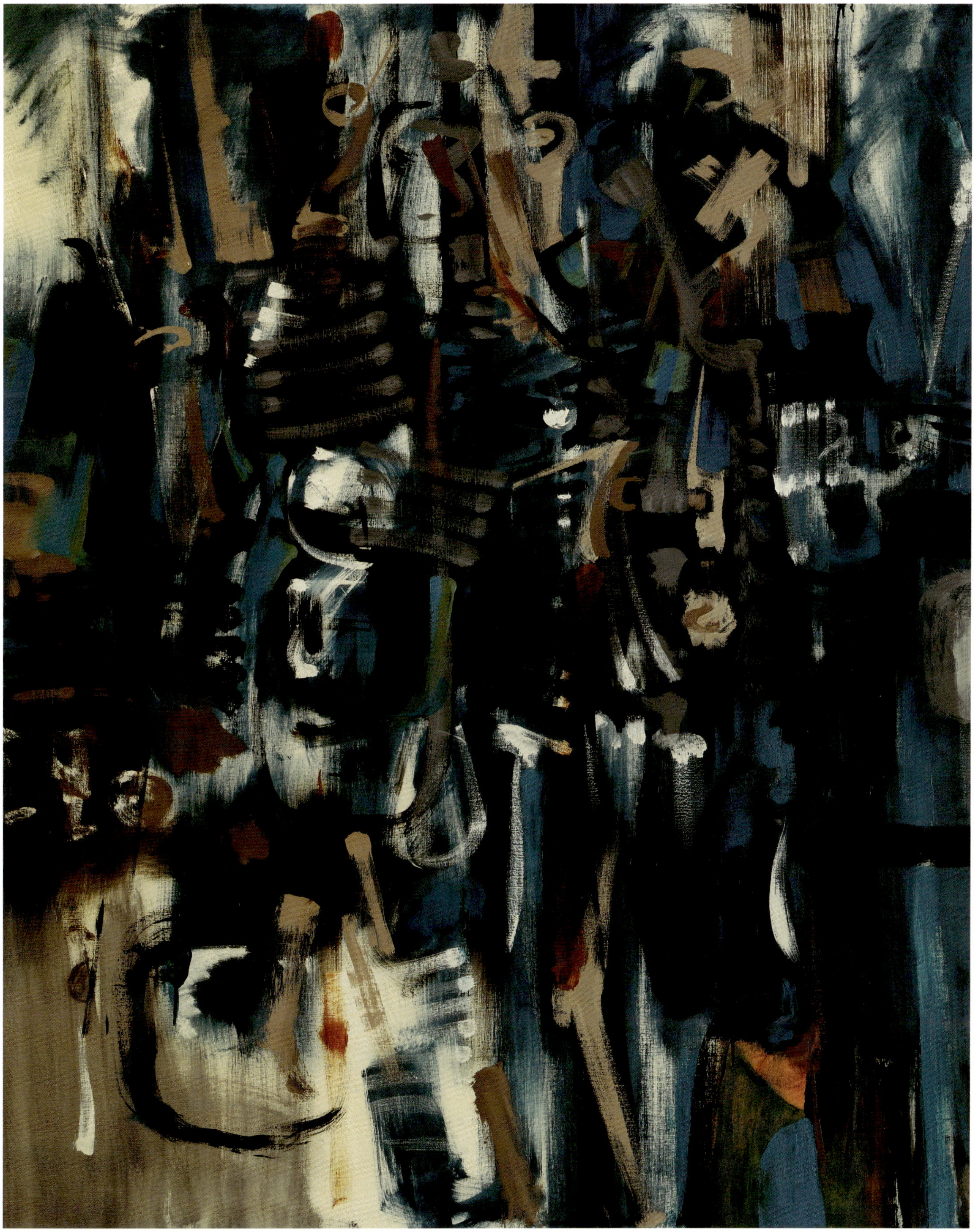

probably posed) Pollock-style in mid-stroke action amid tins of house paint (fig. 127). Around 1960 landscape metaphors became more prominent than ever in Wynter's thinking about his art. A 'process of dynamic versus static elements' is reflected in all his paintings of the early 1960s, from small oil studies (fig. 136) to full-scale works such as *Saga I*, *Dark Traverse*, *Black Diamond*, *Ironstone Journey* and, perhaps most successfully, in the magnificent *Kayak* (figs 129, 130, 128, 131). So, too, is Wynter's observation that the landscape's form 'contains its history'. In these terms, a painting was not 'an event', in Harold Rosenberg's Abstract Expressionist sense, but the record of the history of an event, an accumulation of temporal and spatial (visible or invisible) layers, that constituted its present and its presence.

Such ideas inform a series of twelve paintings on which Wynter worked concurrently (along with other paintings and IMOOS) between 1960 and 1963, to which he gave the title 'Sandspoor' (figs 132, 133, 134, 135). This composite term, invented by Wynter, means simply a track in the sand left by a human or animal foot. But, like his stream metaphor, it also applies to his creative process. A 'spoor' or footprint is a record of movement (as a painting records the artist's movements) that 'contains its own history'. Like a painting, it can be interpreted or 'read'. But, when painted by an artist rather than found in the sand, what kind of reading do such 'spoors' suggest? Do they reflect something seen in the actual landscape, or are they traces of gestures through which the unconscious reveals itself?

Wynter said that the idea for the 'Sandspoor' series came from Wilfred Thesiger's travelogue *Arabian Sands*, which he'd read soon after its publication in 1959. The book recounts Thesiger's exploration during the 1940s of the Rub' al Khali, or Empty Quarter, a vast sand desert covering the southern Arabian Peninsula. Wynter may have identified personally with Thesiger, a privileged Englishman who had devoted his life to exploring, usually on foot, remote regions where traditional ways of life survived, untouched (until his arrival, that is) by Western contact. During these adventures Thesiger insisted on living as the indigenous peoples did. He seemed, in fact, to have been motivated by something not dissimilar to the ideal of anti-materialistic integrity that had led Wynter to adopt the Carn and the Penwith moors as his home in 1945. More specifically, Thesiger described how, during a journey across the sands of Ghanim, his party came across some indistinct tracks in the sand: 'I was not even sure that they were made by camels,' he recalled, 'for they were much blurred by the wind.' But an old man in the group, 'who was noted as a tracker', was able to read even these ambiguous signs:

> the man turned aside and followed them for a short distance. He then jumped off his camel, looked at the tracks where they crossed some hard ground, broke some camel droppings between his fingers and rode back to join us ... 'They were Awamir ... They have raided Januba on the southern coast and taken three of their camels. They have come here from Sahma and watered at Mughsin. They passed here ten days ago.'[31]

The blurred forms of these 'sandspoors', therefore, contained an exact meaning, revealing the detailed history and geography of an event.

In *Sandspoor II* (1961) the softer underlying brushmarks have a wiry, Tobey-esque superscript, as though to give them a 'readable' emphasis. Wynter has also started to group brushstrokes in configurations that suggest schematised ripples or echoes, a technique that becomes more evident in *Sandspoor III*. The slightly programmatic, decorative effect of this sort of mark-making is offset by vaguer, wave-like rhythms that run vertically or obliquely, restraining the more frenetic animation of the sharper calligraphic shapes. Two years later, when he painted *Sandspoor X (Lunar)*, these grouped marks had developed into tilted quivers of

130
Dark Traverse
oil on canvas
152.4 x 122 cm (60 x 48 in)
1961
Osborne Samuel

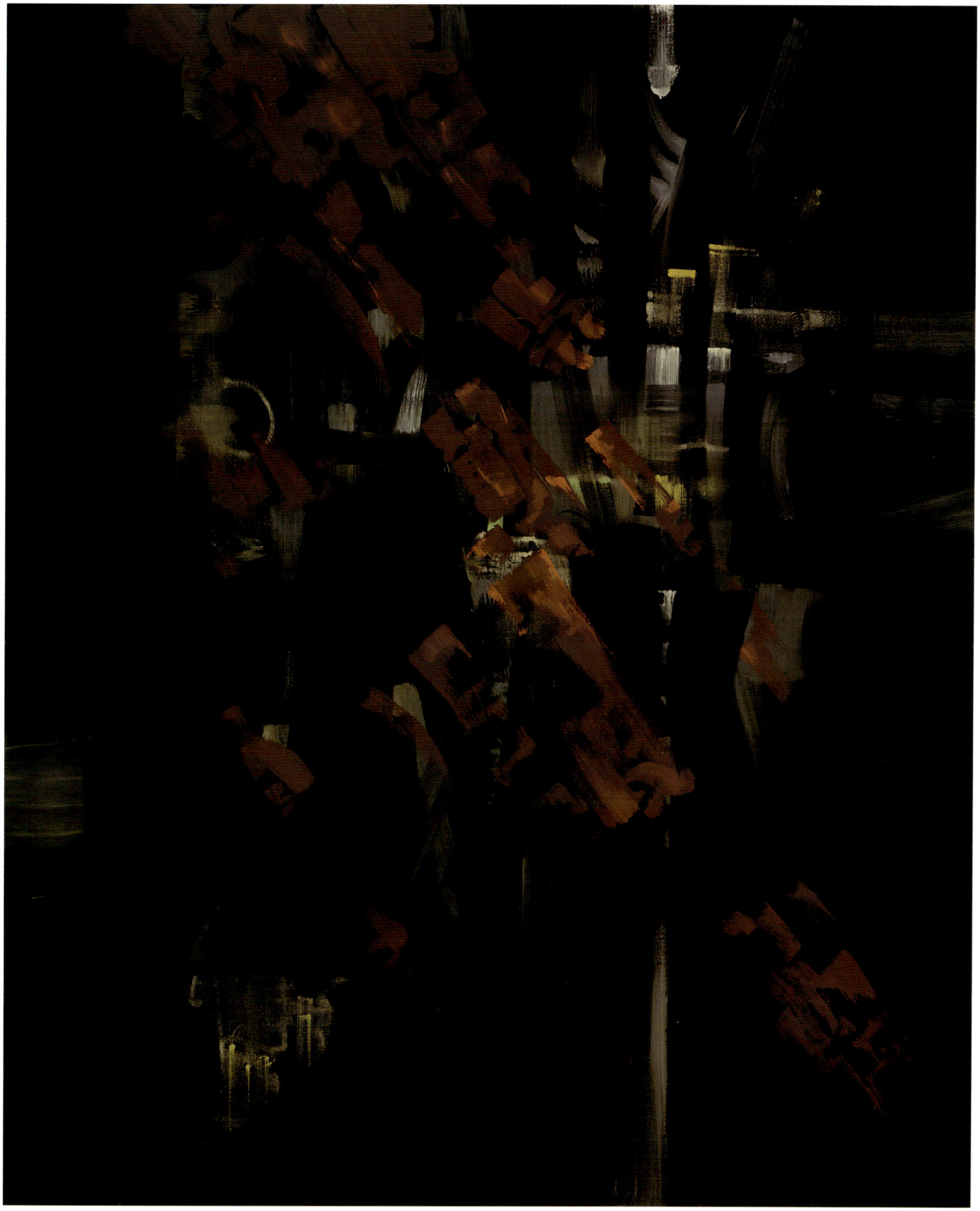

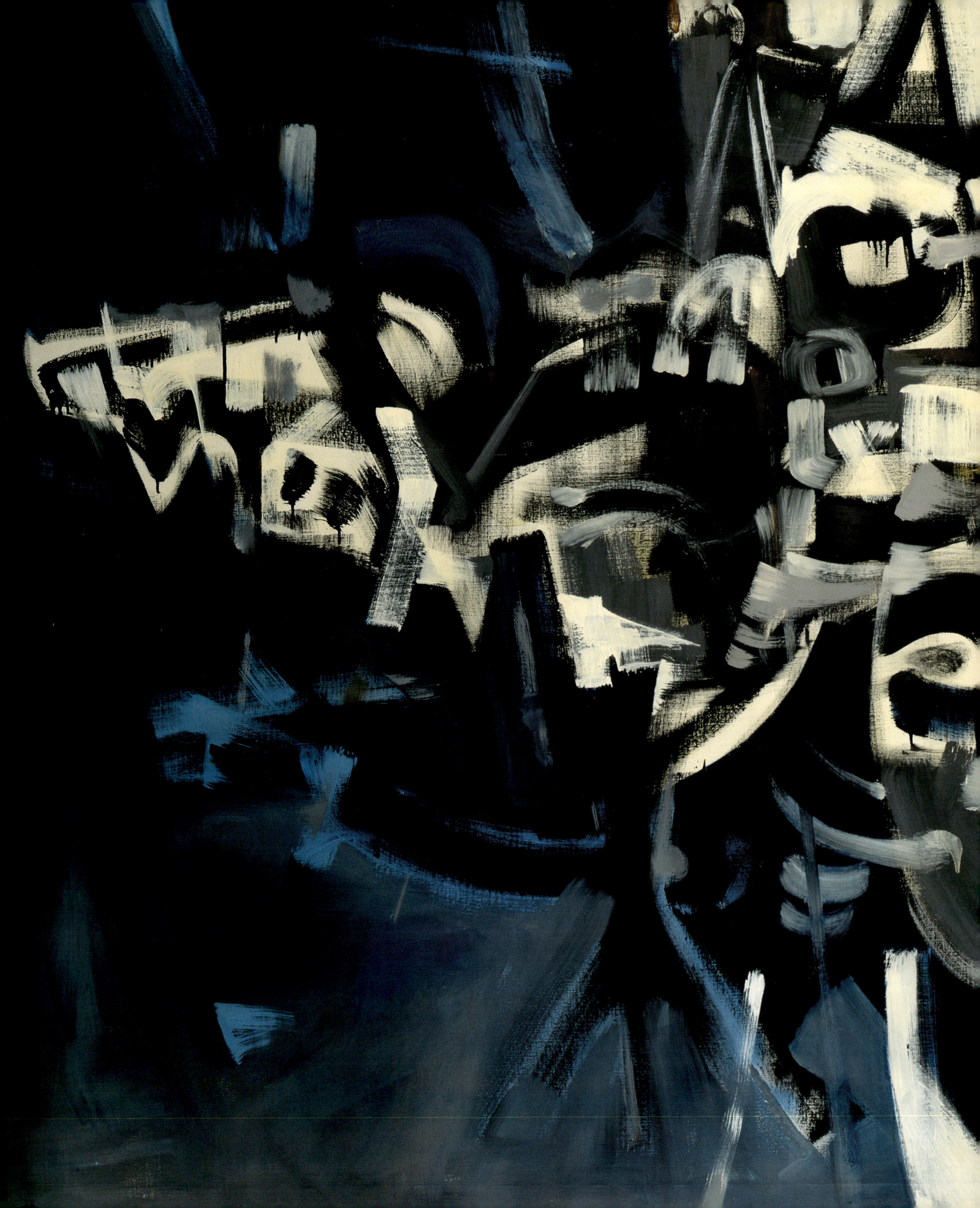

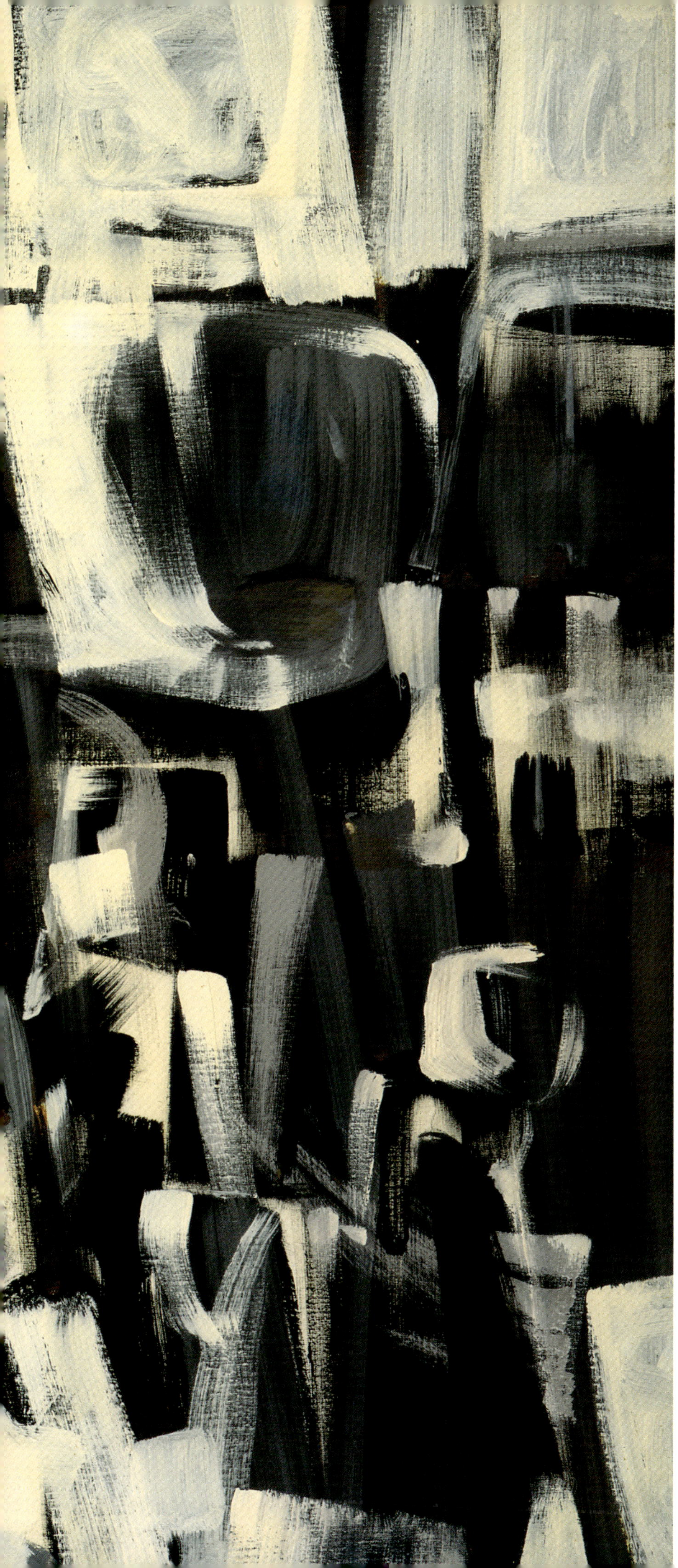

131
Kayak
oil on canvas
122 x 152.4 cm (48 x 60 in)
1961
British Council Collection

parallel hatchings, reminiscent of the fractured illusionism of early Cubism, as though the sand-track had become a mirage and the act of reading physical traces been transformed into an attempt to grasp the most elusive of perceptions. This effect is even more pronounced in *The Black* (1962), where the painting's strong, vertical organisation plays against a sense of mirrored instability, amounting almost to a non-kinetic version of the IMOOS viewer's experience.

In January 1962 Wynter had an exhibition at Galerie Charles Lienhard in Zurich. In his catalogue statement he reflected on what had evidently struck observers as changes in his work, although to Wynter himself they seemed evidence of continuity:

> People tend to say: 'You are using larger forms.' There is a confusion here. 'Form', as usually understood, is not at issue. The small brushmarks function as units of energy rather than as separate formal entities. A stream of such marks may enter and leave the canvas as from outside it. It may encounter another similar stream. The turbulence thus set up engenders new forces which in turn hinder or deflect the original paths. So the painting generates its own laws of development. But painting is an imaginative activity. Each development reflects the predilection of the artist and the life that surrounds him.
>
> These paintings, then, are not pure abstractions. Nor do I abstract from 'nature'. I approach 'nature' from the other side.
>
> I used to be a landscape painter. Am I still influenced by landscape?
>
> The landscape I live among is bare of houses, trees, people; is dominated by winds, by swift changes of weather, by the moods of the sea; sometimes it is devastated and blackened by fire. These elemental forces enter the paintings and lend their qualities without becoming motifs.[32]

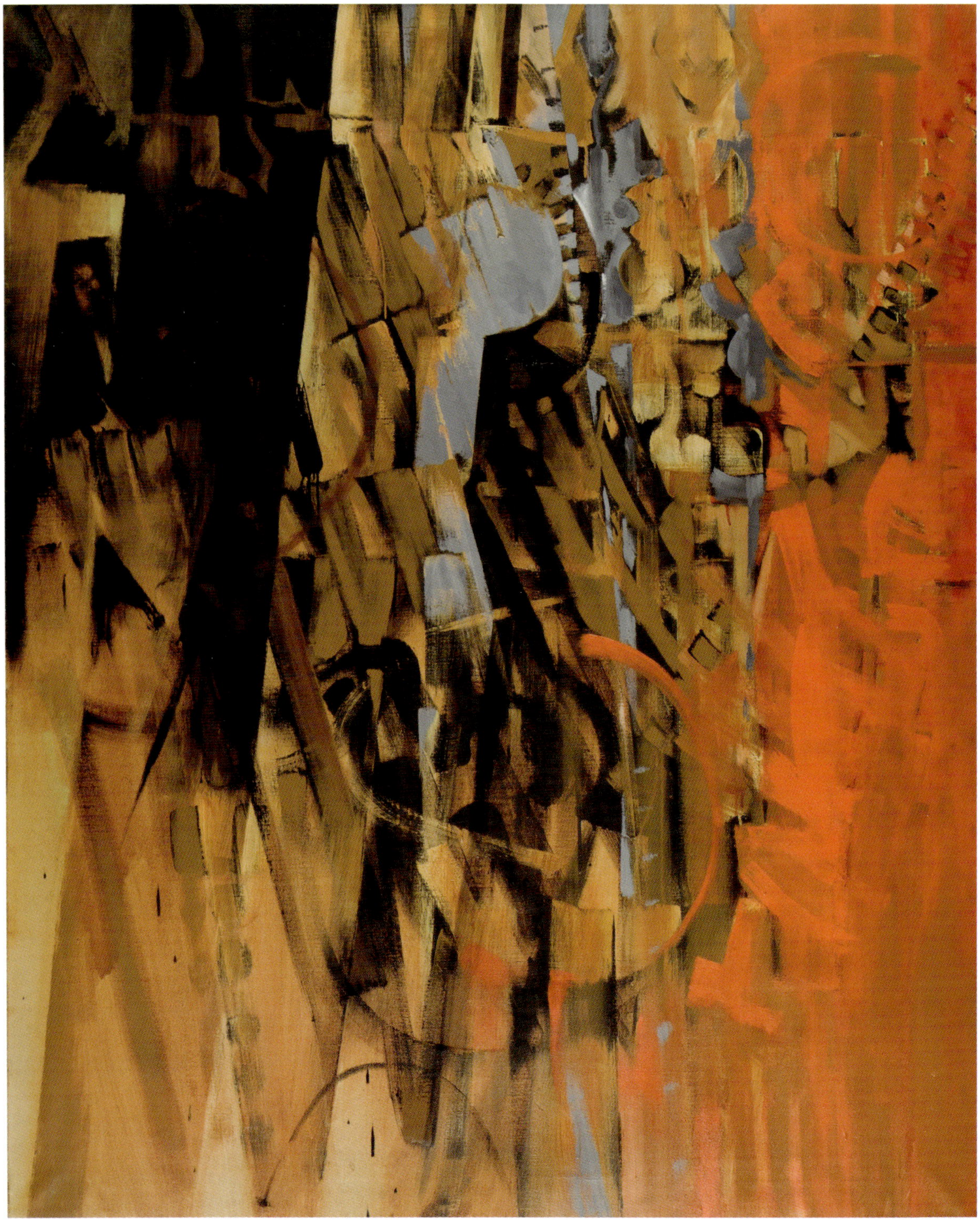

132
Sandspoor VII (Penumbra)
oil on canvas
142 x 111.8 cm (56 x 44 in)
1963
Private collection

133
Sandspoor II
oil on canvas
142.2 x 111.8 cm (56 x 44 in)
1961
Artist's estate

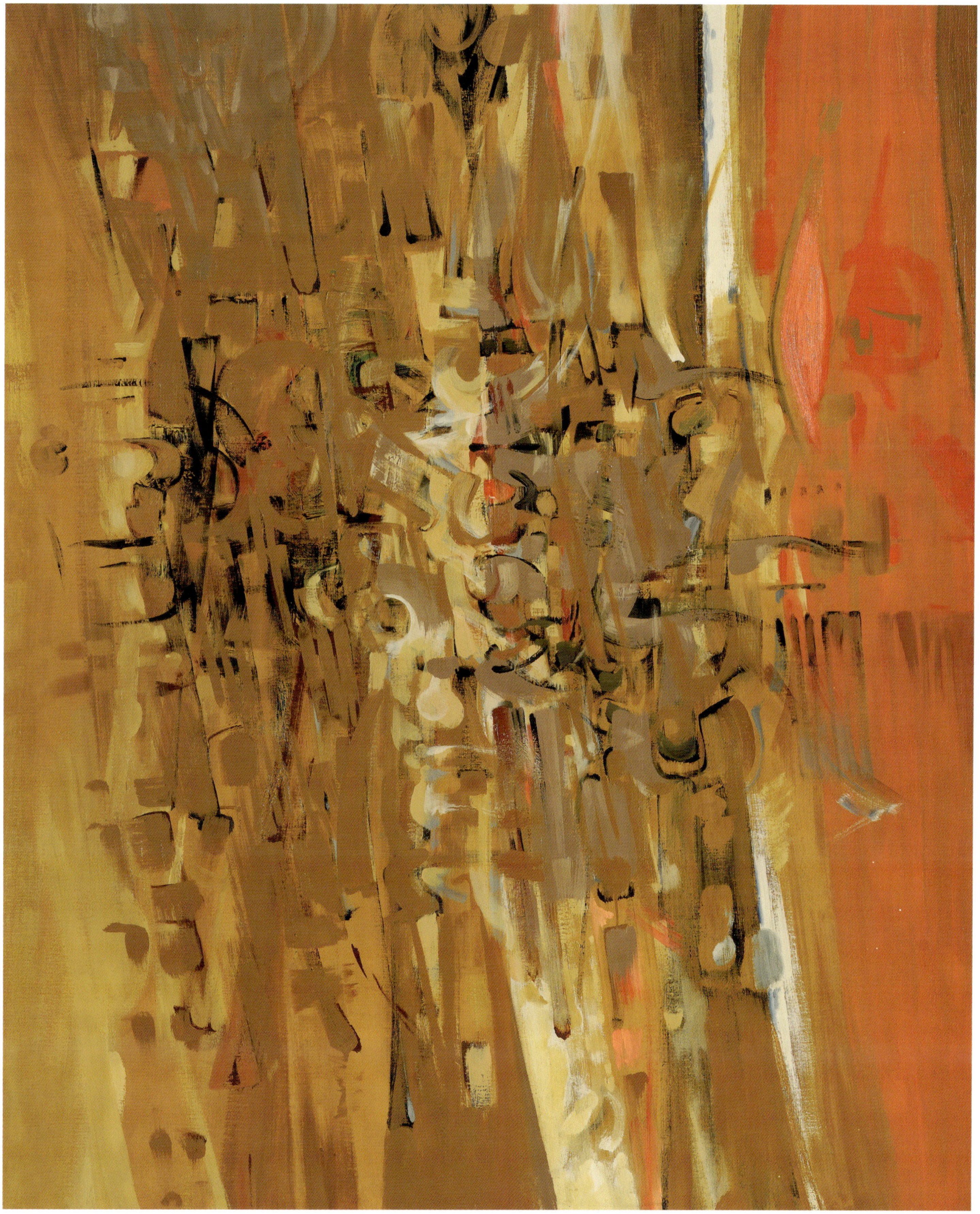

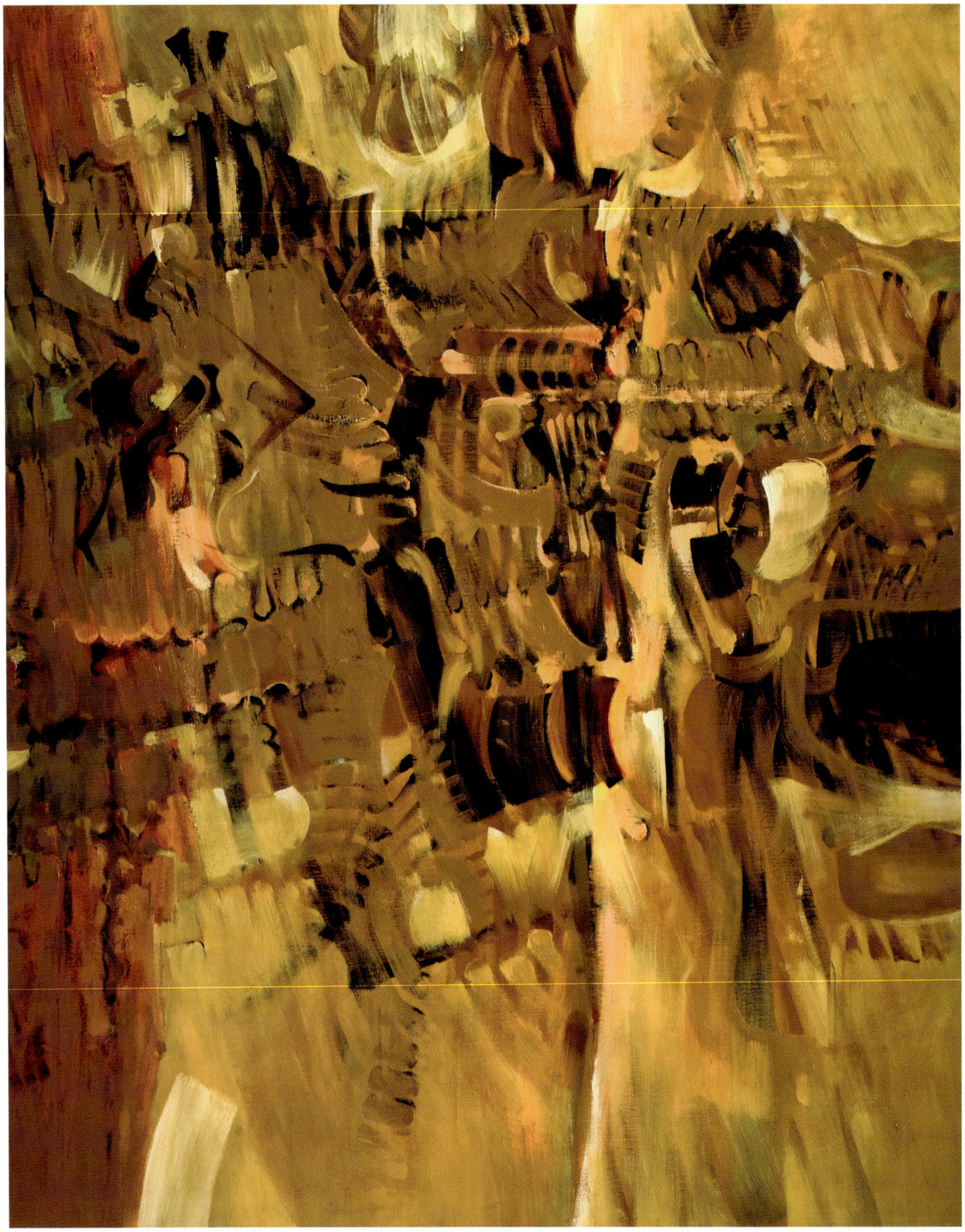

134
Sandspoor III
oil on canvas
152.5 x 122 cm (60 x 48 in)
c.1961
Lincolnshire County Council,
Usher Gallery

135
Sandspoor X (Lunar)
oil on canvas
142.2 x 111.8 cm (56 x 44 in)
1963
Private collection

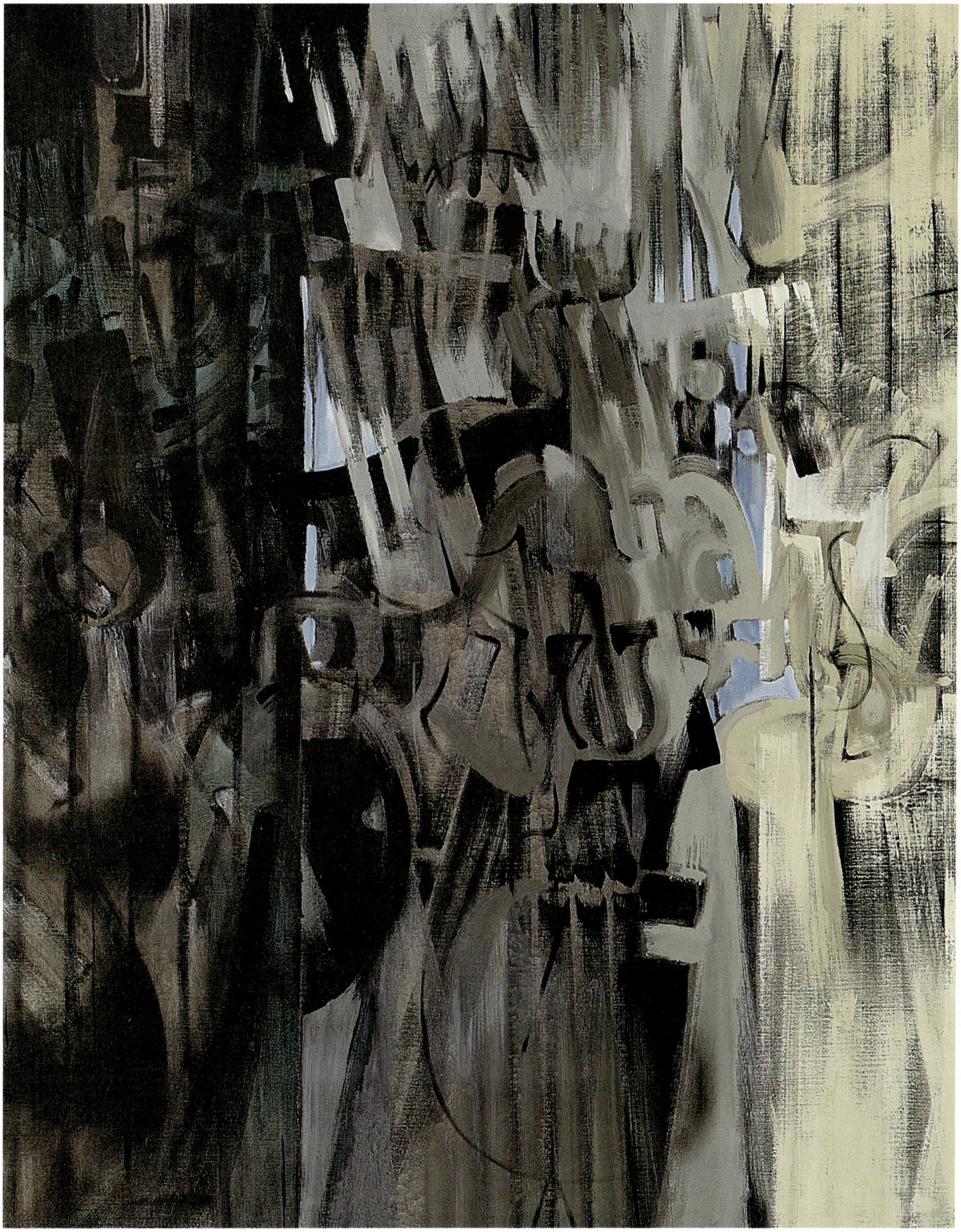

136
Untitled
oil on masonite
39.4 x 24.1 cm (15½ x 9½ in)
1961
Private collection

137
Black White
oil on canvas
101.6 x 80.7 (40 x 31¾ in)
1964
Private collection

Where, exactly, is that 'other side' from which Wynter says that he approaches 'nature'? Does he mean approaching from the psychic to the physical, maybe, or from principle to practice? In the year before the Zurich show he had had an experience that may well have informed this phrase. One evening in early May 1961 the Wynters had been entertaining Patrick and Delia Heron and their guest at the time, Prunella Clough. During the night Wynter was woken by severe chest pains. The doctor was called, and Wynter was ferried by Land Rover to the coast road and thence by ambulance to hospital in Penzance, where he learned that he'd had a heart attack. The treatment in those days, which Wynter was duly prescribed, involved three months of bed-rest at the cottage hospital in St Ives – an enforced absence from the Carn that exposed certain problems with life there for a young family. Monica, with a baby to care for, had not yet learned to drive, and the nearest telephone was several hundred yards away at Eagles Nest. During his long recuperation Wynter found convivial company on the ward, which he shared with another heart-attack victim, the painter Tony O'Malley. But he was shaken; despite his athletic pursuits and love of the outdoors, years of heavy smoking and addiction to fry-ups (what Wynter called 'the blue-smoke school of cookery') had taken their toll. These factors, combined with his growing family (the Wynters' second son, Billy, was born in August 1962), finally led to the decision, in May 1964, to move from the Carn to Treverven, an enormous house near St Buryan, on the milder, south-facing coast of the Penwith Peninsula.

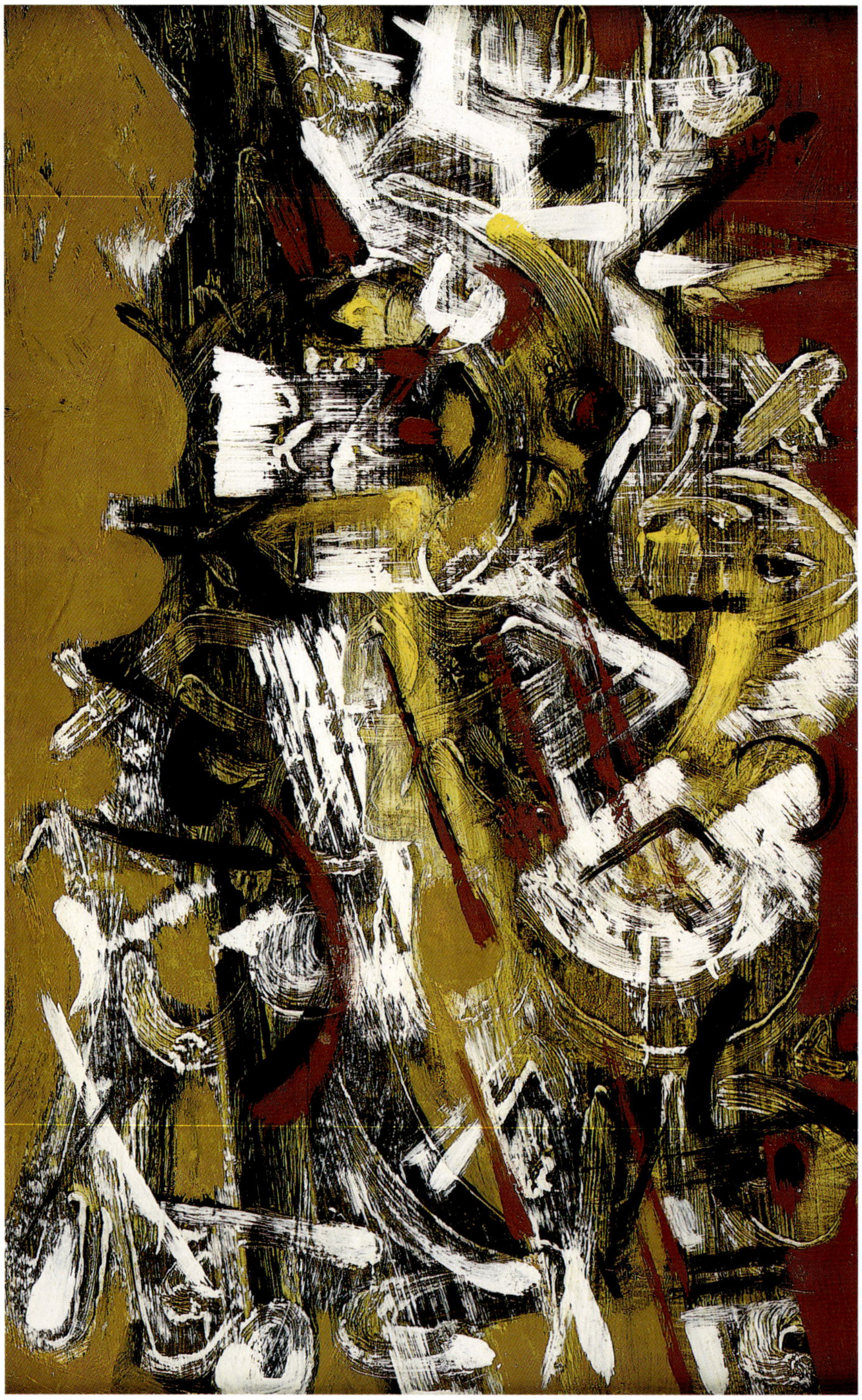

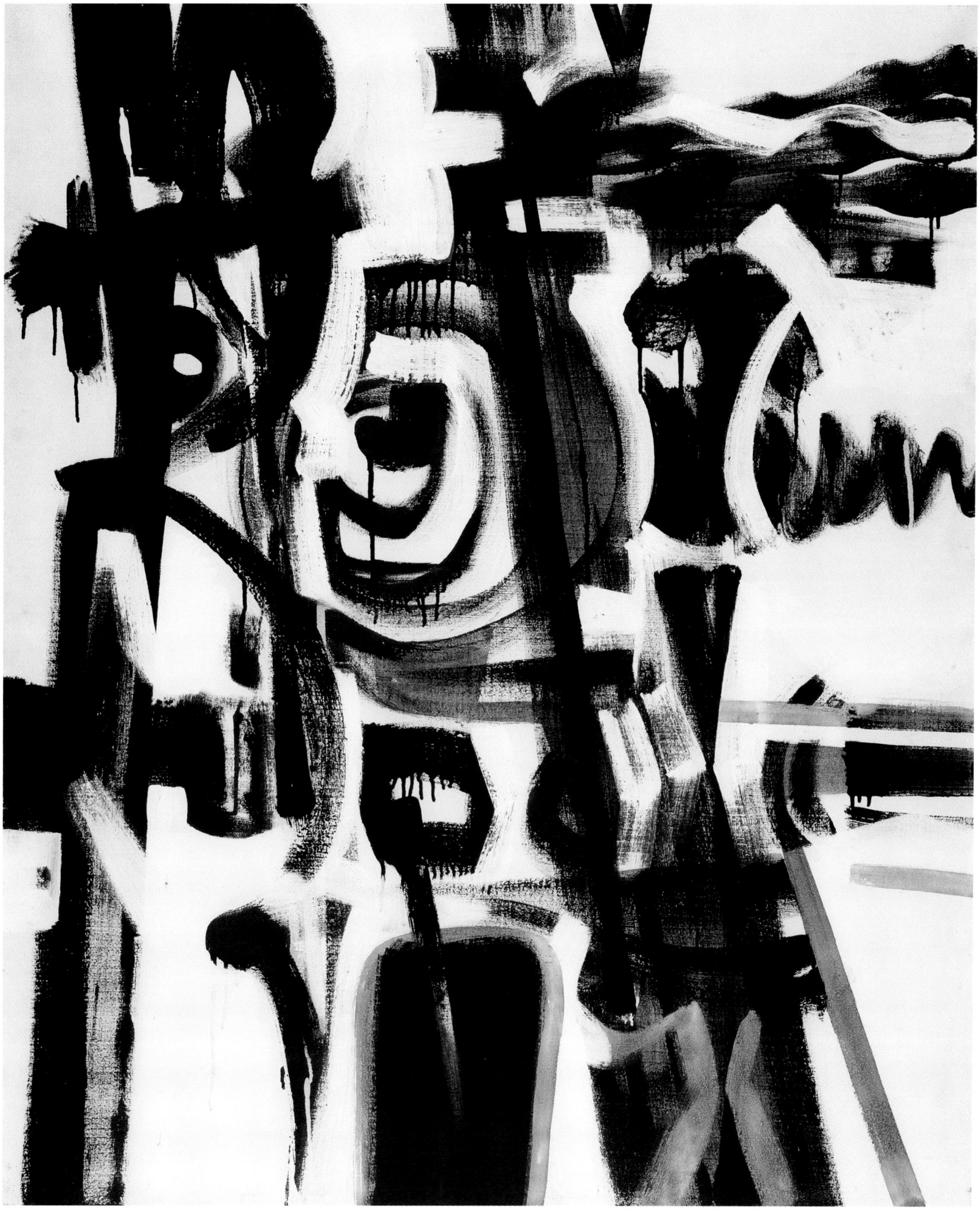

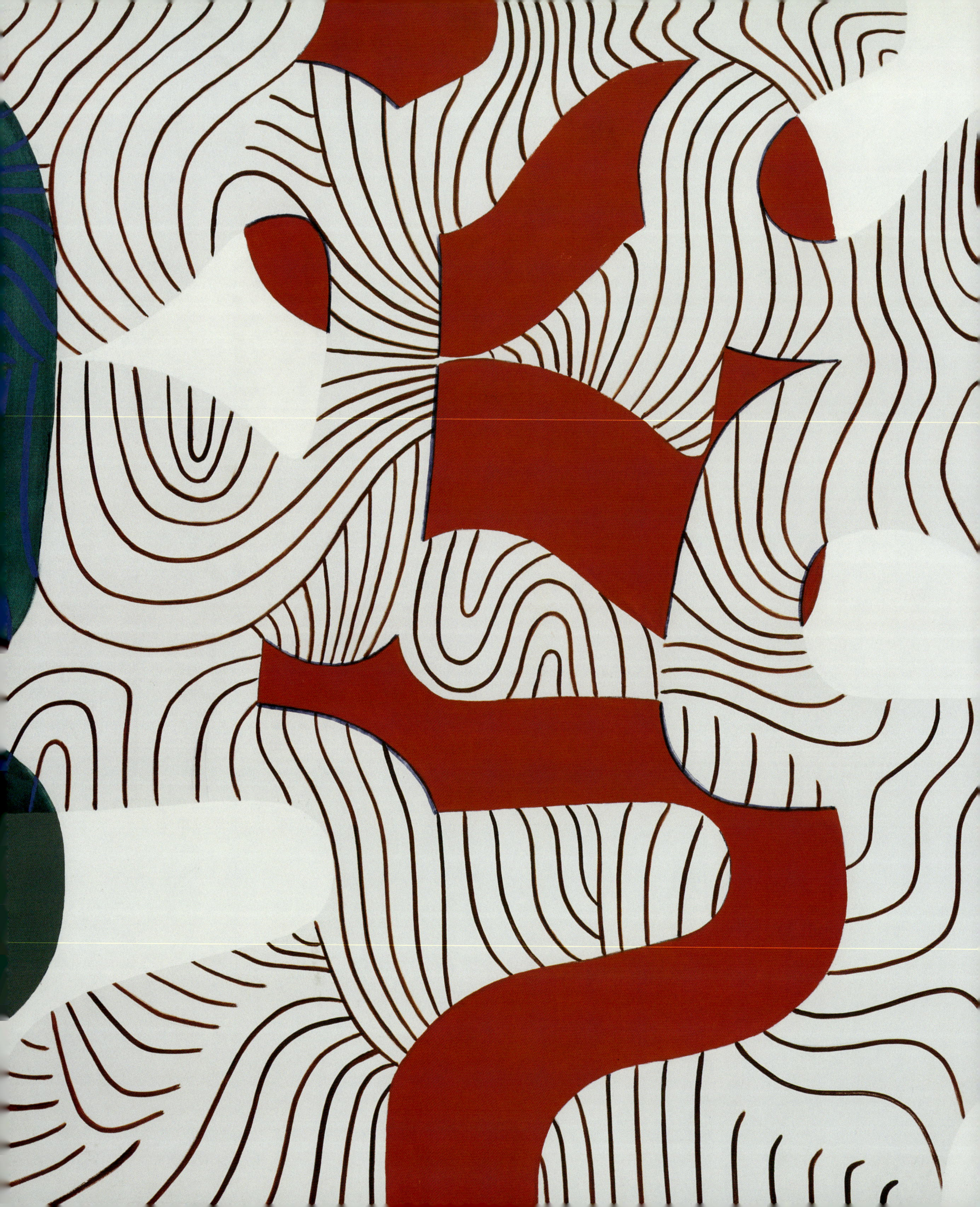

7

'The Alphabet of Nature': Pattern and Process, 1964–75

The Wynters' new home at Treverven presented quite a different prospect from the Carn. Sheltered by rising fields to the north, with the south light pouring in on the other side, where a small valley ran down to the sea, it was a benignly aspected place, altogether on a grander, more comfortable scale. Wynter threw himself into sorting out his new demesne. He bought a rotavator and ploughed a vegetable patch in the large garden that surrounded the house, and hacked through thick bramble overgrowth to clear the path down to the cove below. Like Lanyon, who had moved into Little Park Owles in 1955, and Heron at Eagles Nest, Wynter now occupied one of the larger properties in West Penwith.

There were considerable advantages. The house afforded plenty of space both for work and family life: there were two drawing-rooms (one in the artistic, the other in the social, sense), a photographic dark-room, a workshop outside and ample wall space for hanging even Wynter's largest canvases. Tom Wynter recalls how, growing up there, he and his brother enjoyed the cornucopia of junk their father had acquired, 'out of curiosity, or in case one day it might be useful: relays, transformers, motors, search light mirrors, magnets, sheets of Polaroid filters, bottles of concentrated nitric acid'. Mixing sugar and weed-killer, Wynter created 'improvised but very effective rockets'.[1] While the next ten years were to see further, striking developments in his work, this move marked the effective end of one long-running theme in Wynter's life, his war of resistance against middle-classness. Perhaps he felt able to take on Treverven, which involved constant effort and expense in its upkeep, partly because, in his childhood's ample, well-tended surroundings, the heavier tasks of household and garden management had all been performed by employees.[2]

The move also coincided with changes in Wynter's working practice. In place of the accumulation of marks, carefully executed but never preconceived, of which his great series of all-over abstracts from 1956 onwards had been composed, he began more often to base his work on consciously selected and pre-formed shapes. This may have been a consequence of working on the IMOOS, which required precise calculations and carefully constructed parts in order to function properly. This change also seems to relate to Wynter's increasingly specific and technical application of the 'stream' metaphor to his painting, and to other aspects of his life. In 1961, when he'd painted *Kayak* (see fig.131), Wynter was still balancing a free, gestural manner with an architectonic feeling of structure (reminiscent in its lower left-hand section of Lanyon's contemporaneous *Silent Coast* or *Thermal*). As Bowness observed, there was a sense of 'cosmic energy ... brought into a fruitful conflict with the demands of architecture and spatial organization'[3] – qualities that continue to be felt in his work of the early 1960s, as in *Black White* (fig. 137), painted in 1964. The paint handling in other works from around this time, however, starts to appear at once more fluid and more sharply defined. In *Spate II* (1964; fig. 139) the systematic 'optical' hatching first seen in such paintings as *The Black* (1962) is accented by a crisply marked C shape that was to become a motif of remarkable versatility in Wynter's paintings in the following decade.

The titles of many works from the mid-1960s are specifically to do with kayaking. These include the 'Spate' series (figs 138, 139, 140), *Clapotis* (the term for a standing wave; fig. 143), *Tailrace* (fig. 142), *Tidal Surge* (fig. 141) and *Fall I* (fig. 146). Whereas Wynter's earlier explorations on the water had often involved ocean canoeing and kayaking – activities that, post-heart-attack, were thought unadvisedly strenuous and unpredictable – he now began avidly studying maps of Cornwall for suitably navigable rivers and taking every opportunity to explore the Severn Valley and Welsh rivers with his brother. Manoeuvring a canoe and especially a fibreglass kayak, which sits almost on the water surface and has a natural tendency to float broadside to the

detail of **157**
Meander I, 1964

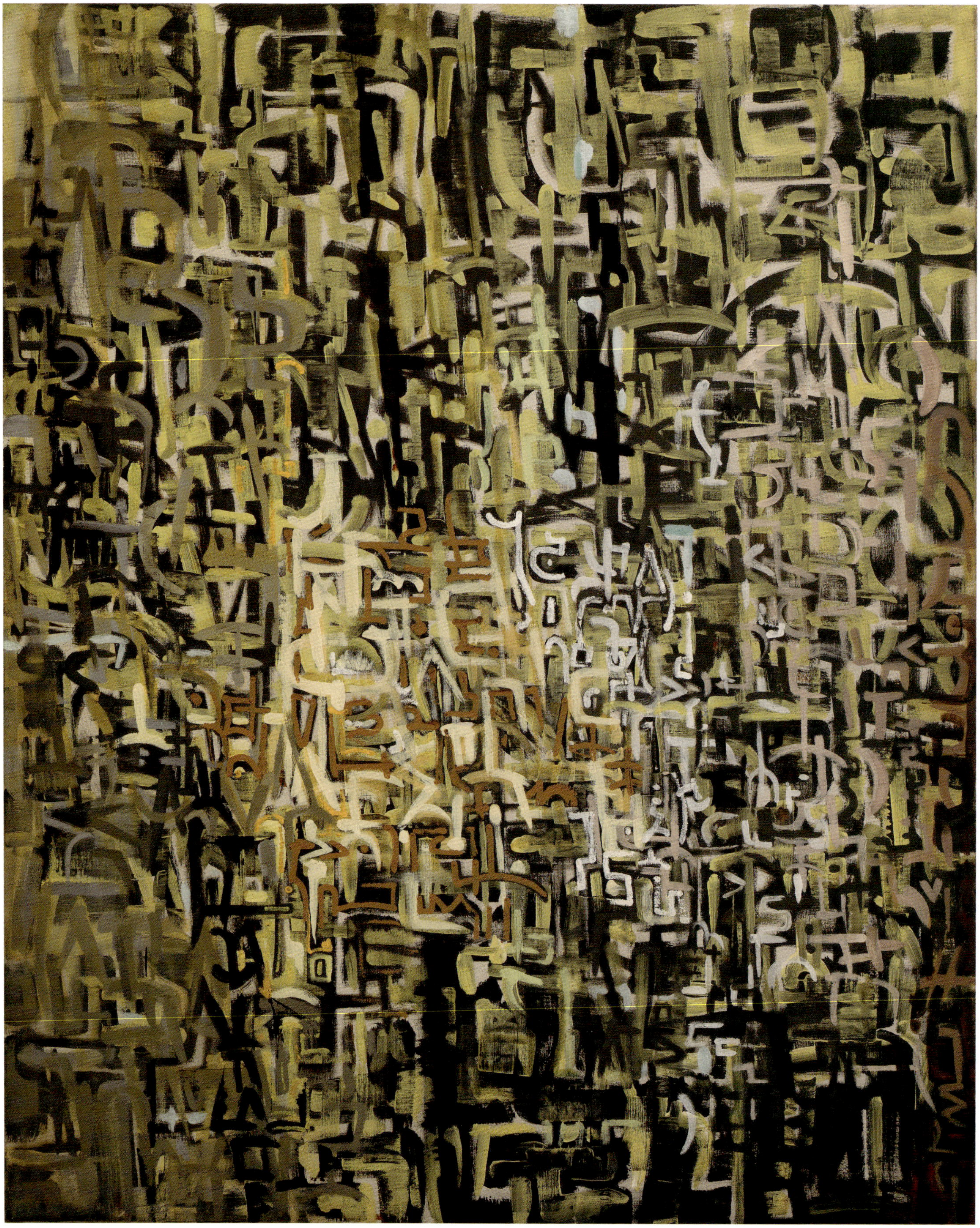

138
Yellow Painting, Spate I
oil on canvas
142.3 x 111.8 cm (56 x 44 in)
1964
Fitzwilliam Museum, Cambridge

139
Spate II
oil on canvas
152 x 122.2 cm (59 7/8 x 48 1/8 in)
1964
Private collection

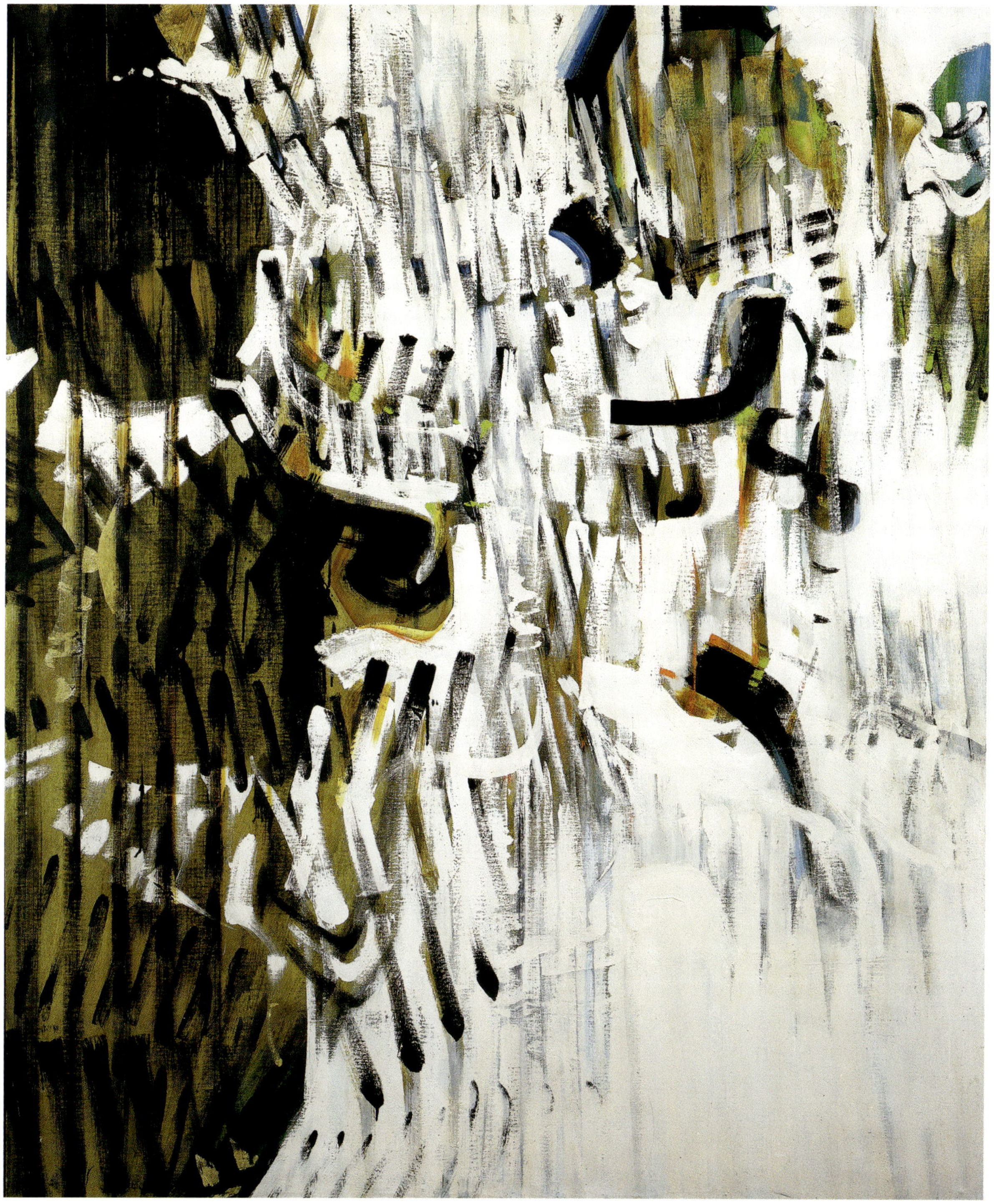

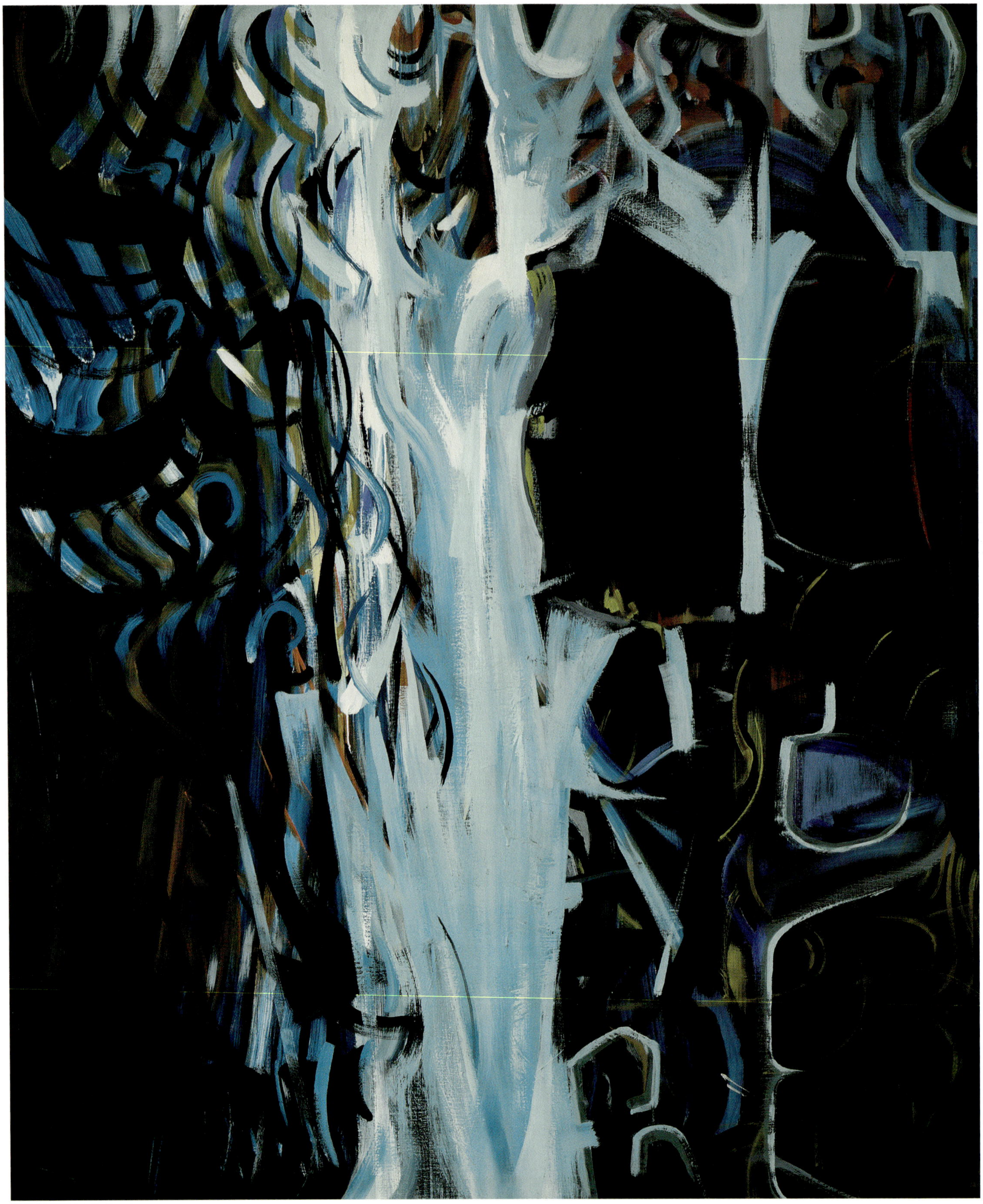

140
Spate III
acrylic on canvas
152.5 x 122 cm (60 x 48 in)
1965
Government Art Collection

current and so capsize, depends entirely on the rower's skill. In order to avoid obstacles and dangers, you need to be able to 'read' water movements in the course ahead, an art that gives this sport a kind of intellectual dimension. Wynter immersed himself in the technical literature on the subject, making detailed notes on treatises such as R. A. R. Tricker's *Bores, Breakers, Waves and Wakes* (there were inevitable family jokes about bores, tidal and otherwise).[4]

Throughout the 1960s kayaking and canoeing expeditions formed the basis for countless Wynter family excursions and camping trips. Wynter researched precise itineraries, studying maps and data about river flow. His physical, imaginative and scientific engagement with, and pleasure in, water – its sensations, movements, properties – was further fired by his discovery in 1965 of the book *Sensitive Chaos: The Creation of Flowing Forms in Water and Air*. Its author, Theodor Schwenk, was an engineer and disciple of the esoteric Austrian polymath Rudolf Steiner. The preface, by Jacques Cousteau, began: 'Ever since that magical moment when my eyes first opened under the sea I have been unable to see, think or live as I had done before.' 'All that life around us', Cousteau continued, referring to the myriad creatures he had encountered in the sea but also summarising Schwenk's overarching thesis, 'was really water, modelled according to its own laws, vitalised by each fresh venture, striving to rise into consciousness.'[5] Among other ideas Schwenk explored was the notion that, since animal embryos grow *in utero* within a fluid medium, the laws of hydrodynamics account for the shape of many living things, including the human form and our inner organs. An understanding of the behaviour of water under different conditions, therefore, enables us to 'read' other natural phenomena:

> These phenomena in water and air may, we think, be regarded as the letters of a script, which it is necessary to learn to use like the alphabet of nature ... Through watching water and air with unprejudiced eyes, our way of thinking becomes changed and more suited to the understanding of what is alive.[6]

'This transformation of our way of thinking', asserted Schwenk, was 'a decisive step that must be taken in the present day' – that is, in a world in which 'A way of thinking that is directed solely to what is profitable' has led to incalculable environmental damage. Wynter took these ideas seriously; their elaboration by Schwenk with reference to detailed analyses of water and air flow, which he then compared both to life-forms such as shellfish, antelope antlers and mammalian intestines, and to art forms ranging from ancient Greek grave stelae to the bronze doors of the church of San Zeno, Verona, mirrored several long-meditated elements in Wynter's thinking. His desire to create a synthesis of scientific objectivity with creative subjectivity had been there since at least the early 1940s. Coupled with this now were Schwenk's photographs and diagrams of flow, which echoed with startling precision certain patterns and rhythms in Wynter's painting, as well as those he had documented in the hundreds of colour slides of natural forms and surfaces he had taken during the previous decade. From the mid-1960s onwards, titles such as *Kayak* and *Tailrace* began to be superseded by terms connoting not water sports but river flow, such as 'Confluence' and 'Meander'.

While these ideas came to preoccupy – not to say obsess – Wynter, to the gallery-going public in 1965 it probably looked as though, after a sell-out show of his IMOOS at Waddingtons that July, he had made a successful transition from abstract painting to kinetic art. With its emphasis on interaction between audience and art work, and on wider environmental factors, such as the choice of location and manner of viewing, kinetic art of the 1960s pointed the way to later developments in, for example, installation art. Of all the Middle Generation

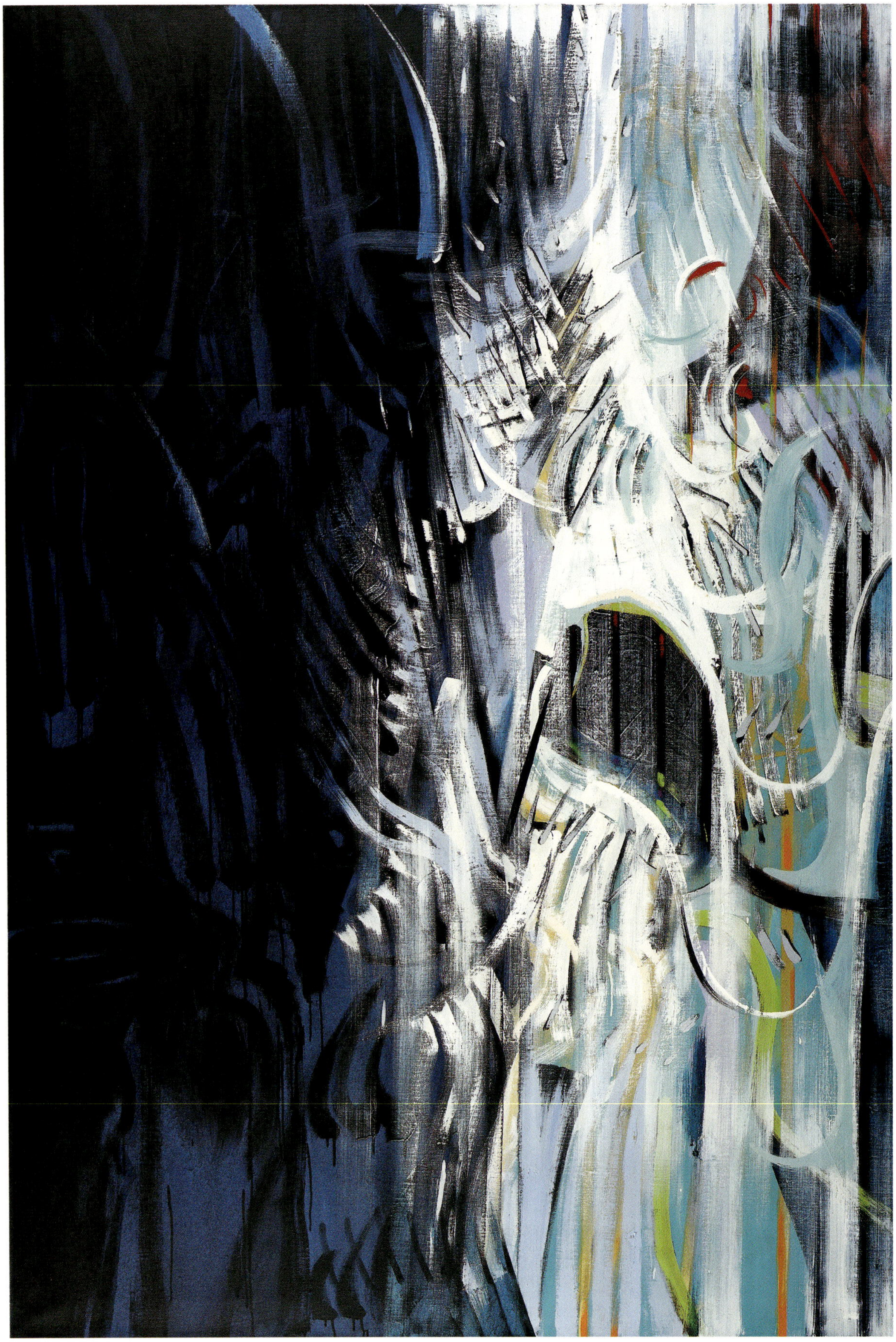

141
Tidal Surge
oil on canvas
182.9 x 122 cm (72 x 48 in)
1964
National Gallery of Wales, Cardiff

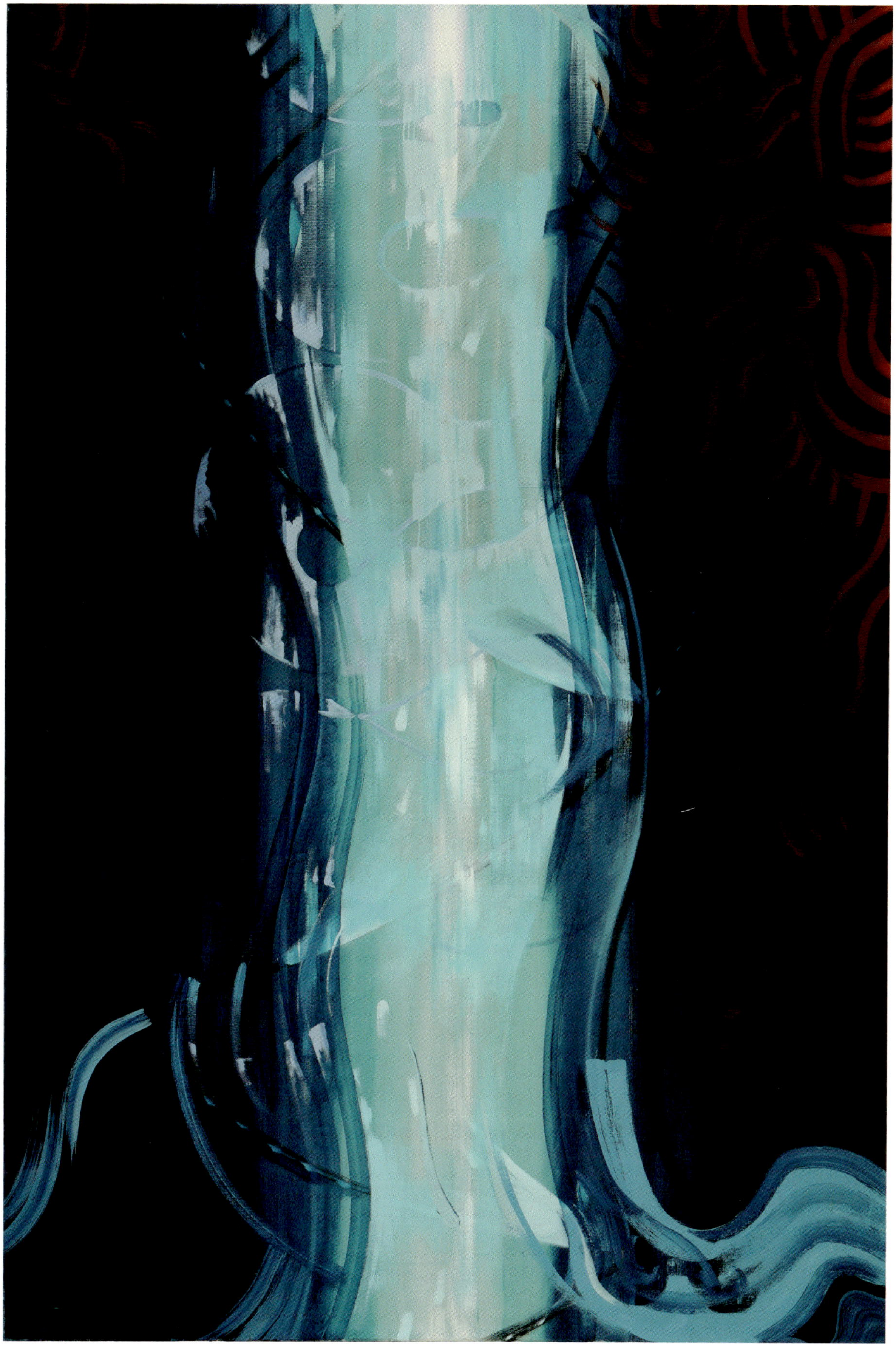

142
Tailrace
oil on canvas
182.9 x 122 cm (72 x 48 in)
1966
Artist's estate

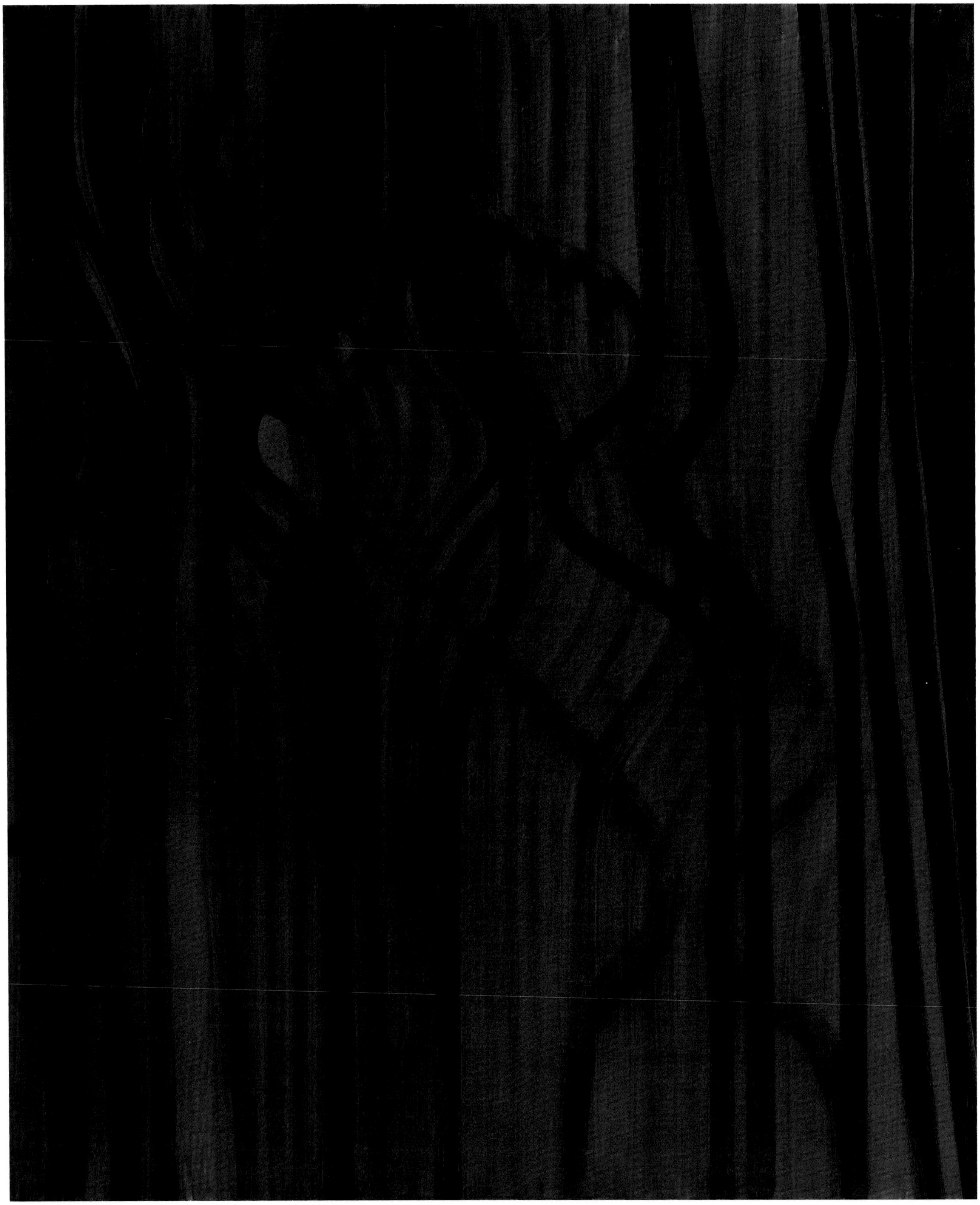

143
Clapotis
oil on canvas
152.4 x 122 cm (60 x 48 in)
1965
Artist's estate

and their associates, Wynter was the only one to break new ground in this way. In the early 1960s Lanyon made a number of Pop-style assemblages and architectural-scale murals, and Frost was later to experiment with soft sculpture, but for the most part the work of Wynter's painter contemporaries remained rooted in the traditional gallery model.

Since kinetic art combined several of Wynter's passions – the rendering of movement, 'flow' and environmental experience in art, and the cross-fertilisation of art and science – the IMOOS seemed exactly the vehicle he'd been looking for. In terms of Wynter's own career, there was a certain consistency in departures of this kind. The fact that 'experimenting in the world of kinetic art' was, as one reviewer commented, 'the last thing one would imagine him doing'[7] was absolutely in character. He had been bracketed in the 1940s with the Neo-Romantics, and in the 1950s with the 'action painters'; now his work could be positioned somewhere between Vasarely's *cinétisme* and Yves Tinguely's Surrealist-inspired meta-mechanical sculptures (which Wynter much admired), on the one hand, and, on the other, the work of artists such as Liliane Lijn and Nam June Paik, which engaged more deliberately with science and technology. By 1965 kinetic art was an established field, as evidenced by the institutional purchases from Wynter's show by the Tate, Manchester University and Bristol City Council. It's possible to imagine him reinventing his career at this stage. Why didn't this happen?

The answer lies, probably, in a combination of professional and personal circumstances. After almost a decade Wynter was teaching again, this time at Falmouth College of Art. Established in the early 1900s as a small local art school, Falmouth was now trying to raise its game to compete with metropolitan institutions. Its principal, Michael Finn, recruited Lanyon, Frost and Wynter – all still resident in west Cornwall in the early 1960s – as visiting lecturers. As at Corsham, Wynter found that teaching sapped his energy for work. Being identified as a senior 'St Ives' artist was also problematic. For one thing, he had always denied being part of any such school or movement, or even that one existed. For another, the younger staff at Falmouth were understandably keen to distance themselves from any perceived allegiance to a 'St Ives' tradition, equated as it was with an outdated vogue for landscape-inspired abstract painting. By 1965 the idea of a St Ives School that Heron had done so much to promote felt like history. In 1958 Nicholson had left for Switzerland; in 1963, with a growing family and in the hope of being closer to sources of regular teaching income, Frost had moved to Banbury; and in August 1964 Lanyon died in hospital in Taunton after complications arising from relatively minor injuries sustained in a botched glider landing. Hilton, meanwhile, who had become almost famous, after winning first prize in the 1963 John Moores Competition and representing Great Britain at the 1964 Venice Biennale, did not move down to live permanently in Cornwall until the following year. Heron, it was true, remained at Eagles Nest, a friend and supporter; but his own work never swerved from its dedication to the principles of pictorial space, which provided only a limited handle on other types of art – kinetics, perhaps, less than most. Finally, despite the success of his show at Waddington Galleries, 1965 was a difficult year for Wynter personally. He suffered a bad bout of depression, which medication did little to alleviate.

In another context Wynter's kinetics might have connected with other developments in the increasingly pluralistic art world of the 1960s. In reality, however, the isolation that probably contributed to his depression was real enough. His work lacked the persuasive critical promoter so necessary to artists, and he was out of the orbit of the kind of collaborative projects or institutional commissions that might have carried his kinetic art forward. Another snag was that, once he had solved the challenges posed by IMOOS construction, his interest moved elsewhere. In the mid-1960s his more technical

144
Drawing
fibre-tip pen on paper
42 x 53.3 cm (16½ x 21 in)
1966
Artist's estate

145
Drawing
fibre-tip pen on paper
42 x 54 cm (16½ x 21¼ in)
1969
Private collection

146
Fall I
oil on canvas
142.2 x 111.7 cm (56 x 44 in)
1966
Private collection

investigations into the nature of 'flow' informed a new system of drawing, which in turn radically influenced the construction of his paintings. Wynter was always eager to experiment with different media, whether 'non-art' materials such as cellophane, which he had used in layers in photographic works in the late 1950s, or newly patented media. Some time around 1966 he constructed a light-box, on which a drawing could be laid so that it could be copied or adapted by placing a blank sheet above the illuminated image. These works, made using Pentel fibre-tip pens, represent hundreds of variations on 'flow' motifs (figs 144, 145, 147, 148). Some are reminiscent of the diagrams in Schwenk's book, one of which shows a series of looping meanders in a river with the caption 'Naturally flowing water always endeavours to follow a meandering course'. The meander, according to Schwenk, is 'an archetypal principle of flowing water that wants to realise itself, regardless of the surrounding material'[8] – that is, whether flowing through rock, sand, air or water. As an example of the last, he cited the Gulf Stream, which has what he described as 'a rhythmical form in *space*, and it is also subject to a rhythmical process in *time* through the changing position of its loops'.[9]

The black Pentel pens with which Wynter produced his drawings were a tool for designers rather than artists, producing a line of uniform thickness, almost uninflected by pressure, the angle at which the pen is held or any of the other variables that animate pencil or dip-pen ink lines. The process was, in fact, a virtual negative of what happened with the IMOOS. In the drawings, the dynamics of flow through time and space became static designs (Schwenk explained that, when water flows around rocks in a stream, 'The wave form remains in the same spot with new water constantly flowing through it'[10]). In the IMOOS, static shapes and colours were transformed by motion and distortion in a mirror. Wynter's Pentel drawings have a hieratic flatness that recalls the graphic style of Pre-Columbian

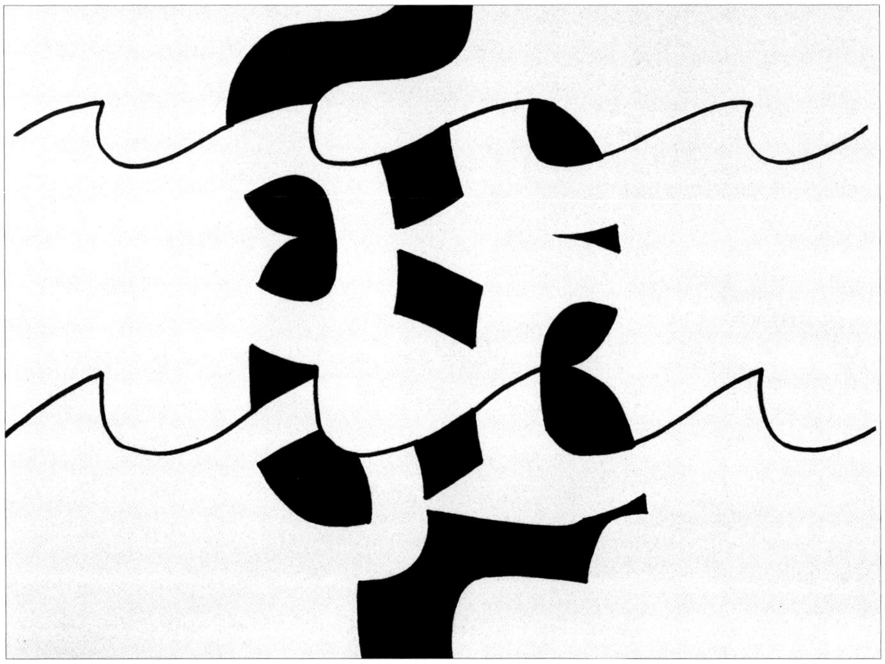

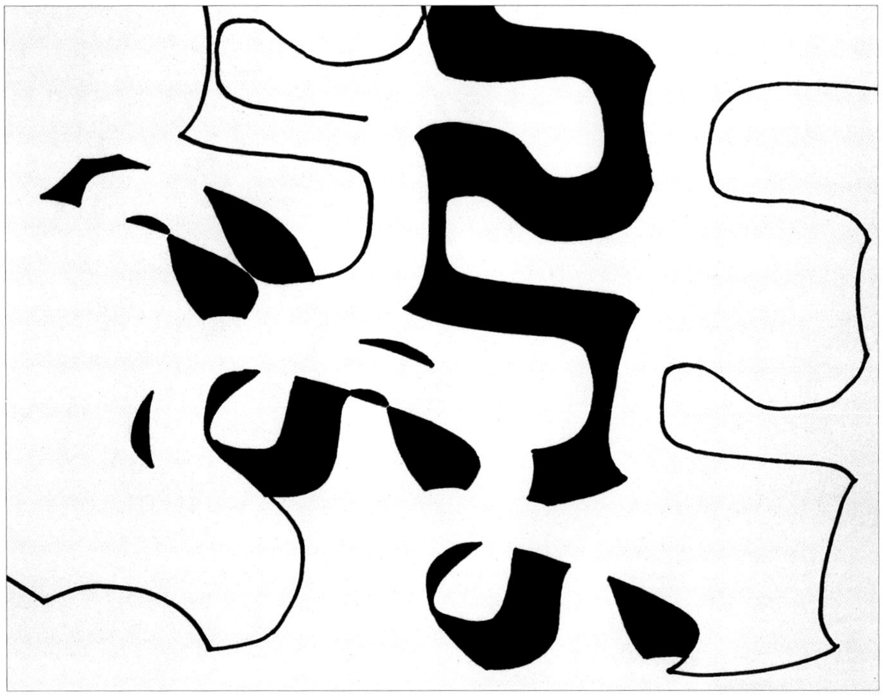

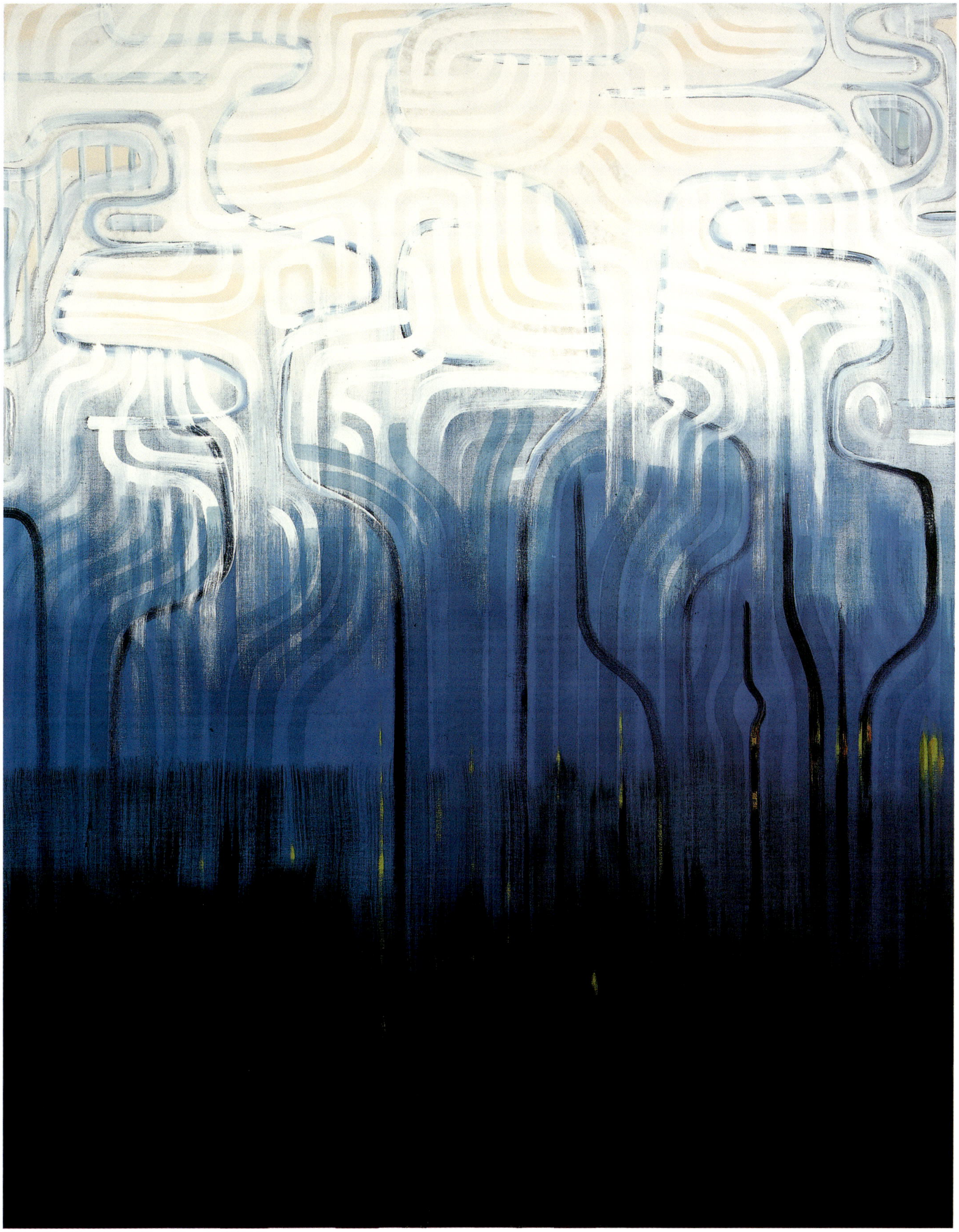

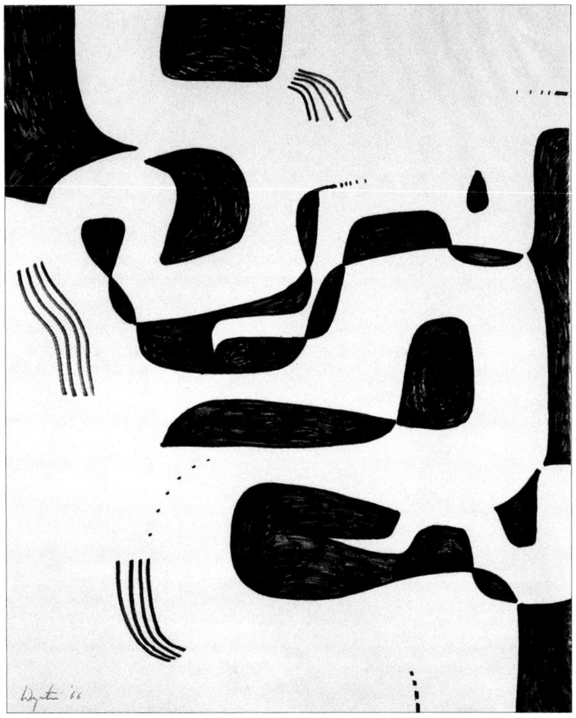

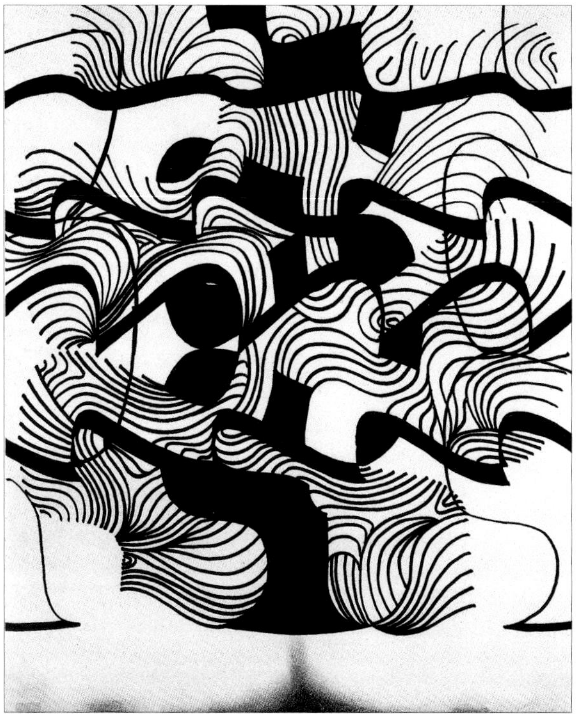

147
Drawing
fibre-tip pen on paper
54 x 42 cm (21¼ x 16½ in)
1966
Private collection

148
Drawing
fibre-tip pen on paper
54 x 42 cm (21¼ x 16½ in)
1969
Private collection

Mesoamerican codices, of which an example was reproduced by Schwenk.[11] Taken together, the series of fibre-tip drawings Wynter produced from 1966 onwards has an ambivalent quality. Here is an artist, you can't help feeling, who is not entirely at ease in this substitution of system for a more expressive, intuitive method. At the same time, however, as with Josef Albers's colour diagrams, fixation generated its own intensity and variation.

The eleven or so 'Confluence' paintings Wynter produced between 1965 and 1967 (figs 149, 150, 152) translate elements from the Pentel drawings into what is, in purely formal terms, the most varied series of his career. *Confluence I* weaves a complex interplay of striated curves into an image of tensile translucency. Wynter's awarness of Op art and Pop can be felt in the uniform, light colours and strong linear definition, but the painting's overall movement encodes his reflections about flow – a way of thinking that had become much more than a pictorial language. In *Confluence IV* (fig. 152) a blue meander snaking obliquely down the left-hand third of the canvas (a typical site of action or division in Wynter's paintings) again has a bright, poster-like, Pop flatness. This time the flow-curves are blackly emphatic but softened by pale over-painted veiling, centred on a white disc that suggests a flashlight's dazzling reflection, or the illumination from within of sun through cloud. In some paintings of the mid-1960s the formalisation of natural movement into semi-diagrammatic patterns results in a cool opulence strangely reminiscent of Art Nouveau. In *Clapotis* (1965) or *Fall* (1966; see figs 143, 146), for example, the expressive colour touches an almost Whistlerish note of midnight watery reflection. In *Confluence VI* (1966; fig. 153) the broader black-and-white design suggests ceramic texture, recalling the Native American-influenced manner of the potter Janet

149
Confluence I
oil on canvas
152.3 x 122.2 cm (60 x 48⅛ in)
1965
Artist's estate

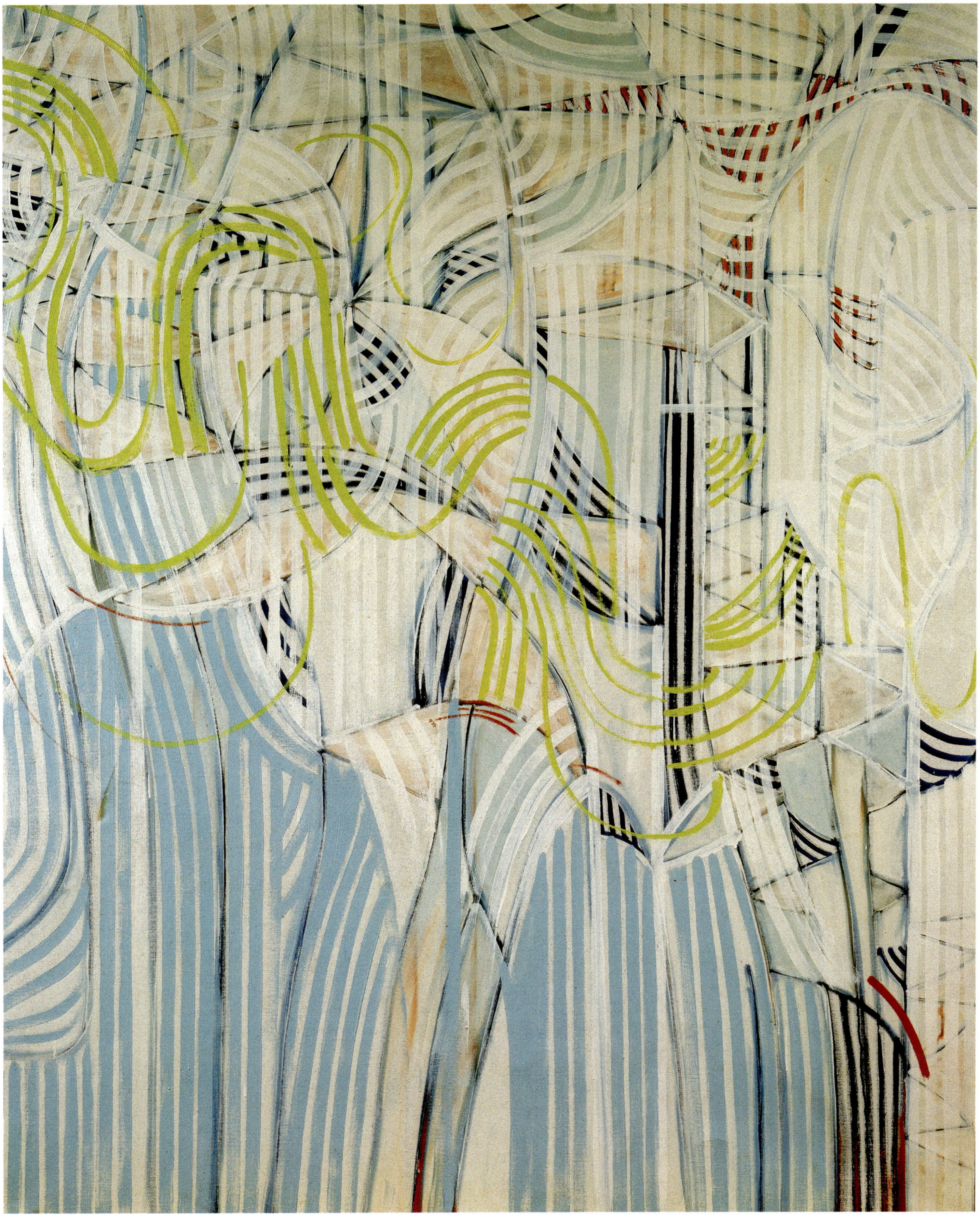

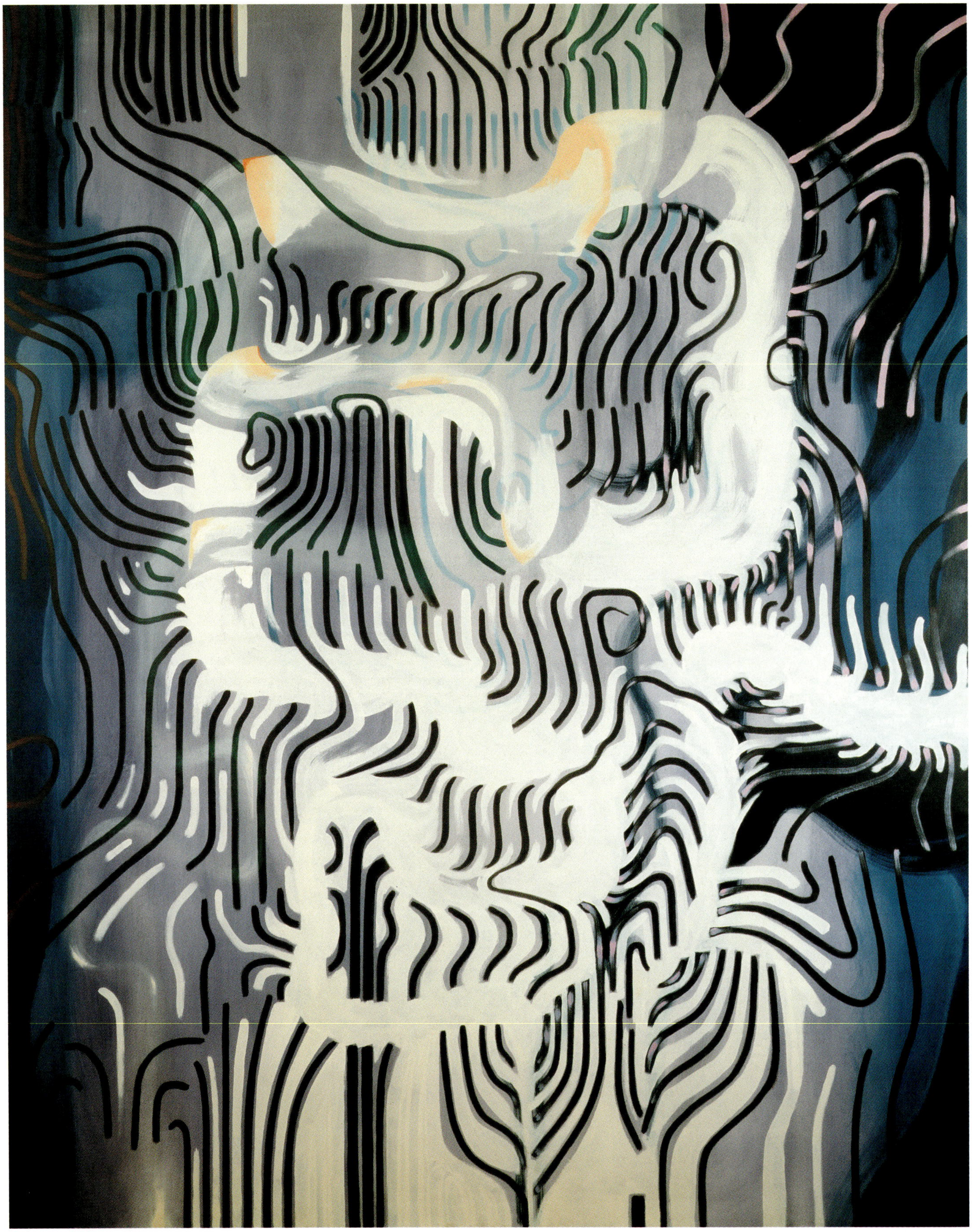

150
Confluence
142 x 111.7 cm (56 x 44 in)
*c.*1969
Private collection

151
Confluence XI
oil on canvas
182.9 x 122 cm (72 x 48 in)
1967
Private collection

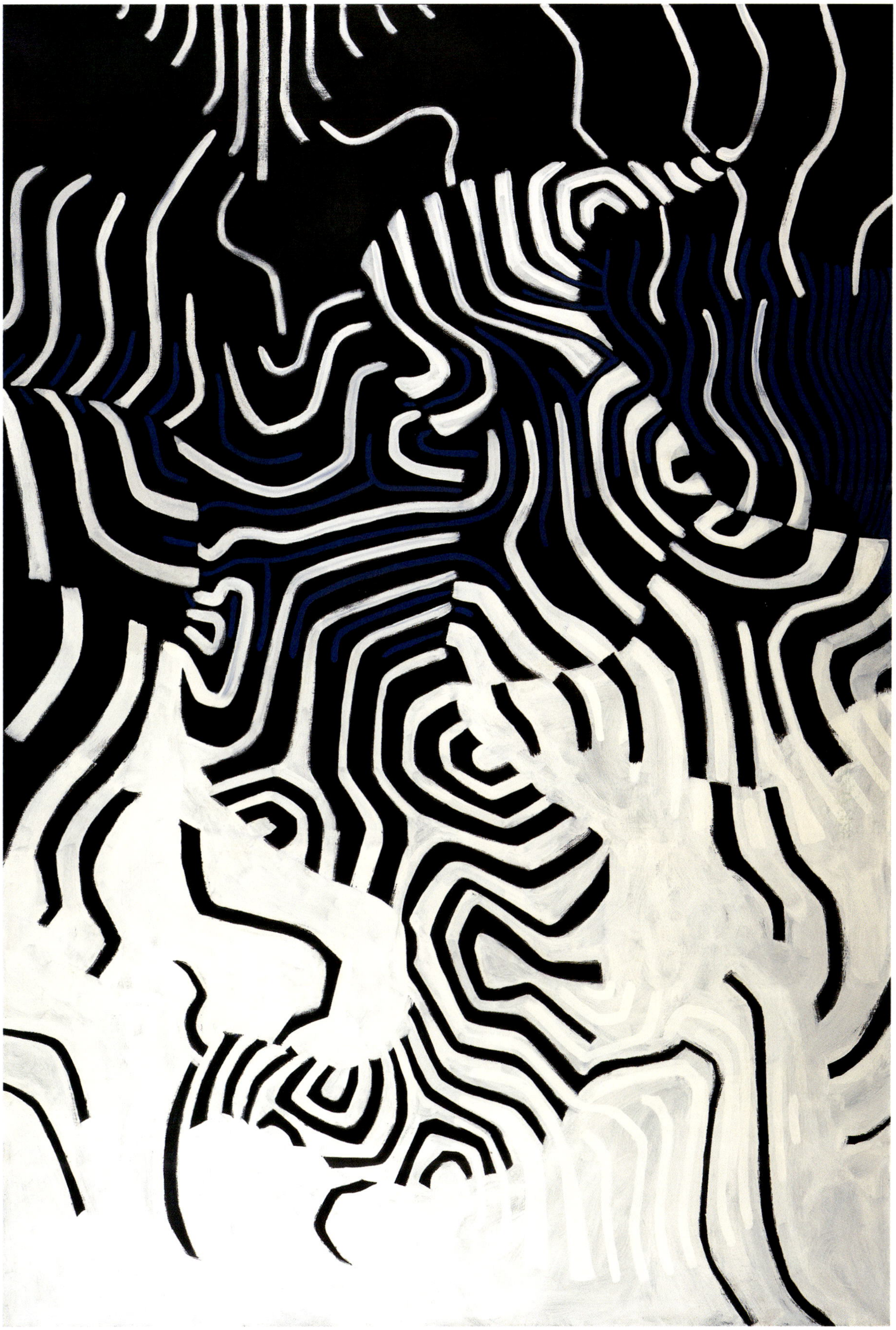

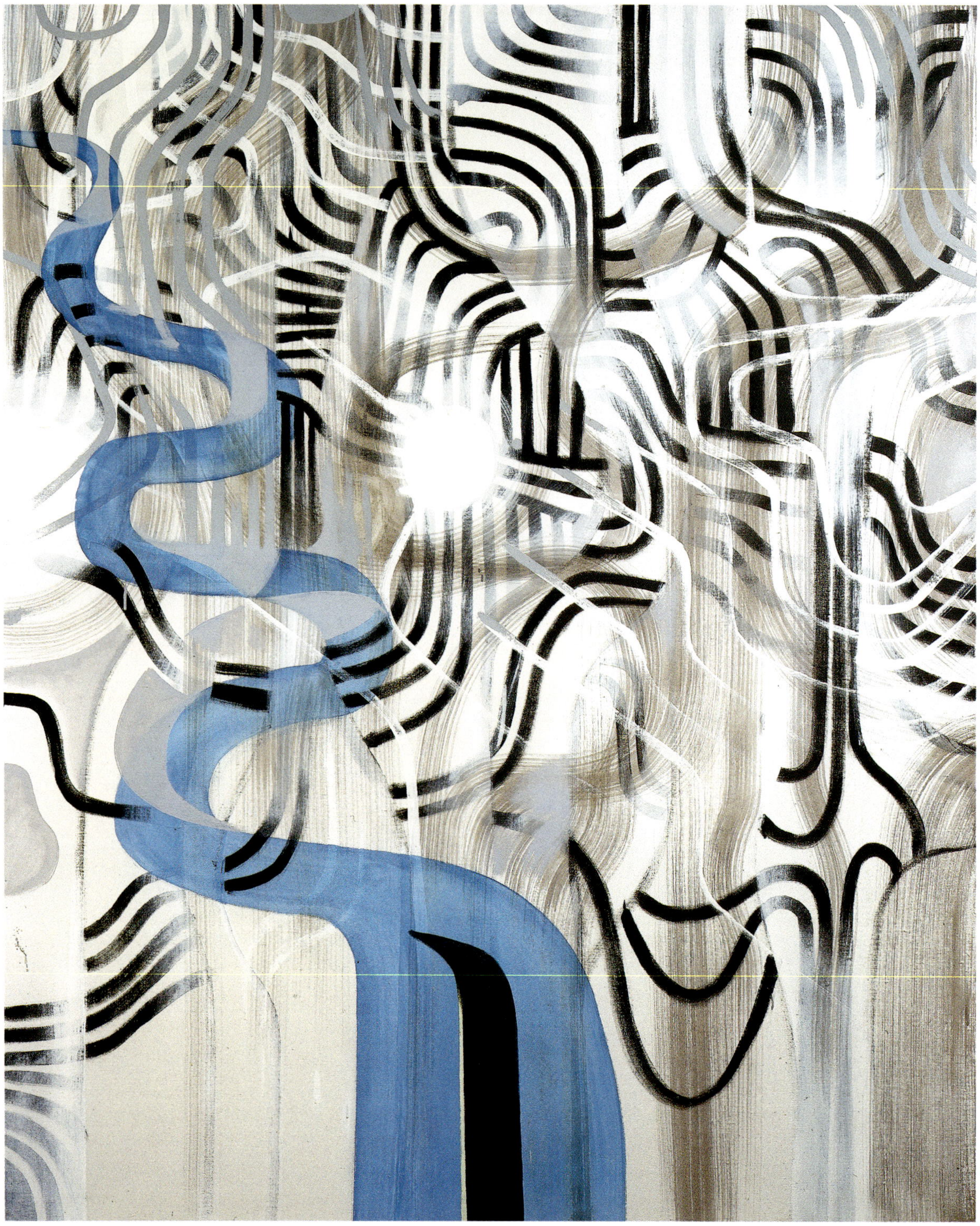

152
Confluence IV
oil on canvas
142.2 x 112 cm (56 x 44 in)
1965
Artist's estate

153
Confluence VI
oil on canvas
182.9 x 122 cm (72 x 48 in)
1966
Artist's estate

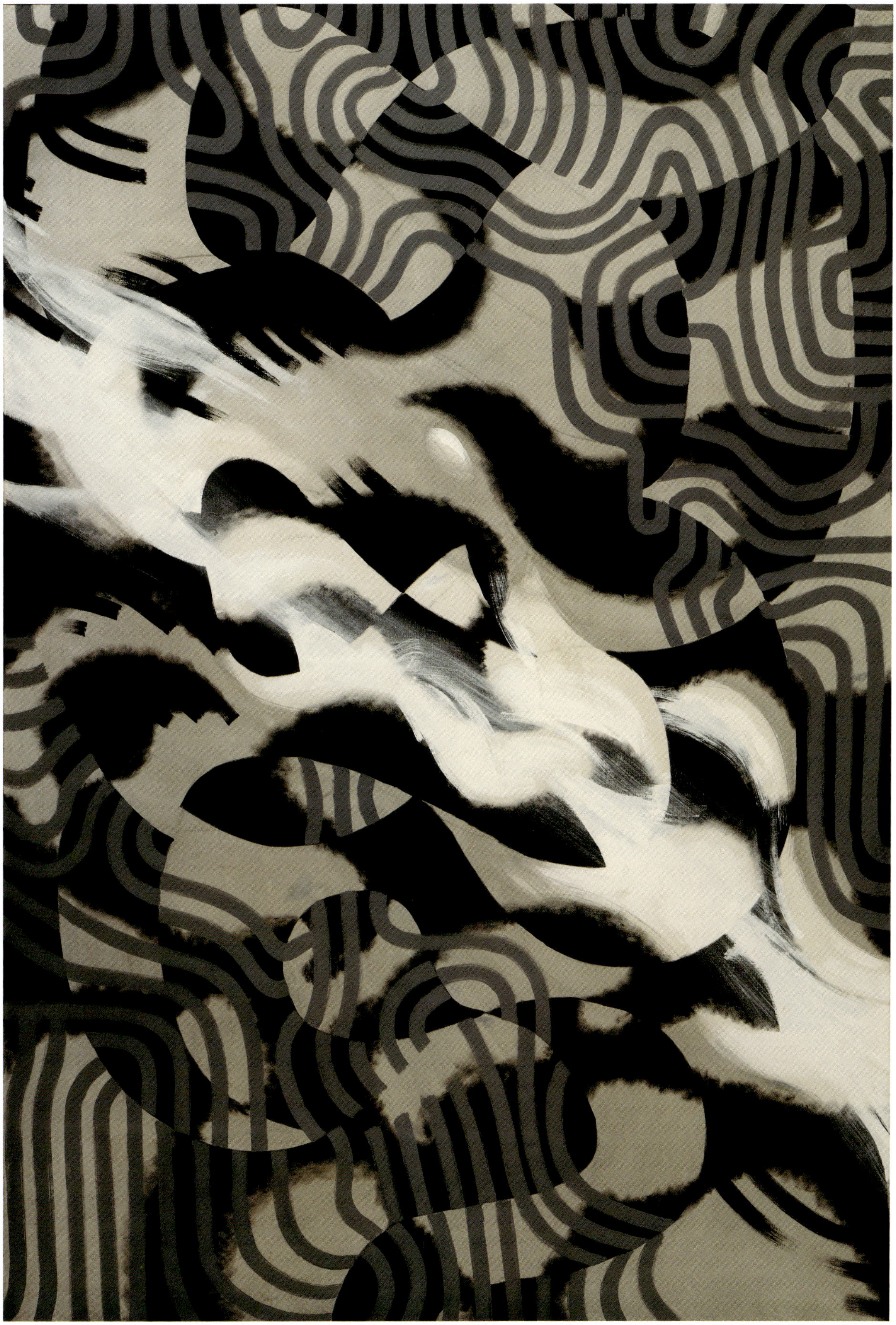

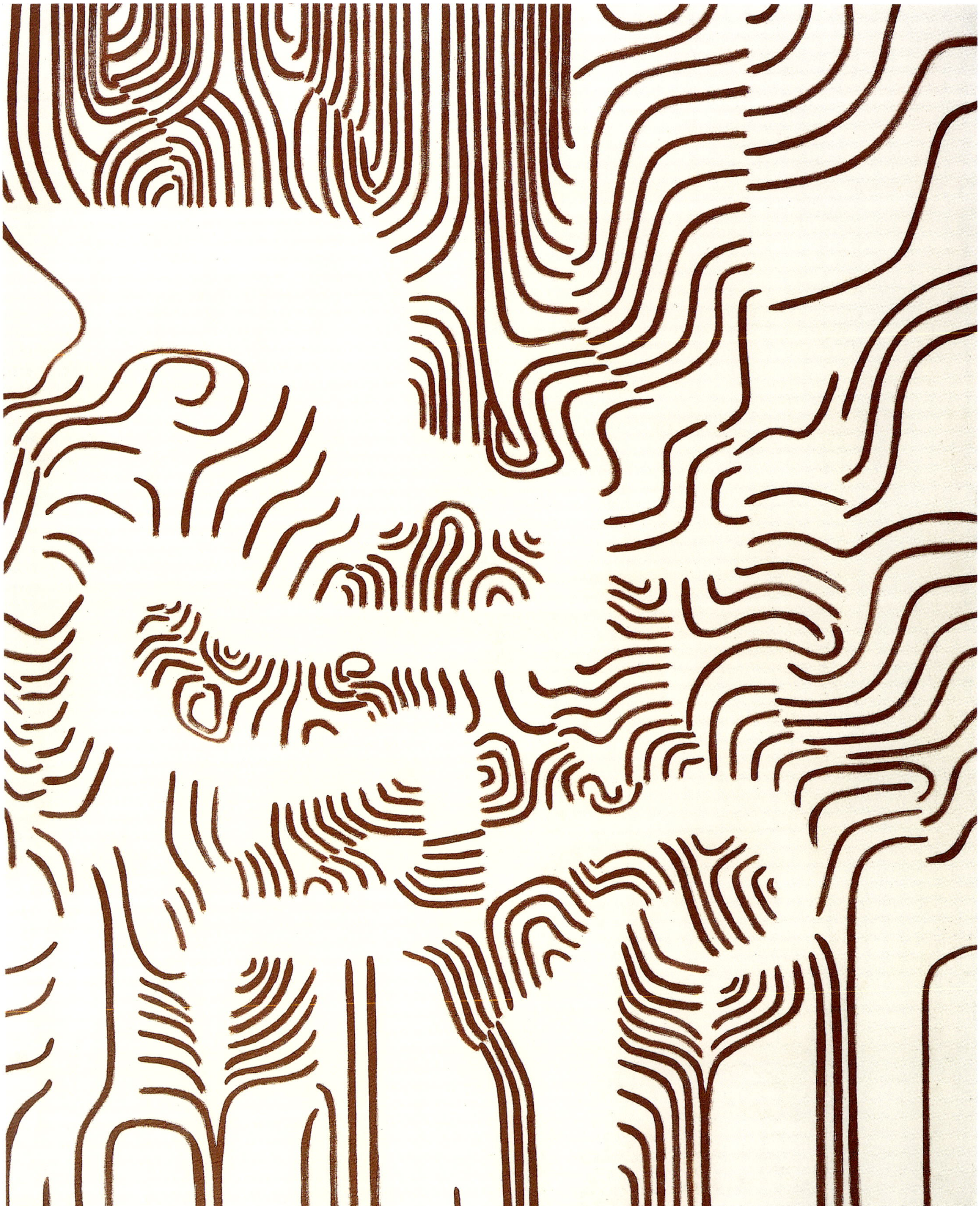

154
Confluence VII
oil on canvas
152.3 x 122 cm (60 x 48 in)
1966
Private collection

155
Confluence VIII
oil on canvas
142.2 x 111.7 cm
(56 x 44 in)
1967
Artist's estate

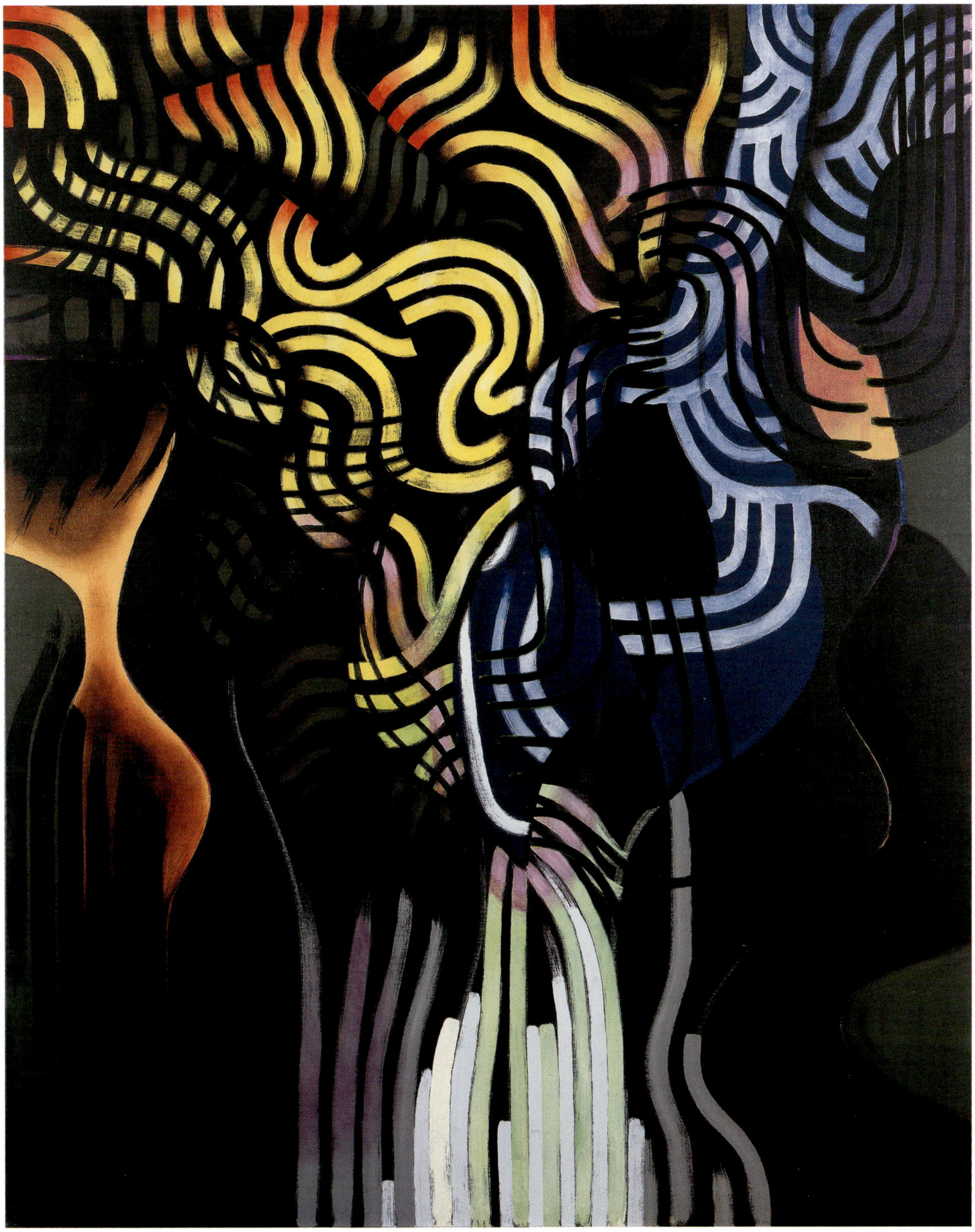

Leach. *Confluence VII* (1966; fig. 154) is a strikingly simple painted version of a Pentel drawing from which gestural mark-making has been all but banished and in which the dominant meander shape is negatively defined, as in a optical illusion. To this neutral opticality *Confluence VIII* (fig. 155) provides a complete contrast in its lurid neon tones and mimicry of airbrush shading.

In September 1966 Wynter showed works from the 'Confluence' series at the Arts Council Gallery in Belfast. The following September further examples were included in his solo exhibition at Waddington's, alongside the first canvases in a new series to which Wynter had given the title 'Meander'. In a poem completed a few years later, 'Wynter And The Grammarsow', Graham greeted his friend in mock-heroic style as a 'Scholar King/ Of rare meanders', a 'Rider of Rivers/ Undiscovered', giving Wynter's multifarious explorations of water a legendary inflection:

> Bryan the Spinner
> In endless eddies
> Above the weir
> Of rushing home.
>
> Fibre-glass swiveller
> Over the weaving
> Strands of water
> In an innocent pool ...
>
> . . . . . .
>
> Masked thinskinned diver
> On the Cornish shelf.
> Wet-suited Seeker after
> The church choir of urchins. ...[12]

The 'grammersow' in the title (intentionally misspelt 'grammar', perhaps as a reference to Wynter and Graham's compulsive word-gaming) is a Cornish dialect term for a woodlouse. Like Wynter himself (who can be imagined observing it with sardonic eye), it is a creature that flourishes in the damp Cornish climate. Wynter the 'Scholar King' both rules and studies the waterscape; circling in a kayak, or like the 'spinner' attached as a lure to a fishing line, he both enters and creates 'the weaving/ Strands of water'. Graham's poem reminds us that, for all the changes that had taken place in Wynter's life and work since he'd arrived in Cornwall in July 1945, his desire to explore the Penwith landscape remained as vivid as when, writing to Hedy Hoffmann that month, he compared it to 'an enthralling book which I cannot lay down'.

As ever, Wynter was keen to initiate others into his current enthusiasm. For Heron, who joined an afternoon's expedition on the sea one afternoon in 1967, the results were to have an impact on his own career. The

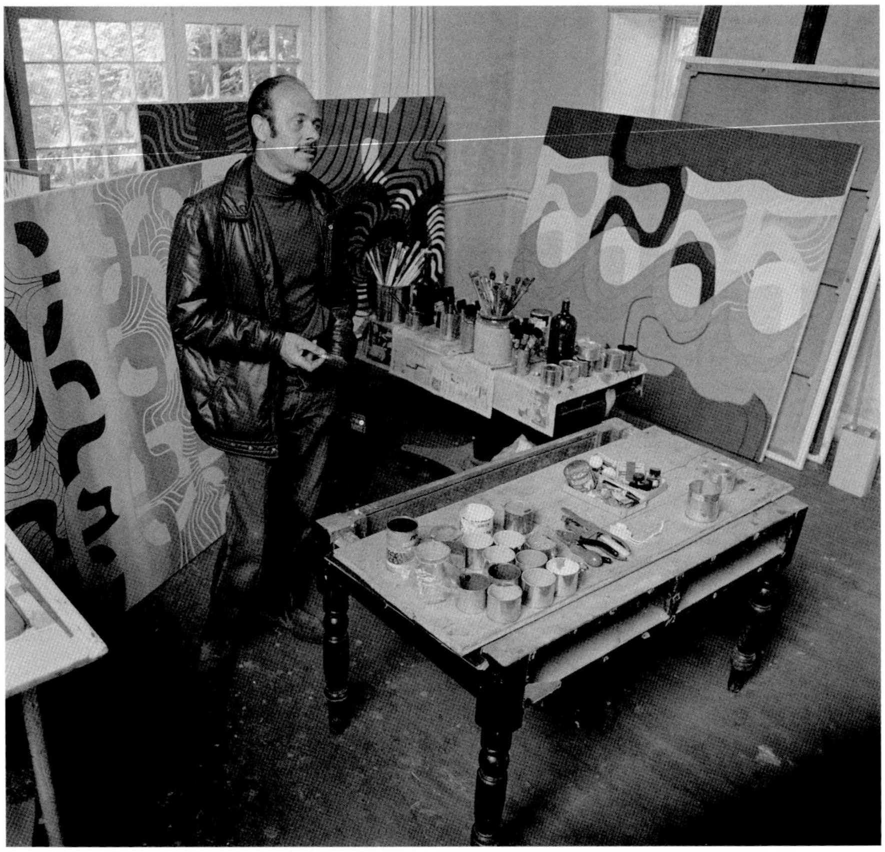

156
Bryan Wynter with 'Meander' paintings in studio, early 1970s photograph by Jorge Lewinski

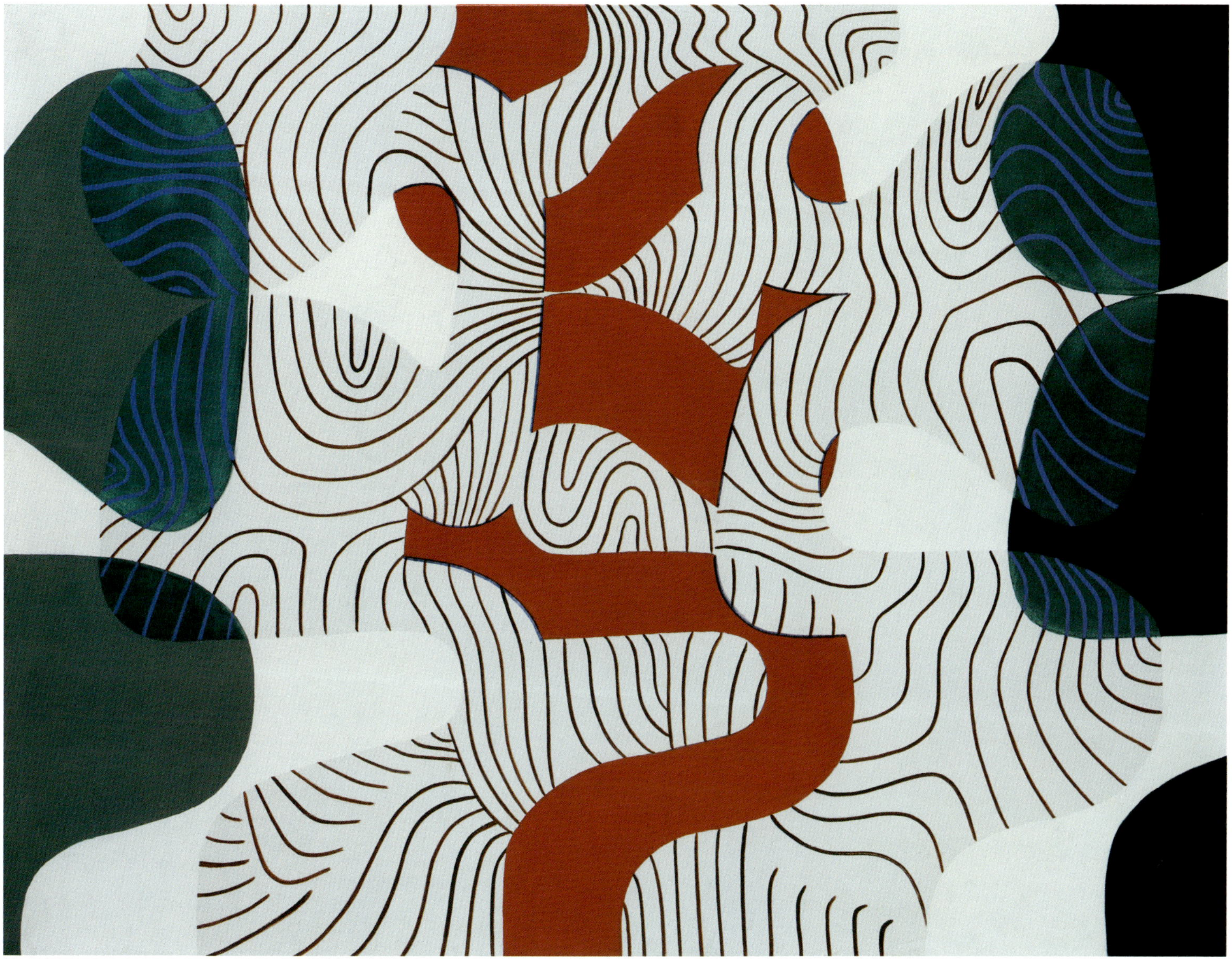

157
Meander I
oil on canvas
168 x 213.4 cm (66 x 84 in)
1967
Tate

party of five set out from Lamorna Cove, near Treverven, in four boats: Heron and his wife, Delia (both novices at this sport), and Wynter in single-seater kayaks, while two guests of the Herons took a two-seater canoe. When the canoeists capsized, Wynter went to their aid, leaving the Herons to return to the granite slipway and extricate themselves from their kayaks as best they could. As Heron clambered free of the cockpit, his boat drifted away and flipped over, then, weighted with water, was flung by an incoming wave hard against him, shattering his right leg. He looked down to see fragments of bone pushing through the skin with seaweed snagged on them.[13] The break was so severe that it was a year before Heron was able to work on large canvases again. He turned instead to producing small, strongly coloured gouaches on paper – a medium in which, it could be argued, he achieved more freedom and intensity than in the rather unmodulated major-key tonality of his large paintings of the later 1960s.

In their flatness and high colour both Heron's (fig.158) and Wynter's painting of this period reflects a general trend in contemporary abstract painting, in which the legacy of the 'Situation' shows and the influence of hard-edge American abstract painters such as Kenneth Noland is easily detectable. Whereas in Heron's work, however, the visual dialogue takes place between colour and shape alone, Wynter's 'Meander' series (figs 157, 159, 160, 169) is clearly informed by something like the 'alphabet of nature' described by Schwenk. There is pleasure in shape, line and colour for their own sake, certainly; but beyond lies a sense that these qualities offer a further meditation on some 'archetypal principle of flowing water'. *Meander I* and *Meander II* are (unusually for Wynter after 1956) landscape-format canvases. Large-scale as they are, these designs feel like sections of a still larger, apparently endless, pattern of flow – an effect that contributes to their steady amplitude, as does the calm sonority with which Wynter infuses these schemata of movement. In place of the intricate weave and complex, not always entirely successful, colour interactions that characterise several of the 'Confluence' paintings, the broad, strong areas of flat colour feel monumental.

It is a fusion of these two themes of the later 1960s – 'Confluence' and 'Meander' – that underlies the luminous, fluid beauty of paintings such as *Night Confluence* (fig. 161), *Saja* (fig. 162) and *Fuente Dé* (fig. 163), all from 1969. Whereas Wynter's layering of a multitude of small paintstrokes in his late 1950s, abstracts captivates but also fractures the attention, in *Night Confluence* the complexities are strongly harmonised. This is an image of dynamic depth, as in the currents and eddies active within a single body of water that Schwenk had described. Like Bridget Riley's Op art images of the mid-1960s, in which a surface of illusory three-dimensionality is defined by pattern, *Night Confluence* maintains a delicate balance between the programmatic and the lyrical. Its elusive, aqueous density, however, feels quite different from the sharply focused clarity of Riley's images.

The titles *Saja, Fuente Dé* and *Pas* (1970; fig. 164) refer to rivers in northern Spain, which Wynter and his brother explored during a joint family holiday in April 1969, when the rivers were swollen by snow melt from the mountains. The echoes of contour lines in the short, bundled curves of the 'Confluence' and 'Meander' paintings add cartographic and geological dimensions to their complex semantics. Since contour lines describe land forms that have been shaped, very often, by the

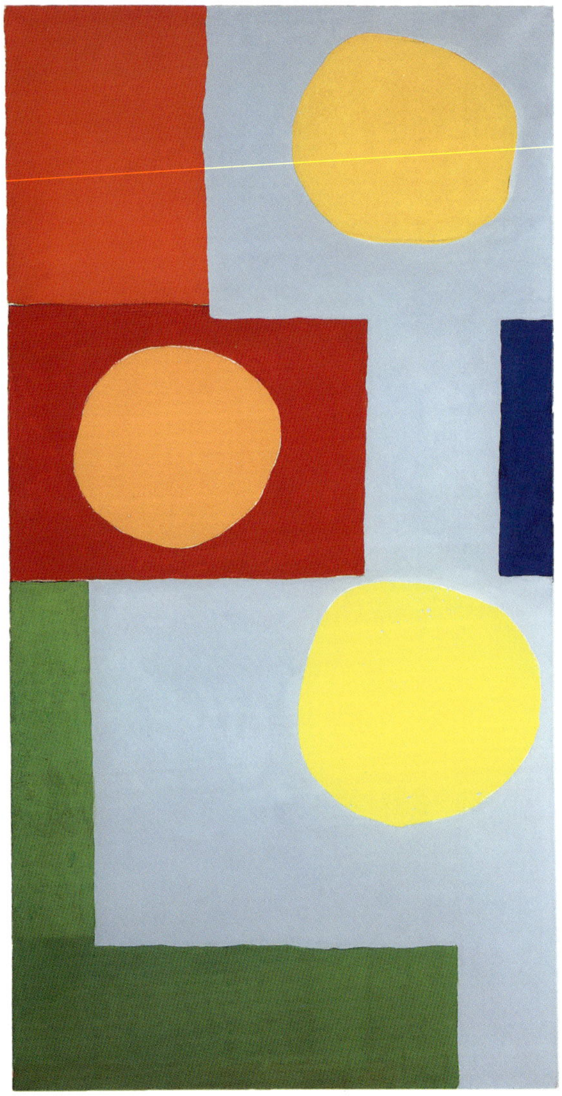

158
Patrick Heron, *May 1965*
oil on canvas
182.9 x 91.4 cm (72 x 36 in)
1965
Private collection

159
Deva
oil on canvas
152.4 x 122 cm (60 x 48 in)
1970
Private collection

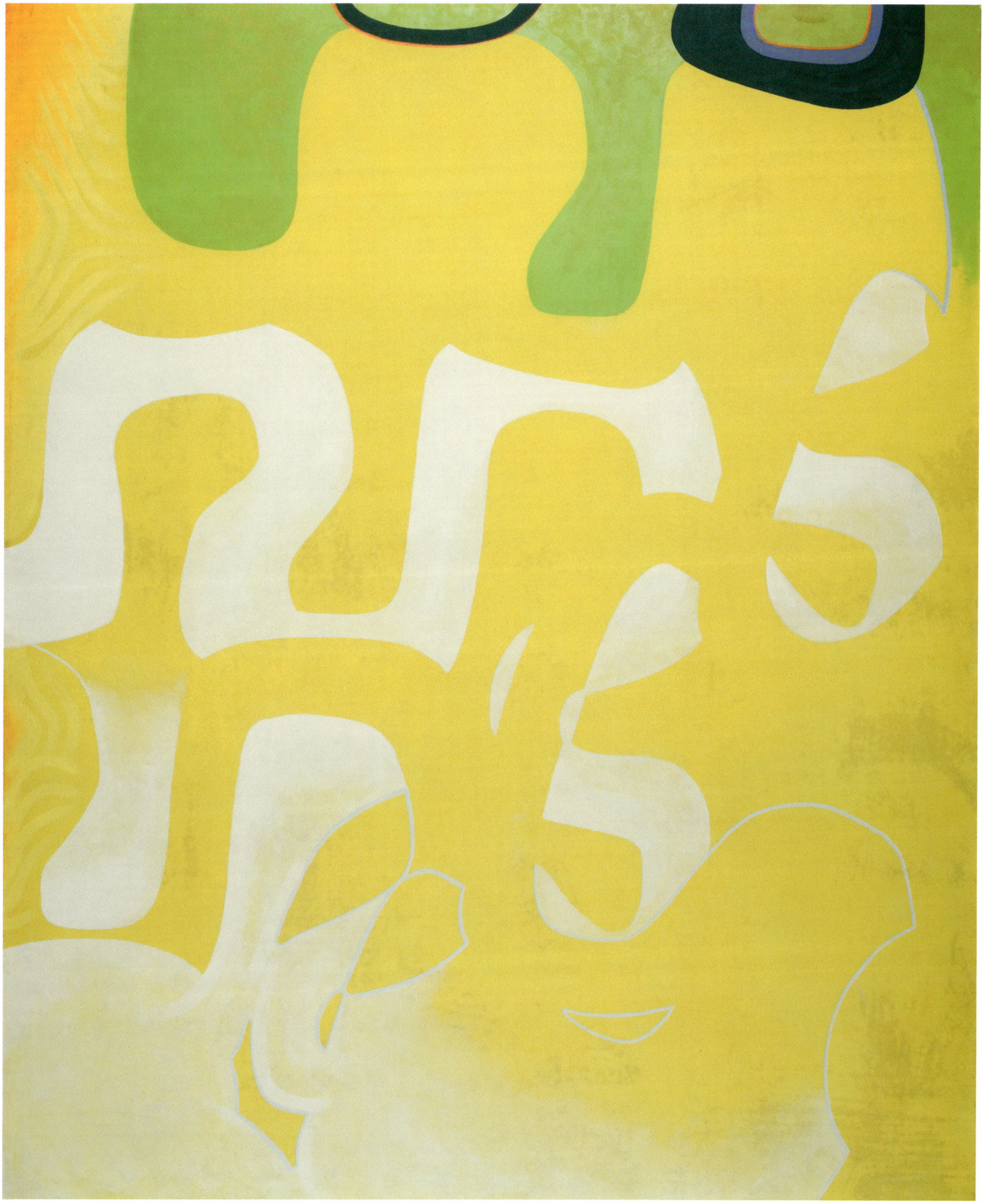

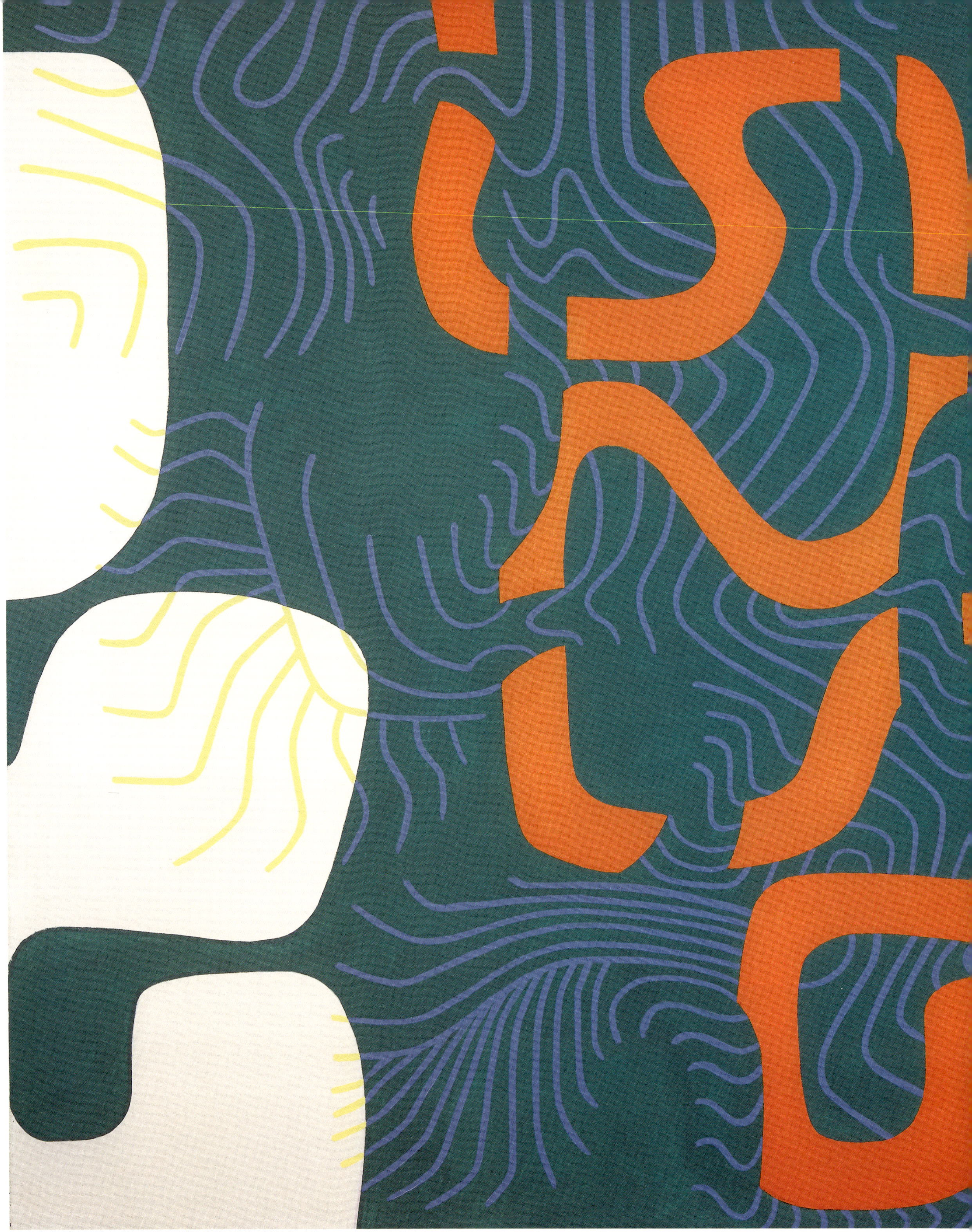

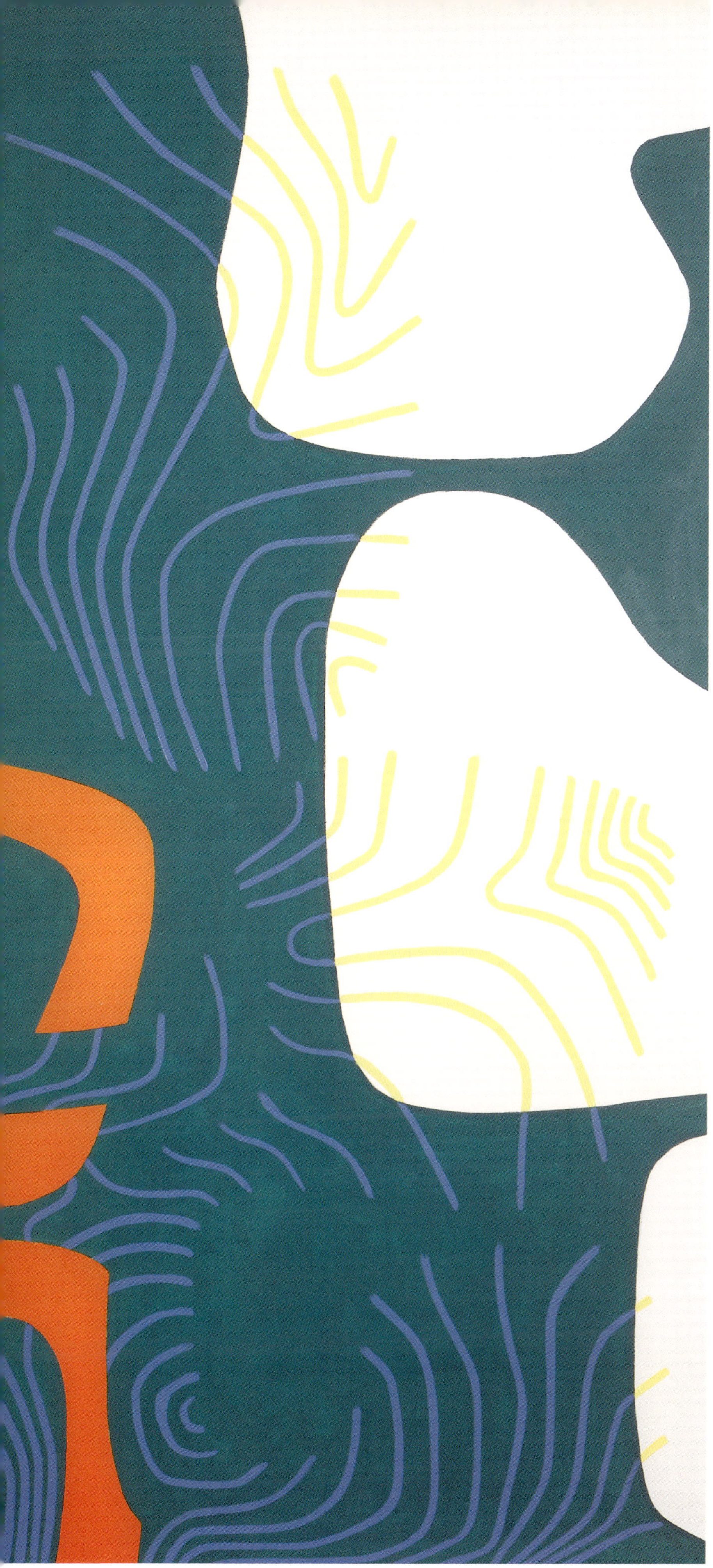

160
Meander II
oil on canvas
167.6 x 213.4 cm (66 x 84 in)
1967
Jonathan Clark Fine Art

eroding action of water, they too reflect the principles of flow experienced by a canoeist negotiating a river. The different time-frames – millions of years on the one hand, on the other a brief few hours on the river – create a paradoxical effect in these paintings, in which shapes resembling timeless sacred glyphs denote rapid flux and instability. Despite his taste for adventure, Wynter seldom travelled abroad (air travel had little attraction for him). The colours in these two paintings – warmer, thinner and paler than Wynter's usual range – register the impact of the landscape around the Picos de Europa, a massif that rises from a coastal plain through thickly wooded valleys to peaks where, even in summer, patches of snow remain. 'Sensuous' is also – unusually in Wynter's *oeuvre* – a word that comes to mind. In *Saja*, in particular, it is as though the sensory and the intellectual, two interwoven strands throughout his work, had fused into a relaxed, radiant apprehension. Perhaps it's the suggestion of anatomical curves, a general feeling of physical ease, in the interlocking wave and meander shapes. Or the soft-toned colour, more invitation than statement. There is, too, a feeling that Wynter is, at last, wielding oil colour as naturally as he'd always used gouache, ink and other water-based media. Here, whatever the gravity or complexity of the image, the medium itself seems to carry no burden of special seriousness.

Apart from the group of works associated with the rivers of northern Spain, Wynter produced few paintings in 1969–70, though he continued to elaborate on the meander motif using his Pentel and light-box method. He was still being represented by Waddington Galleries, but sales were slow. In autumn 1970 Wynter was represented in the Arts Council's survey show of kinetic art at the Hayward Gallery. That year, too, after having for some time shown only infrequently at the Penwith Society of Arts in St Ives, he was persuaded by Barbara Hepworth to submit an IMOOS. This piece was bought by an American architect, Enslie O. Oglesby, who was

161
Night Confluence
oil on canvas
101.6 x 81.2 cm (40 x 32 in)
1969
Private collection

designing new premises for the Bloom advertising agency in Dallas, Texas. Oglesby commissioned Wynter to produce a large IMOOS (1.8 m high) as a focal point for the reception area in an open-plan office; the fee was to be $3,000 (about £1,250 at that time). Work on the 'Bloomobile' occupied Wynter during the early months of 1971 and was followed by his first and only visit to the USA. Oglesby also asked Wynter to ship over several of his paintings, which he was planning to promote to corporate clients. Accompanied by Wynter's detailed assembly instructions, the IMOOS was installed in July 1971, when it featured on the cover of *Interior Design* magazine (fig. 172).[14] (The four shots of the IMOOS in different configurations were, presumably unintentionally, rotated through 90 degrees, giving Wynter's designs the horizontally stratified look of bright indigenous textiles.)

It may have been this renewed commercial interest in Wynter's kinetic works that, also in July 1971, inspired Leslie Waddington to commission a whole new series from him. The deal amounted to a regular income for Wynter of £200 per month for the next couple of years, to be followed by an exhibition. 'I will therefore be purchasing £4800 worth of kinetic sculptures from you',[15] wrote Waddington, sealing what amounted to a considerable investment in this project. This posed a dilemma for Wynter. It was more than ten years since he'd made his first IMOOS; now, when his creative interest in these constructions had waned, it appeared that they represented the most commercially viable side of his work. During the remainder of 1971 and throughout 1972 his studio effectively became an IMOOS production line. There were hundreds of parts, all needing to be individually designed – a process that involved vast numbers of measured drawings and time-consuming fabrication. It was not until 1973 that Wynter seems to have returned full-time to painting and to the themes he had been exploring some two or thee years earlier (see fig. 169).

'Wynter's best pictures are big ones', Alan Bowness had written in 1959. Size was necessary because, he thought, in order for the 'magic' to work, 'One needs to be swallowed into the picture'.[16] In 1973 Wynter completed one of the largest paintings of his career, *Red and Black Streams* (1.83 x 2.75 m), a mural-scale statement of the meander motif (fig. 166). The lessons of seven years of light-box drawings – that infinite series of five-finger exercises – are transformed into an image that combines a monumental serenity with a more human-scale wit and sensual warmth. The repeated meander shapes in black and red are both linked and broken by the central blue meander, while the illusion of intertwining forms injects a playful opticality into his painting. It's hard to decide whether the connotations of this image veer more towards philosophical seriousness (reflecting on a 'chain of being', maybe) or towards a delight in illusionistic *trompe l'oeil*, as the eye attempts to distinguish presence from pattern. Together, the black, blue and red meanders suggest a triad of standing forms, which, relating back to such images as *Hostile Tribe*, offer a version of the figure-in-the-landscape motif. Except, in this case, like the stories woven into Arachne's cloth in the Greek myth, figure and medium cannot be separated. Heron pronounced *Red and Black Streams* a 'magnificent painting'. He interpreted this whole phase of Wynter's work as a 'merger between hard and soft edges, between flat and smooth segments of colour and furry "worms" of linear expression, between opaque planes of pure colour and endlessly rippling lines of demarcation, winding their evenly looped way from edge to edge of the canvas', the whole adding up to 'a personal fusion of differing elements, originally seen in the mobiles'.[17]

More complex in construction but equally serene in their effect are three paintings from the following year: *Green Confluence* (fig. 167), *Confluence V* (see fig. 9) and *Red River* (fig. 168). The colours in all three are subtler and more varied than in *Red and Black Streams*. In the

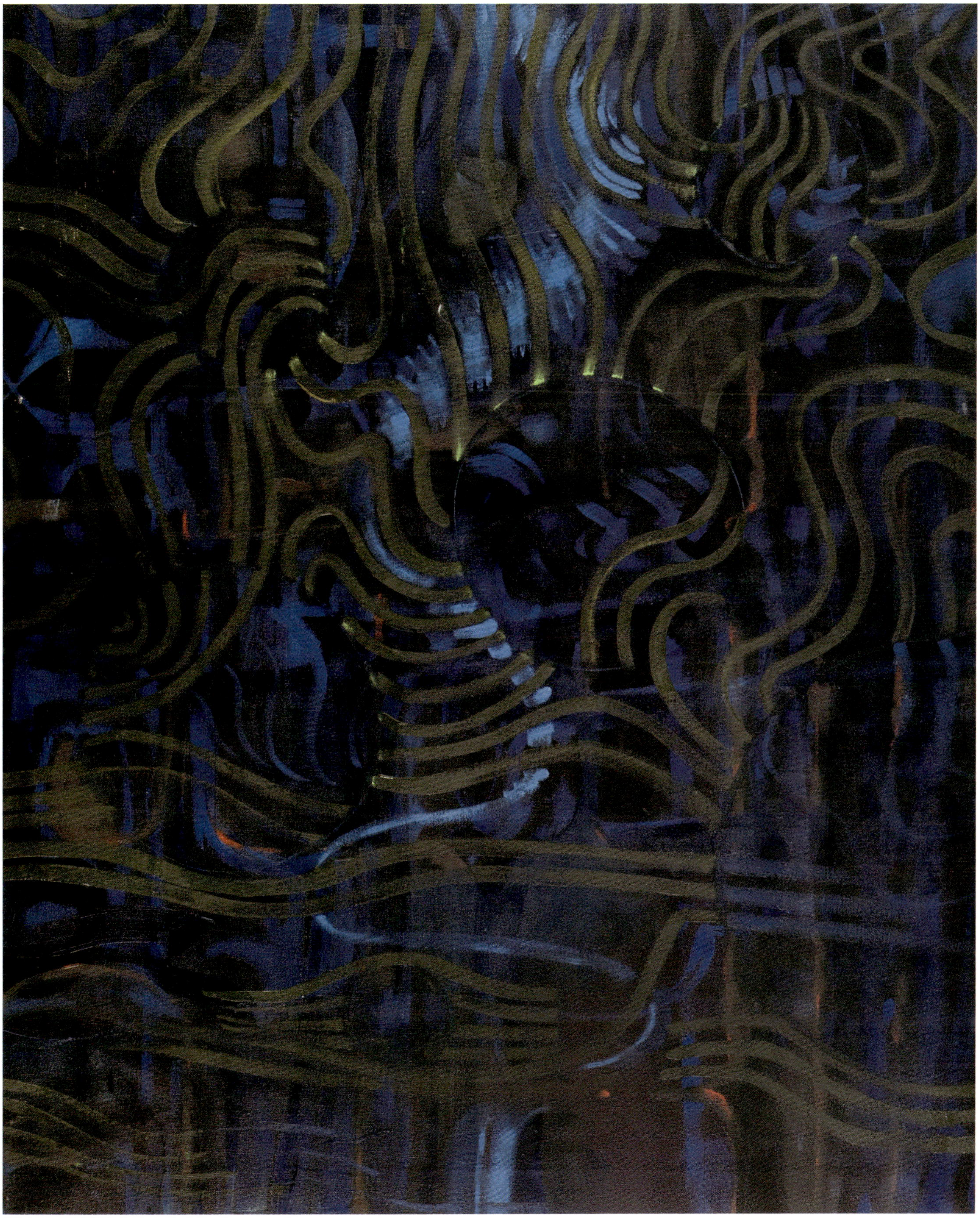

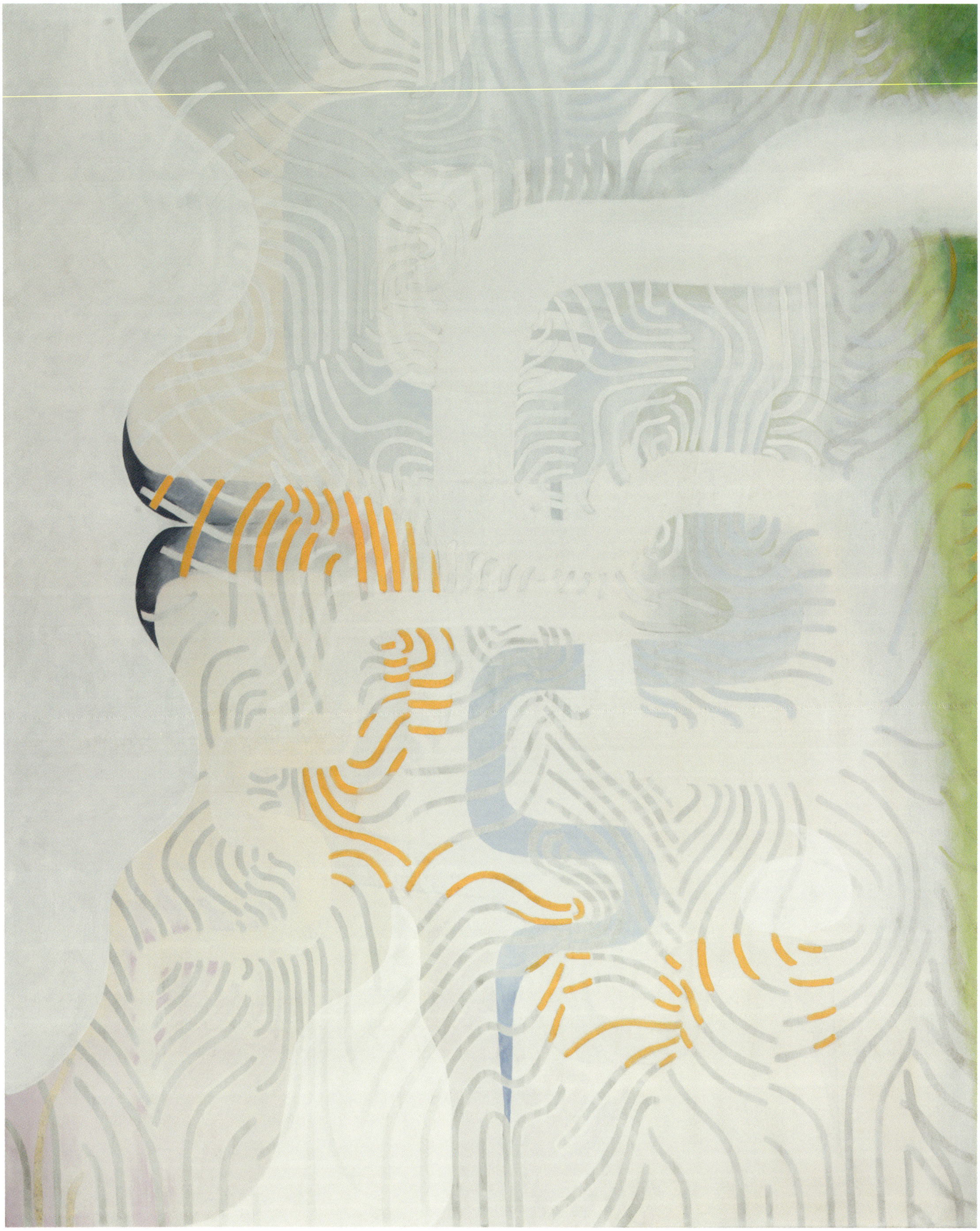

162
Saja
oil on canvas
213.3 x 167.6 cm (84 x 66 in)
1969
Tate

163
Fuente Dé
oil on canvas
182.8 x 142.2 cm (72 x 56 in)
1969
Private collection

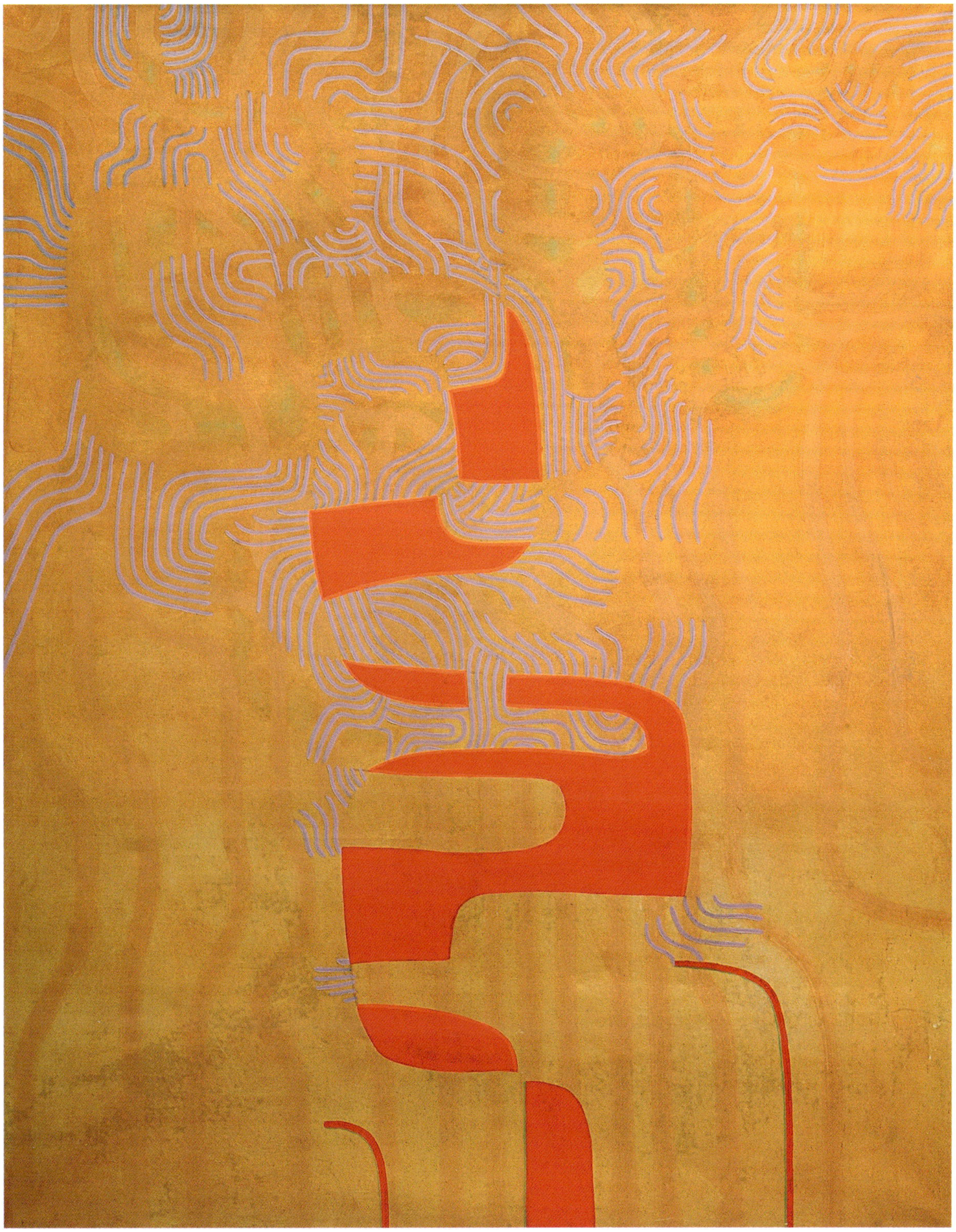

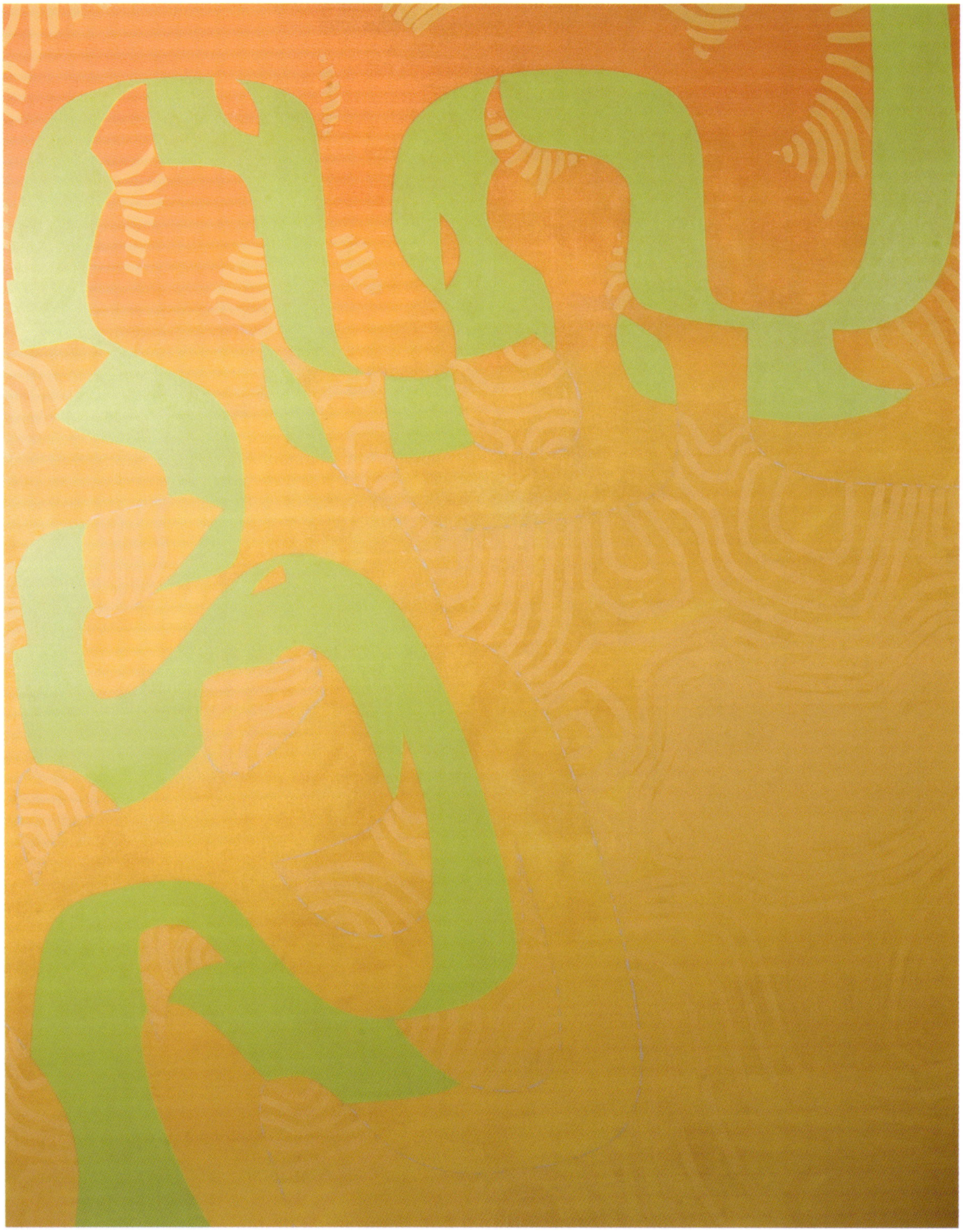

164
Pas
oil on canvas
00 x 00 cm (00 x 00 in)
1970
Plymouth City Museum
and Art Gallery

165
Landscape photographs
colour transparencies
1955–60s

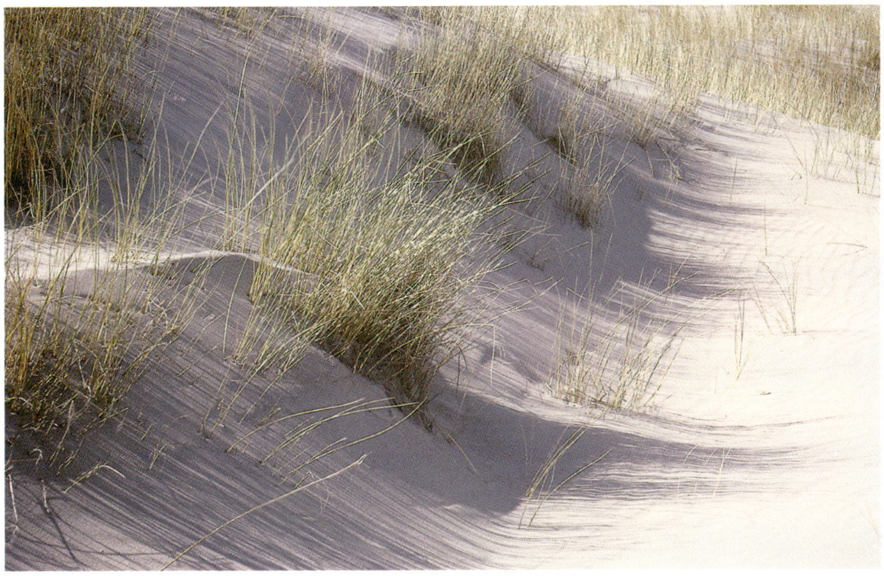
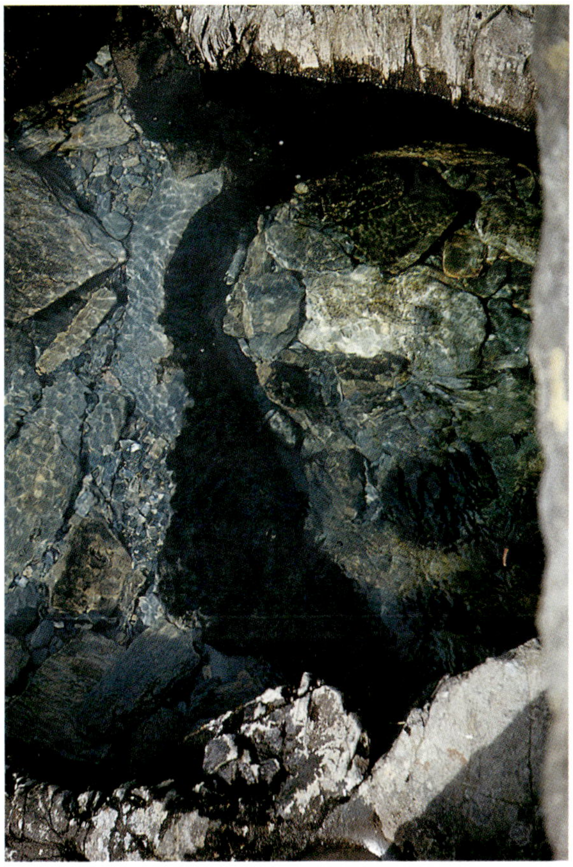
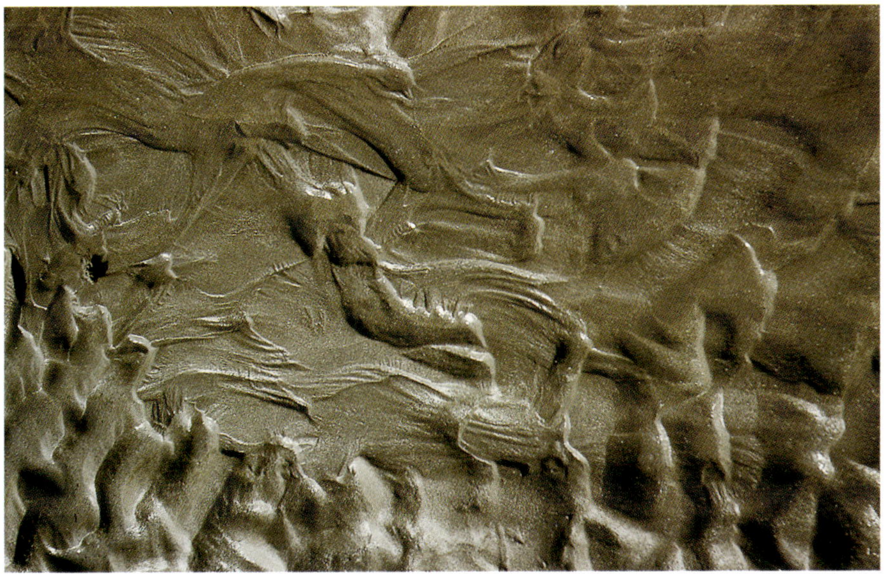
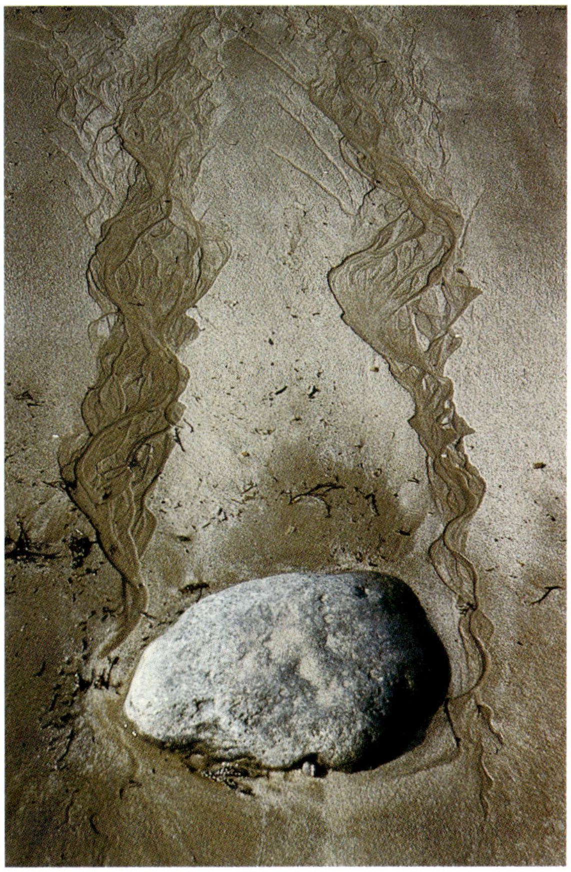
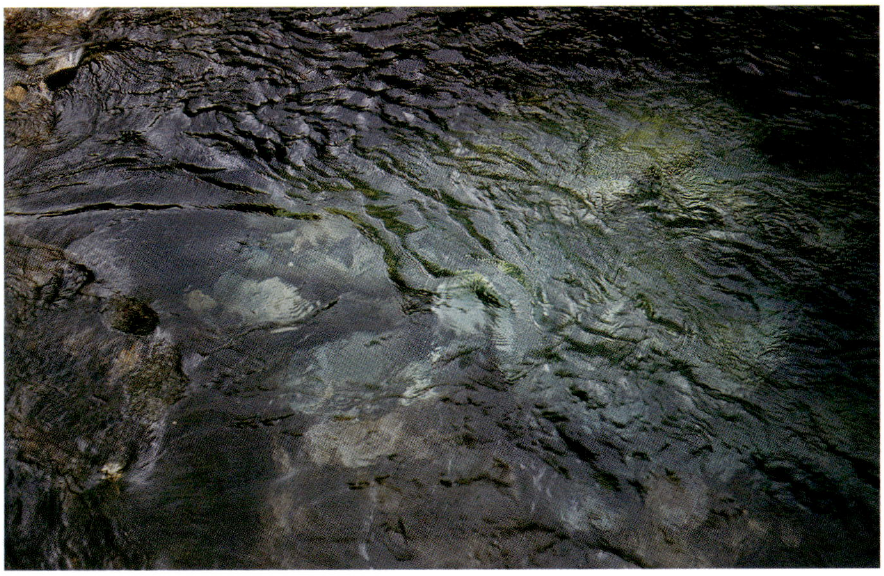

166
Red and Black Streams
oil on canvas
182.8 x 274.8 cm (72 x 108 in)
1973
Private collection

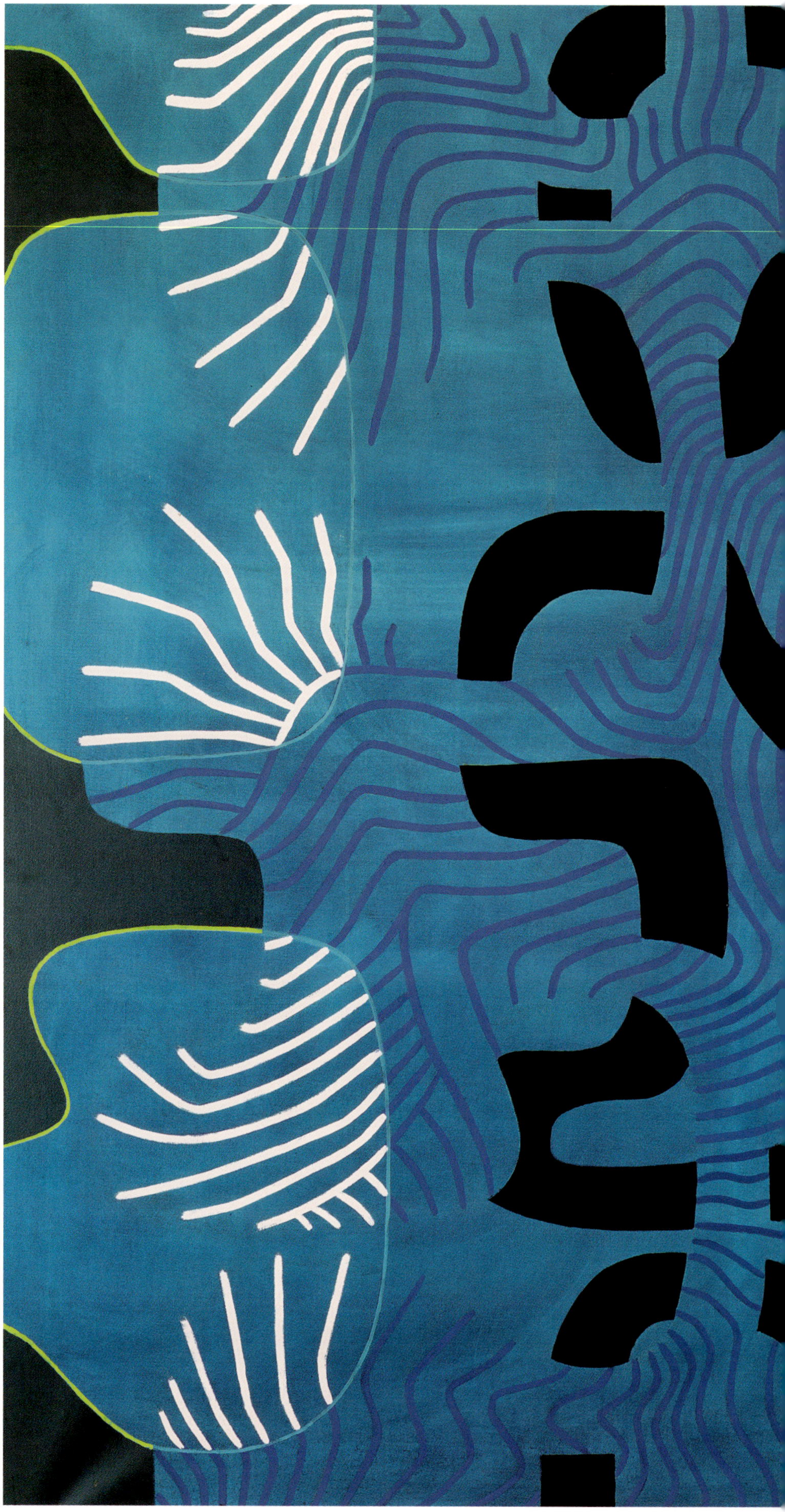

first two, bracken green, gorse-flower yellow, slate or granite grey and the blues of sky overhead or reflected in water provide a chromatic 'alphabet of nature', while the formal language of superimposed, interlocked or abutting curves reads like a map intended to be legible only to initiates. The red spectrum Wynter used in *Red River*, on the other hand, creates a thoroughly corporeal, cardiovascular pulse. This is an image of the meandering, riverine landscape in human bodily form, as though revealed by infra-red photography.

However you interpret Wynter's large oil paintings of 1973–4, it is evident that these works bring home a complex of themes he'd been exploring over several decades. Their place in the wider context of contemporary art, however, was far from clear. During the 1970s in Britain painting *per se* was having a hard time and was increasingly said to have had its day. 'What faces painting ... is a compound of antagonism and indifference', opined the painter and critic Andrew Forge, explaining his selection for the 'British Painting '74' exhibition at the Hayward Gallery, London (in which *Red and Black Streams* and *Red River* were included). 'As objects of commerce', he continued, '[paintings] are OK. But how is a painter going to reconcile this with what he is doing in the studio, where he knows instinctively that the moment he allows these commercial values to move his hand, he has sacrificed his self-respect?'[18]

While confidence in painting languished, other media and art forms were claiming the attention of funding bodies and art schools. When in 1972 the Tate bought *Equivalent VIII*, a sculptural installation by Carl Andre consisting of 120 firebricks, the acquisition caused a public scandal, based partly on the notion that artists deserved to be paid only for work that required some kind of skill or training not possessed by non-artists. Andre's explanation that the sculpture was (like Wynter's meanders) a water metaphor, 'as if you were wading through bricks', failed to disperse the storm. In the confusion between ideas of 'real' art and artists who

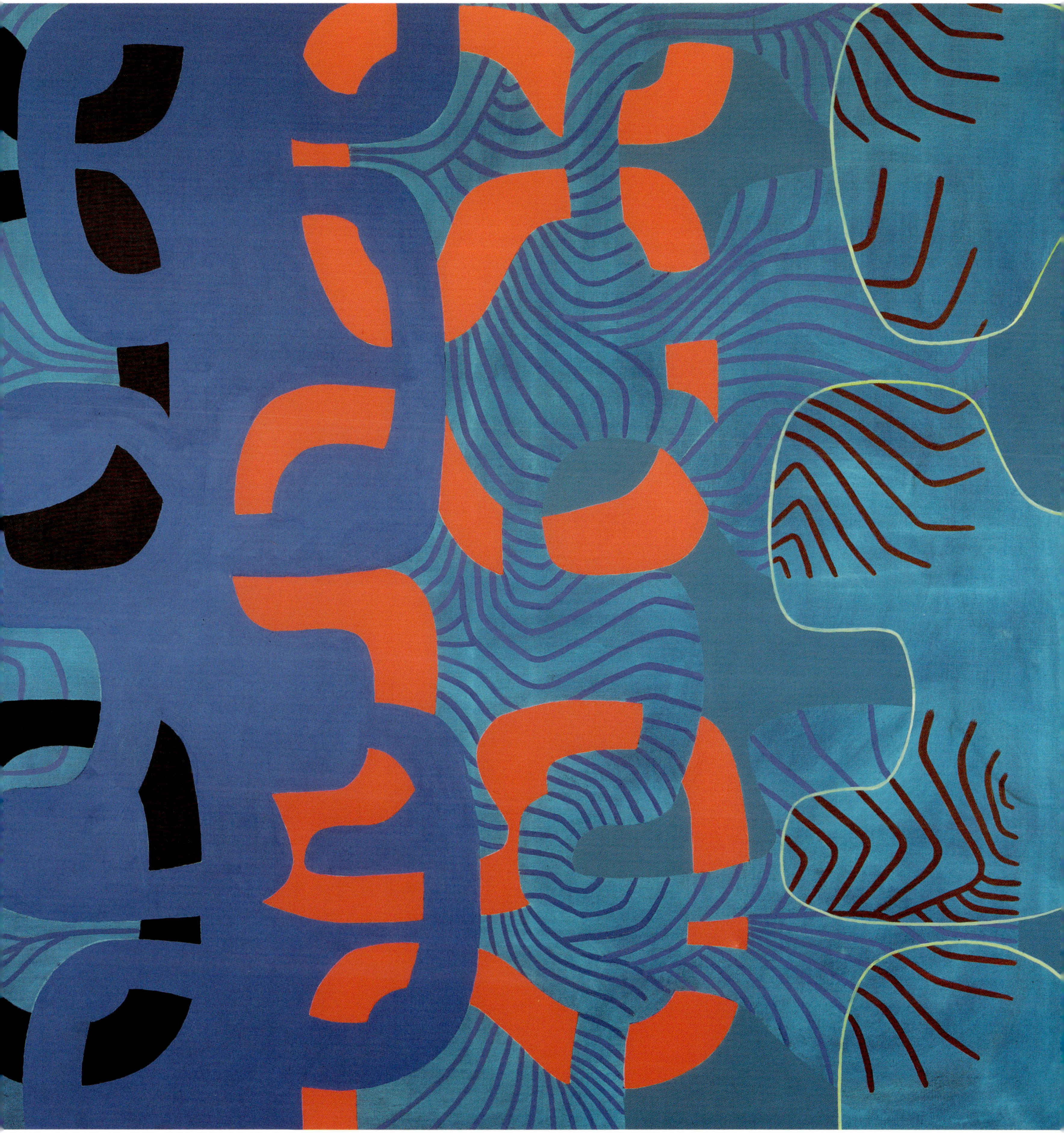

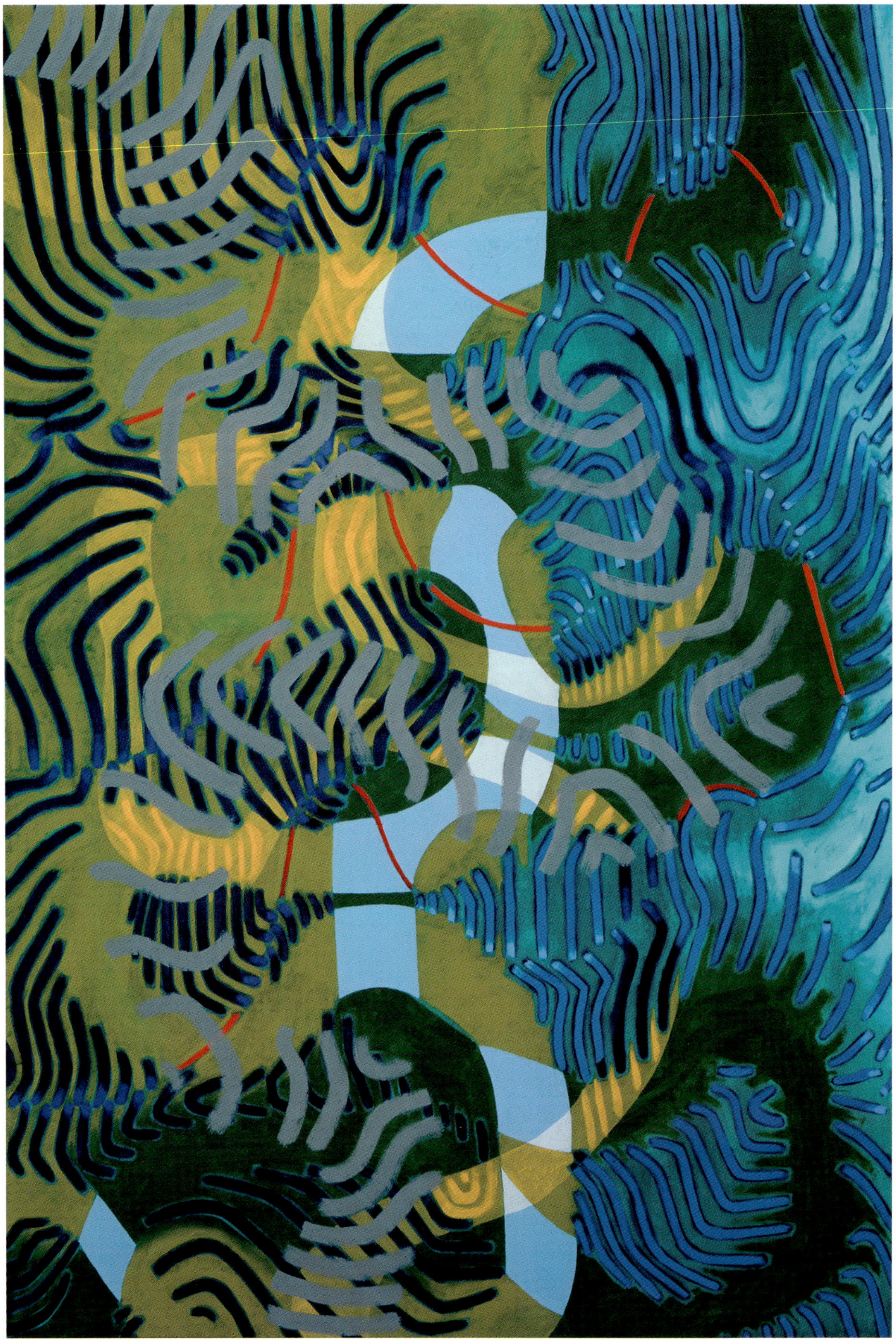

167
Green Confluence
oil on canvas
182.8 x 122 cm (72 x 48 in)
1974
Tate

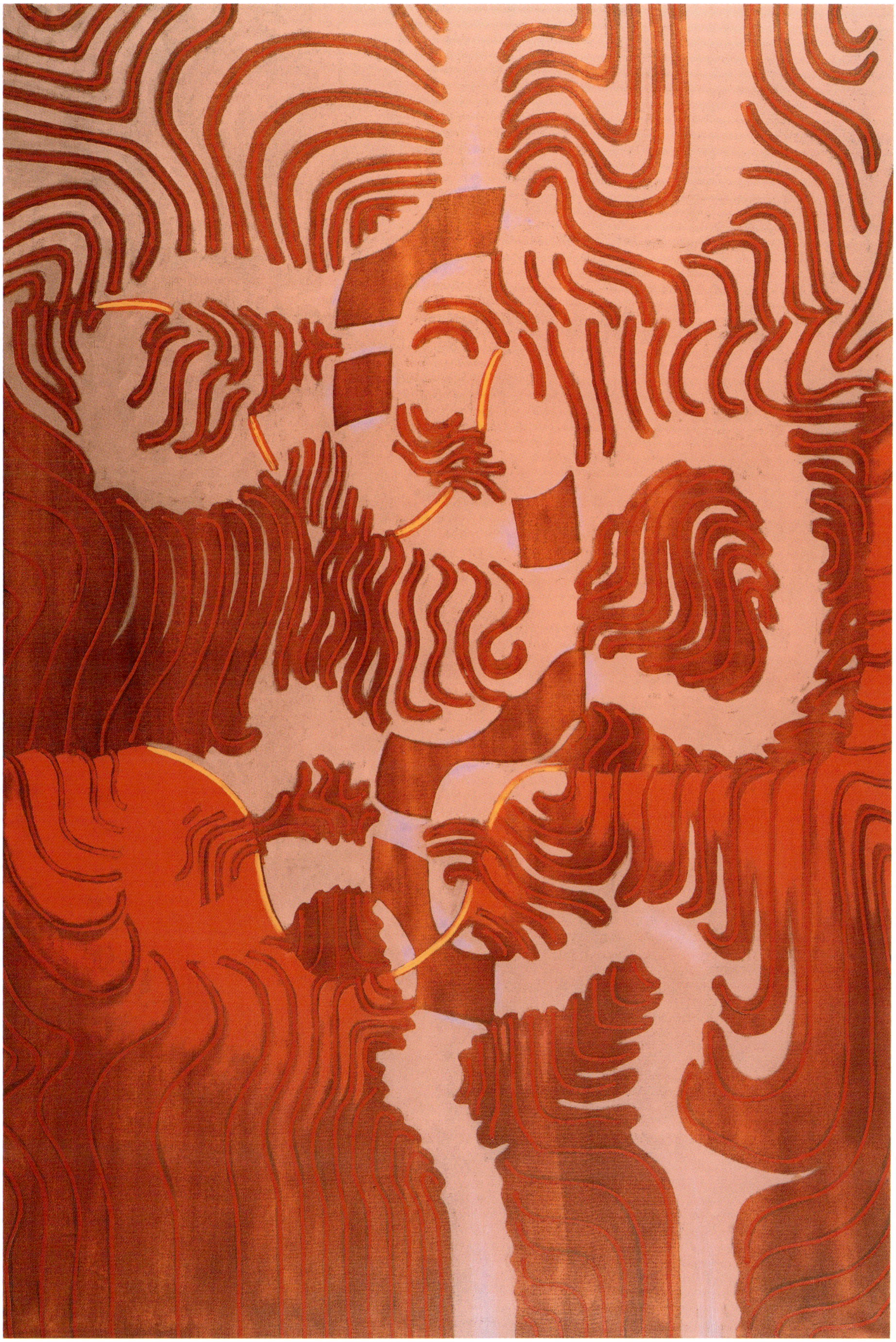

168
Red River
oil on canvas
182.8 x 122 cm (72 x 48 in)
1974
Artist's estate

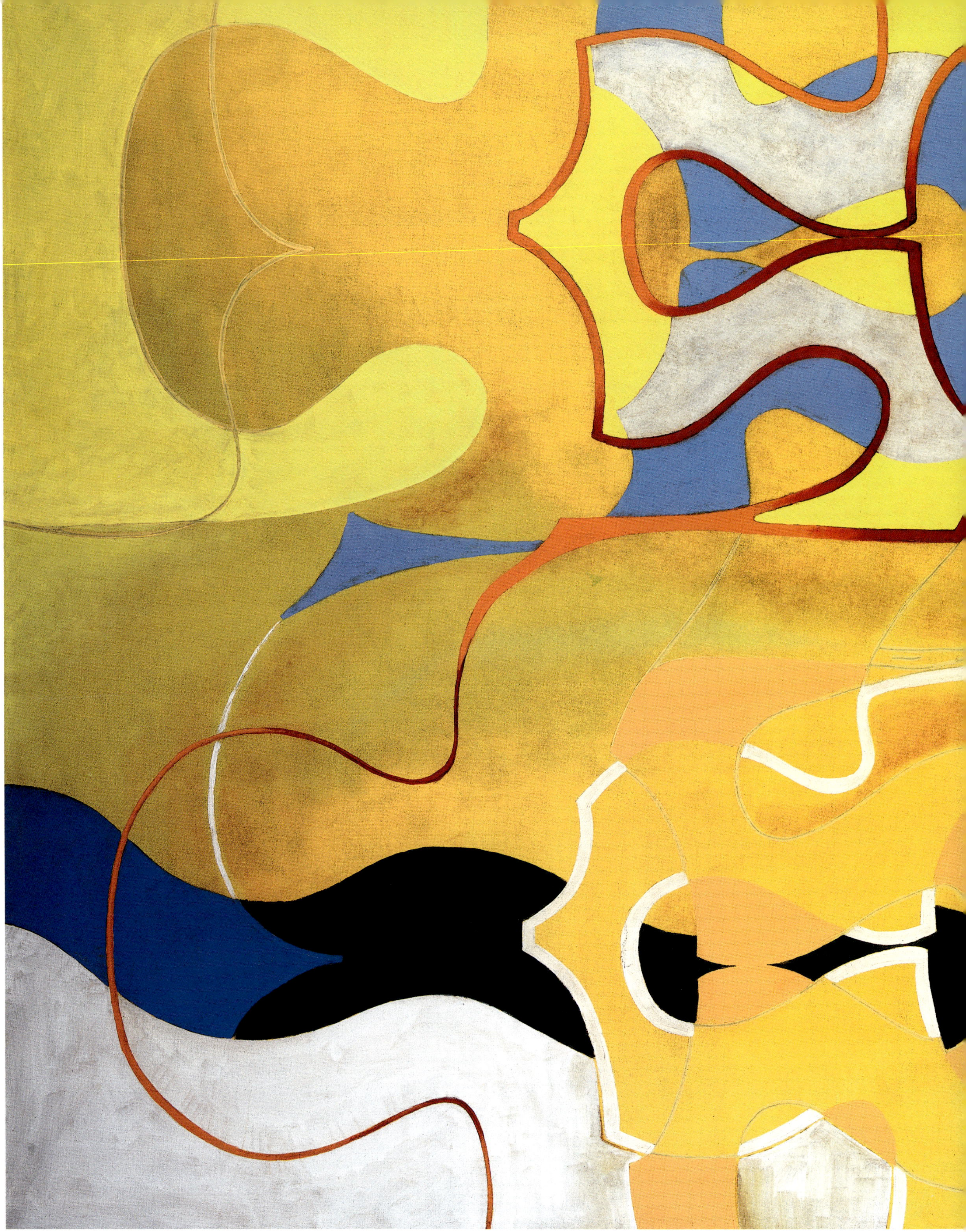

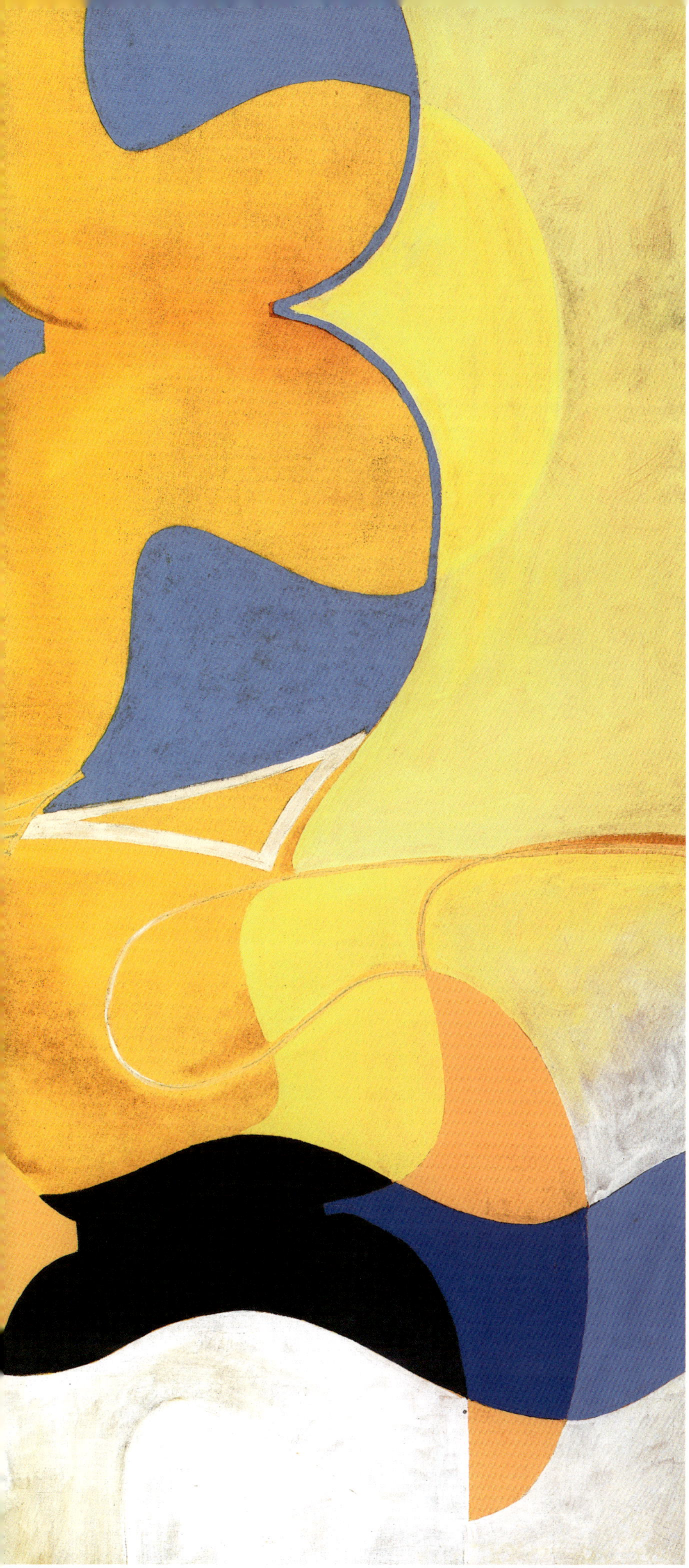

169
Meander III
oil on canvas
111.7 x 142.2 cm (44 x 56 in)
*c.*1972–4
Jonathan Clark Fine Art

were popularly seen to be earning good money just for arranging ordinary objects, Wynter's painting (or Heron's, Hilton's, Frost's – any of their generation) had no place in the argument. And the idea that art was inevitably compromised by commerce was soon to be superseded by more pragmatic approaches to the market.

In 1974 Wynter's future, as it must have seemed to his dealers, lay in his reputation as a kinetic artist. When he had fulfilled the terms of his two-year contract with Waddington Galleries, they duly staged an exhibition of IMOOS that October (figs 173, 174). Nine years earlier, every IMOOS in the show had sold; this time, there was not a single bite on the line. West End galleries, it seemed, had yet to take full account of the rapidity with which art world fashions had been changing in the early 1970s. Wynter continued to work on the 'Meander' series, but such was the dispiriting effect of the IMOOS show and the bleak prospect for sales of any kind that he also contemplated returning to representational landscape drawings and gouaches as a possible source of income. In the first weeks of 1975 he produced several small abstract paintings in acrylic on paper (figs 175, 176. 177). These are in effect a set of fresh variations on the meander motif, opening it out to a different range of colour possibilities and a freer formal interpretation than had been allowed for in images based on his light-box drawings. He seems to have thought of them as a potential starting point for a new series of large paintings.

When Eric Wynter visited in January, he observed, 'I hadn't seen (Bryan) look so well and full of ideas for a long time'. As well as the small acrylics, he had 'turned out some cartoons of preposterous dogs, and bought a very heavy cast-iron bath which had to be unloaded and trundled down to the brook below the house.'[19] One afternoon a few days later Wynter was about to collect his sons from the local primary school, when he noticed that the Mini had a flat tyre. The wheel bolts were seized tight, and after struggling to lever them free, he was overcome with chest pains. When these failed to improve

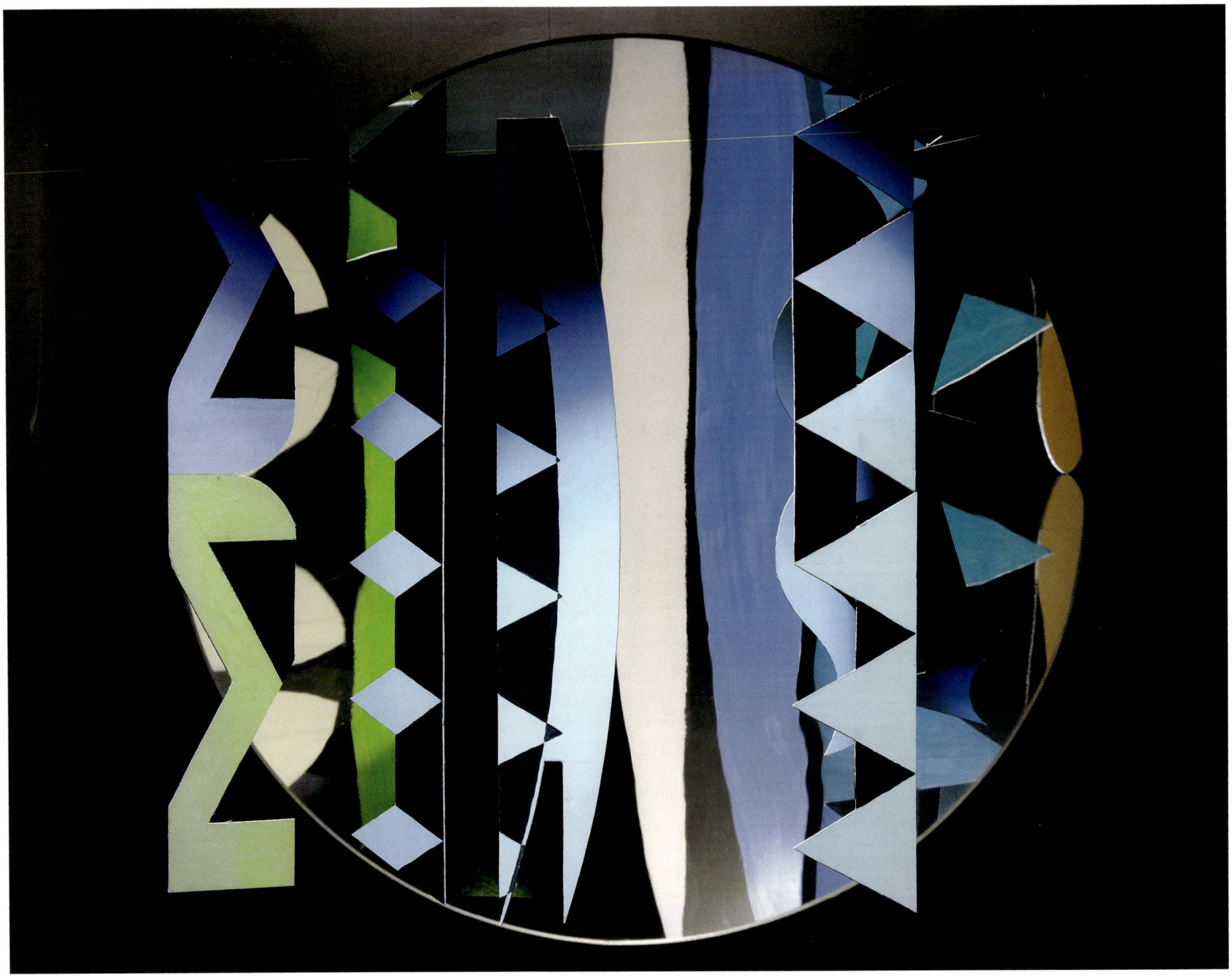

later that evening, he was taken by ambulance to hospital in Penzance. He'll recover, the doctor told Monica, but he won't be as good as he was. Then, on 11 February, he had another heart attack, this time fatal.

After his first coronary, almost fourteen years earlier, Wynter had made a good recovery. But he continued to suffer from angina and was well aware of the probability, and likely outcome, of a further heart attack. In retrospect, Monica Wynter felt that the progressive lightening and greater intensity of colour so noticeable in his painting in the last five or six years of his life might, at some level, be attributable to this awareness – that, although his vitality seemed unaffected, his work had already entered the kind of serene final phase so often seen in artists' careers.[20] (There was to be a comparable lightening in Heron's work during the years before his death in 1999.) For all Wynter's interest in what came to be known as 'alternative' theories and practices, which had begun with Huxley's application of Zen Buddhism to the counter-totalitarian struggle, he didn't have much time for overtly 'spiritual' discourse, or indeed for lofty seriousness of any kind. He floated various irreverent ideas as to what should be done with his mortal remains when the time came. Following cremation, they could, he proposed, be moulded into figurines like the plastic toys given away free in cereal packets.

When the time did finally come, however, such suggestions – true as they were to Wynter's idiosyncratic humour – seemed less appropriate. In the event, he was interred in the churchyard at Zennor. A few yards away is

170
IMOOS 18/1
gouache on card, wire, mirror and light set within a painted wooden box
59.9 x 50.8 x 65.4 cm
(23½ x 20 x 25¾ in)
1972-3
Jonathan Clark Fine Art

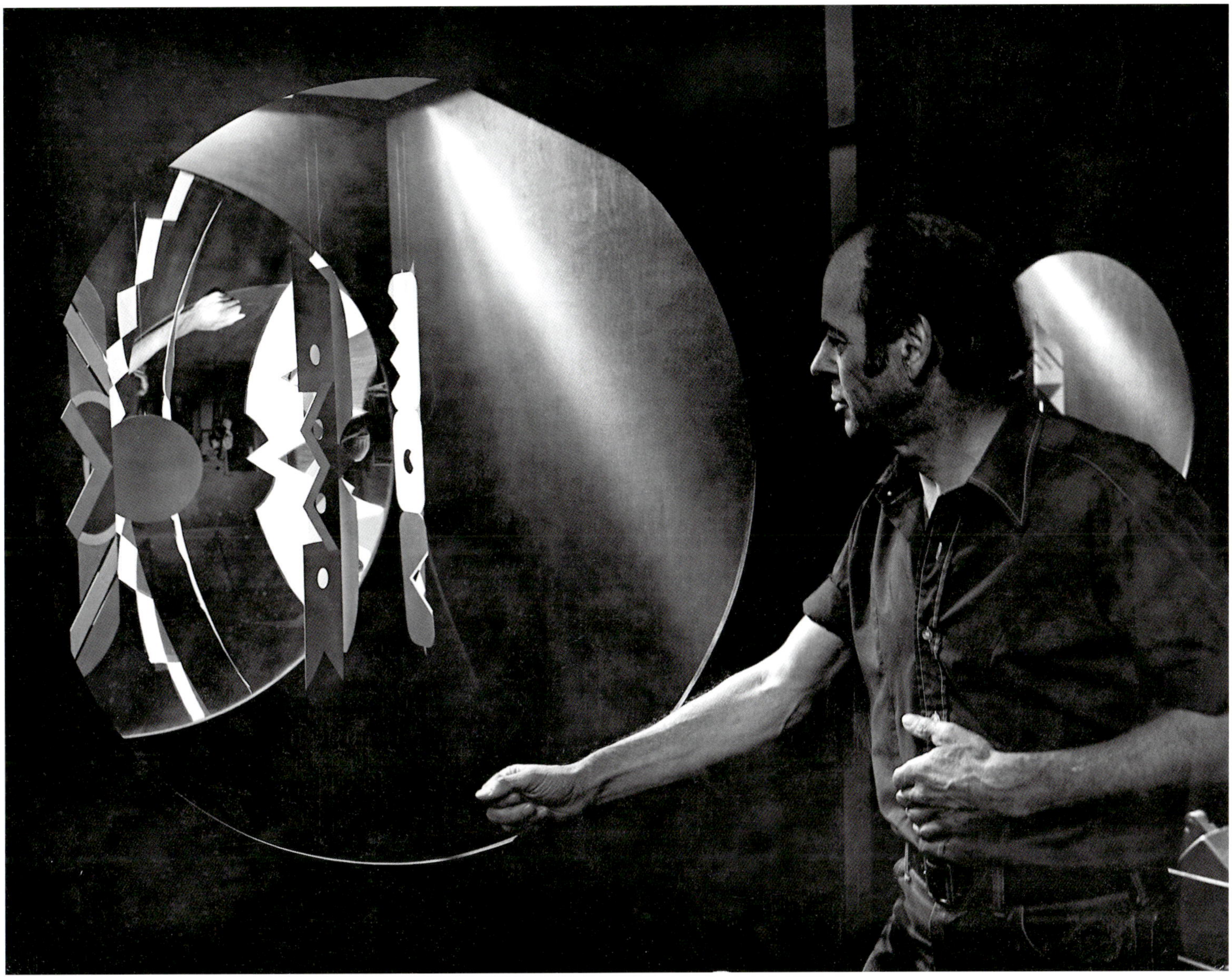

171
Bryan Wynter with IMOOS, 1971

172
IMOOS featured on the cover of *Interior Design*, July 1971

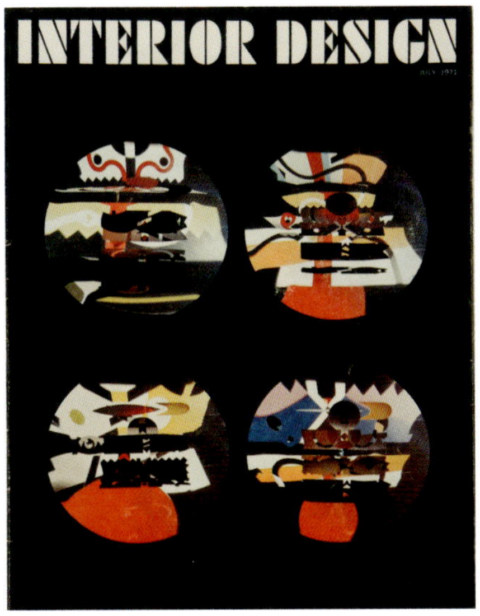

the small outhouse in the vicarage garden that Wynter had rented soon after his escape from Oxford, in impatient anticipation of his move to the Carn. On the other side of the churchyard, away from the village, fields rise towards the coast road, beyond which they break up into moorland and the vigilant outcrop of Zennor Carn. The house itself – a derelict shell next to which the large, light prefabricated studio Wynter erected in 1957 lies flattened by gales – stands just below the sightline. The landscape here is hardly changed from the scene of 'queer rocks, broken ruins, cromlechs & burial grounds' into which Wynter so enthusiastically immersed himself, where 'the present appears as a recent growth upon the past', and where, in the summer of 1945, he had at last 'found release to work as he wanted'.[21]

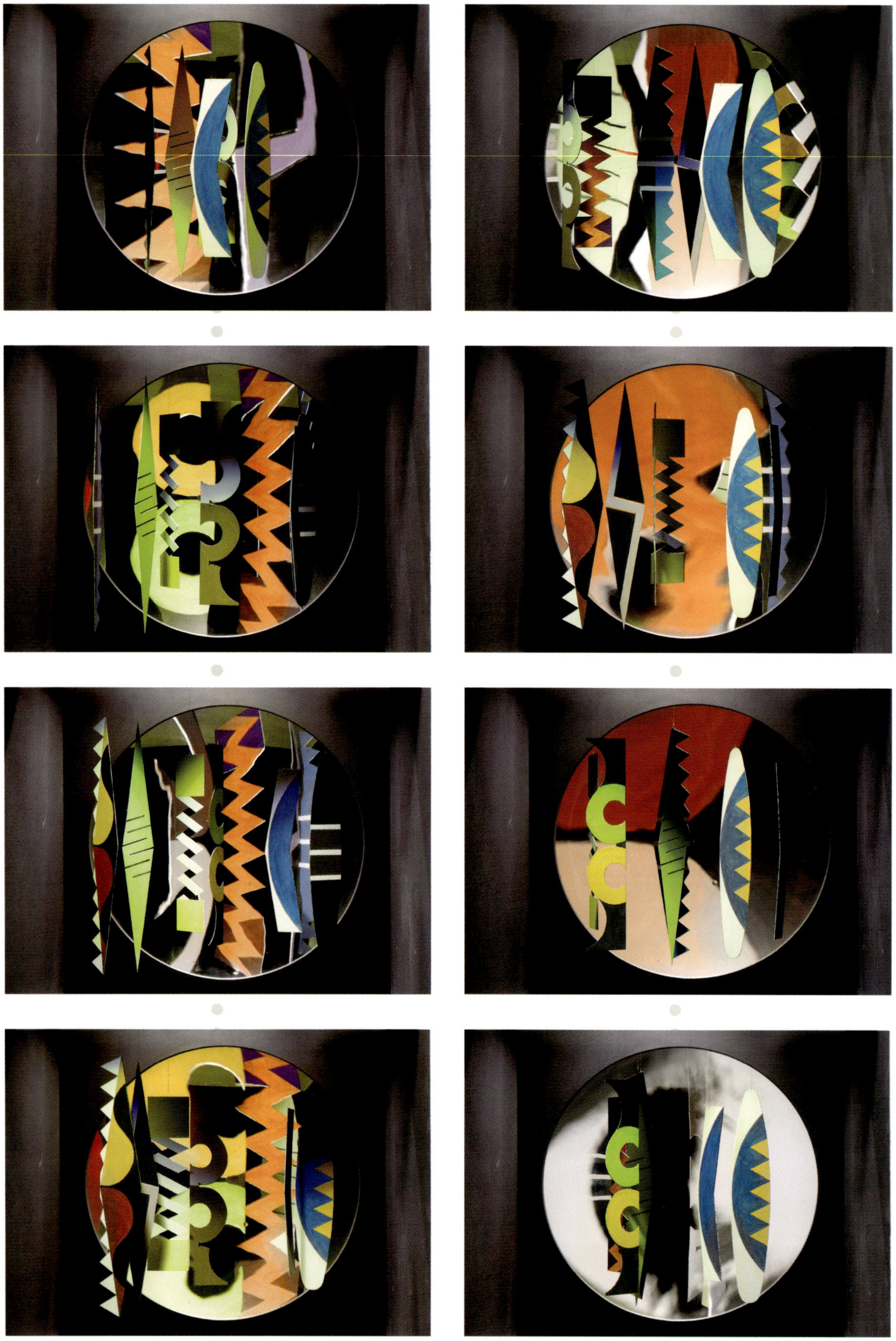

173
IMOOS 18/4
gouache on card, wire, mirror and light set within a painted wooden box
59.9 x 50.8 x 65.4 cm
(23½ x 20 x 25¾ in)
1972–3
Jonathan Clark Fine Art

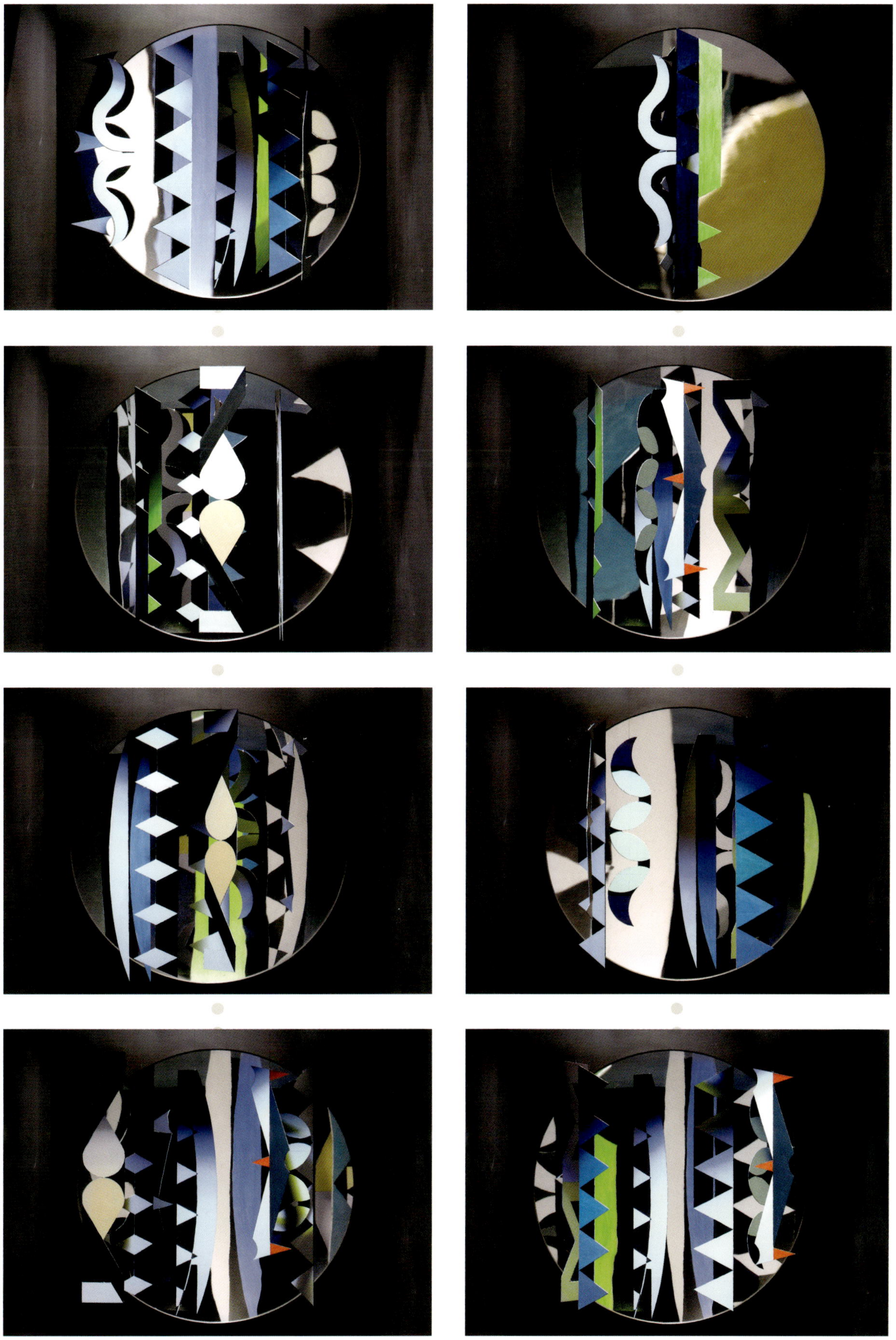

174
IMOOS 18/1
gouache on card, wire, mirror and light set within a painted wooden box
59.9 x 50.8 x 65.4 cm
(23½ x 20 x 25¾ in)
1972–3
Jonathan Clark Fine Art

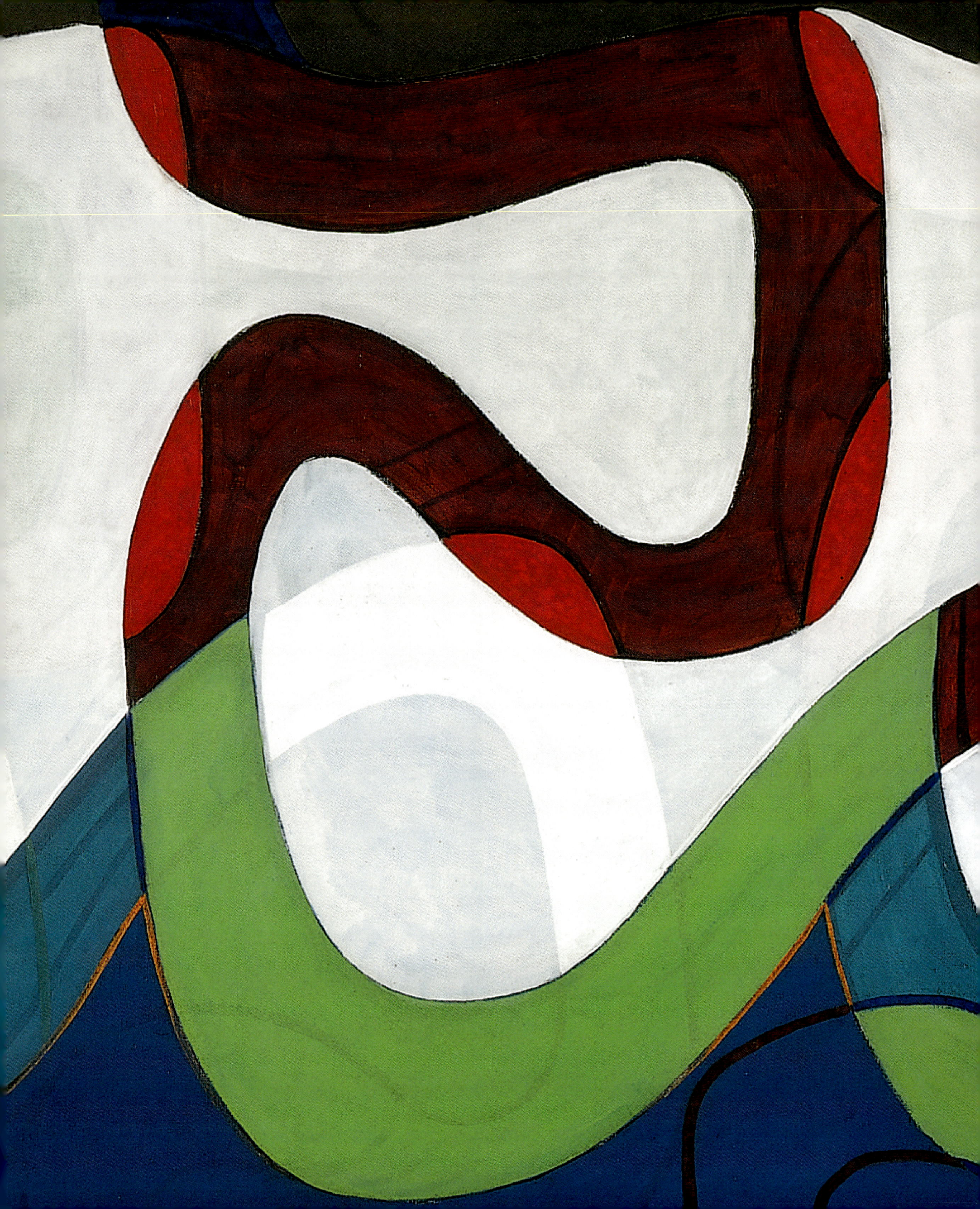

8

Epilogue

Some time in the months after Wynter's sudden death Sydney Graham climbed Zennor Hill to look around the Carn. The foxgloves were out, the mist blowing around the high moors. This visit – or imagined visit, since he knew the place well enough to visualise every detail – formed the setting for his elegy to Wynter. 'Dear Bryan Wynter', it begins:

> This is only a note
> To say how sorry I am
> You died. You will realise
> What a position it puts
> Me in. I couldn't really
> Have died for you if so
> I were inclined. The carn
> Foxglove here on the wall
> Outside your first house
> Leans with me standing
> In the Zennor wind.[1]

In mixing humour and pathos in these lines, Graham measures each quality in the exact proportion that he knows would have appealed to Wynter. Now that Wynter has gone, Graham tells him, he finds it difficult to go 'Beside Housman's star/ Lit fences'. Even worse, 'nobody will laugh/ At my jokes like you'.

Something that still comes through strongly when you speak to people who knew Wynter, or had even just briefly met him, is how sorely he was missed – what a gap his absence left in the landscape. In his obituary for the local paper (he wrote a second, more formal assessment of Wynter's career for *Studio International*) Heron paid tribute to Wynter's 'dazzlingly attractive personality' and 'quite extraordinary originality of mind'. 'No-one', he affirmed, 'who ran into him in a pub or at a private view or a party, ever forgot the sparkling impression of extreme intelligence and vitality – as well as of a true and deep human sympathy.'[2] All right, you think, this was written in grief, in the manner of a funeral oration – let's allow for some overstatement, for a rhetorical turn of phrase that fits the occasion. Yet the terms in which Heron painted his verbal vignette of Wynter – 'charm', 'generosity', 'perceptiveness' and so on – are echoed by people who encountered him in all sorts of different contexts.

Lanyon had thought Wynter 'a very generous human being'.[3] To fellow members of Penzance Canoe Club, with whom Wynter made many expeditions on the Lynher, Inny, Fowey, Camel and other Cornish rivers in the late 1960s and early 1970s, he was 'a fantastic person, easy to talk to', with 'an incredible sense of humour'.[4] The 'great gentleness and kindness' remarked by Sven Berlin on his first meeting with Wynter at the Leach Pottery seems to have struck chance acquaintances in the streets of Penzance three decades later just as forcibly. And, although Wynter 'would talk about inventions, people, jazz, poetry, about underwater, about discoveries on walks', recalled Eric Wynter in his short memoir of 1984, 'He didn't talk much about art at all.'[5] To his friends and associates Wynter's personal qualities seemed to belong to some greater creative enterprise that existed alongside and beyond his art. 'His original thinking', wrote Eric, 'his understanding of the country and his relish in communication had been bringers of freedom.'[6]

Throughout his years in Cornwall, Wynter's involvement with artistic factions and rivalries in St Ives was largely tangential. During one of his few meetings with Ben Nicholson he was struck by the senior artist's frank and business-like admission that, as part of his working routine, he set aside time each day to write letters promoting himself. If Nicholson was offering a piece of well-meant professional advice, however, he was talking to the wrong man. Another frequently observed characteristic of Wynter's was that he shied away from such self-promotion, from what Wyndham Lewis called the 'prize-fighter' behaviour necessary for artistic reputation-building. His modesty, in Heron's well-informed professional opinion, was 'without doubt partly

detail of **178**
Meander V,
*c.*1972–4

175
Untitled, no.2
acrylic on paper
41.9 x 30.5 cm (16½ x 12 in)
1975
Private collection

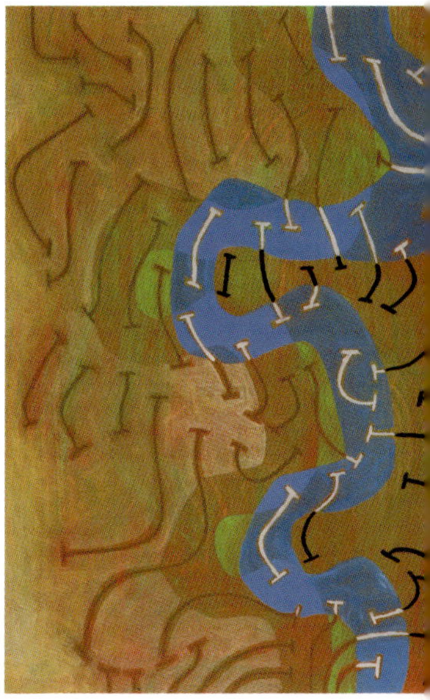

responsible' for the fact that Wynter's reputation had, by the time of his death, suffered a marked decline since its high point around 1959. In this he was not alone; the rehabilitation, not only of Wynter but of a whole group of British painters that also included Scott, Lanyon, Davie, Hilton, Wells, Frost and Heron himself became Heron's critical crusade throughout the following two decades. This group of artists, he announced in 1976, had been 'far less celebrated here at home in England than it had been overseas', although thankfully 'There is at last evidence to suggest that British neglect of this generation is increasingly being rectified.'[7]

His optimism was occasioned by exhibition 'Bryan Wynter 1915–75', a full-scale retrospective at the Hayward Gallery that Heron, aided by Bowness and Leslie Waddington, persuaded the Arts Council to stage in August 1976. The critical response seemed, on the whole, to justify his hopes. Marina Vaizey discerned in Wynter's work 'the intensity of a scientist and the intuition of an artist', most dazzlingly combined in his 'remarkable kinetic constructions which suggest limitless depths'.[8] So far so good; yet Wynter himself might well have felt uneasy at *The Observer* critic's judgement that he 'belongs to the generation who married romantic British landscape to Cubism', adding that 'He was one of the Cornish clan, and his strength seems to derive from the accent developed by that sturdy band'.[9] During the following decade Wynter's career was to become firmly located within a notion of post-war 'St Ives' art. First promoted by Heron as a kind of critical banner beneath which he and his associates could contest the dominance of New York-based abstract art in the late 1950s, it had by 1985 solidified into an art-historical category. In this year the Tate Gallery put on the exhibition 'St Ives: Twenty-five Years of Painting, Sculpture and Pottery', in which ten of Wynter's works were included among those of forty-eight other artists and craftspeople who between the 1880s and the 1980s (the title was something of a misnomer) had had some connection or other with St Ives. Bowness, who had been appointed director of the Tate in 1980, was also involved in the early stages of planning the new Tate outstation in St Ives that would eventually open in 1993.

All this was mixed news for Wynter's reputation. It ensured him a continued presence among a group of his peers whose collective place in the history of modern British art, whatever the vagaries of the market, was now secure. At the same time it aligned his work with certain categories of art into which, in the end, it made at best an awkward fit. There is little to be gained, for example, in making connections between Wynter and many of the artists usually considered quintessential examples of 'St Ives', such as Nicholson, Hepworth, Wells and Frost. Even Lanyon, who outdid Wynter in the complexity and intensity of his theory of landscape in art, provides only limited points of comparison. Heron, meanwhile, whose life and work in so many ways ran parallel to Wynter's, remained loyal to a set of aesthetic principles that hardly begin to explain the mainsprings of Wynter's art.

Bowness described Wynter as 'a natural outsider'.[10] In an art world whose very functioning relies on categories, Wynter's work has proved much harder to assimilate as a single, unified *oeuvre* than that of his peers. There is Heron, for example, the Francophile colourist. Or Frost the unpretentious humaniser of Constructive abstraction, Lanyon the bolshy synthesiser of landscape and abstract painting, and Hilton the wild card, conjuring his unique, unearthly sensuality from a mélange of body parts and semi-abstract entities. But how would you characterise Wynter? Heron thought that his career represented 'four distinct developments': his landscapes of the 1940s; the abstract all-over paintings he produced between 1956 and 1965; the IMOOS; and the final phase, of 'hard-edged *plus* soft-edged imagery', which he predicted 'may come to be looked upon as his best works'.[11] This is a fair summary, from an artist and writer who knew Wynter and his work better than anyone. Even so, Heron's concentration on visual effects,

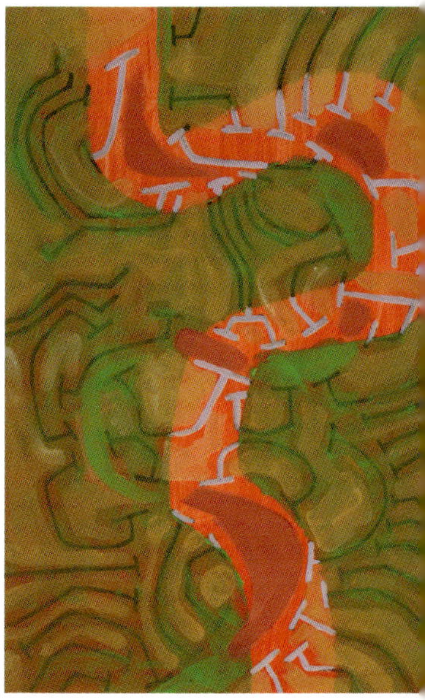

176
Untitled, no.5
acrylic on paper
32.5 x 25.5 cm (14 x 10 in)
1975
Private collection

177
Untitled, no.3
acrylic on paper
32.5 x 25.5 cm (14 x 10 in)
1975
Private collection

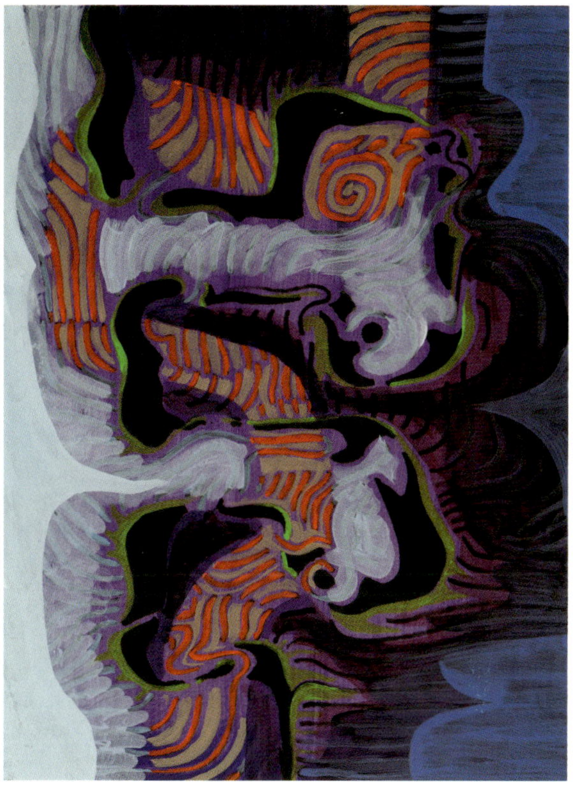

on the primacy of shape and colour, leaves a mysterious void at the centre of Wynter's enterprise.

Let's put aside for a moment the art-historical attempt to place Wynter's career alongside those of his exact contemporaries and look forward a few years. Think, instead, of the development of what came to be termed Land art in 1970s' Britain. In 1967 a former student at the West of England College of Art in Bristol, Richard Long, photographed a track he'd made by walking repeatedly through grass. This was the start of a career based on documenting the artist's passage through different landscapes, in photographs or words, and in bringing elements of those landscapes, in the form of stones, mud or other matter, into gallery spaces. The interweaving of self and environment – the patient, detailed tracking of the artist's physical movement through spaces that feed the imagination as well as fill the journal – relates in many respects to Wynter's preoccupations. In terms of its philosophy and process, Long's approach can sometimes sound almost like continuation of Wynter's concerns by other means. 'The planet', according to Long, 'is full of unbelievably permanent things, like rock strata and tides, and yet full of impermanences like butterflies or seaweed on the beach, which is in a new pattern every day for thousands of years. I would like to think that my work reflects that beautiful complexity and reality.'[12] Like this statement, the cartographic features in the map of Dartmoor that forms part of Long's *A Hundred Mile Walk* (1972) provide a process-based parallel to Wynter's late paintings. Wynter's own vast output of landscape photography, shot from every angle and focal distance, remained a largely private affair. It was a resource intended, like Eugène Atget's haunting photographic record of Paris, to assist in the production of art rather than to become an art work in its own right. It would not have occurred to Wynter to exhibit his slides or have them printed in book form, as a similar body of work with accompanying statements might be displayed today.

Wynter could have exhibited maps of his river trips, films of the huge kite he constructed to pull his kayak, piazza-scale IMOOS. He didn't – not because he wasn't as a rule closely in tune with contemporary interests but because his idea of art, of what an artist's life was ultimately about, remained rooted in the mid-century. In his elegy to Lanyon, Graham described the artist's metier in these terms: 'His job is Love/ Imagined into words or paint to make/ An object that will stand and will not move.'[13] It was this faith in the object – in the power of painting – even more than any particular shared motifs or themes, that bound Wynter to the generation of painters that was promoted, and then defended, by Heron. By the mid-1970s this faith was deeply unfashionable, identified as it was with capitalist values and the commodification of art.

There is now under way, however, a general reassessment of post-war culture. The revisionist view of the period between the mid-1940s and the mid-1970s is coloured by a combination of academic historiography and less cool-headed nostalgia, exemplified by Grayson Perry's introduction to the exhibition 'Unpopular Culture', which he selected from the British Council's art collection in 2008. The post-war period, according to Perry, was an age when 'stories about art did not feature

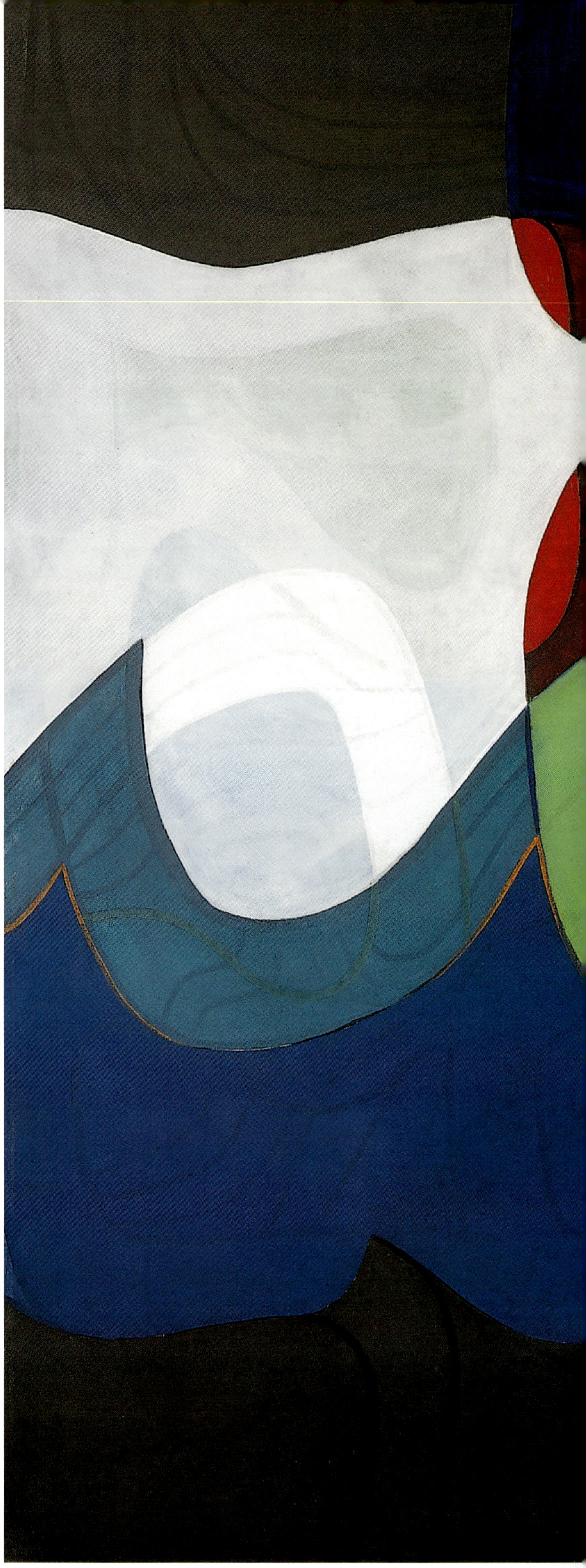

178
Meander V,
oil on canvas
152.4 x 122 cm (60 x 72 in)
*c.*1972–4
Artist's estate

daily in the broadsheets or contemporary artists crop up frequently in gossip columns'. It was a time

> when modern art was an even more rarefied activity, practised and appreciated by other-worldly bohemians and intellectuals. The title (of the exhibition) also refers to a feeling that many artists then made art that could be characterised as subtle, sensitive, lyrical and quiet in contrast to today when much art can seem like shouty advertisments for concepts or personalities. As a group for me these works conjure a nostalgic picture of a post-war, pre-Thatcherite Britain, more reflective, more civic and more humane.[14]

Wynter was represented in this show by *Landscape, Zennor* (see fig. 31), an understated, lyrical gouache that is also, of course, evidence of a time when, for specific historical reasons, the officers of the British Council and Arts Council paid close attention to what was happening around St Ives. But it is true that for Wynter there was indeed something 'subtle, sensitive, lyrical' about art; and there was nothing in his nature that would have made good copy for 'shouty advertisments for concepts or personalities'. He was, as Heron said of Braque, 'One of the most intellectual of painters',[15] yet at the same time an artist whose creative thought was continually drawn to the rhythms of physical movement, of flow and change. 'Am I still influenced by landscape?' Wynter asked himself in 1962, thinking of the strange rocks and cromlechs of the Penwith moors, the upland wilds around the Carn. Perhaps the landscape of which his work makes us most aware, however, is not the 'placeness' of west Cornwall (in Lanyon's phrase) or any other visitable location but the terrain Huxley describes when he observes in *The Doors of Perception* that 'The mind is its own place'.[16]

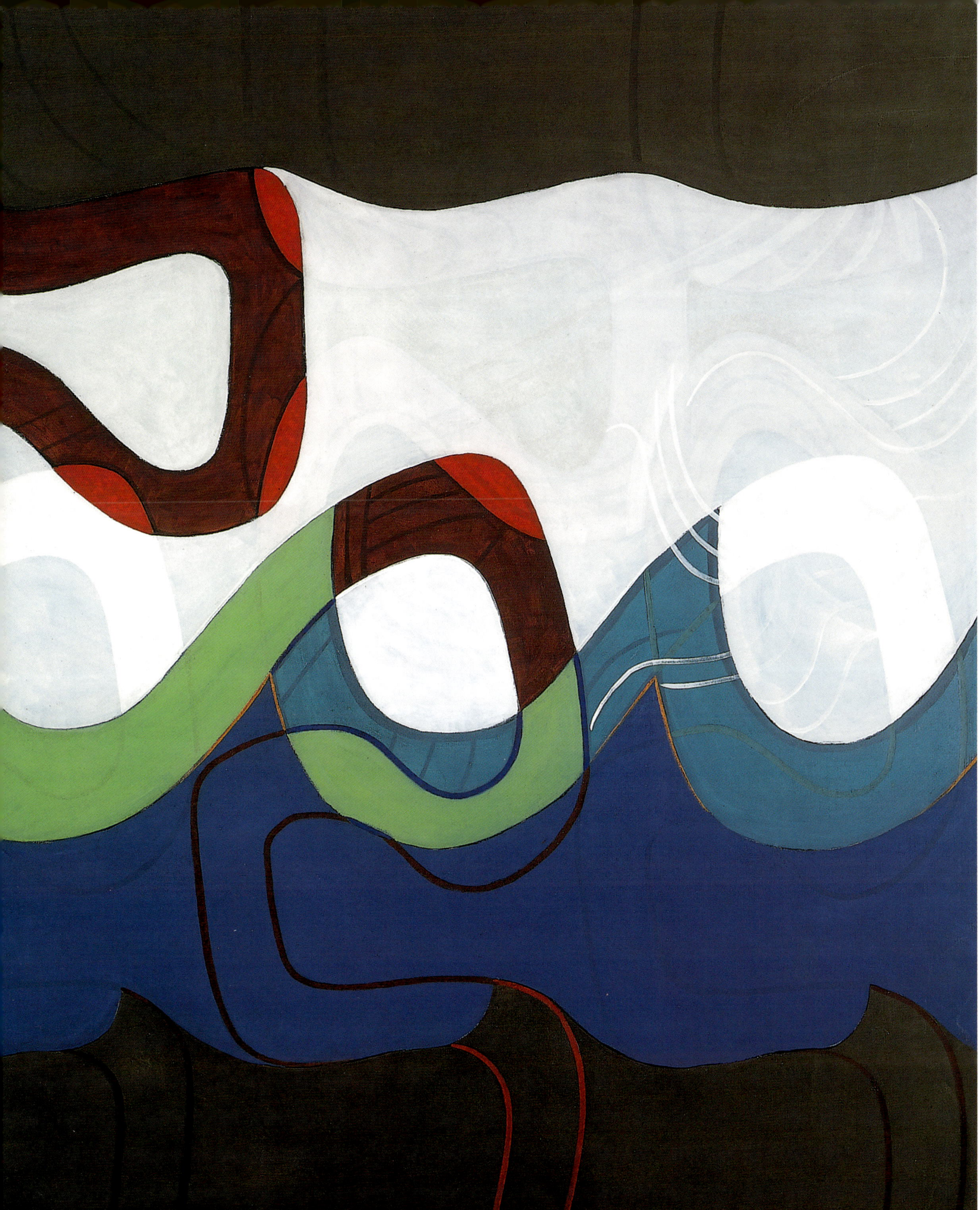

Notes

INTRODUCTION

1 Monica Wynter observed that, as a rule, 'If Bryan was interested in something, he wanted to share it with people'. Conversation with author, August 2009.
2 Alan Bowness, Foreword, *Bryan Wynter 1915–75* (exhib. cat., Hayward Gallery, London, 1976).
3 Bryan Wynter, artist's statement in *Statements: A Review of British Abstract Art in 1956* (exhib. cat., Institute of Contemporary Arts, London, 1957), n. p.
4 Johann Wolfgang von Goethe, quoted by Aldous Huxley in *The Doors of Perception* (London, 1954); edn used *The Doors of Perception* and *Heaven and Hell* (London, 1994), p. 46.
5 Huxley, *Doors of Perception*, p. 47.
6 Bryan Wynter, *Statements*, n. p.
7 Patrick Heron, *The Changing Forms of Art* (London, 1955), p. 174.
8 Ibid, pp. 173–4.
9 In a piece for *Arts* (New York) in November 1956, Heron described Wynter's technique as a 'grille, or network of brushsigns (I think the word "brushstroke" no longer applies where the *stroke* is itself become the chief *object* in the picture)'.
10 Harold Rosenberg, 'The American Action Painters', *Art News* (New York), li (Dec 1952), pp. 22–3.
11 David Sylvester, *Interviews with Francis Bacon: 1962–1979* (London, 1980), p. 61.
12 Patrick Heron, Introduction, *Bryan Wynter 1915–75*.
13 Frank Auerbach in conversation with Catherine Lampert, *Frank Auerbach* (exhib. cat., Hayward Gallery, London, 1978), p. 10.
14 Bowness, Foreword, *Bryan Wynter 1915–75*.
15 Peter Blake and Richard Hamilton both designed album sleeves for The Beatles: *Sgt Pepper's Lonely Hearts Club Band* (1967) and *The White Album* (1968) respectively.
16 Patrick Heron, obituary, *The Cornishman* (13 Feb 1975).
17 Ibid.
18 Graham's comment is recalled by Monica Wynter, conversation with the author, April 2009.
19 Letter to Tate Gallery, March 1966; cited in Chris Stephens, *Bryan Wynter*, St Ives Artists (London, 1999), p. 62.
20 Milein Cosman, conversation with the author, December 2008.

CHAPTER 1

1 See David Wynter's obituary in *The New-Church Herald*, vol. 12, no. 565 (5 Dec 1931), pp. 734–7.
2 Mel Gooding, *Patrick Heron* (London, 1994), p. 27.
3 Quoted in Gooding, *Patrick Heron*, p. 27.
4 Email from Toby Parker, archivist at Haileybury, 13 Jan 2009.
5 'I Hate Painting', interview with Howard Hodgkin, *The Guardian* (13 May 2006).
6 André Breton, *Surrealist Manifesto* (Paris, 1924).
7 Cited in Malcolm Yorke, *The Spirit of Place: Nine Neo-Romantic Artists and Their Times* (London, 1988), p. 54.
8 Letter to Hedy Hoffmann, n. d. (?1944).
9 Monica Wynter, conversation with the author 20 June 2007.
10 As recalled by Paul Nash, quoted in Yorke, *The Spirit of Place*, p. 55, n.
11 Conversation with the author, 19 March 2009.

CHAPTER 2

1 Aldous Huxley, *Ends and Means* (London, 1937), p. 3.
2 Ibid, p. 33.
3 Ibid, p. 141.
4 William Wordsworth, *The Prelude, or Growth of a Poet's Mind* (text of 1805), ed. Ernest de Selincourt (London, 1933; rev. Helen Darbishire 1960; repr. 1969), Book X, ll. 825–6, and Book XII, ll. 367–8.
5 Eric Wynter, 'Bryan – A Memoir', *Catalogue of the Paintings of Bryan Wynter* (exhib. cat., Prema Project, Uley, March 1984), n. p.
6 Quotations from Wynter's letters to Hedy Hoffmann are taken from copies provided by her husband, David King.
7 Letter to Hedy Hoffmann, n. d. (?1942). Wynter opens this letter 'Dearest one' rather than, as in almost all other letters to Hedy, 'My dear Mouse', which suggests that it may come from an early stage in their relationship.
8 Letter to Hedy Hoffmann, n. d. (?spring 1945).
9 Letter to Hedy Hoffmann, 20 June 1945.
10 Carl Gustav Jung, 'On Psychic Energy' (1928), repr. in *The Structure and Dynamics of the Psyche*, vol. 8 of *Collected Works of C. G. Jung* (London, 1960; 2nd edn 1969), p. 45.
11 Letter from Hedy Hoffmann, n. d. (July 1942).
12 Letter to Hedy Hoffmann, n. d. (July 1942).
13 Letter to Hedy Hoffmann, n. d. (July 1942).
14 Michael Meyer, 'Memoir', in *The Collected Poems of Sidney Keyes* (London, 1945), p. xiii.
15 Milein Cosman, 'Memories of Sidney Keyes', www.carcanet.co.uk/cgi-bin/scribe?showdoc=7;doctype=biography.
16 Quoted by Michael Meyer in his 'Memoir', in *The Collected Poems of Sidney Keyes* (London, 1945), p. xiii.
17 Keyes, 'The Wilderness', *Collected Poems*, p. 113.
18 Loose notebook page, datable to 1940–45 by diary references from the same notebook to black-out curtains and neighbours 'digging for victory'.
19 Comment by Vera Leslie, cited in Stephens, *Bryan Wynter*, p. 21, n. 24.
20 Conversation with the author, 19 March 2009.
21 'Foreword', *Counterpoint*, no. 1 (1945), n. p.
22 Ibid.
23 Conrad Senat, letter to Paul Nash, 31 May 1944. Tate Archive TGA 7050/424.

24 Cited in Yorke, *Spirit of Place*, p. 63.
25 Conrad Senat, 'Young English Painters, No. 1: Some Paintings by Bryan Wynter', *Counterpoint*, 1 (1945), n. p.
26 John Heath-Stubbs, 'Virgin and Unicorn', *Selected Poems* (London, 1965), p. 27.
27 According to Senat (letter to Paul Nash, 31 May 1044), *Counterpoint* was 'conceived primarily in opposition to the rather stuffy Liberal standpoint of Horizon'. Its projected series on young English Painters was probably a riposte to the series of such features run by *Horizon*.
28 Read used this phrase in his review of British sculpture at the 1952 Venice Biennale, which included work by Robert Adams, Kenneth Armitage, Reg Butler, Lynn Chadwick, Geoffrey Clarke, Bernard Meadows, Eduardo Paolozzi and William Turnbull.
29 Senat, 'Young English Painters, No. 1'.

CHAPTER 3

1 Letter to Hedy Hoffmann, n. d. (*c.* 9 May 1945).
2 Letter to Hedy Hoffmann, 20 June 1945.
3 Ibid.
4 Ibid.
5 Letter to Hedy Hoffmann, n. d. (*c.* July 1945).
6 Patrick Heron, 'Bryan Wynter', in *Painter as Critic*.
7 Huxley, *Ends and Means*, p. 58.
8 Ibid.
9 Patrick Heron, 'Artists in Cornwall', *New Statesman and Nation* (17 Jan 1948); repr. in *The Changing Forms of Art*, pp. 241–2.
10 Letter to Hedy Hoffmann, 6 July 1945.
11 Ibid.
12 Letter to Hedy Hoffmann, n. d. (July 1945).
13 Letter to Hedy Hoffmann, n. d. (Aug/Sept 1945).
14 Letter to Hedy Hoffmann, 13 Aug 1945.
15 Ibid.
16 Letter to Hedy Hoffmann, 13 Aug 1945.
17 William Wordsworth, 'Preface to *Lyrical Ballads* (1800/1802)', *Lyrical Ballads and Other Poems of Wordsworth and Coleridge* (Ware, 2002), p. 8.
18 Sidney Keyes, 'The Wilderness', *The Collected Poems of Sidney Keyes* (London, 1945), p. 113.
19 T. S. Eliot, 'The Hollow Men', *Complete Poems and Plays of T. S. Eliot* (London, 2004).
20 Letter to Hedy Hoffmann, n. d. (August 1945).
21 Sven Berlin, *The Coat of Many Colours: Autosvenography* (Bristol, 1994), p. 206.
22 Eric Wynter, 'Bryan – A Memoir', n. p.
23 Letter to his mother, 6 Oct 1945.
24 Letter to Hedy Hoffmann, n.d. (Aug/Sept 1945).
25 John Keats, letter to Benjamin Bailey, 22 Nov 1817, *Letters of John Keats: A Selection*, ed. Robert Gittings (Oxford, 1970; repr. 1977), p. 37.
26 Patrick Heron, 'Modern English Romantics', *Changing Forms of Art*, p. 174.
27 Barbara Hepworth, *A Pictorial Autobiography* (Bradford on Avon, 1970), p. 55.
28 Letter to Hedy Hoffmann, Sept 1946.
29 Patrick Heron, Review of 'Braque and Rouault' at the Tate Gallery, London, April–May 1946, *New English Weekly* (July 1946); repr. in *Painter as Critic*, p. 15.
30 Ibid, p. 13.
31 Recalled by Monica Wynter.
32 Interview with Lionel Miskin, quoted in Chris Stephens, *Peter Lanyon: At the Edge of Landscape* (London, 2000), p. 124.
33 The co-exhibitors were Derwent Lees, Elsa Vaudrey and Michael Rothenstein.
34 Review in *The Spectator* (19 April 1947).
35 Maurice Collis, review in *Time and Tide* (19 April 1947).
36 Patrick Heron, review in *New Statesman and Nation* (12 June 1948).
37 Berlin, *The Coat of Many Colours*, p. 211.
38 Sue Murray, conversation with the author, Dec 2008.
39 The business later prospered and expanded; during the 1960s and 1970s its products gained an international reputation and were widely distributed by school suppliers.
40 Letter to Hedy Hoffmann, 10 March 1949.
41 Letter to Hedy Hoffmann, 31 Aug 1945.
42 Letter to Hedy Hoffmann, 10 March 1949.
43 Ibid.
44 Letter to Hedy Hoffmann, n. d. (April 1949).

CHAPTER 4

1 Letter to Hedy Hoffmann, 17 Dec 1949.
2 The second Crypt Group exhibition, in August 1947, included Sven Berlin, Peter Lanyon, Guido Morris, John Wells and Wilhelmina Barns-Graham; the third, in August 1948, included Wynter, Berlin, Barns-Graham, Lanyon, Wells, Kit Barker, David Haughton, Patrick Heron and Adrian Ryan.
3 J. Wood Palmer, introduction to *Contemporary English Painting* (exhib. cat., City Art Gallery, Bristol, 1950).
4 Herbert Read, *Contemporary British Art* (Harmondsworth, 1951), p. 33.
5 Berlin, *The Coat of Many Colours*, p. 206.
6 Patrick Heron, 'Space in Contemporary Painting and Architecture', *Changing Forms of Art*, p. 40.
7 The artist Derek Ellwood studied at Corsham 1951–4.
8 According to David Brown, 'Barbed wire was placed around Monks Park later in an attempt to prevent unauthorized entry by men, following complaints from parents about their daughters' promiscuity. One artist teaching at Corsham in the first half of the 'Sixties described Corsham as being *"full of randy girls."* There were usually many more female than male students. At one time

it was described, unfairly, as being a finishing school for girls. One father who suspected, quite rightly, that his daughter was having an affair with a teacher tried to get him sacked. Stories of close encounters between staff and students are legion. Some teachers married students'. 'Introduction', *Corsham: A Celebration: The Bath Academy of Art 1946–72* (exhib. cat., Michael Parkin Gallery, London, 1989), n. 5.

9 Cited in online catalogue entry for Reg Butler, *Working Model for 'The Unknown Political Prisoner'*, 1955–6 (T02332), www.tate.org.uk.

10 Berlin, *The Coat of Many Colours*, p. 212.

11 Bryan Robertson, introduction to *British Painting and Sculpture 1954* (exhib. cat., Whitechapel Art Gallery, London, 1954).

12 This, at least, was Heron's view in March 1949, when he wrote a short piece, 'To an American Painter', for the New York journal *Magazine of Art*. Heron, *Changing Forms of Art*, p. 242.

13 Mel Gooding, 'Editor's Note: The Writings', in Patrick Heron, *The Painter as Critic*, ed. Mel Gooding (London, 1998), p. viii.

14 'Space in Colour: Hitchens, Scott, Pasmore, Frost, Vaughan, Hilton, Lanyon, Davie: Paintings Selected by Patrick Heron', Hanover Gallery, London, 7 July–7 August 1953.

15 Heron, *Changing Forms of Art*, p. 171.

16 Ibid, p. 173.

17 Ibid.

18 Artist's statement, in *Statements*, n. p.

19 Huxley, *Doors of Perception*, p. 18.

20 Berlin, *The Coat of Many Colours*, p. 212.

CHAPTER 5

1 Monica Wynter, email to author, 1 June 2009.

2 Ibid.

3 *Metavisual, Tachiste, Abstract* (exhib. cat., Redfern Gallery, London, 1957).

4 Paul Feiler, conversation with the author, 19 March 2009.

5 Letter to Eric Wynter, 5 July 1956.

6 Artist's statement in *Statements*, n. p.

7 Patrick Heron, *Arts* (New York) (Nov 1956).

8 Patrick Heron, 'Introduction', *Bryan Wynter, 1915–75*, n. p.

9 Patrick Heron, 'To an American Painter', *Magazine of Art* (March 1949); repr. in *Changing Forms of Art*, p. 244.

10 Clement Greenberg, 'The Present Prospects of American Painting and Sculpture', *Horizon*, vol. 16, no. 93/94 (October, 1947), pp. 25–6.

11 Holger Cahill, Introduction to *Modern Art in the United States: A Selection from the Collections of the Museum of Modern Art, New York* (exhib. cat., London, Tate Gallery, 1956), pp. 21–2.

12 Jackson Pollock, quoted in Selden Rodman, *Conversations with Artists* (New York, 1957), pp. 76–87.

13 Berlin, *The Coat of Many Colours*, p. 212.

14 Patrick Heron, 'Art is Autonomous', *The Twentieth Century* (September 1955); repr. in Heron, *Painter as Critic*, p. 99.

15 Heron, 'Space in Painting and Architecture', *Architect's Year Book*, no. 5 (Jan 1953); repr. in *Painter as Critic*, p. 73.

16 Roger Hilton, artist's statement in *Statements*, n. p.

17 Lawrence Alloway, 'Introductory Notes', *Statements*, n. p.

18 Ibid.

19 Patrick Heron, *Statements*, n. p.

20 Bryan Wynter, *Statements*, n. p.

21 W. S. Graham, 'The Nightfishing', *New Collected Poems*, ed. Matthew Francis (London, 2004), p. 117.

22 A. E. Housman, *A Shropshire Lad*, LII.

23 W. S. Graham, *The Nightfisherman: Selected Letters of W.S. Graham*, ed. Michael and Margaret Snow (Manchester, 1999), p. 162.

24 Bryan Wynter, *Statements*, n. p.

25 The British Sub-Aqua Club (BSAC), for example, was established in 1953.

26 David Sylvester, review of Jackson Pollock retrospective at the Whitechapel Gallery on BBC Radio, 7 November 1958; repr. in *About Modern Art: Critical Essays 1948–96* (London, 1996), p. 63.

27 Denys Sutton, Preface to *Metavisual, Tachiste, Abstract*, n. p.

28 Conversation with the author, 19 March 2009.

29 Heron, *Painter as Critic*, p. 148.

CHAPTER 6

1 'American Explosion', *Art and Artists*, vol. 1, no. 5 (n. s.) (May 1959), p. 1.

2 Alan Bowness, 'The Paintings of Bryan Wynter', *Art News and Review*, vol. 9, no. 4 (14 March 1959), pp. 5, 18.

3 Lawrence Alloway, 'Painting from the Big Country', *Art News and Review*, vol. 9, no. 4 (14 March 1959), pp. 3, 17.

4 Margaret Garlake, *New Art New World: British Art in Postwar Society* (New Haven and London, 1998), p. 26. With its combination of high seriousness and the accidental, action painting was easy game for satirists, most famously Tony Hancock, in his film *The Rebel* (1961).

5 Ralph Rumney, catalogue statement for an exhibition at the New Vision Centre Gallery, 1956; quoted in Garlake, *New Art New World*, p. 126.

6 I am indebted to Monica Wynter for this account of Wynter's working method, which she first observed in his studio at The Boltons in early 1956.

7 Quoted in Alfred H. Barr, Jr, 'Introduction', *The New American Painting* (exhib. cat., Tate Gallery, London, 1959), p. 9.

8 In the 1960s, after Bryan and Monica Wynter's sons were born, Bryan apparently found Mingus especially effective in the studio for drowning out the sounds of children elsewhere in the house.

9 'Notes on My Painting', *Bryan Wynter* (exhib. cat., Galerie Charles Lienhard, Zurich, 1962).

10 Bowness, 'The Paintings of Bryan Wynter'.

11 Alan Bowness attributes the phrase to Heron, who, however, later ascribed it to Leslie Waddington, Victor Waddington's son and business partner.
12 Roger Hilton, statement in Lawrence Alloway, *Nine Abstract Artists: Their Work and Theory* (London, 1954), p. 30.
13 Alan Bowness, introduction to *Four Middle-Generation English Painters* (exhib. cat., Waddington Galleries, London, 1959).
14 Quoted by Mel Gooding, 'Editor's Note: The Writings', in Heron, *Painter as Critic*, p. ix.
15 Bowness, *Four Middle-Generation English Painters*, n. p.
16 Conversation with the author, 29 Aug 2008.
17 David Sylvester, 'English Abstract Art' (revised from a review of 'Dimensions' in the *New Statesman*, 21 and 28 Dec 1957), *About Modern Art: Critical Essays 1948–96* (London, 1996), p. 150.
18 Quoted by Alfred H. Barr, Introduction, *The New American Painting*, p. 9.
19 Letter to Tate Gallery, n. d. [March 1966], quoted in Stephens, *Bryan Wynter*.
20 Unsigned review of Wynter's exhibition at Waddington Galleries in July 1965.
21 Patrick Heron, obituary of Bryan Wynter in *Studio International* (May–June 1975).
22 Peter Brook, *The Empty Space* (London, 1968; edn used Harmondsworth, 1972;, repr. 1980), p. 57.
23 Guy-Ernest Debord, 'Introduction to Critique of Urban Geography', *Les Lèvres Nues*, vol. 6 (1955).
24 Information from Marilyn Weston, whose parents owned and ran the hotel.
25 Letter to the author, n. d. (2008).
26 From a notebook addressed to Bryan Wynter, 19 Nov 1958, *The Nightfisherman*, p. 163.
27 Patrick Heron, 'Art is Autonomous', *The Twentieth Century* (Sept 1955); repr. in Heron, *Painter as Critic*, pp. 94–5.
28 'Unpublished note, 10 January 1960 (for Alan Bowness)', in *Bryan Wynter 1915–75*.
29 There are numerous accounts of this event. I have used those provided by Rose Hilton, Monica Wynter and Dr Roger Slack.
30 Eric Wynter, 'Bryan – A Memoir', *Catalogue of the Paintings of Bryan Wynter* (exhib. cat., Prema Project, Uley, 1984), n. p.
31 Wilfred Thesiger, *Arabian Sands* (London, 1959; edn used London, 2007), pp. 65–6.
32 'Notes on My Painting', *Bryan Wynter*, Galerie Charles Lienhard.

CHAPTER 7

1 Tom Wynter, email to the author, 22 April 2009.
2 I owe this observation to Billy Wynter.
3 Alan Bowness, 'The Paintings of Bryan Wynter', *Art News and Review*, vol. 9, no. 4 (14 March 1959), p. 5.
4 R. A. R. Tricker, *Bores, Breakers, Waves and Wakes: An Introduction to the Study of Waves on Water* (New York, 1964).
5 Jacques Cousteau, 'Preface', in Theodor Schwenk, *Sensitive Chaos: The Creation of Flowing Forms in Water and Air*, trans. Olive Whicher and Johanna Wrigley (London, 1965), p. 8.
6 Ibid, p. 11.
7 Unsigned review of Wynter's exhibition at Waddington Galleries in July 1965.
8 Schwenk, *Sensitive Chaos*, p. 19.
9 Ibid, p. 20.
10 Ibid, p. 27.
11 'The Seven Caves. From the Toltec Legend of the Original Home of the Race', ibid, p. 134.
12 W. S. Graham, 'Wynter and the Grammarsow', *New Collected Poems*, p. 185.
13 Gooding, *Patrick Heron*, p. 189.
14 *Interior Design*, vol. 42, no. 7 (July 1971).
15 Letter of 1 January 1971.
16 Bowness, 'The Paintings of Bryan Wynter', p. 5.
17 *Bryan Wynter, 1915–75*.
18 Andrew Forge, 'Introduction' to *British Painting '74* (exhib. cat., Hayward Gallery, London, 1974), n. p.
19 Eric Wynter, 'Bryan – A Memoir', n. p.
20 Conversation with the author, 6 May 2009.
21 Eric Wynter, 'Bryan – A Memoir'.

CHAPTER 8

1 W. S. Graham, 'Dear Bryan Wynter', *New Collected Poems*, p. 258.
2 Patrick Heron, obituary in *The Cornishman* (13 Feb 1975).
3 Peter Lanyon, interviewed by Lionel Miskin, 1962, Tate Archive TAV 211AB.
4 Graham Coles, conversation with the author, 17 Nov 2008.
5 Eric Wynter, 'Bryan – A Memoir'.
6 Ibid.
7 Patrick Heron, 'Introduction', *Bryan Wynter, 1915–75*, n. p.
8 Marina Vaizey, review in *The Sunday Times* (15 August 1976).
9 Nigel Gosling, review in *The Observer* (15 August 1976).
10 Alan Bowness, 'Foreword', *Bryan Wynter, 1915–75*, n. p.
11 Heron, 'Introduction', *Bryan Wynter, 1915–75*.
12 Quoted in David Sylvester, 'Long', *About Modern Art: Critical Essays, 1948–96* (London, 1996), p. 310.
13 W. S. Graham, 'The Thermal Stair', *New Collected Poems*, p. 164.
14 Grayson Perry and Blake Morrison, *Unpopular Culture: Grayson Perry Selects from the Arts Council Collection* (London, 2008).
15 Heron, *Painter as Critic*, p. 18.
16 Huxley, *The Doors of Perception*, p. 4.

Exhibitions

Solo exhibitions

1947 Redfern Gallery (concurrent with Derwent Lees, Elsa Vaudrey and Michael Rothenstein)
Downing's Bookshop, St Ives
1948 Redfern Gallery (concurrent with David Jones and Derek Hill)
1950 Redfern Gallery, London (concurrent with Kenneth Wood)
1953 Redfern Gallery, London (concurrent with Michael Ayrton, Michael Rothenstein and Graham Sutherland)
1955 Redfern Gallery, London (concurrent with Guillaume Orlix)
1957 Redfern Gallery, London
1959 Waddington Galleries, London
1962 Galerie Charles Lienhard, Zurich
Waddington Galleries, London
1963 Arnolfini, Bristol
Taynton Arts Society, Taynton House, Gloucester
1965 Waddington Galleries, London
1966 Arts Council Gallery, Belfast
1967 Waddington Galleries, London
1969 Sheviock Gallery, Torpoint, Cornwall
1971 University of Exeter
1974 Waddington Galleries, London
1975 Memorial Exhibition, Falmouth College of Art, Falmouth
1976 'Bryan Wynter, 1915–75' (full retrospective), Arts Council, Hayward Gallery, London
1988 University of Essex, Colchester
1981 New Art Centre, London (Part 1)
1982 New Art Centre, London (Part 2)
Penwith Gallery, St Ives
1983 New Art Centre, London
1984 Prema Project, Uley, Gloucestershire
1987 Gillian Jason Gallery (concurrent with Denis Mitchell)
2001 'Bryan Wynter: A Selected Retrospective', Tate St Ives
2002 Jonathan Clark Fine Art, London
2006 Jonathan Clark Fine Art, London

Group exhibitions

1945 Castle Inn, Fore Street, St Ives (and occasionally until about 1951)

1946 Crypt Group (with Sven Berlin, Peter Lanyon, Guido Morris and John Wells), crypt of New Gallery (Mariners' Church), St Ives

1947 Spring Exhibition, Crypt Group, St Ives Society of Artists
Summer Exhibition, St Ives Society of Artists Summer Exhibition, Redfern Gallery, London
Summer Exhibition, Redfern Gallery, London

1948 Third Annual Crypt Group Exhibition, St Ives
Downing's Bookshop, St Ives, with Kit Barker

1949 'Original French and English Lithographs and Monotypes', Redfern Gallery, London
Summer Exhibition, Redfern Gallery, London
First Exhibition, Penwith Society, St Ives
Winter Exhibition, Penwith Society, St Ives

1950 'Contemporary English Painting', Bristol City Art Gallery (selection on tour to Bridgewater, Cirencester, Plymouth Arts Centre, Dartmouth Royal Naval College and Falmouth Polytechnic, by the Arts Council, South-West Region)

1951 'Work by Fifteen St Ives Artists and Craftsmen', Mansard Gallery, Heal's, London
'Sixty Paintings for '51', Arts Council (touring)
'British Watercolours and Drawings of the 20th Century', British Council (touring Spain, 1951–5 and 1957)
Summer Exhibition, Redfern Gallery, London
'Contemporary British Painting', Arts Council, Bristol City Art Gallery

1952 'The Mirror and the Square', Artists' International Association (AIA), New Burlington Galleries, London

1953 'Contemporary British Watercolours', British Council, Brooklyn Museum, New York (and touring)

'Pictures to be Enjoyed', AIA Gallery, London
'Coronation Exhibition, Contemporary British Paintings', Redfern Gallery, London
'West Country Landscape', Arts Council, South-West Region (touring)

1954 'Abstract, Cubist, Formalist, Surrealist', Redfern Gallery, London
'Fifty Years of British Art', Bradford City Art Gallery
'British Painting and Sculpture 1954', Whitechapel Art Gallery, London

1955 'Paintings' (with Paul Feiler, Peter Lanyon and Peter Potworowski), The Octagon, Bath
'Six Painters from Cornwall', Montreal City Art Gallery (and touring Canada, 1955–6)
'British Watercolours and Drawings of the 20th Century', British Council (touring Canada, 1955–7)

1956 'Recent Abstract Painting', Whitworth Art Gallery, University of Manchester
Spring Exhibition, Bradford City Art Gallery
'Vision and Reality', Wakefield City Art Gallery

1957 'Abstract Art', Galerie Creuze, Paris
'Dimensions: British Abstract Art 1948–57', O'Hana Gallery, London
'Statements: British Abstract Art in 1956', Institute of Contemporary Art, London
'Abstract 1957', AIA Gallery, London
'Fourth International Exhibition of Contemporary Art', Tokyo
Summer Exhibition, Penwith Society, St Ives
'The Penwith Society of Arts in Cornwall', Arts Council (1957–8, touring)
'Metavisual, Tachiste, Abstract: Painting in England Today', Redfern Gallery, London
'Contemporary English Painting', Musée des Beaux-Arts, Liège (touring to Geneva and Brussels)
'Contemporary British Painting', Chicago Arts Club (and touring USA)
'New Trends in British Art', New York Art Foundation, Rome
Print Exhibition, Redfern Gallery, London

1958 'Eleven British Artists', Jefferson Place Gallery, Washington, DC
'English Drawings', Aldeburgh Festival, Suffolk
Spring Exhibition, Penwith Society of Arts, St Ives
John Moores Liverpool Exhibition 1, Walker Art Gallery, Liverpool
'British Abstract Painting', Auckland City Art Gallery, New Zealand
'The Christian Vision', Redfern Gallery, London
'Contemporary British Printmakers', St George's Gallery, London
'The Religious Theme', Contemporary Art Society, Tate Gallery, London
Summer Exhibition, Redfern Gallery, London
'Contemporary British Painting', Howard Wise Gallery, Cleveland, OH
'Five Cornwall Artists' (with Terry Frost, Patrick Heron, Peter Lanyon and John Wells), Bear Lane Gallery, Oxford
Print Exhibition, Redfern Gallery, London

1959 'Recent Paintings: Seven British Artists', British Council (touring Australia)
'The Graven Image', Whitechapel Art Gallery
'Four English Middle Generation Painters' (with Patrick Heron, Roger Hilton and Terry Frost), Waddington Galleries, London
Fifth Tokyo Biennale
'Documenta II', Kassel
John Moores Liverpool Exhibition 2, Walker Art Gallery, Liverpool
'Thirteen British Printmakers', Göteborg Museum (touring Sweden, to 1961)

1960 'British Painting 1720–1960', British Council (touring the USSR)
International Exhibition, Tunis
'Art Alive', Northampton City Art Gallery

'Contemporary British Painting', Royal Birmingham Society of Artists
Second International Print Biennale, Tokyo
'Bianco e Nero' (drawings and prints), British Council, Lugano
'Aspects', Waddington Galleries, London
'Artists from the Waddington Galleries', Nottingham University
'Irish Exhibition of Living Art', National Collection of Art, Dublin
'British Painting 1900–1960', Mappin Art Gallery, Sheffield, and Aberdeen Art Gallery
Penwith Society of Arts, 10th Anniversary, Arts Council tour
'Painters in Cornwall', Plymouth City Art Gallery
Luca Scacchi Gracco, Milan (with Francis Bacon, Alan Davie, Roger Hilton, Alexander Mackenzie, Ben Nicholson, John Piper and Graham Sutherland)
'Six British Artists' (with Alan Davie, Merlyn Evans, Terry Frost, William Gear and Roger Hilton), British Council (touring to Mexico, Peru and Kenya into 1961)
'Contemporary British Landscape', Arts Council, Glynn Vivian Art Gallery, Swansea (touring to 1961)

1961 Spring Exhibition, Bradford City Art Gallery
'British Graphics 1961', Linköping (and touring Sweden)
'International Exhibition of Watercolours', Brooklyn Museum, New York
'Middle Roads: Four British Abstract Painters' (with Adrian Health, Patrick Heron and Roger Hilton), Manchester City Art Gallery
Summer Exhibition, Redfern Gallery, London
House Exhibition, Waddington Galleries, London
Sixth Tokyo Biennale
Fourth International Contemporary Art Exhibition, All India Fine Art & Crafts Society, New Delhi (and touring India)
Fore Street Gallery, St Ives (and occasionally until about 1964)
'New Painting 1958–61', Arts Council, Walker Art Gallery, Liverpool (and touring, to 1963)

1962 'West Penwith Painters and Sculptors', Arnolfini, Bristol
'New British Art', Sammenslutningen af Danske Kunstforeninger, Denmark
'British Art Today', San Francisco (and touring, to 1963)

1963 British Council, Budapest
'Some Aspects of Contemporary British Painting', British Council, National Gallery of Canada (and touring)
'British Painting in the Sixties', Contemporary Art Society, Tate Gallery and Whitechapel Art Gallery, London
Summer Exhibition, Redfern Gallery, London
First Commonwealth Biennale of Abstract Art, Commonwealth Institute, London
John Moores Exhibition 4, Walker Art Gallery, Liverpool

1964 'Young British Painters' (with Sandra Blow, Alan Davie, Terry Frost, Donald Hamilton Fraser and Gwyther Irwin), Carolina Museum of Art, Raleigh, NC
'British Contemporary Artists', New Metropole Arts Centre, Folkestone

1965 '9 Painters and 3 Sculptors', Arnolfini, Bristol
'Corsham Painters and Sculptors', Arts Council, Bath Festival (and touring)
'Trends in Contemporary British Painting', Bear Lane Gallery, Oxford
'Frost, Heron, Hilton and Wynter', Waddington Galleries, London
'Patrick Heron and Bryan Wynter', Hume Tower, Edinburgh
'British Watercolours and Drawings of the 20th Century', British Council (touring, including Hong Kong)

1966 'Open Painting Exhibition', Ulster Museum, Belfast
'Five Years', Arnolfini, Bristol
Inaugural Exhibition, Richard Demarco Gallery, Edinburgh
Christmas Exhibition, Richard Demarco Gallery, Edinburgh

1967 'Works on Paper', Waddington Galleries, London
Festival Exhibition, Richard Demarco Gallery, Edinburgh
'Recent British Painting', Peter Stuyvesant Foundation, Tate Gallery, London

1968 'Six Painters and Sculptors', Peterloo Gallery, Manchester
'British Art Today', Hamburg Kunstverein, Hamburg

1969 'Arts Council Collection 1967–68', exhibition of works bought by Alan Bowness and Robyn Denny (touring, to 1971)

1970 'Painting and Sculpture 1970' (with Alexander Mackenzie and John Skelton), Plymouth City Art Gallery
'Kinetics', Arts Council, Hayward Gallery, London

1972 'Contemporary Drawings', Bath Festival and Bath Academy of Art
'Two by Seven', Archer Gallery
'Reflections', Mappin Art Gallery, Sheffield
'Decade 40', Whitechapel Art Gallery, London (and touring)

1974 'British Painting '74', Arts Council, Hayward Gallery, London

1975 'British Painting 1900–1960', Mappin Art Gallery, Sheffield, and Aberdeen Art Gallery

1976 Penwith Gallery, St Ives (with Roger Hilton)
Cornwall Education Committee Art Collection, Penwith Gallery, St Ives

1977 'British Painting 1952–77', Royal Academy of Arts, London
'Cornwall 1945–55', New Art Centre, London

1980 'Pictures from an Exhibition', Whitechapel Art Gallery, London

1982 'The Sea, St Ives and the Seeing Eye', Penwith Gallery, St Ives
'British Drawings and Watercolours', British Council (touring China)

1983 'The British Neo-Romantics', Fischer Fine Art, London, and the National Museum of Wales, Cardiff

1984 'English Contrasts', Art Curial, Paris

1985 'St Ives 1939–64: Twenty Five Years of Painting Sculpture and Pottery', Tate Gallery, London
'Cornish and Contemporary', Worcester City Museum

1986 'The Unbroken Line: 50 Years of British Drawing 1936–86, Part II', Gillian Jason Gallery, London
'British Prints of the Post-War Years', Redfern Gallery, London

1987 'Ayrton, Craxton, Minton, Richards, Vaughan, Wynter', Gillian Jason Gallery, London
'Looking West', Newlyn Art Gallery, Newlyn, and Royal College of Art, London
'The Experience of Landscape', Arts Council (touring)
'Works on paper by Modern British Artists', Austin-Desmond Fine Art, Sunninghill

1988 'St Ives', New Art Centre, London
'A Selection of Post-War British Art', Austin-Desmond Fine Art, London

1989 'St Ives 1920–89', Beaux Arts Gallery, Bath
'100 Years of Art in Cornwall', County Hall, Truro
'The Modern British Artist as Printmaker', Austin-Desmond Fine Art

1990 Spring Exhibition, Redfern Gallery

1998 'St Ives and British Modernism', Jonathan Clark Fine Art, London

2006 'Between a Rock and a Hard Place: The Stone in Art', Kenny Schachter, London

2008 'Unpopular Culture: Grayson Perry Selects from the Arts Council Collection', De La Warr Pavilion, Bexhill on Sea, and touring

Collections

Arts Council of Great Britain
Arts Council of Northern Ireland
Auckland, City Art Gallery
Belfast, Ulster Museum
Birmingham, City Museum and Art Gallery
Bradford, City Art Gallery and Museum
Bristol, City Art Gallery
British Council
Cambridge, Fitzwilliam Museum
Contemporary Art Society
Coventry, Herbert Art Gallery and Museum
Eastbourne, Towner Art Gallery
Kingston upon Hull, Ferens Art Gallery
Lincoln, Usher Gallery
Lisbon, Callouste Gulbenkian Foundation
London, Tate Gallery
London, Victoria and Albert Museum
Manchester, City Art Gallery
Manchester, Whitworth Art Gallery, University of Manchester
New York, Museum of Modern Art
Oxford, Keble College
Plymouth, City Museum and Art Gallery
Rochdale, Rochdale Art Gallery
Wellington, New Zealand, Museum of New Zealand Te Papa Tongarewa
York, City Art Gallery

Picture Credits

THE AUTHOR AND PUBLISHER wish to thank the following individuals, artists' estates, galleries, museums and other institutions for permission to reproduce and/or for supplying photographic sources for the illustrations in this book:

ADAGP, Paris and DACS, London 2009, photo courtesy of Sotheby's: 58; Artist's Estate: 1, 16, 22–3, 25–7, 32–3, 39, 45, 51, 57, 61, 81, 84–5, 91, 93, 102, 109, 123, 125–6, 129, 133, 142–4, 149, 152–3, 155, 168, 178; Arts Council Collection, Southbank Centre, London: 31; Bishop Otter College Collection, University of Chichester: 65; © Bristol Museums, Galleries & Archives: 35, 94, 115; British Council Collection: 2, 79 and 131; The Collection: Art & Archeology in Lincolnshire, Usher Gallery, Lincoln: 134; © John Craxton, all rights reserved, DACS, image courtesy of Tate Gallery, London: 28; © Crown Copyright: UK Government Art Collection: 67, 140; Fitzwilliam Museum, Cambridge: 20, 138; Hedy Hoffman Estate: 21; Jonathan Clark Fine Art: 6, 8, 78, 117, 160, 169–70, 173, 184; © The Lewinski Archive, Chatsworth: 157, 171; © Roger Mayne, photo courtesy of the artist: frontispiece, 89, 122, 127; The Metropolitan Museum of Art, bequest of Florene M. Schoenborn, 1995. Photo © The Metropolitan Museum of Art © ADAGP, Paris and DACS, London: 44; Digital image *c.*2009, The Museum of Modern Art, New York / Scala, Florence: 96; Image courtesy of Sue Murray: 53; National Gallery of Wales in Cardiff: 141; Collection of Newlyn Art Gallery and the Exchange: 50; Osborne Samuel Gallery, London: 130; Peggy Guggenheim Collection, Venice (Solomon R. Guggenheim Foundation, New York): 34; Plymouth City Museum and Art Gallery: 164; Private Collections: 4, 9, 17–19, 24, 29–30, 38, 40–43, 46–7, 49, 52, 55–6, 59, 62, 64, 69–71, 74–5, 77, 83, 95, 97–8, 103–106, 110, 112–14, 118–19, 121, 132, 136–37, 139, 145–48, 151, 154, 159, 161, 163, 166, 175–77; Private collection, image courtesy of Christie's Images Ltd: 135; Private collection, image courtesy of Gillian Jason Modern & Contemporary Art / The Bridgeman Art Library: 86, 101, 124, 150; Private collection © Estate of Patrick Heron, all rights reserved DACS: 90, 158; Private collection, image courtesy of Piano Nobile Fine Art: 128; Private collections, images courtesy of Sotheby's: 66, 80; © St Ives Studio, photo courtesy of the artist's family: 37; Scottish National Gallery of Modern Art, Edinburgh: 88; Southampton City Art Gallery: 87; Collection of the Suter Te Aratoi o Whakatu, Nelson, New Zealand: 54; Tate Archive: 43; © Tate, London: 68, 82, 107, 157, 162, 167; © Bryan Wynter, photograph courtesy of Monica Wynter: 7, 165; Photograph by Bryan Wynter: 76; Courtesy of Monica Wynter: 10–13, 15, 48, 60, 63, 72–3, 92, 120, 172; © V&A Images: 14; The Whitworth Art Gallery, The University of Manchester: 5, 99

Bibliography

Conrad Senat, 'Young English Painters, No. 1: Some Paintings by Bryan Wynter', *Counterpoint*, no. 1 (1945), n. p.

Patrick Heron, 'Moderrn English Romantics: Graham Sutherland, Keith Vaughan, Bryan Wynter', in *The Changing Forms of Art* (London, 1955), pp. 155–74

Patrick Heron, 'London: John Wells and Bryan Wynter', *Arts* (New York) (Nov 1956), pp. 15, and 73

Alan Bowness, 'The Paintings of Bryan Wynter', *Art News and Review*, vol. 9, no. 4 (14 March 1959), pp. 5, 18

J. P. Hodin, 'Bryan Wynter', *Quadrum*, no. 9 (1960)

J. P. Hodin, 'Introduction', *Bryan Wynter* (exhib. cat., Galerie Charles Lienhard, Zurich, 1962)

Patrick Heron, 'Bryan Wynter', *Studio International*, vol. 189, no. 975 (May–June 1975)

Patrick Heron, 'Bryan Wynter' (exhib. cat., Falmouth School of Art, 1975)

Bryan Wynter, 1915–75 (exhib. cat., Hayward Gallery, London, 1976) (essays by Alan Bowness and Patrick Heron)

Tom Cross, *Painting the Warmth of the Sun: St Ives Artists, 1939–75* (Penzance and Guildford, 19874; 2nd edn Penzance, 2009)

Eric Wynter, 'Bryan – A Memoir', *Catalogue of the Paintings of Bryan Wynter* (exhib. cat., Prema Project, Uley, 1984), n. p.

St Ives: Twenty Five Years of Painting Sculpture and Pottery (exhib. cat., Tate Gallery, London, 1985)

Chris Stephens, *Bryan Wynter*, 'St Ives Artists' (London, 1999)

Mel Gooding, 'Bryan Wynter: The Elements of His Art', in *Bryan Wynter* (exhib. cat., Jonathan Clark Fine Art, London, 2002)

Andrew Lambirth, 'Altered States and the Trace of Flux', in *Bryan Wynter: Paintings, Drawings, Kinetic Sculptures, 1960–1975* (exhib. cat., Jonathan Clark Fine Art, London, 2006)

Michael Bird, *The St Ives Artists: A Biography of Place and Time* (London, 2008)

Writings

Artist's statement, in *Statements: A Review of British Abstract Art in 1956* (exhib. cat., Institute of Contemporary Arts, London, 1957), n. p.

'Notes on My Painting', *Bryan Wynter* (exhib. cat., Galerie Charles Lienhard, Zurich, 1962)

'Unpublished Note, 10 Jan 1960 (for Alan Bowness)', in *Bryan Wynter, 1915–75* (exhib. cat., Hayward Gallery, London, 1976)

Index

NOTE: Page numbers in *italics* refer to illustrations.

Y

Z